Landscape as Herit

This edited book provides a broad collection of current critical reflections on heritage-making processes involving landscapes, positioning itself at the intersection of landscape and heritage studies.

Featuring an international range of contributions from researchers, academics, activists, and professionals, the book aims to bridge the gap between research and practice and to nourish an interdisciplinary debate spanning the fields of geography, anthropology, landscape and heritage studies, planning, conservation, and ecology. It provokes critical enquiry about the challenges between heritage-making processes and global issues, such as sustainability, economic inequalities, social cohesion, and conflict, involving voices and perspectives from different regions of the world. Case studies in Italy, Portugal, Spain, Slovenia, the Netherlands, Turkey, the UK, Columbia, Brazil, New Zealand, and Afghanistan highlight different approaches, values, and models of governance.

This interdisciplinary book will appeal to researchers, academics, practitioners, and every landscape citizen interested in heritage studies, cultural landscapes, conservation, geography, and planning.

Giacomo Pettenati is Assistant Professor of Economic and Political Geography in the Department of Cultures, Politics, and Society at the University of Turin, Italy.

Landscape as Heritage
International Critical Perspectives

Edited by
Giacomo Pettenati

LONDON AND NEW YORK

Cover image: Giacomo Pettenati

First published 2023
by Routledge
4 Park Square, Milton Park, Abingdon, Oxon OX14 4RN

and by Routledge
605 Third Avenue, New York, NY 10158

Routledge is an imprint of the Taylor & Francis Group, an informa business

© 2023 selection and editorial matter, Giacomo Pettenati; individual chapters, the contributors

British Library Cataloguing-in-Publication Data
A catalogue record for this book is available from the British Library

Library of Congress Cataloging-in-Publication Data
A catalog record has been requested for this book

ISBN: 978-1-032-04934-2 (hbk)
ISBN: 978-1-032-04623-5 (pbk)
ISBN: 978-1-003-19523-8 (ebk)

DOI: 10.4324/9781003195238

Typeset in Bembo
by Taylor & Francis Books

Contents

Illustrations

Figures

Tables

Contributors

Jully Acuña Suárez is an artist and PhD candidate at the Faculty of Archaeology, Leiden University. She uses art as a research method in cultural heritage and develops collaborative artistic and curatorial practices. Her research seeks to understand how art is used as a colonizing method, and her art is produced from a decolonial perspective, addressing issues such as social justice, the environment, and identity.

Milena Aguillón Chindoy is a Kamëntsá warrior spirit, activist, and mother of three. She is interested in understanding how colonialism has affected and transformed her culture. She is working to recover Kamëntsá history and traditional knowledge to transmit it to her children and new generations.

Ana Rita Albuquerque has a Master's degree in International Studies. She is currently a joint-PhD student in Geography and Heritage Studies at the University of Porto and at the University Paul Valéry of Montpellier, researching online and offline representations and practices of heritage-making and placemaking in urban landscapes in Europe. She has been running capacity-building workshops at several universities, civil organisations, and institutions on project management and monitoring in the field of cultural heritage and sustainable tourism.

Federica Appendino is Associate Professor of Urban Planning at ESPI Paris and Research Associate at ESPI2R and Lab'URBA Research Units. She obtained a joint PhD in Urban Planning and Heritage Conservation in 2017 (Sorbonne University and Polytechnic University of Turin). Dr Appendino's research focuses on sustainable urban planning and environmental assessment procedures.

Melissa Baird is Associate Professor of Anthropology in the Department of Social Sciences at Michigan Technological University. A graduate of the University of California, Berkeley, she earned her Master's and Doctorate at the University of Oregon. Her research has focused on the politics of heritage within the extractive zone and coalition and equity in higher education. She is the current President of the Association of Critical Heritage Studies.

Maria Leonor Botelho, PhD in History of Art, is Assistant Professor at the Faculty of Arts and Humanities at the University of Porto (Department of Heritage Studies), President of the Scientific Commission of the Master in History of Art, Heritage and Visual Culture, and Integrated Researcher of CITCEM. She is part of the UNESCO Chair "Heritage, Cities and Landscapes. Sustainable Management, Conservation, Planning and Design," in the Faculty of Architecture of the University of Porto.

Jacky Bowring is Professor of Landscape Architecture at Lincoln University, and a Fellow of the New Zealand Institute of Landscape Architects. She is the author of *Landscape Architecture Criticism* (2020), *Melancholy and the Landscape: Locating Sadness, Memory and Reflection in the Landscape* (2016), and *A Field Guide to Melancholy* (2008).

Katherine Burlingame completed her PhD in Human Geography at Lund University in 2020. Her dissertation, *Dead landscapes – and how to make live*, received an outstanding thesis award from *Vetenskapssocieteten*. She is currently a postdoctoral researcher at the University of Oslo for the project *Relics of Nature: An Archaeology of Natural Heritage in the High North* funded by the Norwegian Research Council, connecting archaeology, heritage studies, and landscape geography with a theoretical basis in landscape phenomenology.

Philip Burlingame completed his PhD in higher education at the University of Pittsburgh in 1989. He previously served as the Associate Vice President for Student Affairs at Penn State University and was Affiliate Assistant Professor in Higher Education, co-coordinating the College of Education's Master's program in higher education and student affairs. Prior to his work at Penn State, he was Vice President for Student Affairs at the State University of New York Polytechnic Institute.

Benedetta Castiglioni, PhD, is Professor in Geography at the University of Padua, where she coordinates the M.Sc. degree in Landscape studies. Key themes in her researches are the relationship between people and the landscape and the questions concerned, with special attention to education and to heritagisation processes.

Margherita Cisani is Research Fellow in Geography and Lecturer of Tourism Geography: Heritage and Sustainability at the University of Padua (DiSSGeA). She is interested in the interplay between landscapes and mobilities in everyday contexts, in heritage landscapes, as well as in formal and non-formal educational practices.

Dominique Crozat is Professor in Social and Cultural Geography at the Université Paul Valéry – Montpellier 3. His current research interests are the relationship between mobility, space, and identity and the performative effects in the discursive construction of identity (e.g. tourism, festivities and leisure activities). He is a permanent member of the research unit 'Actors, Resources and Territories in Development'.

Shannon Davis is Senior Lecturer in Landscape Architecture at Lincoln University New Zealand specializing in Landscape Planning. She undertakes much of her research within the Lincoln University Centre of Excellence: Designing Future Productive Landscapes, working in the areas of urban and peri-urban food production. Shannon also undertakes research into cultural landscapes.

Mesut Dinler is Assistant Professor at Politecnico di Torino. He has international experience in research projects including the ones managed by US/ ICOMOS, Getty Conservation Institute, Association for the Protection of Cultural Heritage, as well as European research programs. His research interests include politics of heritage, activist movements, and digital humanities.

Anneli Ekblom is Professor in Archaeology and Global Environmental History at Uppsala University with an interest in landscape history and conservation. As an archaeologist by training, she has combined archaeobotanical and palaeoecological tools to reconstruct landscape history. Her research has focused on relations between humans-nature ranging from the very physicality of landscape changes in flora and climate to conflicts and contestations when it comes to conservation and heritage.

Maurits W. Ertsen is Associate Professor within the Water Resources Management group of Delft University of Technology, the Netherlands. He studies how water practices emerge from short-term (inter)actions of human and non-human agents in current, historical, and archaeological periods. In his work, he cooperates with universities, NGOs, and the private sector.

Vincenza Ferrara is an early-stage researcher at the Department of Archaeology and Ancient History (Uppsala University) and Department of Human Geography (Stockholm University). She is interested in the investigation of nature-human dynamics at different spatio-temporal scales, combining methods from historical ecology and critical geospatial analysis so to address contemporary agroecological issues. Vincenza is a practitioner herself, owning and managing some ancient olive orchards in the island of Sicily.

Viviana Ferrario, PhD, is Professor of Landscape Geography at the Iuav University di Venice. Active in the field of landscape studies, she coordinates research projects about agricultural landscape change, urbanization, heritagisation, and energy transition. She is the President of the Comelico-Dolomites Foundation and member of the Scientific Committee of the Alpine Adriatic Rectors' Conference.

Francesca Giliberto, PhD, is Research Fellow at the University of Leeds. She investigates urban heritage conservation and management, heritage for sustainable development, and policy evaluation. Dr Giliberto's work bridges research, policy, and practice, facilitating the implementation of international frameworks, including the United Nations' Agenda 2030 and the UNESCO's Historic Urban Landscape Recommendation.

Juan Sebastián Granada-Cardona is Postdoctoral Researcher at the Instituto de Investigaciones Sociales-UNAM (México). He holds a PhD in Political Science and Sociology from the UNAM (México) and an MA in Social Anthropology from the EHESS-Toulouse (France). His lines of research are memory/history relations; testimonies, literature and memory; heritage and socio-cultural landscape; and contemporary history.

Patrick Hayombe has a PhD in Environmental Planning and Management and Master's in Environmental Planning. He is a Corporate Member in Kenya Institute of Planners (KIP). He has also worked in Jaramogi Oginga Odinga University of Science and Technology as Dean of School of Spatial Planning and Natural Resource Managements and formerly Deputy Director Applied Water Research (2007–2010). He is the current Director/Chief Executive Officer and Secretary to the KEWI Governing Council.

Silvia Jamioy Juajibioy is a Kamëntsá communicator and works for Indigenous radio stations. She has worked on cultural heritage revitalization and develops radio programmes and multimedia content that engage the audience with the issues that affect the rights of Indigenous Peoples. She has a degree in Social Work from the Externado University of Colombia.

Špela Ledinek Lozej, PhD, is Research Associate at the Institute of Slovenian Ethnology of the Research Centre of the Slovenian Academy of Sciences and Arts. She is the head of the multidisciplinary program *Heritage on the Margins*. In addition to heritage-making processes, she also researches alpine pasture, food, dwelling, and collecting practices.

Mirella Loda has been Full Professor of Geography at the University of Florence since 2013 and is Head of the Laboratory of Social Geography (www.lages.eu). She has directed cooperation projects in Herat and Bamiyan (Afghanistan). She is a member of the Expert Working Group for the Safeguarding of the Cultural Landscape and Archaeological Remains of the Bamiyan Valley World Heritage Property.

Sara Luchetta is a cultural geographer and Lecturer in Geography at the University of Padova (Italy). Her research interests are grounded in mountain spaces: she focuses on the relationship between contemporary literature and mountain imagination and on the living connections of (tangible and intangible) culture and landscapes.

Marcelo Marques Miranda is a PhD candidate at the Faculty of Archaeology, Leiden University. His research addresses how cultural policies, museums, and archaeology affect the rights of Indigenous Peoples. Likewise, his research and action seek to decolonize understandings of cultural heritage, develop collaborative curatorial practices, and promote antiracist approaches to education.

Lucas Monsaingeon is currently a PhD student within the laboratories MRTE of CY Cergy Paris University, and LéaV of the National Architecture School of

Versailles, on the evolving and living heritage of the Nord-Pas de Calais Mining Basin. He is actively engaged in the territory as an architect, partner, and project director at Atelier d'Architecture Philippe Prost. In 2016, he was awarded the Richard Morris Hunt Prize for his study on American bridges preservation.

Özgün Özçakır is an architect by training and received his PhD from METU for his thesis entitled "In-Between Preservation and Economics: Establishing Common Ground between Socio-Cultural and Economic for the Sustainability of Urban Heritage Places in Turkey." His research interests include heritage values, conservation policies in Turkey, and heritage impact assessment.

Fredrick Odede has a PhD in Planning and is also a cultural heritage expert from Jaramogi Oginga Odinga University of Science and Technology. He has experience in ecotourism, and socio-cultural and sustainable urban development research and has engaged in the spatial and physical planning of urban centres in Kenya.

Kenneth R. Olwig now professor emeritus, has taught primarily at universities in Denmark, Norway and Sweden, and lectured widely in Europe, Britain and the Americas. He is the author of Nature's Ideological Landscape (2021, orig 1984), Landscape Nature and the Body Politic (2002) and The Meanings of Landscape (2019).

Cecilia Paradiso is an anthropologist. She received her PhD at the EHESS-Marseille in 2022. Her dissertation focuses on socioecological relations and environmental policies, with a fieldwork conducted in Sardinia, around the Archipelago of la Maddalena National Park. Meanwhile, she keeps an interest on landscape, heritagization, and politico-economic processes.

Edilson Pereira is Adjunct Professor at the School of Communication and the Graduate Program in Communication and Culture of the Federal University of Rio de Janeiro. He holds a PhD in Social Anthropology from National Museum, Brazil, with a research internship at the École des Hautes Études en Sciences Sociales, in Paris, and postdoctoral studies at the Universitat de Barcelona.

Beth Perry is Professor of Urban Knowledge and Governance and Director of the Urban Institute at the University of Sheffield. Her research spotlights the theory and practice of co-production in urban governance and research with a focus on addressing urban epistemic inequalities.

Primož Pipan is a human geographer and Research Fellow at Research Centre of the Slovenian Academy of Sciences and Arts (ZRC SAZU). His research interests are in the heritage of landscape, political geography, regional geography, natural disasters, geographical names, and the geography of tourism.

Marjeta Pisk, PhD, is Research Associate at the Institute of Ethnomusicology of the Research Centre of the Slovenian Academy of Sciences and Arts. She intertwines folkloristic research of marginalized genres and practices with the research of heritage-making practices in border regions.

Pavel Raška is Associate Professor in the Department of Geography at the J. E. Purkyně University. His background is in geography and history (MA) and physical geography (PhD). He explores the historical and present-day risks and disasters with respect to community responses and adaptive planning.

Guillem Rubio-Ramon is PhD Researcher in Human Geography at the University of Edinburgh. His work, grounded in Catalonia and Scotland, combines perspectives from human-animal studies, political ecology, and the environmental humanities to explore cases ranging from animal agriculture to biodiversity conservation and environmental conflicts.

Karen Lykke Syse is an agronomist and ethnologist and holds a PhD in cultural history from the University of Oslo, where she is Associate Professor at the Centre for Development and the Environment. Her research interests pivot around landscape history and the cultural history of food.

Maria Luisa Sturani is Professor in Geography at the University of Turin. Her interests are focused on historical geography, with particular reference to the reconstruction of landscape's past dynamics and to the issues of its management as heritage. Her research also relates to the fields of history of cartography and the history of geography.

Maja Topole is a regional geographer and Research Fellow at Research Centre of the Slovenian Academy of Sciences and Arts. Her main research interests are in geographical regionalization and rural geography, focused in geoecology, sustainable development of rural landscape, land use changes, tourism, and natural and cultural heritage protection.

Stéphanie Tselouiko is currently an independent researcher and consultant in environmental anthropology and holds a joint PhD in social anthropology and ethnology at the École des Hautes Études en Sciences Sociales and at the Federal University of São Carlos. At the crossroads of social and environmental anthropology, her doctoral research focused on how the Mebengôkré-Xikrin of the Trincheira Bacajá Indigenous Land (Pará, Brazil) conceive and practice their territoriality in a context of unprecedented transformations.

Mauro Varotto is Associate Professor of Geography and Cultural Geography at the University of Padua. Since 2008 he has coordinated the "Terre Alte" Group of the Italian Alpine Club Scientific Committee; he directed the first Museum of Geography in Italy. Since 2021 he has been the Rector's delegate for museums and collections at the University of Padua. He is the author of over 120 scientific publications.

Leonardo Vilaça Dupin is a journalist and holds a PhD in Social Sciences from the State University of Campinas, with a research internship at the École des Hautes Études en Sciences Sociales. He currently works as a technical adviser to communities affected by mining disasters in Brazil.

Rory Walshe is Research Associate in the Department of Geography at the University of Cambridge. He earned his PhD from King's College London and University College London and specializes in disaster vulnerability and resilience and the role of culture and knowledge in disaster response.

Anders Wästfelt is Professor in Geography, especially Human Geography, at Stockholm University with an interest in historical and contemporary agriculture. As a geographer with a special interest in historical cartography and geographic information systems, he has developed a method to combine satellite image analysis with agriculture geography. His research focus is on landscape heritage, globalization of farming and use rights, with a special focus on commons and lease of agriculture land.

1 Why we need a critical perspective on landscape as heritage

Giacomo Pettenati

Introduction

Many geographers and landscape theorists have recurred to landscape paintings to support their theoretical reflections. It is famously the case of the "new cultural geography", focusing on landscape as "painterly way of seeing" (Duncan, 1995) and on the ideological dimension of landscape pictorial representations (Cosgrove, 1985; Cosgrove and Daniels, 1988). Taking inspiration from these much more important predecessors, I, too, open this introduction with a painting, which – in my opinion – clearly symbolizes the theoretical approach that inspired this volume.

I allude to "The Delights of Landscape" (original title: *Les charmes du paysage*, 1928), one of the less renowned works of the Belgian surrealist painter René Magritte.[1] It represents an empty wooden frame, leaning on a black wall. Besides the frame there is a shotgun and on its lower side, a label describes its content: *paysage* (i.e. landscape). According to the critics, several meanings can be attributed to this painting: the complexity of the relationships between perception and signification (Basque, 2009); the importance of absence in producing meanings (Searle, 2020); the role of frames in visual perception and representation (Ludu, 2016); the invisible meanings expressed through visible images (Jongen, 1994); the violence of power, symbolized by the shotgun, in determining the content and the meanings of representations (Basque, 2009).

All these meanings, concerning the intrinsically political relationships between objects and representations, redirect to the multifaceted, complex, politically charged process of selective framing that involves landscape, when it is recognized as heritage by individuals, communities, or institutions.

During the winding history of its conceptualization, landscape has often been described as a "volatile" (Bender, 2006) concept, as a hazy perspective on the material forms of land (Farinelli, 1991). As Bender (2006: 303) notes:

> The same place at the same moment will be experienced differently by different people; the same place, at different moments, will be experienced differently by the same person; the same person may even, at a given

DOI: 10.4324/9781003195238-1

moment, hold conflicting feelings about a place. When, in addition, one considers the variable effects of historical and cultural particularity, the permutations on how people interact with place and landscape are almost unending, and the possibilities for disagreement about, and contest over, landscape are equally so.

Like Magritte's empty frame suggests, landscape's contents, meanings, and boundaries are never objective. They are, rather, the expression of multiple – individual and collective – subjectivities, which apply frames on reality. This framing process determines what spatial features contribute to compose landscape, what are its meanings (including that of "heritage"), and how it should be lived, experienced, transformed, and managed. Needless to say, this process of material and symbolic framing is imbued with power and politics and often contested. When they are valued as heritage:

> Landscapes are mapped and sung, lived and contested, walked on and turned over, cared for and held. But at the same time, landscapes are sites of negotiations, they are constrained and contested, and mediated within systems of exclusion and oppression.
>
> (Baird, 2017: 99)

This happens at different scales: from the micropolitics that inform individual choices about what landscapes are worthy to invest in, take care about, and reproduce as expression of one own's culture (Rose, 2021); to the power that is exercised at multiple scales during the process of collective identification of those meanings and forms of landscape that become part of an "authorized heritage" (Smith, 2006), which is legitimized by what we may call "authorized *landscape* discourse" (Pettenati, 2019; Santos and Piñeiro-Antelo, 2020). Heritagized landscape can therefore be interpreted as a specific form of "landscape of power", being both material expression of social and economic relations mediated by power (Zukin, 1993). The "authorized landscape discourse" legitimizes and strengthens some specific ways of transforming and representing places. Specific narratives of past and heritage become official, while alternative and dissonant representations are disempowered and disenfranchised (Bell, 2013). Such powerful heritage narratives become "interpretative gateways" (Johnson, 1999), providing insiders and outsiders with new lenses through which reading the landscape and its meanings. They represent an "embedding framework" for the perception and the representation of the links between the past and the future of landscape (Lowenthal, 1993).

Recalling Magritte's painting, the process of heritage-making entails a framing on landscape, which is transformed from a non-discrete and constantly changing entity (Lowenthal, 1978) into a symbolically and materially bounded, manageable, and discrete local (Smith, 2006).

Critical scholars largely agree on the fact that heritage is a version of the past (Atkinson, 2005; Waterton and Watson, 2015) and that the processes of negotiation, conflict, exclusion, resistance, and exercise of power that produce such versions of the past are at the core of heritage-making. The representations of landscape that are produced during the heritage-making processes are highly performative, as they affect how landscape is perceived, managed, transformed, and practiced by local communities, tourists, and any other relevant stakeholders. Moreover, when specific narratives of the past and of heritage become official, other narratives become peripheral. It is often the case of those produced by cultural or political minorities, or by socially marginalized groups. At the same time, counter-narratives can emerge and be mobilized by actors contesting the authorized landscape discourse.

The politics that affect the landscape heritage-making processes are at the core of the critical approach that this volume aims to discuss and to mobilize in the analysis of the several case studies included in the book. This includes the power-related different capacity of actors to implement their understandings of and strategies on landscape; the material and symbolical exclusionary effects of authorized landscape discourses; the impact of heritage narratives on landscape management, transformation, and individual experience; and the production and reproduction of different visions of what is landscape and what are its values.

From a theoretical perspective, most of the contributions in this volume are grounded on a post-structuralist, processual, and relational understanding of landscape (and of heritage). The aim of the book is to contribute to expanding and updating the debate about how critical heritage studies and critical landscape studies can be combined, in order to provide theoretical and methodological tools that allow to understand the complexity of landscape heritage-making in the contemporary globalized and unstable world (for recent accounts of the critical debate about landscape as heritage, see: Harvey and Wilkinson, 2013; Harvey, 2015; Harvey and Waterton, 2015; Baird, 2017).

The contents of the book

The selection of the contributions included in this volume was organized in two phases.

In the first phase, I invited to contribute some of the participants in the session that my colleague Margherita Cisani and I chaired in occasion of the International Geographic Union (IGU) Conference "Heritage Geographies. Politics, Uses and Governance of the Past", organized by the University of Salento (Italy) and held online, due to Covid-19, in May 2021 (originally it should have been held in Lecce, in 2020).

The remaining chapters have been selected through a call for chapters launched in June 2020.

The choice of this selection methodology proved to be a double-edged sword. The advantage is that the themes and approaches of a critical perspective on landscape as heritage are not identified *a priori*, but they emerged spontaneously, through the many proposals I received from different geographical contexts. On the other hand, this selection methodology has prevented the contents of the volume from extensively covering all the themes and perspectives that could be taken into consideration in a critical reading of the heritage-making process concerning landscape. Therefore, the book does not provide an exhaustive account of cutting-edge theoretical contributions on the topic, rather a good and diverse overview on the diversity of the international – mostly non-Anglo-Saxon – debate about landscape as heritage.

Despite the wide geographical diversity of the book's contents, in terms of the nationality of the authors and their workplace, and in terms of location of the case studies, another limitation I want to highlight is the absence of contributions from some cultural areas of the world, in particular Central and Eastern Asia. Critically, as the editor of the book, I have wondered about the reasons for this absence. My hypothesis is that it derives from the channels of circulation of the call for chapters (mostly Western-based academic mailing lists) and – maybe – from the lack of appeal of my proposal among researchers working in those areas of the world. For this and for the other reasons mentioned above, I hope that this volume, far from being exhaustive, will represent a starting point for a critical discussion on the processes of heritage-making regarding landscapes. Such discussion should develop on a global scale, including as many voices as possible and reflecting on the effects that the great social and environmental transformations underway will have on landscape heritagization.

The remainder of this first chapter is divided in two sections. The first outlines the long-time "collaborative conversation" (Harvey and Waterton, 2015) between landscape and heritage studies, trying to answer the call of critical heritage studies for a historically, socially, and politically processual understanding of heritage-making (Baird, 2017). I will specifically focus on the co-evolution between the conceptualization of space-culture tangles and landscape, within the limited, but in my opinion particularly relevant field, of cultural geography.

The second section outlines some of the cornerstones of a critical perspective on landscape heritage-making, emphasizing the urgent need for it, as a way for understanding how landscape and its values are changing in the contemporary world and stressing how it can be a way for tackling the most urgent challenges, in terms of heritage management, sustainability, and social inclusion (Winter, 2013).

Landscape in cultural geography

Critical heritage studies are an inherently cross disciplinary and cross-sectoral (academia, conservation professionals, etc.) field (Winter, 2013), as the high diversity of this book's chapters clearly shows. Nonetheless, the account of the culture-heritage-landscape links outlined in this section mainly (but not exclusively) draws from human geography and notably cultural geography. This is due to my positioning in this field, as a researcher, and to the fundamental role that human geography has played in addressing critical thinking about the role of culture in producing and identifying the meaning and values of landscapes.

Moreover, the evolution of cultural geography theorization of landscape has anticipated (together with cultural anthropology) the critique of a Western-oriented, rational, structural approach to landscape as heritage, which has only recently developed within critical heritage studies (Harrison, 2013; Harvey and Wilkinson, 2013; Harvey and Waterton, 2015; Baird, 2017)

In this discussion I focus on three main approaches, developed mainly – but not only – within the English-speaking cultural geography debate in the 20th-century. I refer to: (a) the "traditional" cultural geography, which developed mostly in the US between the 1920s and the 1970s; (b) the "new cultural geography", which developed primarily in the UK between the 1980s and the 1990s; and (c) the post-structuralist turn that has revolutionized the scholarly debate since the late 1990s and which has laid the foundations for important conceptual and methodological subsequent innovations, such as new materialism and more-than-representational theories (Wylie, 2007).

The concept of landscape has ancient origins and, with different theorizations and meanings, it has flanked a relevant trait of cultural history in many cultural contexts. However, the emergence of the concept of "cultural landscape" – as the expression of the interaction between human actions and natural environment, mediated by culture – is widely attributed to the so-called Berkeley School, whose main representative was the geographer Carl Sauer, who began his career at Berkeley University in the 1920s. According to this perspective: "Culture is the agent, the natural area is the medium, the cultural landscape is the result" (Sauer, 1925). A corollary of this theoretical approach was the conception of landscape as artefactual external materiality, whose morphology can be empirically studied and minutely described and explained through the allegedly homogeneous "way of life" (Williams, 1981) of those who have materially shaped the landscape. The idea of culture on which this perspective is based is that of a monolithic and reified entity, in a vision that has been defined as "superorganic" by critics (Duncan, 1980).

Precisely because of this empirical, a-political, and scarcely differentiated vision of the relationships between culture, places, and landscape, since the 1990s this approach has been broadly criticized, despite a number of relevant voices who defend the theoretical and methodological value of the concept of cultural landscape produced by the Berkeley School (Price and Lewis, 1993), highlighting the severity of its critics (Olwig, 2010). The morphological perspective developed by Sauer and his successors has influenced for decades, and continues to influence, the vision of landscape heritage-making proposed by important international institutions; first and foremost UNESCO, which is explicitly inspired by Sauer's vision in its understanding of "cultural landscapes" (Fowler, 2003; Rössler, 2006) and in the idea of the World Heritage List as a "catalogue" of representatives of the "best heritage" in the world (Rao, 2010).

Starting at the end of the 1980s, particularly in the United Kingdom, a critique of the previous static, homogeneous, and a-political visions of the relationship between culture and landscape developed, initially through Denis Cosgrove's cultural Marxist (as defined by Wyley, 2007) analysis of pictorial representations of landscape, interpreted as a support for the normalization of the dominant social order (Cosgrove, 1984, 1985; Cosgrove and Daniels, 1988). This vision was then further developed by other representatives, defining itself from the beginning as the "new cultural geography" (NCG) (Cosgrove and Jackson, 1987), and expanding this critical "semiotic" gaze to every representation of landscape and to the landscape itself, which started to be read as a text (Jackson, 1989; Duncan, 1990). From this perspective:

> the landscape is not simply a reflection of culture or an expression of cultural patterning. On the contrary, the landscape is an arena of social struggle; a site where dominant social hierarchies struggle to represent what society is and should be in our most everyday spaces.
>
> (Rose, 2021: 962)

As Rose (2021) points out, using Williams' words, the role of culture here is that of a "signifying system" through which "a social order is communicated, reproduced, experienced and explored" (Williams, 1981: 13).

NCG's constructivist approach, in turn later criticized for the reproduction of dominant gazes on landscapes (for instance, masculine: Rose, 1993) and for the progressive detachment from the materiality of the places (Mitchell, 1995), has been further developed by the post-structuralist turn that has revolutionized geography, and more broadly social and humanistic science, starting at the end of the 1990s and that was inspired by the philosophical thinking of authors like Derrida, Baudrillard, Deleuze, Guattari, Foucault, and Latour (Jones, 2013). The post-structuralist impact on geographical thinking, notably in cultural geography, can be roughly summarized into four main points, which have largely impacted landscape research theories and methods. Their common bases are a strongly relational understanding of space (Massey, 2005; Murdoch, 2006): the refusal of any essentialism or search for deep, generative structures beyond the infinite variety of the surface of life (Cresswell, 2013: 207), a key role attributed to power relations and discourses. The first point is about the new relationships between epistemology and ontology, which radically questions a binary vision of knowledge, including the sharp separation between reality and representation typical of structuralism. Referring to landscape, it thus becomes relevant to understand not only how a specific landscape is materially made or intangibly represented, but how the very concept of landscape is constantly produced and reproduced through knowledge and practice. Second, post-structuralist thinking is founded on the acceptance of the constant state of change of reality and its meanings and on the refusal of universalizing and stable explanations. Given this constant state of becoming, post-structuralist landscape research should focus on investigating the relational process of "landscaping" (Wylie, 2007; Crouch, 2013) more than on researching supposedly stable features or explanations. A third key element of the post-structuralist conception of space and, consequently, of landscape, lies in the multiplication of centralities and points of view, overcoming a dichotomous vision of the centre/periphery binomial. According to this perspective, in each place there is not a single landscape, which is supposed to be a unique expression of the culture or way of life of a population, but there are multiple landscapes, in constant material and symbolic transformation, which are perceived, experienced, represented, and shaped through a kaleidoscope of multiple viewpoints. It is easy to understand how this perspective opens the way for the development of alternative understandings of landscape and its meanings, based on previously excluded ontologies of space, expressed for instance by feminist (Rose, 1993) and postcolonial (Baird, 2017; Dang, 2021) approaches. Fourth, drawing on the Foucaldian idea of the ubiquitous spatiality of power, poststructuralism focuses on the spatial performativity of socially and politically produced discourses on norms and deviations, which are mirrored by exclusionary processes and challenged by the development and practice of counter-geographies. Matless (1998) has expanded this vision, working on the tensions between the notions of *property* and *propriety* in relation to landscape, understanding the latter as a "matter of conduct and forms of 'proper' bodily display and performance" (Wylie, 2007: 117), stressing the normative dimension of landscape.

Starting from the kaleidoscopic vision of reality proposed by post-structuralism, a new methodological, and conceptual turn has developed, which has affected landscape and heritage studies in the last two decades, namely the affirmation of the so-called non-representational or more-than-representational theories (Thrift, 2008; Lorimer, 2005). Radically processual and relational, these perspectives detach landscape from its historically rooted visual and representative nature, giving new theoretical relevance to its phenomenology and materiality and focusing on how it is bodily encountered, performed, and affectively and multisensorially experienced, through a constant and mobile interaction of human and more-than-human entities (Waterton, 2018).

As anticipated, this is a very partial synthesis of the relationship between culture and landscape in human geography, which does not consider other important lines of research, such as political ecology (Neumann, 2011), and only marginally refers to very relevant non-Anglophone schools of geographic thought, like the Italian (Minca, 2007a) or French (Raffestin, 1978; Berque, 1994), not to mention the non-Western ones.

I focused on these three major conceptual perspectives because they have strongly affected heritage studies and they represent the theoretical bases of different ways of conceiving the heritage value of landscapes. Moreover, they come from a cultural and political context where most of the cultural (mostly academic) production, able to globally influence the politics of heritage, is still produced.

The Sauerian morphological conception of landscape, as a manifestation of the interaction between human communities and nature, has for a long time constituted the theoretical foundation of a vision of landscape's heritage values based on the material analysis of landscape forms and of their meanings in relation to *the* culture which, presumably, characterizes a territory. This approach still constitutes the theoretical foundation of many policies for the protection of landscapes as heritage, from the many local and national registers of valuable landscapes, to the globally impacting UNESCO World Heritage List (Aplin, 2007), grounding on an "objectivist understanding" of landscape (Minca, 2007a).

On the other hand, the focus on how power is mirrored by landscapes, developed (not exclusively) by NCG's first critical conceptualizations, is clearly reflected in the rich scientific production whose objective is to investigate not only what landscape becomes heritage, but above all why and how the landscape as heritage is politically used to legitimize power (among the many contributions, also with different theoretical origins, see Lowenthal, 1985; Olwig, 2002; Waterton, 2010) and as a part of politics of identity (Whelan, 2016).

Finally, the post-structuralist turn has paved the way for a new manifold understanding of landscape as heritage, interested in issues that were previously underestimated by heritage studies and landscape studies, such as the processual and relational nature of heritage-making; a prospective vision of the past; how landscape is performed as heritage; the emergence of dissonant, alternative voices, excluded by the "authorized heritage discourse"; the more-than-visual bodily encounter between human and non-human agents (Harvey and Wilkinson, 2013; Waterton and Watson, 2013; Harvey and Waterton, 2015; Baird, 2017).

It is on these disruptive theoretical and methodological bases that critical heritage studies have developed, as I will argue in the next paragraph, pointing out the need to focus on a processual and relational understanding of landscape as heritage, in order to deal with the main present and future challenges affecting landscapes.

Critical heritage landscape studies

Although the first scientific works interested in critically questioning the process of heritage-making date back to the 1990s and some still fundamental works, such as *Uses of Heritage* by Laurajane Smith (2006), were published in the 2000s (see the interesting review made by Harrison, 2013), the founding event of critical heritage studies, as a specific front within the vast world of heritage studies, can be identified in the inaugural conference of the Association of Critical Heritage Studies, held in Gothenburg in 2012, with the support of the International Journal of Heritage Studies.

The core ideas of this approach are clearly stated in the manifesto of the newly born association:

> heritage studies need to be rebuilt from the ground up, which requires the "ruthless criticism of everything existing". Heritage is, as much as anything, a political act and we need to ask serious questions about the power relations that "heritage" has all too often been invoked to sustain. Nationalism, imperialism, colonialism, cultural elitism, Western triumphalism, social exclusion based on class and ethnicity, and the fetishising of expert knowledge have all exerted strong influences on how heritage is used, defined and

managed. We argue that truly critical heritage studies will ask many uncomfortable questions of traditional ways of thinking about and doing heritage, and that the interests of the marginalised and excluded will be brought to the forefront when posing these questions.

(Quoted in Smith, 2012)

The initial statements are followed in the manifesto by a number of essential requirements for a critical heritage approach, such as the opening up of the field to a wider range of intellectual traditions; the need of new methods of research and enquiry; the integration of heritage studies with other fields like studies of memory, public history, community, tourism, planning and development; the development of genuinely international and multidisciplinary networks; a democratization of heritage, going beyond elite cultural narratives and embracing the heritage insights of those who have traditionally been marginalized.[2]

Due to its volatile, constantly changing, intrinsically political and ambiguous nature, as "perhaps the only modern concept that refers to both the thing itself – and to its description" (Minca, 2007a: 179), landscape is one of the main objects of interest of critical heritage studies, far before their "official" emergence, as works like Lowenthal's (1978, 1998) or Samuel's (1994) clearly demonstrate, and it is widely discussed in recent contributions (Harvey and Wilkinson, 2013; Harvey and Waterton, 2015; Baird, 2017).

Without denying the contribution of other approaches to a complex vision of the landscape as heritage, a truly critical approach to how the landscape is recognized, perceived, transformed, and represented as heritage is almost inevitably based on a theoretical perspective of post-structuralist inspiration. As Baird (2017) highlights, thinking critically of landscapes as heritage means to be aware of their role in the heritage business; to understand how they work as sites of negotiation and conflict; to adopt multiple understandings of what landscape is and what are its heritage values; to also bring in subjugated, excluded, and weak voices, proposing heritage narratives and performing landscape practices that fall outside the "authorized landscape discourse". Each of these perspectives unavoidably entails a fluid, open-ended, multivocal, and hybrid (human/non-human; material/immaterial; local/non-local) understanding of landscape, like the one proposed by post-structuralist thinking (Wyley, 2007).

Several scholars call for an urgent critical turn in heritage studies (Waterton and Watson, 2015), not only referring to the need of a social and political engagement regarding the "potential of deploying tangible and intangible heritage to address historical and systemic inequalities as a social activist strategy" (Kryder-Reid 2018: 691), but also because it is a way to

better understanding the various ways in which heritage now has a stake in, and can act as a positive enabler for, the complex, multi-vector challenges that face us today, such as cultural and environmental sustainability, economic inequalities, conflict resolution, social cohesion and the future of cities, to name a few.

(Winter, 2013: 533)

Five challenges for thinking and practicing landscape as heritage

Such a perspective helps in understanding some issues that have radically changed the way in which landscape is recognized, managed, and practiced as heritage in the contemporary world. I would like to highlight five, which are strictly interconnected, and which open challenging questions about the multiple meanings of considering landscape as heritage:

Migrations. Even if mobilities have characterized humankind all throughout history, it is widely acknowledged that we live in the age of migrations (Castles et al., 2013). The total number of migrants worldwide, including refugees and asylum-seekers, has dramatically grown in the last three decades; flows have become global and they are rapidly changing; and migrants today represent a significant percentage of population in many countries (Samers and Collyer, 2017). The new magnitude of the migration processes is significantly affecting landscape heritage-making, producing new landscapes of migrations (Blunt, 2007), which deal with complex issues such as the need of migrant people to build new senses of belonging in and attachment to the countries they cross or settle down in (Tolia-Kelly, 2004; Rishbeth and Powell, 2013); the manifold links of the diasporic transnational communities with the landscapes of their places of origin, including the development of new symbolic meanings and the material effects of emigration and remittances (Blunt, 2007); the role of migrants as agents of landscape transformations (like in the case of agricultural workers recalled by Mitchell, 2007, 2011, 2013) and as human elements of landscape as heritage; the new and multifaceted meanings and values attributed to "local" landscapes by increasingly culturally mixed populations, including a growing number of "lifestyle" or "amenity" migrants, that often represent themselves as *stewards* of rural landscapes (Gosnell and Abrams, 2011; Cooke and Lane, 2015); and the identification as heritage of places linked to migrations, like in the case of US historical immigration stations (Hoskins, 2010).

Tourism. Before the dramatic global halt of tourist mobility in 2020, due to the Covid-19 pandemic, the tourism industry contributed about 10% of the global GDP, with almost 1.5 billion international tourist arrivals and more than 330 million jobs created worldwide (WTTC, 2021). Tourism probably represents the main driver of the heritage industry and a prime motivation for the commitment of local actors in aspiring to a heritage designation, like in the case of the World Heritage status. The motivation of many World Heritage nominations is linked to the relevant effects of heritage designations including a locality on the map of international tourism destinations and to the economic effects of increased tourist flows (Bourdeau et al., 2015). From a conceptual standpoint, a critical reflection of the complex links between tourism and heritage has followed a similar path to that of the concept of landscape.

Initially, it focused on the role of tourists in producing and reproducing "ways of seeing" (gazes) places, mediated by the many actors of the tourism industry, and able to affect the way in which those who live those same places perceive, represent, and perform them (Urry, 1990, 1992; Larsen, 2014). At a later stage, authors such as Crang (1997) and Minca (2007b) have enriched reflection on the tourist gaze with greater attention to performances, focusing on the practices through which representations of places and landscapes are produced and reproduced by tourists. In a historical moment in which tourism probably represents the main global industry and the main engine of reflexive processes regarding places, their landscape, and their heritage (D'Eramo, 2017), there is the urgency of a critical perspective, able to further unpack the tourist gaze, understand its role in the heritage-making processes concerning landscapes, and deal with the material impacts of overtourism on heritagized landscapes.

Digital landscapes. In 1988, Cosgrove and Daniels emphasized the importance of landscape representations, referring to the "reality" of landscapes reproduced through "a flickering text displayed on a word processor screen whose meaning can be created, extended, altered, elaborated and finally obliterated by the merest touch of a button" (1988: 8), initiating what Olwig (1996) called "melting of landscape into cybtertextual space" and "disciplinary dematerialization". Despite the theoretical and empirical new interest on the materiality of landscapes that characterize cultural geography's recent "materialist turn" (Kirsch, 2013), digital has undoubtedly become a part of everyone's spatial experience and it is "reshaping the production and experience of space, place, nature, landscape, mobility, and environment" (Ash et al., 2018: 35), becoming a constituent part of contemporary hybrid geographies. Digital space contributes to produce specific "digital imaginations" (Offen, 2013), based on the production, circulation, and reproduction of heritage representations, affecting how landscape is valued and experienced as heritage. Referring to the digital mediation of cultural objects, today almost ubiquitous, Gillian Rose stresses how "Digital 'objects' are not stable, but rather are mutable, multimedial and mass" (2016: 336). Landscape experience to most of us is mediated by the fruition of digital representations. A number of urgent questions therefore emerge. How does the digital experience of landscape (e.g. Google Street View) affect its perception as heritage? How do the digital reproduction and circulation of landscape representations (through social media) produce new hybrid landscapes, with specific values? How does this affect visitors and residents' preferences about landscape and their material experience of it (Giaccardi, 2012)? Will exclusively digital landscapes, like those of videogames (Ash and Gallacher, 2011), social networks or websites, become objects of specific heritage-making processes, or do they already?

Decolonization. The process of landscape and heritage symbolic and material decolonization from the colonial, masculine, dominant power gazes, which forms the basis of much of the authorized heritage discourse, has been a part of scholarly debate and grassroots movement activity for several decades (Rose, 1993; Giblin, 2015). In the first phase, much of the reflection concerned the collective reinterpretation of postcolonial heritage and the construction of a national and indigenous heritage in territories that had gained autonomy from imperialist control (in addition to the several existing regional and local case studies, see: Harrison and Hughes, 2010). Recently, increasing attention has been given to the role that decolonial and postcolonial approaches can play in unravelling the role of power in defining landscape also in the Global North (Naylor et al., 2018), subsuming – and, according to some scholars, diluting (Dang, 2021) – the decolonial perspective into broader discourses on social justice (Tuck and Yang, 2012). In recent years there have been attempts to rewrite cultural heritage and public memory, highlighting the dissonance of the oppressive and colonialist nature of some of the dominant heritage narratives. This is evident in the increasingly frequent actions of anti-racist, feminist, and anti-fascist movements against statues or other material elements of heritage that celebrate the imperialist past. Let's consider the increasingly frequent protest initiatives against statues celebrating the protagonists of the imperial and slavery past by Black Lives Matter activists, which in some cases have led to their removal (Burch-Brown, 2020). It seems inevitable to wonder how much the growing public awareness about the celebration and reproduction of discriminating social systems through cultural heritage (which some disparagingly call "cancel culture") will be reflected in the future in a diffuse questioning of what Duncan and Duncan defined as "landscapes of privilege" (2003); rewriting landscape as heritage in the light of the multiple and fluid identities of contemporary societies.

Climate change. Finally, landscape is increasingly impacted, in its material forms, by what is probably the main environmental phenomenon taking place on a global scale: anthropogenic global warming and the consequent climate change. From a critical perspective, it is impossible not to reflect on the effects that these transformations have on heritage-making processes, which are often based on the production of cultural values and relationships between society and the landscape, resulting from long-term relationships with a physical context inevitably destined to change due to rising temperatures (Aktürk and Dastgerdi, 2021). Let's think, for instance, about the case of vineyard landscapes, whose heritage narratives are based on the history and daily practice of a production that, in a few decades, could disappear or move to higher altitudes. What challenges will climate change bring to the management of landscape heritage sites, which will have to deal with the inevitability of the transformation of some material elements, impossible to safeguard or reproduce in a changed climate context? (Dastgerdi et al., 2019; Guzman et al., 2020).

Some of the issues discussed so far are addressed by the chapters contained in this volume. Other remain open questions. Starting from these open questions, this work aims to stimulate heritage researchers and practitioners, in the development of a critical and political perspective on landscape heritage-making processes. This perspective should deeply question existing knowledge; imagining and practicing new paths, new methods, and new objects of research on landscape as heritage, all of which are consistent with the rapid transformations of contemporary and future societies.

Notes

1 www.wikiart.org/en/rene-magritte/the-delights-of-landscape-1928 (retrieved on 18/01/2022).
2 www.criticalheritagestudies.org/history (retrieved on: 28/01/2022).

References

Aktürk, G. and Dastgerdi, A. S. (2021). Cultural Landscapes Under the Threat of Climate Change: A Systematic Study of Barriers to Resilience. *Sustainability* 13(17): 9974.

Aplin, G. (2007). World Heritage Cultural Landscapes. *International Journal of Heritage Studies* 13(6): 427–446.

Ash, J. and Gallacher, L. A. (2011). Cultural Geography and Videogames. *Geography Compass* 5(6): 351–368.

Ash, J., Kitchin, R., and Leszczynski, A. (2018). Digital Turn, Digital Geographies? *Progress in Human Geography* 42(1): 25–43.

Atkinson, D. (2005). Heritage. In D. Atkinson, D. Sibley, N. Washbourne, and P. Jackson (eds.) *Cultural Geography: A Critical Dictionary of Key Concepts*. New York: Tauris.

Baird, M. (2017). *Critical Theory and the Anthropology of Heritage Landscapes*. Gainesville: University Press of Florida.

Basque, J. (2009). Ceci n'est pas un texte sur Magritte. Réflexions sur les oeuvres de Magritte, la perception et la signification. *Commposite* 12(1): 39–57.

Bell, J. S. (2013). The Politics of Preservation: Privileging One Heritage Over Another. *International Journal of Cultural Property* 20(4): 431–450.

Bender, B. (2006). Place and Landscape. In C. Tilley, W. Keane, S. Kuechler, M. Rowlands, and P. Spyer (eds.) *Handbook of Material Culture*. London: Sage, 303–314.

Berque, A. (1994). *Cinq propositions pour une théorie du paysage*. Ceyzérieu: Editions Champ Vallon.

Blunt, A. (2007). Cultural Geographies of Migration: Mobility, Transnationality and Diaspora. *Progress in Human Geography* 31(5): 684–694.

Bourdeau, L., Gravari-Barbas, M., and Robinson, M. (eds.) (2015). *World Heritage, Tourism and Identity: Inscription and Co-production*. Abingdon: Routledge.

Burch-Brown, J. (2020). Should Slavery's Statues Be Preserved? On Transitional Justice and Contested Heritage. *Journal of Applied Philosophy* 1: 59–86.

Castles, S., de Haas, H., and Miller, M. (eds.) (2013). *The Age of Migration: International Population Movements in the Modern World*. London: Palgrave McMillan.

Cooke, B. and Lane, R. (2015). How Do Amenity Migrants Learn to Be Environmental Stewards of Rural Landscapes? *Landscape and Urban Planning* 134: 43–52.

Cosgrove, D. (1984). *Social Formation and Symbolic Landscape*. London: Croom Helm.

Cosgrove, D. (1985). Prospect, Perspective and the Evolution of the Landscape Idea. *Transactions of the Institute of British Geographers*, 10(1): 45–62.

Cosgrove, D. and Daniels, S. (eds.) (1988). *The Iconography of Landscape: Essays on the Symbolic Representation, Design and Use of Past Environments*. Cambridge: Cambridge University Press.

Cosgrove, D. and Jackson, P. (1987). New Directions in Cultural Geography. *Area* 19 (2): 95–101.

Crang, M. (1997). Picturing Practices: Research Through the Tourist Gaze. *Progress in Human Geography* 21(3): 359–373.

Cresswell, T. (2013). *Geographic Thought: A Critical Introduction*. Oxford: Wiley-Blackwell.

Crouch, D. (2013). Landscape, Performance and Performativity. In P. Howard, I. Thompson, E. Waterton, and M. Atha (eds.) *The Routledge Companion to Landscape Studies*. Abingdon: Routledge.

Dang, T. K. (2021). Decolonizing Landscape. *Landscape Research* 46(7): 1004–1016.

Dastgerdi, A. S., Sargolini, M., and Pierantoni, I. (2019). Climate Change Challenges to Existing Cultural Heritage Policy. *Sustainability* 11(19): 5227.

D'Eramo, M. (2017). *Il selfie del mondo*. Milano: Feltrinelli.

Duncan, J. (1980). The Superorganic in American Cultural Geography. *Annals of the Association of American Geographers* 70: 181–198.

Duncan, J. (1990). *The City as a Text: The Politics of Landscape Interpretation in the Kandyan Kingdom*. Cambridge: Cambridge University Press.

Duncan, J. (1995). Landscape Geography, 1993–94. *Progress in Human Geography* 19(3): 414–422.

Duncan, J. and Duncan, N. (1988). (Re)reading the Landscape. *Environment and Planning D: Society and Space* 6(2): 117–126.

Duncan, J. and Duncan, N. (2003). *Landscapes of Privilege*. Abingdon: Routledge.

Farinelli, F. (1991). L'arguzia del paesaggio. *Casabella* 575: 10–12.

Fowler, P. (2003). World Heritage Landscapes, 1992–2002: A Review and a Prospect. *World Heritage Papers* 7: 16–32.

Giaccardi, E. (ed.). (2012). *Heritage and Social Media: Understanding Heritage in a Participatory Culture*. Abingdon: Routledge.

Giblin, J. (2015). Critical Approaches to Post-colonial (Post-conflict) Heritage. In E. Waterton and M. Watson (eds.) *The Palgrave Handbook of Contemporary Heritage Research*. London: Palgrave Macmillan, 313–329.

Gosnell, H., and Abrams, J. (2011). Amenity Migration: Diverse Conceptualizations of Drivers, Socioeconomic Dimensions, and Emerging Challenges. *GeoJournal* 76(4): 303–322.

Guzman, P., Fatorić, S., and Ishizawa, M. (2020). Monitoring Climate Change in World Heritage Properties: Evaluating Landscape-based Approach in the State of Conservation System. *Climate* 8(3): 39.

Harrison, R. and Hughes, L. (2010). Heritage, Colonialism and Postcolonialism. In R. Harrison (ed.) *Understanding the Politics of Heritage*. Manchester: Manchester University Press.

Harrison, R. (2013). *Heritage: Critical Approaches*. Abingdon: Routledge.

Harvey, D. (2015). Landscape and Heritage: Trajectories and Consequences. *Landscape Research* 40(8): 911–924.

Harvey, D. and Wilkinson T. (2013). Landscape and heritage. Emerging landscapes of heritage. In P. Howard, I. Thompson, E. Waterton, and M. Atha (eds.) *The Routledge Companion to Landscape Studies*. Abingdon: Routledge, 176–191.

Harvey, D. and Waterton, E. (2015). Landscapes of Heritage and Heritage Landscapes. *Landscape Research* 40(8): 905–910.

Hoskins, G. (2010). A Secret Reservoir of Values: The Narrative Economy of Angel Island Immigration Station. *Cultural Geographies* 17(2): 259–275.

Jackson, P. (1989) *Maps of Meaning*. London: Unwin Hyman.

Johnson, N. C. (1999). Framing the Past: Time, Space and the Politics of Heritage Tourism in Ireland. *Political Geography* 18(2): 187–207.

Jongen, R. M. (1994). *René Magritte ou la pensée imagée de l'invisible*. Bruxelles: Presses de l'Université Saint-Louis.

Jones, J. P. (2013). Poststructuralism. In N. C. Johnson, R. Schein, and J. Winders (eds.) *The Wiley-Blackwell Companion to Cultural Geography*. Oxford: Wiley, 23–28.

Kirsch, S. (2013). Cultural Geography I: Materialist Turns. *Progress in Human Geography* 37(3): 433–441.

Kryder-Reid, E. (2018). Introduction: Tools for a Critical Heritage. *International Journal of Heritage Studies* 24(7): 691–693.

Larsen, J. (2014). The Tourist Gaze 1.0, 2.0, and 3.0. In A. Lew, M. Hall, and A. Williams (eds.) *The Wiley Blackwell Companion to Tourism*, Chichester: Wiley-Blackwell, 304–313.

Lorimer, H. (2005). Cultural Geography: The Busyness of Being-more-than-representational. *Progress in Human Geography* 29(1): 83–94.

Lowenthal, D. (1978). Finding Valued Landscapes. *Progress in Human Geography* 2(3): 373–418.

Lowenthal, D. (1985). *The Past Is a Foreign Country*. Cambridge: Cambridge University Press.

Lowenthal, D. (1993). Landscape as Heritage. National Scenes and Global Changes. In J. D. Fladmark (ed.) *Heritage: Conservation, Interpretation and Enterprise*. Abingdon: Routledge, 3–15.

Lowenthal, D. (1998). *The Heritage Crusade and the Spoils of History*. Cambridge: Cambridge University Press.

Ludu, A. (2016). *Boundaries of a Complex World*. Berlin-Heidelberg: Springer.

Matless, D. (1998). *Landscape and Englishness*. London: Reaktion Books.

Massey, D. (1995). *For Space*. London: Sage.

Minca, C. (2007a). Humboldt's Compromise, Or the Forgotten Geographies of Landscape. *Progress in Human Geography* 31(2): 179–193.

Minca, C. (2007b). The Tourist Landscape Paradox. *Social and Cultural Geography* 8(3): 433–453.

Mitchell, D. (1995). There's No Such Thing as Culture: Towards a Reconceptualization of the Idea of Culture in Geography. *Transactions of the Institute of British Geographers* 20 (1): 102–116.

Mitchell, D. (2007). Work, Struggle, Death, and Geographies of Justice: The Transformation of Landscape in and Beyond California's Imperial Valley. *Landscape Research* 32(5): 559–577.

Mitchell, D. (2011). Labor's Geography: Capital, Violence, Guest Workers and the Post-World War II Landscape. *Antipode* 43(2): 563–595.

Mitchell, D. (2013). Labour's Geography and Geography's Labour: California as an (Anti-) Revolutionary Landscape. *Geografiska Annaler: Series B, Human Geography* 95 (3): 219–233.

Murdoch, J. (2006). *Post-structuralist Geography*. London: Sage.

Offen, K. (2013). Historical Geography II: Digital Imaginations. *Progress in Human Geography* 37(4): 564–577.

Olwig, K. (1996). Recovering the Substantive Nature of Landscape. *Annals of the Association of American Geographers* 86(4): 630–653.

Olwig, K. (2002). *Landscape, Nature, and the Body Politic*. Madison: University of Wisconsin Press.

Olwig, K. (2010). The "British Invasion": The "New" Cultural Geography and Beyond. *Cultural Geographies* 17(2): 175–179.

Naylor, L., Daigle, M., Ramírez, M. M., and Gilmartin, M. (2018). Interventions: Bringing the decolonial to political geography. *Political Geography* 66: 199–209.

Neumann, R. P. (2011). Political Ecology III: Theorizing Landscape. *Progress in Human Geography* 35(6): 843–850.

Pettenati, G. (2019). *I paesaggi culturali Unesco*. Milano: Franco Angeli.

Price, M. and Lewis, M. (1993). The Reinvention of Cultural Geography. *Annals of the Association of American Geographers* 83(1): 1–17.

Raffestin, C. (1978). Du paysage à l'espace ou les signes de la Géographie. *Hèrodote* 9: 90–104.

Rao, K. (2010). A New Paradigm for the Identification, Nomination and Inscription of Properties on the World Heritage List. *International Journal of Heritage Studies* 16(3): 161–172.

Rishbeth, C. and Powell, M. (2013). Place Attachment and Memory: Landscapes of Belonging as Experienced Post-migration. *Landscape Research* 38(2): 160–178.

Rose, G. (1993). *Feminism and Geography: The Limits of Geographical Knowledge*. Minneapolis: University of Minnesota Press.

Rose, G. (2016). Rethinking the Geographies of Cultural 'Objects' Through Digital Technologies: Interface, Network and Friction. *Progress in Human Geography* 40(3): 334–351.

Rose, M. (2021). The Question of Culture in Cultural Geography: Latent Legacies and Potential Futures. *Progress in Human Geography* 45(4): 951–971.

Rössler, M. (2006). World Heritage Cultural Landscapes: A UNESCO Flagship Programme 1992–2006. *Landscape Research* 31(4): 333–353.

Samers, M. and Collyer, M. (2017). *Migration*. Abingdon: Routledge.

Samuel, R. (1994). *Theatres of Memory*. London: Verso.

Santos, X. M. and Piñeiro-Antelo, M. D. L. Á. (2020). Landscape and Power: The Debate Around Ugliness in Galicia (Spain). *Landscape Research* 45(7): 841–853.

Sauer C. (1925). The Morphology of Landscape. In J. Leighly (ed.) (1963). *Land and Life: A Selection of Writings of Carl Ortwin Sauer*. Berkeley: University of California Press, 315–350.

Searle, A. (2020). Absence. *Environmental Humanities* 12(1): 167–172.

Smith, L. (2006). *Uses of Heritage*. Abingdon: Routledge.

Smith, L. (2012). Editorial. *International Journal of Heritage Studies* 18(6): 533–540.

Tolia-Kelly, D. P. (2004). Materializing Post-colonial Geographies: Examining the Textural Landscapes of Migration in the South Asian Home. *Geoforum* 35(6): 675–688.

Thrift, N. (2008). *Non-representational Theory: Space, Politics, Affect*. Abingdon: Routledge.

Tuck, E. and Yang, K. W. (2012). Decolonization Is Not a Metaphor. Decolonization: Indigeneity. *Education and Society*, 1(1): 1–40.

Urry, J. (1990). *The Tourist Gaze*. London: Sage.

Urry, J. (1992). The Tourist Gaze "Revisited". *American Behavioral Scientist* 36 (2): 172–186.

Waterton, E. (2010). *Politics, Policy and the Discourses of Heritage in Britain*. Basingstoke: Palgrave.

Waterton, E. and Watson, S. (2013). Framing Theory: Towards a Critical Imagination in Heritage Studies. *International Journal of Heritage Studies* 19(6): 546–561.

Waterton, E. and Watson, S. (eds.) (2015). *The Palgrave Handbook of Contemporary Heritage Research*. London: Palgrave Macmillan.

Waterton, E. (2018). More-than-representational Landscapes. In P. Howard, I. Thompson, E. Waterton, and M. Atha (eds.) *The Routledge Companion to Landscape Studies*. Abingdon: Routledge, 91–101.

Whelan, Y. (ed.) (2016). *Heritage, Memory and the Politics of Identity: New Perspectives on the Cultural Landscape*. London: Routledge.

Williams, R. (1981). *Culture*. London: Fontana Press.

Wylie, J. (2007). *Landscape*. Abingdon: Routledge.

Winter, T. (2013). Clarifying the Critical in Critical Heritage Studies. *International Journal of Heritage Studies* 19(6): 532–545.

Woods, M. (2010). Performing Rurality and Practising Rural Geography. *Progress in Human Geography* 34(6): 835–846.

WTTC – World Travel and Tourism Council (2021). *Travel and Tourism Economic Impact 2021*. London: WTTC.

Zukin, S. (1993). *Landscapes of Power: From Detroit to Disney World*. Berkeley: University of California Press.

2 Landscape, heritage, and justice

What place for education?

Margherita Cisani

Learning landscape as heritage

Landscape and heritage are commonly considered vital in ensuring social wellbeing and quality of life (Council of Europe, 2000; 2005; Egoz and De Nardi, 2017; Wylie, 2009; Williams 2019; Wood and Martin, 2020), and they both strongly rely on the ability to preserve and transmit a tangible and intangible capital from a generation to the next. Education is one of the tools of this crucial exchange between generations, but, as affirming that landscape and heritage are directly linked to wellbeing and social justice can be contentious – landscape appearance often hides social injustices – so it is for education, which is a complex and all but straightforward process. This chapter deals precisely with this issue, pinpointing to the pivotal role of education in relation to landscape as heritage, and discussing its place in what is to be considered as a process rather than fact (Harvey, 2015; Harvey and Waterton, 2015).

The evolving debate around landscape and heritage and on heritage landscapes (Harvey and Wilkinson, 2018) showed how both fields of research have to benefit from an intertwined discussion, which should regard especially their temporality and communal nature, as "without temporal depth and a critical concern for others, they end up being both presentist and solipsistic" (Harvey, 2015: 918). Harvey's words call into question the very understanding of the notions of landscape and heritage, which necessitate of a complex and holistic interpretation (Smith, 2006; Wylie, 2007; Antrop and Van Eetvelde, 2017) as well as a critical posture (Harrison, 2012; Mitchell, 2003; Winter, 2013). Although now well established in the academic debate, this interpretative shift towards a dynamic and political stance on heritage landscapes is not completely reflected in the public discourse, and especially in the educational realm (Castiglioni and Cisani, 2020). In addition, landscape and heritage scholars rarely considered the educational issues at stake in the process of landscape heritagization. Among such considerations, education has been primarily treated as a variable, a perceptual lens in relation to landscape (Howard, 2013: 49) or as a means of increasing awareness on the authorized heritage (Smith, 2006).

Recently, however, the role of education with regard to landscape has gained a greater attention (Jørgensen et al., 2019; Sgard and Paradis, 2019; Cisani, Castiglioni and Sgard, 2022) and it has been one of the indicators for the assessment of the European Landscape Convention (ELC) application by the signatory parties, with

DOI: 10.4324/9781003195238-2

the 20th anniversary celebrated in 2020. Joining this momentum, this chapter aims at reflecting specifically on the heritage-landscape nexus in relation to education, considering it with a critical stance, highlighting its interactions with landscape democracy (Egoz, Jørgensen, and Ruggeri, 2018). Before proceeding with the chapter, it is worth clarifying the terms "landscape education", "heritage education", as well as their association in the notion of "landscape-as-heritage education".

"Landscape education" – or education towards landscape and landscape's values – is explicitly considered as the primary task of the parties that signed the ELC (Council of Europe, 2000); Antrop and Van Eetvelde define it as "the continuous process of learning about the land, environment and society that are manifested in the landscape" (2019: 31), and it is widely agreed that landscape education has not only disciplinary purposes – as an object of study in geography, architecture and art, planning and urban studies, anthropology and archaeology, and so on – but also wider and transversal pedagogical meanings, in relation to sustainability education, citizenship education and, of course, heritage education (Castiglioni and Cisani, 2020).

The significance of "heritage education" is similarly promoted by international organizations such as the European Commission and presented as the direct experience or analysis of cultural heritage, through which learners gain knowledge, intellectual skills, and a wider range of competences on issues such as cultural heritage maintenance or societal wellbeing,[1] going therefore well beyond the simple teaching of History and History of Art (Delgado-Algarra and Cuenca-Lòpez, 2020: 2). Nevertheless, as the authors of the recent *Handbook of Research on Citizenship and Heritage Education* declare,

> despite the existing connections between citizenship education and heritage education, there are still needs in terms of citizen participation and civic awareness of the value of heritage as a source for citizenship education or the importance of citizen education in the critical conservation of heritage.
>
> (ibid: xx)

Already Smith, in her renowned work on the "authorized heritage discourse" (AHD), in fact, highlighted the lack of concern or acknowledgement of the educational values of heritage places (2006: 137). Naturalising heritage as simply something that "just is" (ibid: 300), leads in fact to considering it as educational per se, without questioning the reasons, the means, and the values conveyed by a visit to a heritage site.

As noticed, among others, by Harvey and Waterton (2015), landscape and heritage have seen an increased popular interest in recent years, and for various reasons – including the efforts from the Council of Europe with the Conventions of Florence in 2000 and Faro in 2005 – the two are often coexisting in the same educational process, to the point that we could speak of a "landscape-as-heritage education". This notion, however, has two possible interpretations: the first is linked to a narrow identification of landscape as made up only of heritage sites and values, while the second broadens its scope and leads to a heritagization of every landscape, all worthy of an "heritage gaze". Both views are controversial, the former mainly for its tendency to convey taken-for-granted and authorized discourses on the importance of landscape as the mere repository of heritage, history and identity (Harrison, 2012; Smith, 2006), the latter for the a-critical and "flattened" vision of landscape, seen as a direct and neutral expression of community belonging and local identity, ignoring coexisting but underrepresented aspects, conflicting values, or power inequalities.

Drawing from previous considerations, the exit way from this impasse could be considering landscape-as-heritage education as a relational process rather than a goal, enhancing awareness on the role of knowing, reading, interpreting, and inhabiting landscapes in heritagization processes, and shedding light on the actors involved as well on those excluded.

In light of the above, the following section of the chapter will explore the nexus between landscape-as-heritage education and social justice.

And education to landscape as heritage "justly arrived at"

On the one hand, learning the language of landscape (Spirn, 2005), exercising the so-called "landscape literacy", should enable individuals to access, in a comprehensive way, to landscape as a source of justice, in terms of wellbeing, citizenship expression, and belonging. On the other hand, the languages, images, and discourses through which landscape is communicated – in the governance but also in educational practices – may convey different messages and ideas of landscape. Landscape education, therefore, can be a tool for generating justice as well as injustice, especially when it delivers a top-down and narrow definition of landscape. Insights from a research conducted in 2018 on several landscape education projects in Italy show that links between landscape and citizenship are often based on the heritage discourse and that an understanding of landscape as a dynamic entity, a shared heritage collectively built, is poorly represented and isolated, if compared with an interpretation of landscape as an area of outstanding beauty or as the repository of pre-established and authorized cultural and natural exceptional values, to be protected from change, often with limited and controlled access (Castiglioni and Cisani, 2020). As previously noticed, the assumption that landscape-as-heritage education is directly linked with a positive outcome in terms of social engagement and justice is contentious, calling therefore for throughout analysis and critical perspectives, as those presented in this chapter.

A reflection on the epistemological assumptions on which landscape-as-heritage education processes are based upon might help in forging a critical approach in their analysis. For the sake of this chapter, this critical stance can be oriented primarily on those approaches where landscape and heritage are both considered as tools for enhancing wellbeing and social cohesion. In these regards, it is possible to identify two lines of thought: one mainly devoted to landscape stewardship and the other to landscape justice (Castiglioni and Cisani, 2020). Educational practices based on the first approach aim at promoting participation of the population in the recognition of landscape values and in stewardship actions (García-Martín, Plieninger, and Bieling, 2018), while those adopting a more transformative and critical stance seek to questioning the processes by which landscapes are produced, highlighting their links with democracy and spatial justice (Freire and Macedo, 1987; Egoz, Jørgensen, and Ruggeri, 2018), their political dimension and the way in which the discourse about landscape-as-heritage is built and conveyed, for example through textbooks (Kühne, 2018: 152).

Following this second vein, it is possible to adapt and perhaps renew Mitchell's "new axioms for reading the landscape" (Mitchell, 2008), focusing in particular on their usefulness in connecting landscape, heritage discourses, and justice. Adopting a materialist point of view over Peirce Lewis' axioms proposed at the end of the 70s in order to learn how to read the cultural meaning of all landscapes, Mitchell discusses a series of six new axioms that culminate with the idea that "landscape is the spatial form that social justice takes" (Axiom 6). Despite "both everyday history ... and extraordinary events ... shape the land, and shape the possibilities for the future" he argues that

> the representation of history in landscape (and all that goes with it, including identity and identification, the politics of inclusion and exclusion, the production of "national" landscapes, memorialization, and so forth) is not somehow immanent in the landscape itself (in the bricks and mortar, lawns and shrubs); rather it is a product of struggles over meanings – the meanings that are attached to landscape and the ones that are made to stick (see, generally, Loewen 1999). History matters in this case because landscape as historical representation is obviously an expression of power.
>
> (Mitchell, 2008: 41)

Speaking directly to the issues relating landscape-as-heritage education, he continues arguing that

> the trick for us is to use our analysis, design, and other skills both to show how [the history of landscape] does still belong to the people and to counter the heavy weight of alienation that is so much a part of the capitalist production of landscape.
>
> (ibid: 47)

Although it is not possible to directly "read" the landscape in any satisfying sense,

> it is possible to analyze it: to search for how it is made, to explore its functions, to examine the other places that are foundational in its production and meaning, to understand its history and trajectory, to uncover how power works in and through it, and *therefore*, to learn what it says about the status of and possibility for a just world in the here and now ... Only by analyzing the social relations that go into its making, that we can begin to really learn (and learn from) what we are looking at. In doing so, we ought to be able to learn how better to intervene into the landscape, to make better

guesses about the reasons for and impacts of our designs, our solidarity work with activist groups, or just to do a better job of telling the landscape's story, and through that to gain a better purchase on how the totality of social relations operates in particular places and at particular times.

(ibid)

Therefore, interpreting Mitchell's words, learning and teaching landscapes are practices strictly related to social justice and ought to concur in challenging the naturalized landscape-as-heritage discourses. A landscape-as-heritage education "justly arrived at" implies therefore such a complex, dialectic, and dynamic understanding of landscape (Mels and Mitchell, 2013: 219).

The abovementioned research on the Italian context indicated though that considerations of diversity and justice in questioning landscapes within pedagogical processes are greater when problems and conflicts are evident, while it is more superficial in cases of landscapes with exceptional and consolidated heritage values, where a simplified approach risks the forced appeasement of any form of landscape conflict (Castiglioni and Cisani, 2020; Ruggeri, 2018). That is why it is crucial to consider issues of democracy, access, belonging, and justice especially in relation to heritage landscapes.

Placing education in landscape heritagization

Having clarified some possible meanings of landscape-as-heritage education as well as its connections with social justice and with the debate on landscape democracy, this paragraph reflects on the place of education in the heritagization of landscape, with the aim of providing a rather simple framework that should help in recognizing the, often underestimated, role of pedagogical initiatives in such processes.

Educational activities materialize in various ways, ranging from the more formal and structured – such as those provided within the school systems and according to national guidelines – to the informal and non-formal initiatives of lifelong learning; thus, the depth and the complexity of their critical reading varies significantly in relation to the context and the participants. The following brief categorization will present and juxtapose three examples representing some of the possible nexus between landscape education, heritage, and justice.

In short, educational activities relating to landscape-as-heritage could emerge in different phases of the process of heritagization of landscape: i) *before* the recognition of a patrimonial value, ii) *during* the process of institutionalization, and iii) *after*, as part of its management, as a revitalization initiative or as a challenge to an established heritage. Needless to say, further variables to take into account relate to the number and type of actors involved as well as to the scale of the initiative, from the local to the global. The examples provided here will follow the sequencing-based categorization proposed, acknowledging though the possibility to explore the matrix derived from the intersection of the variables and, of course, recognizing that what is here proposed is a forced schematization and that each case is part of a more complex continuum.

Table 2.1. Details of landscape-as-heritage educational projects mentioned in the chapter

Title of the project (main institutions involved)	Location (scale)	Description	Place in landscape heritagization
In20amoilpaesaggio (*University of Padua, AIIG and Veneto Region Landscape Observatory*)	Veneto, Italy (*regional level*)	Students (lower secondary schools) are invited to choose one local landscape, to explore it, and to imagine its future, envisioning actions of care, transformation, and enhancement.	Before
Re-telling the Walls. Le mura di Bergamo verso UNESCO. Unesco raccontato ai bambini. I bambini raccontano le mura (*University of Bergamo and Bergamo Municipality*)	Bergamo, Italy (*local level*)	Students (primary schools) explore and co-create the multiple meanings (natural and cultural) associated to the landscape of the Venetian Walls in the city of Bergamo. A short guide to the site and an animated videoclip constitute the outputs of the project.	During
Migrantour: a European network of migrant driven intercultural routes to understand cultural diversity (*Fondazione ACRA, Viaggi Solidali, Oxfam Italia, and others*)	Italian and other European cities (*international level*)	Citizens and students participate in migrant-led tours, in order to discover, through the words of migrants, facets often unknown to even born and bred locals, tackling improper and discriminative representations of local heritage, migration and cultural diversity.	After

Activities taking place prior the official recognition of the heritage are the most difficult to identify, but they can be related, for instance, to research–action initiatives aimed at eliciting, mapping, and studying landscape perceptions among the population, with particular attention to youngsters. An example is the "in20amoilpaesaggio" project,[2] realized by the University of Padova with the Italian Association of Geography Teachers and the Veneto Region Landscape Observatory, that led to the creation of an online map that collect 54 "landscapes of care", or "imagined landscapes", chosen by the students involved (all belonging to lower secondary schools), challenged in identifying feasible actions of protection, management, or valorization. Within this project, the use of a broad notion of landscape, according to the ELC approach, opened up a space of expression that was employed by students and teachers to bring to the fore some minor and marginal landscapes that, however, are considered as heritage for the school and the local community, such as local green and recreational areas, everyday landscapes of the school premises, abandoned or undervalued buildings, or heritage sites related to local history. What is relevant in this project is that students acknowledged their power – albeit sometimes small in relation to other decision makers' agency – in identifying what is worth considering as heritage and which are the actions that can be carried out to enhance it.

The phases during which institutions actively proceed towards an official recognition of landscape as heritage, for example via landscape and territorial plans – at a local scale – or promoting a UNESCO World Heritage candidacy – on a global scale – is often characterized by the activation of participatory processes, among which the involvement of schools and students is commonly foreseen. Primary school students were involved, for instance, in educational activities related to the exploration of the cultural and natural significance of the landscape of the Venetian Walls in the city of Bergamo (Italy), two years before its official inclusion in the WHL among the Venetian Works of Defence serial and transnational site.[3] This initiative was explicitly considered by the promoters of the candidacy – the municipality and the local university among all – as one of the evidences of the local community's engagement towards this particular heritage landscape (Bonadei, Cisani, and Viani, 2017). The title of this project *Unesco raccontato ai bambini. I bambini raccontano le Mura* (UNESCO explained to children. Children narrate the Walls) well describes the dual relation between the institutional discourse around the extraordinary heritage value of the Venetian Walls, as exceptional testimony of architectural and military culture, and the other various and subjective meanings that are attached to this complex landscape by the children of the primary school located within the perimeter of the Walls. Eventually the site became listed as UNESCO World Heritage and – although the official criteria (iii and iv) do not mention it – the natural, cultural, emotional, and experiential values associated to the landscape of the Walls are well recognized in the public representations of this heritage landscape. This negotiation of meanings well exemplifies the complex interplay between different landscape and heritage notions as well as the possible role of educational activities in the making of an AHD.

When the heritagization process reaches the public and the institutional recognition, landscape becomes the object of several representations and performances highly related to education: from its inclusion in school programs to cultural visits and school trips. These initiatives might be encompassed in the management of heritage landscapes, in their revitalization or, finally, heritage landscapes might as well be subject to counter-readings that propose unconventional and underrepresented views that challenge the AHD.

Borrowing Ruggeri's words, "stories are powerful agents of change" (Ruggeri, 2018: 140) and they can help in rewriting wicked or contested heritage, such as in the Zingonia 3.0 project, described by Ruggeri himself, in which students were invited in rewriting local heritage and degradation narratives. A similar example is the Migrantour[4] project, that proposes cultural tours led by migrants in several Italian and European cities, mostly to secondary school students but also to citizens and tourists. The aim of this initiative is offering job perspectives to migrants and refugees – as they are trained for leading the tours – as well as new and alternative stories and perspectives on the urban landscapes of intercultural cities. These Migrantours were firstly launched in Turin (Italy) in 2010 and are now offered in a growing network of EU cities, being also funded by several EU programs (Vietti, 2019). Beside challenging the dominant narrative that describes metropolitan areas subject to significant migration as landscapes of poverty and degradation, these tours also promote a different gaze on traditional and iconic cultural heritage sites, such as the heart of the city of Bologna with the different cults it is possible to encounter, or the city of Rome with its landscape marked by ancient multiculturalism and by a complex history of colonialism. The fact that these tours are primarily offered as educational activities in school trips is a sign of the crucial role played by education in the dissemination of alternative and less represented discourses and, ultimately, in the construction of more inclusive heritage landscapes.

Towards a processual and critical approach

The great variety of educational projects and the overlapping meanings and uses of landscape-as-heritage that transpire from this brief analysis can be puzzling, but it testifies to the vitality of educational practices in the context of heritage landscapes. This chapter aimed at promoting a greater acknowledgement of education as strictly entangled in the production, management, valorization, and transformation of landscapes as heritage, highlighting its role before, during, and after the patrimonialization of landscapes. Moreover, exploring some of the links among landscape, heritage, and social/spatial justice, a processual and critical interpretation of learning practices has been suggested. First, considering education towards landscape and heritage as processes of enskillment entails "a deep level of personal, ecological and cultural experience" (Wattchow and Prins, 2018: 108) and features the active role of learners/teachers within the performances in/of heritage landscapes (Smith, 2006: 304). Second, and avoiding the risk of an excessively individualistic and subjective relationship with landscape as heritage, education should also be considered as a continuous challenge to the AHD, via place-based learning and critical pedagogies able to rework, renew, contest, and criticize consolidated and mainstream approaches towards landscape as heritage.

Further research – including action-research initiatives featuring education practices – should be devoted to deepening the analysis on the way through which education might contribute to democratizing the landscape-as-heritage discourse, via direct engagement with individuals, promoting re-workings and counter-readings of landscapes as heritage, increasing the opportunities for people to access to landscape as a source of justice.

Notes

1 https://ec.europa.eu/culture/cultural-heritage/cultural-heritage-eu-policies/cultural-heritage-and-education (retrieved on 20 April 2021).
2 https://in20amoilpaesaggio.it/ (retrieved on 29/04/2021).
3 https://whc.unesco.org/en/list/1533/ (retrieved on 17/12/2021).
4 www.mygrantour.org/en/ (retrieved on 17/12/2021).

References

Antrop, M. and Van Eetvelde, V. (eds) (2017). *Landscape Perspectives*. Dordrecht: Springer Netherlands.

Antrop, M. and Van Eetvelde, V. (2019). From Teaching Geography to Landscape Education for All. In K. Jørgensen, N. Karadeniz, E. Mertens, and R. Stiles, R. (eds), *The Routledge Handbook of Teaching Landscape*. Abingdon: Routledge, 31–44.

Bonadei, R., Cisani, M., and Viani, E. (2017). City Walls as Historic Urban Landscape: A Case study on Participatory Education. *Almatourism – Journal of Tourism, Culture and Territorial Development*, 8(7): 75–88.

Castiglioni, B. and Cisani, M. (2020). The Complexity of Landscape Ideas and the Issue of Landscape Democracy in School and Non-formal Education: Exploring Pedagogical Practices in Italy. *Landscape Research*, online first, 1–13. Retrieved at: doi:10.1080/01426397.2020.1741528.

Cisani, M., Castiglioni B. and Sgard, A. (2022). Landscape and Education: Politics of/in Practices. *Landscape Research*, 47(2): 137–141.

Council of Europe (2000). European Landscape Convention. Florence 20/10/2000, ETS No 176, Council of Europe.

Council of Europe (2005). Convention on the Value of Cultural Heritage for Society. Faro 27/10/2005, ETS No 199, Council of Europe.

Delgado-Algarra, E. J. and Cuenca-Lòpez, J. M. (2020). *Handbook of Research on Citizenship and Heritage Education*. Hershey: IGI Global.

Egoz, S. and De Nardi, A. (2017). Defining Landscape Justice: The Role of Landscape in Supporting Wellbeing of Migrants, a Literature Review. *Landscape Research*, 42(S1): S74–S89.

Egoz, S., Jørgensen, K., and Ruggeri, D. (2018). *Defining Landscape Democracy: A Path to Spatial Justice*. Cheltenham: Edward Elgar.

Freire, P. and Macedo, D. P. (1987). *Literacy: Reading the Word and the World*. Abingdon: Routledge.

García-Martín, M., Plieninger, T., and Bieling, C. (2018). Dimensions of Landscape Stewardship across Europe: Landscape Values, Place Attachment, Awareness, and Personal Responsibility. *Sustainability*, 10(1): 263.

Harrison, R. (2012). *Heritage: Critical Approaches*. Abingdon: Routledge.

Harvey, D. (2015). Landscape and Heritage: Trajectories and Consequences. *Landscape Research*, 40(8): 911–924.

Harvey, D. C. and Waterton, E. (2015). Editorial: Landscapes of Heritage and Heritage Landscapes. *Landscape Research*, 40(8): 905–910.

Harvey, D. and Wilkinson, T. (2018). Landscape and Heritage: Emerging Landscapes of Heritage. In P. Howard, I. Thompson, E. Waterton, and M. Atha (eds), *The Routledge Companion to Landscape Studies*. Abingdon: Routledge, pp. 176–191.

Howard, P. (2013). Perceptual lenses. In P. Howard, I. Thompson, E. Waterton, and M. Atha (eds), *The Routledge Companion to Landscape Studies*. Abingdon: Routledge, pp. 43–53.

Jørgensen, K., Karadeniz, N., Mertens, E., and Stiles, R. (2019). *The Routledge Handbook of Teaching Landscape*. Abingdon: Routledge.

Kühne, O. (2018). *Landscape and Power in Geographical Space as a Social-Aesthetic Construct*. Cham: Springer International Publishing.

Mels, T. and Mitchell, D. (2013). Landscape and Justice. In N. C. Johnson, R. H. Schein, and J. Winders (eds), *The Wiley-Blackwell Companion to Cultural Geography*, Hoboken: Wiley and Sons, pp. 209–224.

Mitchell, D. (2003). Cultural Landscapes: Just Landscapes or Landscapes of Justice? *Progress in Human Geography*, 27(6): 787–796.

Mitchell, D. (2008). New Axioms for Reading the Landscape: Paying Attention to Political Economy and Social Justice. In J. L. Wescoat and D. M. Johnston (eds), *Political Economies of Landscape Change: Places of Integrative Power*. Dordrecht: Springer Netherlands, 29–50.

Ruggeri, D. (2018). Storytelling as a Catalyst for Democratic Landscape Change in a Modernist Utopia. In S. Egoz, K. Jørgensen, and D. Ruggeri (eds), *Defining Landscape Democracy: A Path to Spatial Justice*. Cheltenham: Edward Elgar, 128–142.

Sgard, A. and Paradis, S. (2019). *Sur les bancs du paysage. Enjeux didactiques, démarches et outils*. Geneve: MétisPresses.

Smith, L. (2006). *Uses of Heritage*. Abingdon: Routledge.

Spirn, A. W. (2005). Restoring Mill Creek: Landscape Literacy, Environmental Justice and City Planning and Design. *Landscape Research*, 30(3): 395–413.

Vietti, F. (2019). Migrantour: Intercultural Urban Routes. *Antropologia Pubblica*, 4(2): 125–140.

Wattchow, B. and Prins, A. (2018). Learning a Landscape: Enskilment, Pedagogy and a Sense of Place. In P. Howard, I. Thompson, E. Waterton, and M. Atha (eds), *The Routledge Companion to Landscape Studies*, Abingdon: Routledge, pp. 102–112.

Williams, A. M. (2019). Therapeutic Landscapes. In D. Richardson, N. Castree, M. F. Goodchild, A. Kobayashi, W. Liu, and R. A. Marston (eds), *International Encyclopedia of Geography*, Hoboken: Wiley.

Winter, T. (2013). Clarifying the Critical in Critical Heritage Studies. *International Journal of Heritage Studies*, 19(6), 532–545.

Wood, N. and Martin, D. (2020). "I'm a Foreigner There"; Landscape, Wellbeing and the Geographies of Home. *Health and Place*, 62: 102274.

Wylie, J. (2007). *Landscape*. Abingdon: Routledge.

Wylie, J. (2009). Landscape, Absence and the Geographies of Love. *Transactions of the Institute of British Geographers*, 34(3): 275–289.

3 Mapping landscape from the past to the future

Critical reflections on the governance of landscape as heritage from the case of the Xikrin Indians of Brazil

Stéphanie Tselouiko

Introduction

Increasingly common in Indigenous environmental and territorial management projects since the 1960s, ethnomapping is a form of participatory mapping, that is, the development of maps by local people in partnership with public authorities, private institutions, scientists, NGOs, and so on, generally in order to support property rights claims and negotiate measures to protect their land – for example in industrial development areas – and as decision-making tools in spatial planning projects.

The production of these maps consists in transcribing ethnic knowledge about the landscape, its cultural use, the history of the group in given places and in relation to the Others, as well as the environmental threats and impacts that affect ways of life in the context of development projects. This involves identifying and spatializing the constituent elements of the territory, such as sacred or habitation sites; the toponyms given by the occupants; the inventory of plant, animal and mineral resources; the places travelled by people during their life; and the ecologically fragile areas.

In this kind of projects, basically two types of ethnomaps can be produced: on one hand, mental maps, and on the other, Euclidean and geo-referenced maps. Mental maps are "cartographic expressions of a subjective representation of space" (Staszak, 2003, in Lefebvre et al., 2017), the transcription of a vernacular geographical knowledge (or ethno-geographical knowledge) which are intellectual constructions grounded in an ontological and daily experience of space and the environment and which engage all the senses. They differ from Euclidean cartography in the nature of the data mobilised (discourses that may introduce philosophical reflections, beliefs, dreams or emotions, for example), the scale of the representations (individual scale or small group), and the free forms of representation which also can be produced with various materials, like textiles (e.g. the Andean Awayu),[1] strings (e.g. the khipus[2]), and techniques, like drawing in the sand or in the ashes of a campfire, or on bark or animal skins.

DOI: 10.4324/9781003195238-3

Given the different aspects that mental maps record, there are no fixed patterns through which these maps are expressed. Strongly marked by individual interpretations, "they are necessarily subjective and contextualised, and can therefore only be plural" (Collignon, 2005: 325). In short, each individual has its own way of understanding and mapping his/her territory even when their singular way is broadly shared by an entire social or cultural group. However, this loosely formalised knowledge does not tend to be theorized and it is therefore difficult to communicate it to actors external to the community, who don't share the same ontology of time and space.

So, to be read and used as a tool for dialogue, these mental maps are generally translated into the language of a discursive knowledge: the single one accepted as "scholarly geographical knowledge, thanks in particular to the objectification that underpins it and legitimizes its claim to a certain universality, formalized in a theoretical mode, concerned with objectification and communicability out of context" (Collignon, 2005: 325). This operation tends to transcribe the collected qualitative information into a more conventional form, starting with the application of a background map, the use of certain conventions (spatial and temporal scale, orientation, etc.), and the employment of symbols shared by all map-makers and understood by every reader of these maps. Ultimately, that means that these mental maps are transformed into geo-referenced maps, based on Western ontologies, epistemologies, and mapping techniques (in particular GIS techniques), which require that all the elements that make up the map have their global coordinates (latitude and longitude) precisely established. This is why geo-referenced maps which are valued by funders for territorial management as being more precise, more objective, more concrete, and more reliable are often favoured from the beginning. This way of approaching "ethnomapping" often implies defining objectives (territorial demarcation, management plan associated with one or more resources, etc.) which will influence the cartographic protocol by directing the questions to be asked, the scale of precision of the data, the source of the data (the informants in the community concerned).

This is why, despite the fact that this second form of ethnocartography (i.e. Euclidean and geo-referenced maps) is increasingly presented by public policies and their consultants as an essential tool for intercultural dialogue,[3] it is often considered inadequate by some authors (Roth, 2009; Mazurek, 2013; Reid and Sieber, 2016) to transcribe the dwelling space of Indigenous communities because its implementation raises ontological, epistemological, methodological, and ethical problems.

It is, among other things, often criticized for "reproducing hegemonic methods of land classification, resource classification and border demarcation, for supporting the processes of state domination and the capitalist system" (Sletto et al. 2013: 194) and obeying Western epistemologies and forms of representation (Harley 1989). Moreover, the geo-referencing of the map requires that a range of advanced technologies – satellite maps, Geographic Information Systems (GIS), sophisticated software, and so on – be used to produce geo-referenced maps. Therefore, the production of this type of map requires the formulation of a data collect protocol and the participation of trained technicians (who are rarely Indigenous) to participate in the ethnomapping process.

The reflections on ethnocartographic practice and its objectives are part of the discussion about ethnosciences in general, which are often criticized for considering the ordering of the world on the basis of Western categories that do not necessarily have a reference point in non-Western societies (Roué, 2012). In so doing, they

> reify certain parts of indigenous knowledge by *making them compatible with the modern division of sciences*, since the boundaries of the field are established a priori according to the classes of entities and phenomena that the corresponding disciplines have gradually carved out as their own objects in the fabric of the world.
>
> (Descola, 2005, my italics)

Ethnosciences also aim at finding correspondence for terms between different regimes of knowledge. In the context of ethnocartography, this is the case with the object "landscape", which has to be characterized in different types and spatialized, in order to address their cultural uses and their heritage value for a given human group, at a point in time t. According to the geographical concept as used in these ethnomapping projects, the landscape designates a part of the territory resulting from the action of natural and/or human factors and their interrelations.

> in this conception, the landscape is a kind of place of memory, as a place where the imprints deposited over time by modes of use of space are superimposed, imprints recognised to a certain extent as its own by a particular human group.
>
> (Descola, 2012: 651–652)

However, this geographical conception of landscape involves a temporal ontology which can fundamentally differ from Indigenous conceptualizations which states that it is more complex than a linear passage of time from the past, to the present, and towards the future (Reid and Sieber, 2016). This ontological difference also challenges the application of the notion of heritagization. Yet, the heritagization of an object or a natural space requires, on the one hand, that it be managed in such a way as to ensure its intergenerational passage and, on the other hand, that it be the object of a certain "patrimonial awareness" (Cormier-Salem and Roussel, 2002). But, at this point in time t, in an environment as changeable as the Amazon rainforest, most of the traces left by the group become materially imperceptible, especially in the case of mobile populations. So, in the intercultural context of these projects, how can landscapes be defined considering their mutability over time? What are we referring to when we talk about landscape as heritage and how can it be governed?

By combining ethnographic surveys and archival study, this chapter proposes a critical reflexion about governance of landscape as heritage for an historically itinerant group in Brazil, the Xikrin Indians of the Indigenous Land of Trincheira Bacajá (Terra Indígena Trincheira Bacajá – TITB).

The TITB is part of a multi-ethnic complex in the region known as Medio Xingu, facing the agrarian colonization front in the Transamazonian region, in the state of Pará. With an area of approximately 1,500,000 hectares, the TITB was delimited and formalized in 1996.

Since 2009, with the arrival of the Belo Monte hydroelectric plant (UHE Belo Monte), the implementation of a compensation programme (Plano Básico Ambiental – PBA), including the construction of roads that connect each village to the Transamazonian, the TITB has been marked by unprecedented political, economic, and ecological transformations that have only worsened since then, including the invasion of the region by settlers, loggers, and illegal gold diggers. In 2013, an environmental and territorial management project was initiated in all the villages of the TITB within the framework of a programme of the National Policy of Indigenous Environmental and Territorial Management – PNGATI (Política Nacional de Gestão Ambiental e Territorial Indígena) under the aegis of the National Indian Foundation – FUNAI, with the participation of the NGO The Nature Conservancy – TNC. The goal of this project based on ethnomapping is to construct a territorial management plan with priority actions towards the empowerment of Indigenous communities, territory protection, and sustainable management of natural resources.

We will question, first, the notion of landscape as heritage and see how the heritage governance of the landscape is rooted in the demarcation process. Second, from the study of an ethnomapping process in the context of PNGATI, we will analyse what happens when landscape is translated into a form outside its own materiality using mapping tools and to what extent do these tools allow the emergence of alternative meanings of landscape. Finally, we will observe what heritage-making in the ethnomapping process says about the relationship between Indigenous communities and the dominant society and how ethnomethodology can overcome the limits of ethnomapping.

Heritage-making through territory demarcation

The Xikrin say that before contact, the elders moved from a savannah ecosystem of Central Brazil to the equatorial forest ecosystem of the Bacajá River basin, today delimited and named Terra Indígena Trincheira Bacajá (TITB). Mobility was, above all, a matter of preference, motivated by a desire for conquest, which at the same time gave them the opportunity to assert themselves through their differences with other groups (Cohn, 2005), as well as within the group itself (Tselouiko, 2018).

Historical studies estimate the settlement of the Xikrin on the banks of the Bacajá River between 1924 and 1928 (Fisher, 1991, 2000) where they kept moving from one habitat to another until the early 1960s, when the Xikrin were contacted by the SPI[4] and were settled in a village on the banks of the Bacajá River in order to benefit from Western medical assistance on which they became dependent. The "peaceful" contact with the national society changed their way of inhabiting the space considerably. From then on, the Xikrin only trekked for a few weeks at a time, on a cyclical basis and no longer on a continuous basis, and instead of moving from one settlement to another they systematically returned to the same village, which had become permanent. This implied reduced spatial mobility and therefore a diminished territorial stake.

In 1979, the first demarcation of a territory of the Xikrin of Bacajá was carried out, encompassing an area of 192,125 hectares. However, this was contested by the Xikrin because the northern, southern, and eastern boundaries did not include their main *castanhais*, [5] which they had exploited since contact and which constituted their main source of income. In addition, the western boundary also excluded many important hunting and gathering areas. At the same time, the Parakanã, Asurini, and Araweté territories, to the south and west of the Xikrin respectively, were also being demarcated. Given the considerable mobility of the various groups in the region, the major difficulty encountered in these demarcations was that the physical or oral marks of appropriation (toponyms) covering this large forest area could overlap from one group to another. It was therefore proposed to delimit a large area of 2,391,600 hectares called the Koatinemo-Ipixuna-Bacajá Indigenous Area, which would encompass the four Indigenous groups in the region. This proposal to create a continuous zone of Indigenous protected areas was presented as a solution to this problem, yet it implied attributing a common heritage to all four groups at the expense of the multiplicity of elements and processes involved in the Indigenous ways of establishing their communities, and thereby denying their differences. According to Vidal (1985), this proposal was abandoned, without further clarification, and each territory was demarcated separately. Spanning an area of approximately 1,500,000 hectares, the TITB was demarcated and formalized in 1996.

There are no records available to indicate exactly how this demarcation took place. However, as we can see from satellite imagery, a river serves as a demarcation line between the TITB and the Koatinema Land of the Asurini, while an arbitrary north–south straight line separates the TITB from the Ipixuna Land of the Araweté (Vidal, 1985). Moreover, contact with civil society served largely as a temporal marker, since the places marking the northern, southern, and eastern boundaries refer to the *castanhais* that the Xikrin have exploited since this event.

Far from calling into question the validity or indeed the necessity of granting Indigenous populations their own territories, from a scientific point of view, the demarcation process raises a number of questions, in particular the equivocal nature of the constitution of borders based on specific spatiotemporal markers in a process of landscape heritagization.

For the Xikrin, who were highly mobile throughout the Central Brazil region, boundaries were never fixed, but dynamic. They allowed the Xikrin to constantly redefine themselves in a relationship of difference with others through movement in a space that constituted a "whole". To move (in the forest) is said to be *me ɣ* (or *me ɣry ten*) in the Mẽbêngôkre language, where *me* is "people", *ɣ* is "seed", and *ten* is "walk". *Yry* is used to mean "to go to meet", but *yry* is also a synonym for "to become". *Me ɣ* is a deeply poetic way that the Xikrin have of expressing movement in space, as an organic action, giving form to that action through the creation of paths and landscapes. The delimitation of a part of this space as Trincheira Bacajá Indigenous Land means subtracting places from this "whole" and denying a large part of the heritage of this mobility as an agent of continuity between the past, present, and future. In other words, when something is highlighted or evoked in order to generate a formal or "official" narrative that gives to a given space the shape of a territory, something else is pushed aside and abandoned.

Furthermore, the employment of "geospatial technologies emphasize a more static view of the world that is often inconsistent with Indigenous perspectives on space and time" (Reid and Sieber, 2016: 248) because it presumes that the relationships between the living beings (human and non-human) of the environment must be inscribed in a temporal continuum, to the detriment of a local conception of historicity in which space, more than time, serves as the basis for measurement and where movement disturbs the scale. Demarcation produces an "abstract space" which "is a static, bounded, homogenous space, existing apart from the observer and meant to be separate from the specificity of place. ... Rather than being neutral, abstract space and its mapping are thoroughly political" (Roth, 2009: 209). With the collective appropriation of a territory in the legal sense, the Xikrin have been transformed into historical subjects recognized as such by the state. In other words, by fixing the space of the Xikrin, their identity was also fixed, and with it, some landscapes that have been essentialized as factors of identity.

The close link created between territory and identity gives meaning to the notion of landscape as heritage. For this reason, when it is a matter of guaranteeing the continuity of an Indigenous community, ethnomapping logically appears to be the most effective way of giving visibility to the territory and making the notion of heritage concrete, by reaffirming its borders and reifying its landscapes.

Ethnomapping: revelation or abstraction of landscape as heritage?

The ethnomapping workshops started in April 2014 with training in the use of GPS. From this, the newly trained ethnomappers were expected to autonomously collect relevant resource points to be marked on the ethnomaps. This notion of "autonomy" needs, however, to be discussed here because the ethnomappers have been oriented on what to look for in a generic way – such as "fishing", "hunting", "gathering" resources and so on, all of which are considered as useful categories for a territorial management plan, but which ultimately leave little evidence of other endemic categories that would make sense in their cosmography like, for example, the living places of the spirits of the dead which are better to avoid. Then, these points were retrieved by the consultants of the NGO in charge of the project and were integrated into a GIS. In October 2014, a workshop was organised to produce the ethnomaps. The Xikrin cartographers, mostly young, single men or even young, married men with small children, were designated to participate in this workshop because, compared to women and the elderly, they are more literate, speak more, and are more familiar with technological devices, which favours their learning to use GPS and cartographic techniques.

The choice of the young male Xikrin for ethnomapping projects also derives from a dominant ideological basis that assigns specific skills for mapping. But if they were at greater advantage in learning to use GPS and cartographic techniques, on the other hand, because they belong to relatively young age groups and a single gender, they have a partial knowledge of the territory (especially given their sedentary lifestyle, which contrasts with that adopted by the elders in the pre-contact era). They also have a different conception of the notion of heritage and what it entails compared to women, who give more importance to individual heritage elements, such as the transmission of cultivars from mothers to daughters, and to the elderly, who put more emphasis on the bellicose relationship with other groups in their conquest of the territory and its resources. Moreover, the use of communication technologies, such as Geographic Information Systems (GIS) and GPS, can potentially lead to the exclusion of traditional knowledge held by elders and create inequality with regard in particular to access to and legibility of maps.

The workshop made it possible to produce four large-scale maps of the entire TITB, each conveying distinct information: the history of occupation of the territory, the resources (gathering, fishing, hunting) it contained, and the threats posed to it (gold panning, fishing, timber extraction, dams, roads, etc.). This division into classes of information was suggested by the consultants, "so as not to clutter up a single map with too much information", which would make it unreadable. The collection of GPS points was used to construct the resource maps, while the historical map of the occupation of the territory was based on the speeches of the ancients which made it possible to trace the trajectories of the group during the period preceding the contact. The map shows the sites of temporary habitation as well as the places where important rituals were performed. However, the stories of the elders only began at the official border of the actual territory, as if beyond the border their memory had no meaning.

The Bacajá River basin contains very little relief, but it is characterised by a dense hydrographic network where each stream bears one or more names that reference an anecdote, a key person, an old settlement site, or the name of a species that is particularly prevalent in the area. The riverbed of the Bacajá River is strewn with numerous rocks that shape its course through waterfalls and currents that are clearly identified and characterised by the Xikrin. Together with the confluence points, these characteristic places along the river serve as descriptive reference points (Surrallés, 2004) that create "a first level of landscape semantics that allows everyone … to speak through space" (Mazurek,

2013: 137) to talk about their history. On the subject of topographical writing, Santos-Granero (1998: 141) argues that "a person walking along the trail ... could and actually does, 'read' their histories, either partially (by reading single topograms) or in their totality (by reading interrelated topograms)". But the consultants asked the Xikrin to mark and name the various landscapes on the maps and for each of them they had to describe the type of soil and vegetation encountered, to state its importance in terms of use, and in particular the presence of animals and plants collected, and finally, to specify who goes there (men, women, everyone, etc.). In other words, it was essentially an ecological notion of landscape that it was asked to present. Among the different categories of forest environments presented by the Xikrin cartographers, there is notably *bà kapryt*, "empty forest", that is, "empty of humans" because, according to their explanations, if the elders used to go there before, nowadays people don't go there anymore, *mar kêt*, they don't know how to go there, they don't know what to find there, even if it represents almost half of the territory. This area has been redefined by these young cartographers as a game breeding area, *mry te ami kam kradjire kadjy*, "where the animals go to reproduce". This was translated as *area mãe* in Portuguese ("mother area", i.e. the breeding area) (Figure 3.1).

As we saw with this example, the ethnomaps are either related to the perception and management of natural resources as such, or to memory, but without being linked together, which makes difficult to understand the historical process of the formation and significance of the different landscapes and thus their heritage value. The methodology adopted here prevents an integrated conception of space by imposing disjointed and independent spaces, it "hence unwittingly produce fixed, impermeable boundaries in landscapes defined by movement, networks, and

Figure 3.1. Presentation of ethnomaps to the community. The map-makers Xikrin presenting to the community the map they made during ethnocartography workshops
Source: photo from an audiovisual recording by the author in December 2014

fluctuating social relationships" (Sletto, 2009: 148) which defines territoriality. Territoriality is understood as the set of existential and social relationships that individuals, both in groups and collectively, maintain with the space that they produce and perpetually reproduce, consistently with the production and reproduction of their society. This perspective contrasts with the objectified understanding of "territory" proposed by Western thinking, which evokes a modern legal notion of appropriation of space as reified, described, and defined by borders. "The rigidity of this form of cartography, enclosed in a Euclidean context, does not allow any appropriation of the social forms of territorial construction, except a forced representation of these territorialities" (Mazurek, 2013: 118). And this constitutes a violence to the way in which the Xikrin may apprehend the places they inhabit since, in fact, it is the result of living, of the experience of dwelling and perceived through various practices of meaning and significance (Bender 1993, Tilley 1994, Descola, 2014) that values landscape as heritage.

Conclusion

Korzibsky (2007) tells us that "a map is not the territory", but a language that reflects in its structure a vision of the world as it is conceived at a point in time *t*. It is a subjective representation of a vision of the territory, in the image of its authors. Built on a dominant ideological basis, maps are instruments of power, communication, and discourse, and ethnomaps in particular raise the question of the commensurability of representations of space.

Together with socio-ecological analysis, ethnomapping serves as means of constructing scenarios regarding the use and conservation of the living space, inviting the community to project towards the future and to formulate a collective project. This implies that this space first had to be recognized and delimited through a process of territorial (and social) demarcation that gives any social reality a temporal duration and spatial consistency. But as we saw with this example, the process of demarcation has led to a reification of the territory and the idealization of the landscape by public policies which, through the identification of signs and the use of spatiotemporal markers, encouraged their heritagization. And this is the adoption of this heritage approach that has gradually enabled the Xikrin to articulate their territorial knowledge with the modern legal notion of territory and to use this historical narrative in a performative sense to serve their interests, particularly in environmental and territorial management projects through the development of ethnomaps.[6] However, heritage does not exist a priori, it is never given nor acquired, it is "made" (Heinich, 2009) to provide an action in the present that pretend to have direct material consequences: the perennity of the TITB in the actual context of environment disturbs.

Beyond appropriating new forms of territorial representation, the Xikrin cartographers also demonstrate their appropriation of the Western discourse on heritage, showing that they understood the challenge of creating these maps to defend their future interests (Tselouiko, 2020).

If we do not take care of the land, they will hasten to bring out the law [PEC 215] to destroy our land. We must act, watch, protect for those who are being born. Today we are here, but tomorrow we will not be. We must prepare the land for those who are being born.

(Interview with Tedjere, 2016, my translation)

By legitimizing the administrative boundaries and historical regime (Hartog, 2003) imposed by the dominant society, ethnomaps run the risk of confusing notions of territoriality and territory, thus confusing Indigenous and non-Indigenous policies of heritagization. The methodological challenges go well beyond the recognition of the boundaries of a territory, and concern more the representation of the elements of territoriality and the meaning of landscape as heritage. It is a matter of assimilating the cultural components of the spaces constructed by these populations to finally understand it by using ethnography which has the potential to bring out the experienced landscape that is continually constituted by and constitutive of social processes. To do this, it seems appropriate to combine field observation and discourse analysis. As this is not very formalized knowledge and is often non-discursive, observation which enables knowledge to be grasped in action is essential.

Notes

1 These textiles carry very strong symbolism as representation of a conception of the World since they are marked by a vertical, highly symmetrical organisation because the world is symmetrical, ordered, and segmented.
2 Khipus are made up of strings, of various colours, assembled in a dichotomous way, and a series of nodes indicating either the geographical coding of the place or the phonetics of the places or products.
3 In Latin America, mapping has played an important role in securing legal recognition of community property rights, through the documentation of land and resource use and occupation.
4 Serviço de Proteção aos Índios (Indian Protection Service), the predecessor of the current FUNAI - Fundação Nacional do Índio (National Foundation for the Indian), which is a state administration responsible for assuring the rights of Brazil's Indigenous peoples.
5 In Portuguese, this term means the grouping of many Brazilian chestnut trees (*Bertholletia excelsa*) in one area.
6 See the territorial and environmental management plan in Trincheira Bacajá Indigenous Land "Aben Kaben Marimei" (The Nature Conservancy, 2018).

References

Aben, K.M. (2018). *Plano de Gestão Territorial e Ambiental, Povo Xikrin da Terra Indígena Trincheira Bacajá.* Sao Paulo: The Nature Conservancy do Brasil.

Bender, B. (1993). *Landscape. Politics and Perspectives.* Oxford: Blackwell.

Cohn, C. (2005). *Relações de diferença no Brasil Central: os Mebengokré e seus outros.* Thèse: Anthropologie sociale et ethnologie: Faculdade de Filosofia, Letras e Ciências Humanas, USP, São Paulo.

Collignon, B. (2005) Que sait-on des savoirs géographiques vernaculaires? *Bulletin de l'Association de géographes français.* n.3, pp. 321–331.

Cormier-Salem, M.-C. and Roussel, B. (2002). Patrimoines et savoirs naturalistes locaux. In J.Y. Martin (ed.) *Développement durable? Doctrines, pratiques, évaluations.* Marseille: IRD Éditions, pp. 125–142.

Descola, P. (2005). *Par-delà nature et culture.* Paris: Gallimard.

Descola, P. (2012). *Anthropologie de la Nature – Les formes du paysage* I. Cours au Collège de France, chaire Anthropologie de la nature. Retrieved from: www.college-de-france.fr/site/philippe-descola/course-2011-2012.htm.

Descola, P. (2014). *Anthropologie de la Nature – Les formes du paysage* III. Cours au Collège de France, chaire Anthropologie de la nature. Retrieved from: www.college-de-france.fr/site/philippe-descola/p1377594533312_content.htm.

Fisher, W. (1991). *Dualism and its Discontents: Social Organization and Village Fissioning among the Xikrin-Kayapo of Central Brazil.* Thèse: Anthropologie sociale et ethnologie, Faculty of the Graduate School of Cornell University.

Fisher, W. (2000). *Rainforest Exchanges: Industry and Community on an Amazonian Frontier.* Washington: Smithsonian Institution Press.

FUNAI/BSB/0707/79, proposta de criação da Reserva Indígena Araweté. Retrieved from: https://acervo.socioambiental.org/acervo/documentos/processo-n-funaibsb070779-proposta-de-criacao-da-reserva-indigena-arawete.

Harley, J.B. (1989). Deconstructing the Map. *Cartographica,* 26(2): 1–20.

Hartog, F. (2003). *Régimes d'historicité. Présentisme et expérience du temps.* Paris: Le Seuil.

Heinich, N. (2009). *La fabrique du patrimoine: "de la cathédrale à la petite cuillère",* Paris: Éditions MSH.

Korzibsky, A. (2007). *Une carte n'est pas le territoire.* Paris: l'Éclat.

Lefebvre, F., Bonnet, E., and Boyer, F. (2017). Une méthode de cartographie participative des pratiques et représentations urbaines à Ouagadougou (Burkina Faso), *EchoGéo* [Online], 40 | Online since 30 June 2017, connection on 10 August 2021. doi:10.4000/echogeo.14978.

Mazurek, H. (2013). Cartographie: vision ou reflet? Une réflexion autour des références indigènes. *Information géographique* 77(4): 109–148.

Reid, G. and Sieber, R. (2016). *Comparing Geospatial Ontologies with Indigenous Conceptualizations of Time,* International Conference on GIScience Proceedings, pp. 248–251.

Roué, M. (2012). Histoire et épistémologie des savoirs locaux et autochtones, *Revue d'ethnoécologie,* 1 (online). Retrieved from: https://journals.openedition.org/ethnoecologie/813.

Roth, R. (2009). The Challenges of Mapping Complex Indigenous Spatiality: From Abstract Space to Dwelling Space. *Cultural Geographies,* 16: 207–227.

Santos-Granero, F. (1998). Writing History into the Landscape: Space, Myth and Ritual in Contemporary Amazonia. *American Ethnologist,* 25(2): 128–148.

Sletto, B. (2009) Indigenous Cartographies. *Cultural Geographies,* 16(2): 147–152.

Sletto, B., Bryan, J., Torrado, M., Hale, C., and Barry, D. (2013). Territoriality, Participatory Mapping, and Natural Resources Policy: The Latin American Experience. *Cuadernos de Geografía Revista Colombiana de Geografía,* 22(2): 193–209.

Surrallés, A. (2004). Horizontes de intimidad. Persona, percepción y espacio en los Candoshi. In A. Surrallés and P. Garcia Hierro (eds.), *Tierra adentro. Territorio indígena y percepción del entorno.* Copenhagen: IWGIA, pp. 137–162.

Tilley, C. (1994). *A Phenomenology of Landscape: Places, Paths, and Monuments.* Oxford: Berg.

Tselouiko, S. (2018). *Entre ciel et terre. Socio-spatialité des Mēbêngôkre-Xikrin. Terre Indigène Trincheira Bacajá (TITB, Pará, Brésil).* PhD thesis of Université Paris Sciences et Lettres. Ecole Doctorale de l'EHESS.

Tselouiko, S. (2020). Notre terre vue du ciel, *Revue d'ethnoécologie*, 17, online. Retrieved from: http://journals.openedition.org/ethnoecologie/6072.

Vidal, L. (1985), *Relatório à companhia Vale do Rio Doce. A situação atual dos indios Xikrin do Bacajá.* Pará assistênci ao projeto de apoio Ferro-Carajás.

4 Community-based organizations in Kisumu

A necessary but not sufficient condition for managing polyvalent heritage landscapes

Fredrick Odede, Beth Perry and Patrick Hayombe

Introduction

Community-based organizations (CBOs) are an institutional response to a number of different challenges in managing landscapes as heritage, representing mechanisms to enhance the agency of local communities to shape and benefit from heritage preservation and development, and pay attention to local heritage practices (Coombes et al., 2014; Ndoro, Chirikure, and Deacon, 2018). Yet their constitution also positions CBOs as active political agents in "heritagization from below" (Harrison and Hughes, 2010; Chung and Bains, 2020) – meaning the processes of making and re-making heritage which, intentionally and unintentionally, prioritize certain heritage values over others.

Through a case study of heritage sites in Kisumu County, Kenya, we demonstrate that CBOs are both a necessary, but also insufficient, part of the local institutional architecture of landscape management. Local community organizations provide mechanisms for better promotion of local interests, effective site management, retaining the economic benefits of site development locally, and strengthening community capacity to resist efforts to "capture" the sites by local administrations or developers. However, CBOs simultaneously produce tensions and risk different forms of capture, due to the multi-scalar governance contexts in which they sit and the conflicting rationalities that inform local landscape management. To this extent, although they are critical actors in heritage governance in both theory and practice, they are a necessary but not sufficient condition for local engagement in heritage management, in the absence of wider structural, funding, and policy changes required to dismantle the legacies of colonialism in the context of a globalized political economy.

This chapter builds on a project funded by the UK British Academy's Sustainable Development Programme (SDP2\100190) called *Whose Heritage Matters*. The project was designed to explore how cultural heritage could be mobilized to support more sustainable and just urban futures, and included mapping and making activities around four cultural heritage sites in Kisumu County (Perry et al., 2021). Here we focus on the specific roles of CBOs at three of those sites – Abindu, Dunga Beach, and Kit Mikayi. First, we set out

DOI: 10.4324/9781003195238-4

the background and methodology underpinning the research, before considering the different values of and for heritage at the sites and the roles of CBOs in managing conflicts which result.

A co-productive case study design

Kisumu City is located on the shores of Lake Victoria and is Kenya's third largest city, with a population of about 700,000 people: 60 per cent of the population reside on 5 per cent of the land within the city, which has high levels of poverty, food insecurity, and low employment, particularly for young people and women. Kisumu boasts diverse cultural heritage resources that are uniquely and spatially distributed on the landscape, laced with scenic landforms that traverse the city and its environs. Historical, archaeological, and cultural sites bear testimony to the vibrancy of the areas' tangible and intangible heritage. The case study focusses on three cultural and sacred sites – at Dunga Beach, Kit Mikayi, and Abindu.

Dunga Beach is a fishing and tourism destination, a peninsular on the shores of Lake Victoria, dominated by rocky surfaces, wetlands, hills, cliffs, and springs. Footpaths, murram, and tarmac-covered roads lead to mud-walled houses made of stones and soil, alongside permanent houses made of bricks and blocks with iron roofs. The site consists of residential, commercial, and recreation buildings, with a boardwalk leading to the lake shore, made of timber with a tin roof. The pier forms a docking area for fishing boats and tour boats which stretch into Lake Victoria. Kit Mikayi is a rock formation of seven boulders, made of uniquely layered graphite stones, with underground bat-dwelling caves and a flat rock formation. The five-acre site is surrounded by rare medicinal trees, and, at its center, there is a shrine used by religious groups. The site has an office space and a traditional hut, used as a cultural museum with traditional artifacts (see also Benter et al., 2016). Abindu is located to the north of Kisumu City, and sits 5 km above sea level. The huge rock formation is composed of 12 different rock shelters, used primarily for different religious or sacred purposes. Springs are scattered around the site, which is surrounded by indigenous plants, such as the baobab tree, 'siala', 'midat', and 'mboto', and medicinal herbs, as well as wild animals such as leopards, hyenas, baboons, and monkeys.

These landscapes have been informally recognized as heritage for a long time. One history of Dunga Beach dates back to 1901 with the arrival of Indian settlers who built the railway line and settled at Dunga to promote fishing. Kit Mikayi – known as the "rock of the first wife" – is shrouded in myth and legend, long recognized by Luo elders as a sacred site. Abindu has deep ancestral roots, recognized since the early ages as a site for rituals and sacred offerings, such as animals, to appease the gods. In 1970 a foreseer from Gem sub-county, by the name Abuor Adet, rediscovered the site and increased local awareness of the site as heritage. In each site, local people acted as "owner-cultivators" and custodians of the land prior to any formal recognition.

Figure 4.1. Dunga Beach Boardwalk and Recreation Centre
Credits: Whose Heritage Matters project

Researchers at the Jaramogi Oginga Odinga University of Science and Technology (JOOUST) had been working with the sites over a few years. Motivated by concern that low community awareness of the cultural value of the sites was leading to their degradation, researchers sought to develop eco-tourism strategies to mobilize resources and catalyze policy change (Omondi, Hayombe, and Agong, 2014; Jernsand and Kraff, 2015; Odede et al., 2020). The *Whose Heritage Matters* project offered an opportunity to build on this prior work, through better understanding the values and conflicts that arise through competing cultural heritage values, and to support community-based organizations in developing their roles and plans. A central plank of the approach was to foster peer learning between four cultural heritage sites so they could learn from each other and build critical mass to represent collective interests.

Our work around the sites was intended to draw on a co-productive methodology (Hemström et al., 2021) – comprising interviews, site visits, community surveys, and data generated through a collaborative process, with community elders, women and youth groups, site management committees, and policy makers. This co-production methodology, informed by a pragmatist orientation, was undertaken to avoid an extractive research practice, whilst simultaneously "giving back" to the sites. Value mapping, where values are considered as both intrinsic and extrinsic to the sites, was undertaken via a collaborative workshop in April 2019, where 46 community members, cultural organizations, and site leaders were asked to draw what "cultural heritage" meant to them. This was supported by ten qualitative interviews, using a standard template, following which the data was coded and analysed for commonalities and differences across the sites. When the COVID-19 pandemic struck, we had to redesign the project to be less proximate and more distant, relying on social media platforms such as WhatsApp to engage with site leaders, and traditional forms of data collection – such as interview questionnaires – which could be used in a socially-distanced way, once travel to and from sites was possible.

Figure 4.2. Kit Mikayi, "The Rock of the First Wife"
Credits: Whose Heritage Matters project

Mapping values: plurality and contestation

Such sites have plural values for different groups, reflecting the evolution of use values associated with the landscapes over time, in both practice and policy (see Table 4.1).

Rather than fixed or static, such values reciprocally shape and delimit each other, and are mediated through different circuits of formal and informal recognition, interacting to produce changing hierarchies of value over time. The relationship between values can be mutually reinforcing, for instance there is a positive link between religious, spiritual, and environmental values whereby the sacredness of the sites has promoted stewardship (Taylor and Lennon, 2011).

Formal recognition has both safeguarded certain heritage values, whilst introducing competing rationalities. Since 2000, the three sites have been

Figure 4.3. Inscriptions in the Rocks at Abindu Cave
Credits: Whose Heritage Matters project

formally recognized through a number of different processes. Dunga is recognized by the national government through the National Museums of Kenya and acknowledged by the Kisumu County Government since the devolution of cultural heritage responsibilities in 2010. Dunga Wetland is also marketed as an Important Bird Area (IBA) by Nature Kenya and Birdlife International. Kit Mikayi has the highest status, recognized as a National Monument in 2003 and designated a UNESCO World Heritage Site in 2019. Abindu was recognized in 2008 by the Department of Culture for Kisumu City. In the last few years, the County Government of Kisumu has formally recognized the Lake Region Tourist Circuit as a key node in the cultural, heritage, and community strategies of the region.

   In securing formal recognition as heritage, the sites have been opened up to both funding opportunities and visitors, from domestic to international tourism. County Development Funds at Dunga and Kit Mikayi support public participation, cultural activities, and infrastructure. Dunga Beach receives funds for the promotion of fishing activities, whilst in Kit Mikayi, the County paid for a Cultural Resource Center and fencing of the site. Large-scale infrastructure

Table 4.1. Valuing landscape as heritage: polyvalency at sacred and cultural sites in Kisumu County

	Dunga	Kit Mikayi	Abindu Caves
Economic value	Aside from income from fishing, the site has become a tourist destination for local and international visitors, which generates employment and income through sales of cultural products, boat rides, entry fees and education fees.	Employment opportunities created for local people through cultural activities, including craft, art, dance, song and tour guiding, as well as the sale of cultural products. Domestic and international tourism is a key part of the economic value of the site.	Abindu is less developed as a tourist destination. The CBO aims to develop Abindu as an international tourist hub, produce and commercialize clean water from Abindu spring, and generate income from new cultural ventures. Income is raised by the sale of local agricultural produce, such as mangoes, guavas, pawpaw, oranges and banana. Fee charges are levied from both the local and international visitors to the site.
Spiritual value	Offerings are made to appease spirits after a good harvest and during high fish season.	The landscape is associated with a range of myths and legends concerning the origins of the Seme people and ethnic groups in the Lake Victoria basin. Powerful religious and political leaders converge on this destination to enrich their lives.	The legends and myths surrounding Abindu caves have significant cultural value and promote cultural identity. Religious groups converge to the site for spiritual nourishment and cleansing. Traditional healers derive their supernatural powers from the site for healing purposes.

	Dunga	Kit Mikayi	Abindu Caves
Religious value	Baptisms and the scattering of ashes take place at the site, and sacrifices such as marking the birth of a child by cutting hair and throwing it in the water.	The rocks are used by religious groups, particularly the Legion Maria denomination. Sacred caves are the site of meditation, fasting and worship. Traditional diviners draw power from the site and engage in traditional healing and exorcism. Holy water at Kit Mikayi is used for such purification purposes.	The rocks are a sacred site, used for ritual ceremonies and religious purposes. The rocks display biblical inscriptions, like the "twelve loaves of bread", and some geographic features are said to represent the map of Africa and Kenya. Independent African Christian Church followers pray, meditate, and fast as facets of their religious worship.
Cultural value	Fishing is valued as a cultural practice, involving around 70 per cent of residents. There is an annual Sitatunga boat race, Fish Night Festival and fish competition. Arts and crafts include weaving, pottery and dancing by the Chiela dance troupe. The recreation centre forms a cultural museum to display artefacts.	A range of intangible cultural heritage practices take place at the site, including dancing, crafts, pageants, arts festivals, and tour guiding. Traditional Luo artefacts are displayed in the museum and there is a Creative Arts Centre on the site which promotes talent, especially for young people, and sports.	The focus of activities is on the preservation of the tangible cultural heritage and its use for worship. There are plans to develop further cultural activities, and some cultural events have already taken place, such as a wrestling event in 2020 at a nearby hotel.

	Dunga	*Kit Mikayi*	*Abindu Caves*
Social value	A range of welfare interventions are undertaken, including food donations, paying school fees, and donating trees to local families. Around the site, families get together, and community relationship bonding and recreational activities take place.	The CBO helps the community through purchasing blankets for the elderly, and paying school fees and uniforms for poorer students, as well as helping orphans and widows. Bonding sessions for couples or families experiencing relationship difficulties take place. Recreational activities take place which are valued for breaks from working and family life.	The CBO provides financial relief, pays school fees and donates to support the community's economic welfare. The site provides a picnic space for those who want to enjoy a quiet environment away from the busy and bustling city life of Kisumu.
Medicinal value	Some of the traditional fish species like lung fish and omena have medicinal value in the treatment of skin disease and measles.	Traditional herbalists visit the site for medicinal plants used to treat and cure various conditions including infertility, stomach pain, skin conditions, diarrhoea, colds and vomiting.	The site attracts herbalists and local people who obtain traditional herbs to treat various human ailments skin rashes, stomach ache, colds, diarrhoea, etc.
Environmental/geological value	The landscape provides a habitat for different bird species; Lake Victoria is rich in aquatic life, with traditional fish species and natural marine flora. The shores are also home to hippos and reptiles.	The natural indigenous vegetative cover, laced with the graphitic rocky landscapes and the intermittent rock tors of the Seme region present an environment rarely found in other regions of Kenya.	The natural rock boulder landscape, covered by a dense thicket of indigenous trees, ranging from dials, oyieko, and ochol, to baobab, provide a natural landscape, which provides a habitat for wild fauna.

	Dunga	Kit Mikayi	Abindu Caves
Aesthetic value	A scenic landscape is provided by the sunset viewing point, wetland papyrus reeds, and flowers, cultural objects, and waters of Lake Victoria.	A rocky landscape with indigenous plants, the rock tors of Seme, the caves, and religious paintings provide a scenic landscape of great natural beauty.	The vantage point of the rocks provides high visibility of Kisumu City along the shores of the Lake basin, the rock tors, and the traditional vegetation in its natural habitat.
Pedagogic, scientific, and archaeological value	Educators and researchers visit the site for field trips and conduct research and surveys. Primary pupils and secondary school students are exposed to various practical experiences on different subjects.	Alongside school and college visits, scientific surveys and research studies, capacity building and training activities also take place at the site.	Local primary and secondary schools visit the site to learn about history, religious values, and practices, as well as geology and environmental awareness. Scientists and researchers also come to the site to research local traditions, practices, and cultures as well as indigenous plant species and fauna.

developments, such as tarmacking the main road connecting Dunga village to Kisumu City, have increased access to local markets to sell fish and crafts, and better signage has also been supported at county level, whilst national government funds have enabled the construction of a tarmac shed for fishmongers (Dunga) and the (partial) fencing of the site at Abindu.

Non-governmental collaborations have also been important in the recognition of the sites as heritage, especially with researchers. As noted above, academics have mobilized resources and catalysed policy change (Omondi, Hayombe, and Agong, 2014; Odede et al., 2020). Local research studies have led to international collaborations, such as support for a boardwalk at Dunga Beach from the French Embassy in Nairobi and the Mistra Urban Futures (MUF) in Gothenburg, Sweden (Jernsand and Kraff, 2015). Along with German international cooperation, Mistra Urban Futures enabled training support and development for fisherfolk on fish farming and the sustainable use of water hyacinths. Such networks plugged local researchers into further international partnerships, for work on festivals (Perry, Ager, and Sita, 2019) and the research underpinning this chapter.

Formal recognition brings acknowledged benefits by local people, but also produces hierarchies of values. Governmental interventions have tended to focus on heritage sites as attractions, eligible for largely infrastructural investment due to their potential for employment and income generation. As the reputation of the sites grows, for instance, via the World Heritage Site designation, this is seen to confirm the importance of these landscapes in the context of a tourist-based, cultural economy. Research partnerships have mobilized a different combination of values through the idea of "eco-tourism" and support for community-based organizing, mapping the plural values of the site (such as in Table 4.1), beyond the purely economic.

Indeed, recognition of these landscapes as heritage has predominately led to a prioritization of their economic value over other values, such as the use and practice of traditional medicine. This points to tensions between an international political economy that continues to be shaped by western and colonial ideas of whose and what heritage matters, how it relates to capitalist modes of production and local heritage values (Bennett, Dibley, and Harrison, 2014). The environmental conservation of the sites is undermined when visitor numbers lead to environmental degradation and increased waste, where there are no marked disposal areas, whilst efforts to maintain and improve access has also led to the loss of grasses and trees. At Dunga Beach, hotel development has encroached on riparian land and displaced wildlife, leading also to increased fatalities from crocodile attacks and hippo bites. In different sites, deliberate untended wildness, reflecting a non-interventionist relationship between nature and culture, has given way to narratives of "neglect", leading to a focus on tidiness and cleanliness. At Kit Mikayi tensions persist between religious groups using the site and tourists, in terms of cultural dress and behavior. Whilst tourism brings much needed income, a sense of local cultural erosion is felt.

Making heritage: recognizing and managing heritage "from below"

Local community governance of the sites is the result of, and implicated in, the official designation of these landscapes as heritage, and the tensions and conflicts that result. A Dunga Beach management unit was founded in 1997 by an act of parliament calling for the formation of such units along the lakes and oceans in Kenya, with the CBO not created till after formal recognition in 2003. In Kit Mikayi the first management group was Kit Mikayi Cooperative Society, formed in 2009 by bringing together seven local landowners and their families. The National Museums of Kenya subsequently intervened to create a CBO in 2014, with a Board of Management, to ensure that the proceeds from the site could be received by and deployed for the community. Abindu was considered a hiding den for hard-core criminals, with high levels of crime at the site. The process of forming the CBO, initiated in 2009, was a direct response to these threats and the desire to protect tourists and worshippers from theft, following the advice of Kisumu municipality.

The legal status of the sites provides an authority and recognition both within and outside the community. Each CBO is registered through the relevant departments and ministries (for youth, sports and gender, or social services) and has a similar structure, comprising a series of committees overseen by a Board of Management (BOM). The CBOs operate as member organizations, with key roles such as Chair, Secretary, and Treasurer, and a range of sub-committees for different activities, including environment, welfare, ICTs, resource mobilization and conflict resolution (Dunga), or land, culture, and training, and human resource and finance (Kit Mikayi).

These structures allow for differential levels of involvement. In Kit Mikayi, the membership organization .enables different groups, some of which were previously excluded from decision-making, to have representation and voice in the CBO, such as Kangeso traditional dancers, the Kadol widows group which sells traditional food, a co-op and a youth group that maintains the site. In Dunga, fishermen, tour operators, school leavers, professionals, and artists are involved in the CBO, whilst in all three sites, different groups support income-generating activities, like banking, welfare, and savings.

The CBOs receive funding from grants, loans, and external funds, as noted above, but are also financed by member contributions, gate and entry charges, as well as income-generating activities such as boat rides and tour guiding, dancing, and selling of products and refreshments. The CBO structure enables local people to make decisions on how to generate and spend these funds, as well as on membership, site management, the preservation of different use values at the sites, and marketing and branding activities. This places them at the heart of heritagization processes, where localized conflicts arise (between different religious groups) or globalized rationalities compete (between tourism, economic development and environmental conservation).

The impact of CBOs on heritagization in Kisumu

These CBOs are a critical part of heritagization strategies from below, that seek to ensure that local communities – rather than distant agencies or developers – benefit from the recognition of these landscapes as heritage, as well as to protect local people from land dispossession and appropriation. This is particularly important as in several places, such as Dunga, local people donated land for the construction and development of the beach front.

The CBO, first and foremost, provides a mechanism for community participation in local management of the sites. Decisions can be made about future priorities and grassroots infrastructural developments, such as roads and power supplies around Abindu. A key function of the CBOs is the marketing and promotion of the sites, through radio, online, word of mouth, and social media, as well as providing site branding and signage. Kit Mikayi's trajectory to World Heritage status was in part enabled by a series of coalition-building activities, such as enrolling political support through visits from members from the County Assembly and Parliamentary Department for Culture and Heritage. Although many members are aware of the dual-edged sword of cultural tourism, interviews suggest that it has also led to the transformation of "abandoned heritage places, into living cultural places". The external recognition of the sites has raised local awareness of the importance of the sites and, through visibilizing multiple values for different communities, garnered grassroots support.

Critically, CBOs support the local capture of income-generation and employment opportunities, through small businesses like selling sodas, *uji, maragwe*, and cultural objects within the sites. This provides the means through which different values can be guarded at the sites, such as social welfare, education, and training. As detailed in Table 4.1, the three sites all engage in outreach and charitable income redistribution, through payment of school fees or the provision of food. Educational and environmental awareness programs, such as enforced waste management, the naming and tagging of trees, and wetland conservation (Dunga), are supported, along with cultural activities such as boat racing, festivals, pageants, and creative arts exhibitions. Such activities provide routes for both formal and "everyday" cultural participation (Miles and Gibson, 2016). In Abindu and Kit Mikayi, different communities from sub-locations across Kisumu also collaborate through the CBO which enhances cohesion and a sense of community while creating checks and balances against emergent land ownership disputes.

The formal organization provides additional training in governance, management, and leadership for committee members. National Museums of Kenya have provided training on how to manage and safeguard sites, whilst researchers have supported the acquisition of technical skills on tour guiding, governance, and tourism management, for instance. Where this works well, the CBOs and BOMs play key roles in resolving tensions, for instance at Abindu where competition between religious groups over the use of space, especially the caves, has led to fights between adherents of different sects. Importantly, the CBOs also strengthen the political power of the community in protecting local rights and interests against reported efforts to take over management and income-generating potential of the sites by organizations such as the National Museums of Kenya or County Government. The formal recognition afforded the sites, alongside legal registration under local control of the CBOs and BOMs, enables greater local resistance to such encroachments and opposition to development initiatives by local villagers, such as the building of beach hotels in Dunga. In Abindu, the CBO provides a route to challenge larger tourism organizations, where it is reported that some tour firms have used the site to obtain funds as a means to supplement their own incomes, whilst never implementing – or even visiting – the sites.

Yet at the same time, the CBOs are not disinterested arbiters between competing heritage values, rather are active in processes of validating whose and what heritage matters. Despite concern for eco-tourism, environmental conservation can be relegated to secondary importance in face of the opportunities to attract tourists and generate local employment and incomes. Funding is limited, which leads to trade-offs between different uses and values of the sites. The interests of CBOs may conflict with other groups using the sites: for instance in Kit Mikayi, tensions have arisen between management and religious groups over the payment of gate fees by worshippers, or the practices of the different religious groups in blocking entrances to caves and degrading the site through candle waste.

The question of land remains hotly contested (Obange and Wagah, 2019). In Kit Mikayi, landowning families traditionally held power through the Kit Mikayi Cooperative Society prior to the subsequent "imposition" of a CBO by National Museums of Kenya. This has left some landowners feeling that they were not adequately compensated for their land and increased demands to reclaim site management. The CBO also bridges between communities at East and Central Seme sub-locations whose land co-constitutes the site, and some Central Seme residents have reported feeling excluded from site management via a BOM that privileges East Seme communities.

As the landscapes have become more visible and recognized, so land price values have increased. Most of these landscapes do not have secure land tenure, title deeds are often missing, and who owns land can be contested. This has led to a rise in individual ownership claims over plots of land and concerns that the CBOs support existing landowners who retain income amongst themselves rather than investing in the conservation of the sites. Where individual landowners are dominant in the CBOs, activities with immediate economic return may be prioritized, such as charcoal burning, deforestation, and quarrying with impacts on the local environment.

CBO structures give form to such contestations and potentially provide routes for dealing with arising issues – for instance, with committees dedicated to conflict resolution (Dunga) and land disputes (Kit Mikayi). However, the effectiveness of such arrangements depends on the constitution and operation of memberships themselves. The CBOs may decide their own membership (Dunga), be constituted through representation from the committees, with additional members elected during Chief's public meetings (Kit Mikayi), or be elected under the supervision of the County Director of Tourism (Abindu).

Such processes are always and inevitably political and subject to social and cultural influence. It was, for instance, considered a defining feature of progress to greater gender equality when a female leader was in position at Kit Mikayi, and widows groups at Dunga and Kit Mikayi have raised the standing and income of traditionally marginalized women. However, the emergence of educated women leaders to control and manage CBOs has also been resisted by other groups. In the case of Kit Mikayi – and in the light of the designation of the site as World Heritage – what has been described as a "coup d'état" took place in 2020 in which the female leader was effectively removed and replaced by different leadership. Cultural heritage practices, like officiating in sacred offerings, engaging in rituals at sacred shrines, or narrating stories or myths, have been a preserve of senior male elders, and women are not able to inherit land. Women are often viewed as migrants to a landscape when they arrive as a result of marriage. Often, site management remains a domain for men, young people are relegated to cleaning duties at the sites, whilst women dance, cook, and craft, a division of labour which has been criticized for "rendering them mostly as objects of development 'solutions'" (Harcourt and Stremmelaar, 2012: 3).

Conflicts over leadership stem also from the tenuous position that committee members can hold within the site. Reports from Abindu suggest that members of the CBO do not respect the offices held by executive members, as they are drawn from the community. This lack of respect is seen to result in greater leadership wrangles where officials are not seen as experts, either in or for their communities. The intermediary function of the CBO in safeguarding plural values and interests is also challenged by conflicts with the BOM. On the one hand, the dual-pronged structure is seen as complex and hindering decision-making and implementation. On the other hand, BOMs have been accused of political interference. In the case of Kit Mikayi, the legal status of the BOM is drawn from the National Museums of Kenya, and officials are seen as "outsiders" without the appropriate skills, and divorced from day-to-day management, positioning authority and power beyond the purview of the CBO.

Conclusion: a necessary but insufficient condition

The case study of three cultural and sacred sites in Kisumu City, Kenya, has shown the critical role that CBOs play in the local management of cultural heritage, in line with contemporary theory and practice (Chirikure, Mukwende, and Taruvinga, 2016). We have shown how CBOs are both a response to and active in processes of heritagization and provide a means to counter the "recognition and misrecognition of community heritage" (Waterton and Smith, 2010). As one response to the "unfulfilled promise" of community participation in cultural heritage in Africa (Chirikure et al., 2010), these institutions sit in sometimes uncomfortable intermediary spaces between development and conservation, facing a series of different trade-offs on how to manage between plural, competing, and sometimes contested heritage values. Following Ndoro, Chirikure, and Deacon's (2018: 248) call for "adaptive heritage management" that enables "daily and situational adaptation to ensure that Africa's heritage resources are sufficiently cared for", we do not suggest that there is any "right" way to address these concerns. Rather, understanding tensions and contradictions enables better evidence on which to make informed decisions, in imperfect environments, about local heritage management and how it benefits different social groups.

How then to make conditions *more sufficient* for community governance of local heritage sites? Building coalitions between different CBOs may be part of the answer. Our project has funded peer-to-peer learning networks to enable CBOs to share knowledge and practices. Funding and conducive cross-sectoral policy frameworks that recognize and enable local decision-making are also key, given that: "the use and accumulation of value addition is certainly shaped by institutional arrangements and capacities at local levels...an overarching concern is how agencies can contribute most effectively to the sustainability and institutionalisation of local capacities" (Saha, Singha, and Xaxa, 2017: 11).

Finally, rather than contrasting heritage from above and below, the case study shows how the process of heritagization is co-constituted in a multi-actor space. Tensions and contradictions result from the clash between intrinsic and extrinsic values, and are shaped in the context of legacies of westernized, colonial ideas and practices of heritage conservation. CBOs can strengthen the agency and autonomy of local groups, but cannot guard against internal tensions and contradictions alone. Neither can they resolve the complexity or the irreconcilability of competing rationalities. The process of management is, in this sense, fundamentally unsettled, like processes of heritagization themselves.

Acknowledgements

We acknowledge the funding of the British Academy for the project "Whose Heritage Matters?" (SDP2\100190) and from Mistra Urban Futures and the Swedish International Development Agency. We also thank Dr Rike Sitas and Dr Victoria Habermehl as collaborators on the project. We specifically acknowledge the support of local groups in the three sites for supporting this research.

References

Bennett, T., Dibley, B., and Harrison, R. (2014). Introduction: Anthropology, Collecting and Colonial Governmentalities. *History and Anthropology*, 25(2): 137–149.

Benter, O., Bosco Mukundi, J., Onyango Watako, A., and Aggrey Adimo, O. (2016). Significance of Traditional Oral Information and Natural Artefacts for Heritage Conservation at the Kit-Mikayi Cultural Site. In A-M. Deisser and M. Njuguna (eds.), *Conservation of Natural and Cultural Heritage in Kenya: A Cross-disciplinary Approach*. London: UCL Press, pp. 172–179.

Chirikure, S., Manyanga, M., Ndoro, W., and Pwiti, G. (2010). Unfulfilled Promises? Heritage Management and Community Participation at Some of Africa's Cultural Heritage Sites. *International Journal of Heritage Studies*, 16: 1–2, 30–44.

Chirikure, S., Mukwende, T., and Taruvinga, P. (2016). Post-colonial Heritage Conservation in Africa: Perspectives from Drystone Wall Restorations at Khami World Heritage Site, Zimbabwe. *International Journal of Heritage Studies*, 22(2): 165–178.

Chung, T. and Bains, S. (2020). The Punjabi Canadian Legacy Project: Possibilities and Limitations of Institutional Heritagisation from Below. *International Journal of Heritage Studies*, 26(3): 221–236.

Coombes, A., Hughes, L., and Karega-Munene (eds.) (2014). *Managing Heritage, Making Peace: History, Identity and Memory in Contemporary Kenya*. New York: I.B. Tauris.

Harcourt, W. and Stremmelaar, J. (2012). Women Reclaiming Sustainable Livelihoods: An Introduction. In W. Harcourt (ed.), *Women Reclaiming Sustainable Livelihoods: Spaces Lost, Spaces Gained*. Basingstoke: Palgrave Macmillan, pp. 1–11.

Harrison, R. and Hughes, L. (2010). Heritage, Colonialism and Postcolonialism. In R. Harrison (ed.), *Understanding the Politics of Heritage*. Manchester: Manchester University Press, pp. 234–269.

Hemström, K., Simon, D., Palmer, H., Perry, B., and Polk, M. (eds.) (2021). *Transdisciplinary Knowledge Co-production: A Guide for Sustainable Cities*. Rugby: Practical Action.

Jernsand, E. M. and Kraff, H. (2015). Participatory Place Branding Through Design: The Case of Dunga Beach in Kisumu, Kenya. *Place Branding and Public Diplomacy*, 11(3): 226–242.

Miles, A. and Gibson, L. (2016). Everyday Participation and Cultural Value. *Cultural Trends*, 25(3): 151–157.

Ndoro, W., Chirikure, S., and Deacon, J. (eds.) (2018). *Managing Heritage in Africa: Who Cares?* Abingdon: Routledge.

Obange, N. and Wagah, G. (2019). Land Tenure Challenges in Kisumu City, Kenya. *Net Journal of Social Sciences*, 7(4): 85–91.

Odede, F., Hayombe, P., Agong, S., and Owino, F. (2020). Upscaling Tourism Product Development for Enhancing Local Livelihoods at Dunga and Miyandhe Beach Destinations in Kisumu City, Kenya: A Co-production Approach. *American Journal of Tourism Management*, 9(1): 24–33.

Omondi, F. O., Hayombe, P. O., and Agong, S. G. (2014). Participatory and Innovative Design Guidelines to Planning and Managing Urban Green Spaces to Transform Ecotourism. *International Journal of Current Research*, 6(12): 10397–10402.

Perry, B., Ager, L., and Sitas, R. (2019). Cultural Heritage Entanglements: Festivals as Integrative Sites for Sustainable Urban Development. *International Journal of Heritage Studies*, 26(6): 603–618.

Perry, B., Odede, F., Hayombe, P., Sitas, R., and Habermehl, V. (2021). *Whose Heritage Matters? Mapping, Making, Mobilizing Cultural Heritage in Kisumu*. Sheffield: Sheffield Print and Design. Retrieved from: heritagematters-rjc.org.

Saha, D., Singha, R., and Xaxa, V. (2017). Introduction. In V. Xaxa, D. Saha, and R. Singha (eds.), *Work, Institutions and Sustainable Livelihood: Issues and Challenges of Transformation*, Singapore: Palgrave Macmillan, pp. 1–14.

Taylor, K. and Lennon, J. (2011). Cultural Landscapes: A Bridge Between Culture and Nature? *International Journal of Heritage Studies*, 17(6): 537–554.

Waterton, E. and Smith, L. (2010). The Recognition and Misrecognition of Community Heritage. *International Journal of Heritage studies*, 16(102): 4–15.

5 A vineyard landscape, a UNESCO inscription and a National Park

A historical–anthropological analysis of heritagization and tourism development in the Cinque Terre (Italy)

Cecilia Paradiso

Introduction

The Cinque Terre (whose meaning is "Five Lands", with reference to their five main villages) are among the best-known Italian destinations, famous for their terraced landscape and their little seaside villages. Their international reputation grew rapidly in the 1990s, when they entered the global tourist market as a place where international guides found an embodiment of the "Mediterranean essence". At the time, local politicians had begun a heritagization project, culminating with this area being added to the UNESCO heritage list and with the creation of a National Park, conceived to protect the agricultural landscape and balance the development of tourism. At present, the outcomes of this process are problematic: while mass and fast tourism increase, those huge visitor flows have not created the agricultural revitalization that this project had anticipated when it was first launched.

To understand how the idea of landscape heritagization gained credibility in local political circles concerned with the survival of viticulture, it is necessary to analyse the historical process preceding the creation of the National Park institution. At the same time, it is necessary to analyse what happened to landscape representations during this process.

Reconstructing the developments of the "modern world system" from the rise of capitalist agriculture in the 16th century, I. Wallerstein wrote that "in the course of social interaction small initial differences are reinforced, stabilized, and defined as 'traditional'. The 'traditional' was then, and always is, an aspect of and creation of the present, never of the past" (1974, p. 98). Building on local history, environmental history, and critical anthropological literature on heritagization and conservation, I study images of the past conveyed in the heritagization process at the Cinque Terre, to highlight which historical and environmental knowledge they conceal, and which visions of the future and practices of the present they support – or not. To this aim, the relationships between the local politico-economic level and international and global configurations must be considered. Through an anthropological approach attentive to scales and frictions (Tsing, 2005), it is possible to appreciate how local poetics

DOI: 10.4324/9781003195238-5

and local socioecological configurations move in a globalized world, not being simply absorbed, but entering wider and different processes than those where they belong. I consider that such a perspective allows to thickly analyse contemporary issues concerning tourism regulation and landscape conservation at the Cinque Terre.

This text is based on ethnographic research conducted since my Master thesis (2012). To the first corpus of field and bibliographic data, I recently added new participant observations and semi-structured interviews. The participants in this research are winegrowers, agronomists, elected representatives, conservation agents, tourism entrepreneurs, local historians, and associated actors.[1]

Landscape heritagization as a political tool

The name Cinque Terre has been used for centuries to indicate a steep section of the eastern Ligurian coast, in Northern Italy, where five villages shelter close to the sea. These towns are historically known for their agricultural products, the most important of which is wine. The production and sales of Cinque Terre wines increased under the Genoese domination, which grew towards the second half of the 12th century, even if environmental archaeological surveys may attest to more ancient terraced slopes.[2] Viticulture represented the main cultivation – and indeed the main economic activity – over several centuries, even if through alternate phases and always accompanied by to other crops. This until the second post-war period, when agricultural land abandonment became increasingly evident, intensified by professional conversions to tourism entrepreneurship.

The name Cinque Terre started to be institutionalized during the last quarter of the 20th century, first through the attribution of a quality assurance label to wines,[3] then with reference to different organisms committed to environmental conservation. To retrace the history of this institutionalization and of its recent renown, we need to go back to the 1970s, when a small group of young winegrowers and municipal administrators started a new political path, by founding an agricultural cooperative and organizing meetings to discuss the survival of local viticulture. This project was mostly based in Manarola and Riomaggiore, the two villages of the Cinque Terre located farthest to the east. Those two villages were entering the touristic era in a different way than others: while the communities of Monterosso and Vernazza[4] were orienting their development toward seaside tourism, people in Manarola and Riomaggiore were starting to look for alternative development solutions. Indeed, the eastern half of the Cinque Terre coast is steeper and deprived of natural harbours. Here, due also to socio-historical differences, viticulture was still thriving and important at the time when tourism emerged as a potential new economic sector. The new political project conducted at the agricultural cooperative of Manarola and at the Riomaggiore municipality started by addressing some claims to the Region of Liguria, asking for concrete help for winegrowers as well as stronger regulations against food speculation and fraud, which had been a problem with big wine merchants. During the 1980s, these same socio-political actors rephrased their demands, asking that the tourism sector – which had based its marketing on the fame of the terraced landscape – contribute to rebalancing the economic benefits of development by participating in the organization of a system of wineries.

Participants in my research recall the first joint effort undertaken during the 1990s by all the town governments and communities of the Cinque Terre. At this time, under the same leadership of local politicians based in Riomaggiore and Manarola, proceedings began in an effort to remove the Cinque Terre from the large *Cinque Terre Regional Park*, which included different areas of eastern Liguria, from the regional border with Tuscany, to the edge of the Gulf of Tigullio. Concerns for the use of the famous toponym were then joining the demands for instruments of territorial regulation fitting the touristic-agricultural configuration of the Cinque Terre. A political and symbolic struggle was launched, to obtain more autonomy for the three city governments which encompass the five little villages of Monterosso, Vernazza, Corniglia, Manarola, and Riomaggiore. The addition of the terraced vineyards landscape on the UNESCO heritage list in 1997 represented a crucial passage to attaining legitimacy and, thereafter, the institution of a National Park for the conservation of this same landscape in 1999.

The synergy behind these accomplishments started with the aversion to the watering down of its own peculiarity and fame in a wide Regional Park, and in the recognition of some changes that had occurred at the national and international level, allowing for an upswing of older projects connected with viticulture. First, the same political actors that had been engaged in local politics since the 1970s succeeded in convincing a wider part of the communities that a new national law on protected areas (Law No. 394/1991) represented an opportunity to enhance local development. This regulation was introduced in the national legislation and represented an innovative model for creating protected areas, built upon sustainable development principles and the involvement of mayors and associations inside the decision-making bodies of national parks. Furthermore, in the 1990s, projects of local autonomy and empowerment could count on the increased international celebrity of the Cinque Terre. This process was part of a changing vision of tourism, towards the promotion of cultural exploration and ecological and environmental experiences, often depicted in nostalgic and romantic tones (Appadurai, 1996).

Selecting and concealing: towards a simplified landscape

As we can see in the Cinque Terre case, definition of heritage elements is a lengthy process, involving selection and negotiation. Ethnographic observation brings new insights to this process, gathering different points of view and memories of the people involved in it. At the Cinque Terre, the vineyard landscape, with its terraces and dry-stone walls, has been the principal subject of heritagization. First, local political actors saw the demarcation of "their" landscape as a necessary step to negotiating the limits of the National Park to be instituted, assuring a prominent representation in its decision-making bodies to the five villages. Then National Park's executives very soon engaged in industrious territorial marketing activities, promoting town or geographic areas twinning (the more resounding one with the Great Wall of China), organizing educational and familiarization trips and participating in tourism exhibitions, thus reinforcing their authority and their tales. During the first decade after its institution, the National Park promoted the exposition of photographs and mural paintings in public spaces, on walls and urban furniture. Old black-and-white photographs and great colourful wall-paintings display images having a vague temporal collocation, representing rhetorical contrasts between orographic hardness, strict geographical isolation, and harmony of man's work in nature, mostly reproducing literary topics from authors of different periods in history. Peasants and winegrowers (more rarely fishermen) are their archetypal characters and, on walls and billboards, they occupy the public space with a monumentalized narrative of the past. Those images and their related narratives have also been largely adopted in private advertising and marketing campaigns, as in souvenirs and packaging manufacturing: daily discursive and productive practices participated in reflecting and multiplying the heritagization process.

Landscape is a complex subject and anthropology largely explored it, appreciating how its physicality and interpretations are permanently under construction (Ingold, 2000). This occurs among ecological dynamics, economic and productive activities, social relations, and symbolic representations (Hirsch and O'Hanlon, 1995). However, in order to achieve the goals of heritagization, a strong territorial identity, deeply rooted in space and time, needs to be highlighted, drawing attention to a consensual facade that often conceals conflicts and disagreements (Siniscalchi, 2007). The UNESCO model treats local rivalry, nationalism, and universalism in a peculiar way: attitudes compete and simultaneously integrate with each other, assimilating local poetics and their resignifications in the global sphere (Palumbo, 2003). In those processes, history itself changes its functions, from a knowledge to be elaborated upon to a resource to be unearthed (Fabre, 2001). By making hegemonic partial and romanticized historical interpretations, other, more complex analysis are overshadowed.

In this case, it is particularly true in regard to a rich and eminent literature developed since the 1970s, about the Ligurian region and the Republic of Genoa's economic, political, and territorial organization.[5] Following this local historical tradition or drawing from environmental and agricultural history approaches, detailed historical researches deconstruct a complex of stereotypes at the forefront of the heritagization process. Historians have focused on the fluctuation of vine-growing and wine-making in the Cinque Terre, attesting to the integration of this area in the Genoese dominion (Iacoponi, 2007). This meant a high degree of dependence to foreign merchants in order to satisfy the communities' economic and food needs. It also meant a quite dramatic pursuit of market orientations, especially since taxes and impositions from Genoa increased in the second half of the 16th century. The Republic of Genoa used to establish customs rules favouring the town, without reinvesting in its territories, leading the communities it controlled into a high specialization of agriculture and to the adoption and abandonment of different crops, in relation to their market value. In this regard, at the Cinque Terre the spread of vine-growing, the changes in vine varieties towards more productive ones, and the decline of the quality of average wines was the result of their subaltern position in the Genoese mercantilist economic space, and not the choice of peasants engaged in a timeless struggle with their environment. Concerning the image of homogeneous communities of hard-working peasants, it has been attested that little property was effectively common, but socio-economic inequalities and differential personal and group relations were also present (Casavecchia and Salvatori, 1997). Moreover, geographical isolation was never so complete as rhetorical narratives assume. Agricultural specialization imposes commerce, but there were also thick networks of exchange with close communities, especially from the villages located inland: vital practices often obstructed by the supra-local powers. Furthermore, whether it was seasonal, daily, or more permanent, close or distant migration also has been an important resource across the centuries, permitting, together with nautical activities, a diversification of family incomes (Gibelli, 1994) and assuring preferential relations for the commercialization of local products (Casavecchia and Salvatori, 2002). It seems possible to affirm that the combination of male migration and female assumption of the greatest part of the agricultural tasks preserved the terraced landscapes until the last half of the preceding century (Iacoponi, 2007). Indeed, in olden days terraced agricultural landscape was common to the entire Ligurian coastal area (Terranova, 1989), even if maybe less suggestive then on the Cinque Terre slopes: it is a complex interweaving of social, politico-economical, ecological, and historical factors that created the landscape particularity of this area and its longevity.

Narratives emerging from the heritagization process tend to oversimplify and partly deny other socioecological interconnections. Recent historic-ecological and archaeoecological research reveal the weight of transhumance systems (between coastal areas and communal lands on the Apennine Mountains), essential in maintaining soil fertility for specialized viticulture (Cevasco et al., 2020, pp. 94–102). The progressive monocultural and exploitative vine-growing practice contributed to deforestation processes, intensifying hydrogeological risks, especially on recently abandoned terraces (Pepe et al., 2019). It also exposed communities and plants to the hazards of pests, the most dramatic one occurring in the 1920s with the *phylloxera* pandemic.

Incidentally, interdisciplinary studies combining historical, geographical, and archaeological approaches help in discerning a more complex territorial reality than the one promoted in the heritagization process. Beyond being involved in a variety of marginal productive and extractive activities, communities of the Cinque Terre were growing complementary crops, were part of transhumance and exchange circuits, and engaged in capillary care practices for the maintaining of woods and water canalizations (Gabellieri, Pescini, and Panetta, 2020, Pescini, Montanari, and Moreno, 2018).

Discourses and practices

The progressive adoption of a landscape simplifying gaze is not without consequences and seems to fit with some paradigmatic frames of prevailing institutional conservation policies. An interdisciplinary study on historical landscape configurations (Gabellieri, Pescini, and Panetta, 2020) compared its results with different planning instruments concerning the Cinque Terre.[6] A great discrepancy between this study's approaches and those adopted by the plan's authors concerns the artificial distinction between "natural" and "anthropic" spaces: while planners recognize the latter ones as needy and worth of human intervention, the former are the object of reforestation and re-naturalization regulations, formally impeding any interference. However, this imposition of the human/nature divide doesn't take sufficiently into account the socioecological complexity we illustrated and, beyond inducing the loss of landscape historical evidences, it doesn't properly address hydro-geological risks.[7] This critique is supported by a number of geological surveys, pointing to recently abandoned terraced zones as the most unstable ones (Pepe et al., 2019) and suggesting a more nuanced comprehension of reforestation role in consolidating soils (Agnoletti et al., 2019; Cevaso & Moreno 2015). Gabellieri and his co-authors (2020, p. 324) propose to pay more attention to changes undertaken to those landscapes over time. What are now generally labelled as "traditional practices" are just a minimal part of the minute practices and activities, which were a fundamental part of past territorial maintenance. Furthermore, identifying traditional landscapes with maximum expansion of vineyard terraces doesn't consider that that configuration was consistent with specific historical and politico-economical moments, while, at other times, landscapes were characterized by more varied human-environment interactions.

Conservational approaches built upon global organizations' guidelines have also numerous social consequences (Brockington and Duffy, 2010). As mentioned by several winegrowers,[8] regulations may interfere with agricultural activities. For example, they constrain agricultural work to expensive maintaining activities and reduce innovation, by imposing some construction techniques or restricting the possibility to modify terraces. This interference may be increased by the institutional and political conflicts overwhelming planning processes, which often take decades to complete, "freezing" the territory under general temporary regulations. Simultaneously, it is true that the National Park provides some concrete support to farmers (to be added to those guaranteed by regional and communitarian institutions) and assures territorial promotion. But, beyond those ambivalences, ethnographic surveys show how this Park didn't became an aggregation actor for contemporary peasants and, if new agricultural projects start, they are carried out at great individual effort and often facing old problems never profoundly addressed. Moreover, national parks have demonstrated to participate in economic development primarily by fostering an idea of natural heritage as a resource, encouraging its consumption in different ways.[9] The participation of the Cinque Terre National Park in the mass promotion of tourism of the area and the rise of new dominant politico-economical actors (as the Harbour Authority of La Spezia, controlling its Cruise terminal) support such critical views (Paradiso, forthcoming).

Ironically, the visions expressed in the early years of the winegrowers' struggles and a few publications supported by the National Park in its first period were aware of the dangers of simplifications and romanticization.[10] Somehow those suggestions have been forgotten, together with the complexity they were advocating for. Nowadays, another oversimplification, the touristic one, seems to prevail, leaving very little space for alternatives to be discussed collectively. The observation of local political life, mainly during electoral campaigns and political meetings, suggests that critics to this new monoculture – and indeed critics to the very concept of monoculture – are not on the forefront, even if some unexpected events recently shew local socioecological fragilities. I think to a flood in 2011, aggravated by land abandonment, and to the pandemic in 2020, when local employment was drastically affected by the tourism crisis.

Conclusions

Once spectacularized, tradition becomes the cornerstone that allows the merger of territory, knowledges, and local products, authorizing economical practices linked to tourism to get in dialogue with the identity dimension (Siniscalchi, 2002). As a process of difference production in a world of culturally, socially and economically interconnected and interdependent spaces (Gupta and Ferguson, 2001), landscape heritagization spreads when many landscapes intended to be places of production become consumption goods (Stacul, 2010). Nonetheless, every conservation effort entails some degree of selection and concrete modifications, taking place in a local dimension which is never homogeneous in terms of power relations (Herzfeld, 2010). In the Cinque Terre as elsewhere, the cultural capital linked to viticulture has been remoulded in light of new goals, progressively enacting a naturalization of some territorial specificities (Ulin, 1996), to be used tactically, both in terms of political carriers and commercial efficiency in expanding contexts (Gouez and Petric, 2007). Moreover, to retrace the origins of this heritagization project allows us to notice how even rooted perspectives stiffen while entering into the so-defined Authorized Heritage Discourse (Smith, 2006). Mark out a territory, promote its own specificity, highlight an exclusive identity: those are processes that profoundly influence contemporary visions and politics at the Cinque Terre. Those dynamics show how difficult it becomes to defy ontological divides, building more inclusive concepts of heritage (Harrison, 2013) and considering landscapes as a starting point to observe human and non-human assemblages, as they emerge and overlap historically (Tsing, Mathews, and Bubandt, 2019; Mathews, 2018).

Being the aim of this text to link patrimonial visions to the possible futures they authorize or not (Carter et al., 2020), I try to put into dialogue the Cinque Terre case with a rich anthropological and political ecology literature, as well as with my other field's studies.[11] It seems to me that the specific patrimonial visions arising in the sustainable development "historic bloc" (Igoe, Neves, and Brockington, 2010), doesn't propose instruments, both intellectual and practical, suited to imagine and realize futures that are moulded into the complexity of socioecological dynamics. Massimo Quaini, geographer, fine expert of Ligurian landscapes and brilliant thinker, reminds us that, to conserve a "self-sustainable landscape" we need to maintain "social continuity between past and present-future", building on historic-geographical interpretations able to take account of "genesis and transformations, of relative balances and perpetual dynamics, abandoning a static concept of identity and an aesthetic-emotional concept of landscape" (Quaini, 2015, pp. 209–210 [my translation]). Inspired by his work, I then argue that prevailing sustainable-developmentalist patrimonial visions don't enhance "convivial landscape utopias" (Quaini, 2006), beyond competition logics among territories, identity sclerosis, and anthropocentric productivism.

Notes

1 In addition to the editor and co-authors of this book, I would like to thank Diego Moreno, Valentina Pescini, Emanuele Raso, Rachel Black, and Katherine Little for their revisions and their stimulating comments. I sincerely thank all my interlocutors in the field.

2 Those are findings under study and under publication, as referred to me by scholars involved in research projects on those topics.

3 A label for Quality Wines Produced in Specific Regions, in Italian *Denominazione di Origine Controllata*. The D.O.C. Cinque Terre has been instituted in 1973 and concerns two wines: a white one and the famous straw one, under the quite recent name *Sciacchetrà*. The white wine of the Cinque Terre must be obtained from specific vine varieties: *Vermentino, Bosco*, and *Albarola*, with the permission of a percentage of local ancient vine varieties.

4 Five villages compose the Cinque Terre, from West to East: Monterosso, Vernazza, Corniglia, Manarola, and Riomaggiore. They are subdivided in three municipalities: Monterosso, Vernazza-Corniglia, and Riomaggiore-Manarola.

5 I think especially to the influential and articulated work conducted by a heterogeneous and little formalized group of researchers, based at the University of Genoa and in the scientific committee of the revue *Quaderni storici*. We can mention a few of its members and some of their works that have been relevant for the construction of a local history, either as an approach and as a body of knowledges about Liguria. Edoardo Grendi was an economic historian. One of his most famous works focuses on the politico-economic articulations between different territorial entities (Grendi, 1993). He also largely contributed to epistemological and methodological reflections (e.g. Grendi, 1977, where the Cinque Terre and the community of Monterosso are used to exemplify how political and market relations can be heuristic subjects to redefine spaces and social entities) and his contribution to the fundamental book edited by Jacques Revel (1996), *Jeux d'échelles. La micro-analyse à l'expérience* (Grendi, 1996). Another historian, Osvaldo Raggio, explored familial and group dynamics to understand local heterogeneity and conflicts (e.g. Raggio, 2018). Some geographers have been very close to this group, adding a particular interest for environmental and ecological data in the historical and archaeological research (e.g. Moreno, 2018).

6 The *Piano del Parco* of 2002 (abrogated after a legal affair in 2010): an important planning instrument, which is superior than town planning. Other plans considered

by Gabellieri, Pescini, & Panetta (2020) are the UNESCO Management Plan of 2016 and the SCI-SPA plan for the Mesco Site of Community Importance.

7 An institutional-technical interlocutor informed me that the new *Piano del Parco* (currently under discussion) could help in nuancing the divide between "natural" and agricultural areas, instituting vast areas of "agricultural protection" on relatively recently abandoned terraced lands.

8 I could profitably cross my own data and analysis with those of Francesco Bravin (*Cinque Terre, dalla patrimonializzazione all'etnopoiesi*, PhD dissertation, Università degli studi di Genova, 2015), whom I would like to thank for the rich confrontation.

9 I base my analysis on a nowadays very ample literature crossing anthropology, environmental history, and political ecology looking to national parks as an integral part of modern (earlier) and neoliberal (more recently) projects for the natural resources' management. Those works address conservation complementarity with industrial activities and their participation in touristic promotion (e.g. Graf, 2010; Gissibl, Höhler, and Kupper, 2012). They also investigate more recent implications of paradigms such sustainable development, ecological restoration, and emission markets (e.g. Brockington *et al.* 2008; Igoe, Neves, and Brockington, 2010, Büscher, Dressler, and Fletcher, 2014).

10 Among the publications supported by the National Park, and beyond the works of Casavecchia and Salvatori, one should mention a volume edited by the urbanist Mariolina Besio (2002). This latter one collects several contributions originating from an interdisciplinary congress on landscape planification. Even if supported by a less attentive historical and critical gaze than the local history and ecological archaeology works mentioned above, this volume contains analysis from some distinguished scholars as the historian of material culture Tiziano Mannoni and the urbanist Alberto Magnaghi.

11 In particular my PhD research on the environmental policies implemented around the archipelago of la Maddalena National Park (Sardinia): for an overview see Paradiso (2021).

References

Agnoletti, M., Errico, A., Santoro, A., Dani, A., and Preti, F. (2019). Terraced Landscapes and Hydrogeological Risk. Effects of land Abandonment in Cinque Terre (Italy) during Severe Rainfall Events. *Sustainability*, 11(1):235.

Appadurai, A. (1996). *Modernity at Large: Cultural Dimensions of Globalization*. Minneapolis: University of Minnesota Press.

Besio, M. (2002). *Il vino del mare Il piano del paesaggio tra i tempi della tradizione e i tempi della conoscenza*. Padova: Marsilio.

Brockington, D., Duffy, R., and Igoe, J. (2008). *Nature Unbound. Conservation, Capitalism and the Future of Protected Areas*. Dunstan House: Earthscan.

Brockington, D. and Duffy, R. (2010). Capitalism and Conservation: The Production and Reproduction of Biodiversity Conservation. *Antipode*, 42(3): 469–484.

Büscher, B., Dressler, W., and Fletcher, R. (eds.) (2014). *Nature Inc. Environmental Conservation in the Neoliberal Age*. Tucson: University of Arizona Press.

Carter, T., Harvey, D. C., Jones, R., and Robertson I. (eds.) (2020). *Creating Heritage: Unrecognised Pasts and Rejected Futures*. Abingdon: Routledge.

Casavecchia, A. and Salvatori, E. (1997). *Vino Contadini Mercanti. Il libro di conti di un viticoltore riomaggiorese del Settecento*. Sarzana: Lunaria.

Casavecchia, A. and Salvatori, E. (2002). *Il parco dell'uomo 1. Storia di un paesaggio*. Riomaggiore: Parco Nazionale delle Cinque Terre.

Cevasco, R. and Moreno, D. (2015). Historical Ecology in Modern Conservation in Italy. In Kirby, K. and Watkins, C. (eds.), *Europe's Changing Woods and Forests. From Wildwood to Managed Landscapes*. Wallingford: CABI Publishing, pp. 227–242.

Cevasco, R., Gabellieri, N., Pescini, V., and Stagno, A. M. (2020). Area III. Cinque Terre e Val di Vara. In Gabellieri, N., Pescini, V. and Tinterri, D. (eds.), *Sulle tracce dei pastori in Liguria. Eredità storiche e ambientali della transumanza*. Genova: Sage, pp. 94–102.

Fabre, D. (2001). L'histoire a changé de lieux. In Bensa A. and Fabre, D. (eds.), *Une histoire à soi. Figurations du passé et localités*. Paris: Éditions MSH, pp. 13–41.

Gabellieri, N., Pescini, V., and Panetta, A. (2020). The "'5T.ERA" Project: Bridging Research with Application for the Management of the Cinque Terre Rural Landscape. *Quaderni storici*, 164(2): 311–341.

Gibelli, A. (1994). La risorsa America. In Gibelli, A. and Rugafiori P. (eds.), *Storia d'Italia. Le regioni dall'Unità ad oggi. La Liguria*. Torino: Einaudi, pp. 585–651.

Gissibl, B., Höhler, S., and Kupper, P. (eds.) (2012). *Civilizing Nature: National Parks in Global Historical Perspective*. New York: Berghahn.

Gouez, A. and Petric, B. (2007). *Le vin et l'Europe: Métamorphoses d'une terre d'élection*. Paris: Institut Jacques Delors.

Graf von Hardenberg, W. (2010). Act Locally, Think Nationally. A Brief history of Access Rights and Environmental Conflicts in Fascist Italy. In Armiero, M. and Hall, M. (eds.), *Nature and History in Modern Italy*. Athens: Ohio University Press, pp. 141–159.

Grendi, E. (1977). Micro-analisi e storia sociale. *Quaderni storici*, 35(2): 506–520.

Grendi, E. (1993). *Il Cervo e la repubblica: il modello ligure di antico regime*. Torino: Einaudi.

Grendi, E. (1996). Repenser la micro histoire. In J. Revel (ed.), *Jeux d'échelles. La micro-analyse à l'expérience*. Paris: Gallimard/Le Seuil, pp. 233–243.

Gupta, A. and Ferguson, J. (2001). Beyond "Culture". Space, Identity, and the Politics of Difference. In A. Gupta and J. Ferguson (eds.), *Culture, Power, Place: Explorations in Critical Anthropology*. Durham: Duke University Press, pp. 33–51.

Harrison, R. (2013). *Heritage. Critical Approaches*, Abingdon: Routledge.

Herzfeld, M. (2010). Engagement, Gentrification, and the Neoliberal Hijacking of History. *Current Anthropology*, 51(2): 259–267.

Hirsch, E. and O'Hanlon, M. (eds.) (1995). *The Anthropology of Landscape: Perspective on Place and Space*. Oxford: Oxford University Press.

Iacoponi, V. (2007). Popolazione e paesaggio in mutamento. Storie di Vernazza e delle Cinque Terre tra Ottocento e Novecento. *Annali dell'Istituto Alcide Cervi*, 29: 105–204.

Igoe, J., Neves, K., and Brockington, D. (2010). A Spectacular Eco-Tour around Historic Bloc: Theorising the Convergence of Biodiversity Conservation and Capitalist Expansion. *Antipode*, 42(3): 486–511.

Ingold, T. (2000). *The Perception of the Environment: Essay on Livelihood, Dwelling and Skill*. Abingdon: Routledge.

Mathews, A. S. (2018). Landscapes and Throughscapes in Italian Forest Worlds: Thinking Dramatically about the Anthropocene. *Cultural Anthropology*, 33(3): 386–414.

Moreno, D. (2018). *Dal documento al terreno. Storia e archeologia dei sistemi agro-silvo-pastorali*. Genova: Genova University Press.

Palumbo, B. (2003). *L'Unesco e il campanile. Antropologia, politica e beni culturali in Sicilia orientale*. Roma: Meltemi.

Paradiso, C. (2012). *Cinq Terres, un parc. La création d'un parc national aux Cinque Terre en Italie: la définition du Patrimoine territorial en perspective historico-anthropologique, entre carrières politiques, développement touristique et production vitivinicole*. Master thesis, EHESS Marseille.

Paradiso, C. (2021). Du sable, des plantes, des microorganismes, des gens. Un regard anthropologique sur l'érosion côtière à l'archipel de la Maddalena (Italie) et sur des politiques situées. *VertigO – la revue électronique en sciences de l'environnement*, 21(1) (online). Retrieved from: http://journals.openedition.org/vertigo/31065.

Paradiso, C. (forthcoming). Parchi nazionali e sviluppo turistico. Il caso delle Cinque Terre o dell'impossibile convivenza nelle monoculture. In G. Salerno and A. Esposito (eds.), *Oltre la monocultura del turismo. Per un atlante delle resistenze e delle controprogettualità*, Roma: Manifesto Libri.

Pepe, G., Mandarino, A., Raso, E., Scarpellini, P., Brandolini, P., and Cevasco, A. (2019). Investigation on Farmland Abandonment of Terraced Slopes Using Multi-temporal Data Sources Comparison and Its Implication on Hydro-Geomorphological Processes. *Water*, 11: 1552.

Pescini, V., Montanari, C. A., and Moreno, D. T. (2018). Multi-proxy Record of Environmental Changes and Past Land Use Practices in a Mediterranean Landscape: The Punta Mesco Cape (Liguria – Italy) between the 15th and the 20th century. *Quaternary International*, 463: 376–390.

Raggio, O. (2018). *Feuds and State Formation (1550–1700): The Backcountry of the Republic of Genoa*, Cham: Palgrave McMillan.

Quaini, M. (2015). Leggere il passato per progettare il futuro. In N. Gabellieri and V. Pescini (eds.), *Biografia di un paesaggio rurale. Storia, Geografia e archeologia ambientale per la riqualificazione di Case Lovara (promontorio del Mesco – La Spezia)*. Sestri Levante: Oltre Edizioni, pp. 209–211.

Quaini, M. (2006). *L'ombra del paesaggio. L'orizzonte di un'utopia conviviale*. Parma: Diabasis.

Siniscalchi, V. (2007). Sapere antropologico, potere e patrimonializzazione dei saperi in Francia. In A. Caoci, and F. Lai (eds.), *Gli "oggetti culturali". L'artigianato tra estetica, antropologia e sviluppo locale*. Milano: Franco Angeli, pp. 148–161.

Siniscalchi, V. (ed.) (2002). *Frammenti di economie. Ricerche di antropologia economica in Italia*, Cosenza: Luigi Pellegrini Editore.

Smith, L. (2006). *Uses of Heritage*. Abingdon: Routledge.

Stacul, J. (2010). Contesting Consumption: Changing Meanings of Landscape in Northern Italy. In P.-J. Stewart and A. Strathern (eds.), *Landscape, Heritage, and Conservation: Farming Issues in the European Union*. Durham: Carolina Academic Press, pp. 227–241.

Terranova, R. (1989). Il paesaggio costiero agrario terrazzato delle Cinque Terre in Liguria. *Studi e Ricerche di Geografia*, 13(1): 1–57.

Tsing, A. (2005). *Friction: An Ethnography of Global Connection*. Princeton: Princeton University Press.

Tsing, A., Mathews, A., and Bubandt, N. (2019). Patchy Antropocene: Landscape Structures, Multispecies History, and the Retooling of Anthropology. *Current Anthropology*, 60(20): 186–197.

Ulin, R. C. (1996). *Vintages and Traditions: An Ethnohistory of Southwest French Wine Cooperatives*. Washington: Smithsonian Books.

Wallerstein, I. (1974). *The Modern World-System I: Capitalist Agriculture and the Origins of the European World-Economy in the Sixteenth Century*. New York: Academic Press.

6 Storytelling and online media as narrative practices for engaging with the Historic Urban Landscapes (HUL)

The case study of Porto, Portugal

Ana Rita Albuquerque, Maria Leonor Botelho and Dominique Crozat

Introduction

Over the last two decades, Porto (Portugal) has undergone a deep rehabilitation of its urban buildings and public spaces, accompanied by demographic transformations and a profound change in the ways of experiencing the city. The UNESCO label in 1996 and the designation of Porto as 2001 European Capital of Culture opened a new phase in the urban rehabilitation process (Antunes 2019). More recently and until early 2020, Porto has experienced an increase in tourist flows. In 2019, the number of non-resident tourist arrivals in Portugal reached 24.6 million, 7.9 per cent more than in 2018 (INE 2020).

Social changes, the rise of gentrification, touristification, and real estate pressures have posed significant threats to the idealised image of Porto as both historic and contemporary city. The preservation of urban heritage is no longer focused solely on the protection of material and historical assets, but also on the management of transformations taking place in the urban landscape (Bandarin and Van Oers, 2012; 2014; Ginzarly, Pereira Roders, and Teller, 2019).

The UNESCO Recommendation on the Historic Urban Landscape (hereafter HUL) is a heritage management tool providing guidelines for heritage and landscape management in an urban context, in every city, not necessarily only on those that have World Heritage (WH) properties. It was established in the Vienna Memorandum (UNESCO, 2005) and was officially adopted in November 2011.

The Recommendation defines the HUL and distinguishes heritage attributes and values:

> The historic urban landscape is the urban area understood as the result of a historical layering of cultural and natural values and attributes, extending beyond the notion of "historical centre" or "ensemble" to include the broader urban context and its geographical setting.

DOI: 10.4324/9781003195238-6

The attributes refer to both intangible and tangible heritage that is preserved, while the values concern the motivations and why the heritage resource needs to be protected (UNESCO, 2011).

Following the UNESCO Recommendation, it is crucial to develop accurate, both bottom-up and top-down, tools and methods to identify HUL attributes and values, and to understand the complex cultural, visual, spatial, and urban system of meanings, experiences, and interactions.

Porto is a relevant case for exploring the HUL approach, not only because it is a multi-layered urban settlement in a dynamic landscape, but also due to its own urban conservation history (Ferreira and Silva, 2019). The city's Historic Centre was the stage of one of the pioneer studies on urban conservation in Portugal. The *"Estudo de Renovação Urbana da Ribeira Barredo"* (Távora, 1969) is a multidisciplinary and integrated study including urban, architectonic, physical, and human elements, as well as the legal framework and policies proposals. The idea behind this work "to continue innovating" connects with today's urban rehabilitation pro-grammes and the objective of HUL approach 50 years later (Ferreira and Silva, 2019).

Since 1996, the historic centre of Porto has been included in the World Heritage List. This property has a perimeter of 51 hectares and a buffer zone of 186 hectares (UNESCO, 1996). The elements that determine the extent of this perimeter are linked to the Douro River and the medieval layout of the town (Loza, 2000; ICOMOS, 2018).

The role of social media for the implementation of the HUL approach just recently started to draw attention (Ginzarly, Pereira Roders, and Teller, 2018; Van der Hoeven, 2019, 2020). Urban-oriented social media platforms, as well as individual accounts or profiles, contain a wide range of memories, informa-tion, historic audio-visual material, and stories related to the heritage and urban past and present. Since the COVID-19 pandemic, the generalization of social media to tell stories has increased. It also changed our perception of space and time and our landscape experience.

The purpose of this chapter is to address the role of storytelling and social media in the engagement of the inhabitants with the urban landscape and in the awakening of Porto's heritage as a resource. Therefore, we pose the fol-lowing research questions: how does storytelling constitute our experience of urban landscapes? How is it used to legitimise what to preserve and transmit to future generations?

This chapter is structured as follows. First, we present the theoretical framework drawn upon literature from the field of cultural geography and heritage studies, as well as digital ethnography and urban conservation. Second, we discuss the methodological approach. Third, we present the research findings by defining heritage categories, situating attributes, and identifying social and affective values, and the significance attached to the urban landscape.

Theoretical framework

Storytelling in heritage landscape studies

New approaches to storytelling have been explored and proposed in heritage landscapes. Geographers have conceived concepts of narrative and storytelling as part of a relational and material turn within the discipline and of non-representational and (post)phenomenological theory (Thrift, 2008; Daniels and Lorimer, 2012; Burlingame, 2020). Davis (2011) provides an environmental history conciliating different landscapes representations from both top-down and bottom-up approaches. Daniels and Lorimer (2012) offered a synopsis of landscape as "a narrative medium" and the impact in reconstructing some key geographical concepts such as landscape. Mossberg (2008) and Moscardo (2020) formulated the relation between creating unique stories, experience, and tourism. More than a *narrative turn*, they talk about the importance of a story *turn*.

Storytelling is also relevant in the production of urban narratives, as highlighted by urban studies (Goldstein et al., 2015). Narrative is an essential element in the formulation of urban systems and in the understanding of transformative change.

Applied to the specific study of HUL, we recall the work of Van der Hoeven (2019; 2020) in the field of media and communications studies about how people engage with urban heritage through participatory heritage websites. Nevertheless, in his work the spatial dimension is less addressed, and he fails to assess how it can be integrated in heritage policies.

In the context of the present chapter, we use the terms story and narrative interchangeably. Three dimensions can be highlighted. The first dimension is the spatial one. Narrative does not exist without spatiality of the characters that "anchor" the narrative and set them in scene (Certeau, 1990 [1980]). Then we have the narrative experience, attached to the temporal dimension that deals with shared experiences of space (Ricoeur, 1983, p. 17). The third dimension is about the performative function of these narratives and upholds the "layers of lived experiences" through body postures, movements, and juxtaposition of spaces: presence, co-presence, and absence.

Heritage "from below" through the lens of storytelling, co-presence, and lived experience

Heritage "from below" (HFB) is often simply addressed as a counter-narrative of what constitutes one's heritage. These counter-narratives are particularly useful in revealing the partiality and selectivity of official versions of the past or in representing counter-sites that the "authorised heritage discourses" (AHD) (Smith, 2006) excluded or forgot (Robertson, 2016). There is a tendency in the literature to romanticise alternative heritage formulations, as subservient to dominant official discourses, driven by only selected grassroots (Muzaini and Minca, 2018).

Drawing on "critical heritage studies" (Winter, 2013), in this chapter we adopt a definition of heritage "from below" (Robertson, 2016) applied to cases where individuals and groups manifest alternative or forgotten types of heritage attributes and values, thus problematising the ways the past and present are engaged. We argue that HFB and AHD should not necessarily be seen as antithetical but possibly complementary to one another.

The concept of co-presence means the online and offline engagement, the mutual interweaving of sense perception, emotions, and materiality in the construction and articulation of space, place, identity, and knowledge (Hjorth et al., 2017). Storytelling and social media are also means to structure perception and contribute to the new (post)phenomenology approach. They constitute a space of flow in which the values participate in the redefinition of the materiality and in the redistribution of the sensible (Thrift, 2008, p. 46). Co-presence can also occur without sharing the same physical space, as long as the actors share a mutual perception.

Methodology

The methodology employed in our work is combining digital ethnography (Boellstorff et al., 2012; Hjorth et al., 2017; Hine, 2020), photography analysis, observation, and information gathering in situ (semi-structured interviews and institutional data).

For the visual documents analysis, we have drawn upon the work of Gillian Rose on visual methodologies about the dimensions and modes of interpretation applied to the field of urban, geographical and heritage studies (Rose, 2016).

Our paper is based on a fieldwork that took place in two main phases between 2018 and 2020. Parallel to the systematic analysis of 35 Facebook and Instagram accounts and pages from Porto locals, we carried out semi-directive interviews divided into three parts: general social media and digital behaviours; images and representations of the city and heritage; online behaviours and offline practices connected to the urban and heritage fabric.

The selection of the inhabitants' social media accounts was done in two steps. First, they were chosen to follow three criteria: place of residence (Greater Porto), belonging to the 25–45 age group, and active presence on social networks. Two techniques were used to refine the selection: the use of one of the three hashtags #Porto, #portoponto, #cidadedoPorto and/or the methodological sampling technique called the "snowball effect", where the people selected for the study propose new participants from their network of friends and acquaintances.

Data analysis

The interview was composed of 30 questions. There were 15 questions with direct answers. The open answers invited interviewers to react to different statements about the current heritage-making processes, urban transformation, and its impacts in Porto (touristification, real estate pressures, housing rights and gentrification).

Interviewers were asked to choose two to four of their own social media photos of Porto and its heritage. They had to describe the images and justify their choices. When developing their arguments, they used personal memories and factual descriptions of the place or element. For the interviewers, the photographs often serve as a support to the discourse, but they also have a force all by themselves and allow them to think of the image as a social fact. We collected 90 photos that allowed us to specify and detail the relationship of the inhabitants with the city and their heritage, the way they feel and practice space, and finally the opportunity to speak about their representations in order to capture the collective narrative on urban heritage. Almost all of these photos were taken with mobile phones when the interviewers were walking between their homes and work, or just randomly around the city.

Data was further analysed considering the spatial distribution and localisation of the city regarding WH property: inside the limits, buffer zone, city centre (downtown), or other parishes (mainly oriental zone).

We used a thematic analysis to identify the kind of heritage preserved or not preserved (attributes) and the significance and meanings attached to it (values). Data was first organised into five heritage categories of attributes: built environment and public space; social-cultural elements and urban environments; cultural activities; intimate heritage; and heritage deprived of their status. For each category of attributes, interviewers assigned multiple values. We distinguish nine kinds of heritage values: aesthetical, historical, artistical, ecological, social, political, economic, scientific, and experiential. Data was organised to the frequency that each category of attributes was mentioned by the interviewers and identified in the photos.

The analysis of photos reveals additional information and highlights that are not detected through the analysis of geographical location or simply through the interviews. While some photos focus on a specific category of attributes (e.g., built environment), others have a broader scope by including several categories and multiple attributes.

To complete the analysis, tags were assessed automatically through a quantitative and a categorical analysis: it was meant to show the most and least used tags in the ensemble of the photos and to help identify tag patterns. We obtained information on how the users refer to the different assets and attributes of the HUL and give insights on how they value them and how they relate socio-cultural practices, meanings, and places.

Such qualitative research methods allow a detailed understanding of the ways in which people perceive and value heritage and provide us with information about the lived experience of Historical Urban Landscapes. Instead of the exclusive top-down approach, it enables the values and attributes to emerge and to be studied inductively.

Findings and discussion

Perceiving the landscape and locating data: attributes on their place

When asked about which heritage attributes were more representative of the city and what they wanted to preserve, all the interviewers initially answered the "whole city", the "ensemble", or the "urban landscape". They addressed the HUL as a coherent whole. They perceive it as a dynamic and inter-connected entity. They were not focusing on specific categories, But instead, they combined all dimensions and attributes as a whole.

As the interview progressed, more specific attributes were redefined, and they began to share the stories behind them. The results revealed that the most cited and photographed category of attributes is the built environment and public spaces (cited 85 times): urban landscape, waterfronts, the Douro River and its bridges, the main monuments of the city and its architectural details. Public spaces, such as gardens, squares and streets are also indicated. These attributes are for the most part located inside the limits of the WH property (26 per cent) or in the buffer zone or city centre (37 per cent).

Another important category of attributes cited was the socio-cultural elements and urban ambiance (cited 70 times). This goes beyond visual appearance and includes the character of the city and the social fabric, tra-ditional crafts, street art, gastronomy, traditional shops, and local traditions connected to the festivities.

Inside this category, several important attributes were cited. Most are located between the buffer zone and the oriental part of the city. Interviewers cited the same number of issues and attributes as those located inside the WH property (26 per cent).

The *Calçada das Carquejeiras* was cited as an attribute of those two categories several times. This place (known as *Calçada da Corticeira* until 1992) is a long, steep climb of 220 metres located in the hillside in the *Fontainhas* district between the Douro River waterfront and the *Alameda das Fontainhas*.

This walk is visible from several places on both sides of the Douro River between the Ponte Dom Luís I bridge (550 metres away) and Ponte Infante Dom Henrique bridge. It depicts the story of a group of poor women of *carquejeiras* (gorse women) from the end of the 19th century until the early 20th century, who spent their days bent over carrying bunches of *carqueja*. This shrub-like plant was harvested in the Douro Valley and transported by boat to Porto. Then, these women would transport them from Ponte Dom Luís I bridge, to the bakeries and the stately homes located in the upper part of the city.

Today, this part of the city is characterised by a profound and rapid trans-formation of the escarpment and the development and creation of new tourist areas. Telling these stories sheds light on areas where heritage boundaries are challenged, and alternatives to dominant narratives can be articulated. These areas create spaces, in which heritage values are in permanent evolution and transformation. They reveal heterogeneity and diversity and provide a platform to rethink the HUL (Albuquerque and Botelho, 2019).

Telling the stories and co-presence: practices of remembering together

> For me, the most representative place of Porto is the viewpoint of Fontainhas. When I was young, I used to come here to visit my grandmother. She told me stories about this place. We used to walk around and visit the abandon chapel and the vegetable gardens in the middle of the ruins.
>
> (Interview, 2020)

Remembering this place means to know about the history and identity of the Porto urban landscape and rediscover a less tourist part of the city with strong industrial and fluvial ties. Through the attributes and stories, we obtained information regarding the factories, storage houses, and ruins of former economies and social activities of Porto (e.g., "ilhas" traditional social housing, the old ceramic factory of *Carvalhinho* from 1841 and the ruin of the *Senhor do Carvalhinho* Chapel).

The process of the reactivation of collective memories began in 2015 with the foundation of the civil organisation *Homenagem às Carquejeiras do Porto*.[1] This organisation allowed a greater recognition of the dignity of these characters, strangely forgotten by the institutional leaders, as well as by most of the inhabitants of the city of Porto. This allows for a multifaceted and general critique of both the historical narrative and modernity.

Today Porto faces strong development of new tourist areas; cultures and practices have emerged as a result of the visitor's desire to go beyond the central districts, to experience the city and to interact with the local community.

Since the 2010s, visiting "ordinary" places has become common practice for visitors and residents alike (Maitland, 2007).

The tours offered by local associations in the oriental part of the city contribute as well to the collective urban narrative. Local organisations such as *The Worst Tours* (2012) and *Slow Motion Tours* (2015) stem from an alternative conception of tourism in Porto. These tours, set up during the economic crisis that shook Portugal and other countries (2008), propose practices such as urban walking combined with photography and walking debates. They offer a collective and shared experience of the urban landscape, representing a shift from passive contemplation to social exchange and tourism as an act of citizenship and active participation (Istasse, 2017).

Through their guided tours, we discover places beyond the historic centre, but also through the walking debates, we have access to information about the austerity measures imposed by the Troika[2] and their perverse effects, the impact of tourism in the local economy and its repercussions, the similarities and differences with other European cities, and potential solutions for the problems presented.

These tours are important tools for mediation, initiating a conversation, and recounting experiences in the city. The interactive walking stimulates the exchange of very personal experiences between participants. All the photos and other materials are shared in the social media groups or pages from the organisations where they continue to interact after the visit ends.

The photos capture the contemporary and quick transformations of the urban fabric, but also different points of view of the different layers of the landscape. Subsequently, posting on social media enables urban and heritage information that might otherwise remain unknown to be shared. These practices enhance public knowledge of Historic Urban Landscapes on a daily basis.

Identifying values through storytelling and lived experiences

Storytelling enables people to express their attachments. This ties in with the objectives of the HUL approach. The HUL Recommendation calls for civic engagement tools that facilitate dialogues between people about the key values in their urban areas (Article 24, UNESCO, 2011). Storytelling and social media are relevant because they make the affective and social values associated with historical heritage emerge, through the account of daily practice, personal and intimate experiences, individual and collective memories and feelings. Storytelling practices invite citizens to actively engage with urban heritage in virtual spaces. In this way, urban residents who might otherwise not physically meet are brought together in the virtual space, facilitating practices of remembering together.

We distinguish the categories of experiential, social, and affective values. These different categories are not exclusively tied to specific heritage attributes. One heritage attribute or category of attributes can have multiple values attached to it. No matter which category of attributes were cited by the interviewers, we noticed a high level of the ensemble's presence in these three categories of values.

By social value we consider a collective attachment to the place that embodies meanings and values that are important to a community, or communities, providing a basis for a sense of belonging and social interaction (Jones, 2017).

Figure 6.1. Screenshot of one of the interviewer's Instagram account: Corticeira street, transversal to the Calçada das Carquejeiras

When I took this picture, several feelings came to my mind. I saw the two bridges, the ruined landscape, I remembered the stories of these women. When I climbed this *calçada*, I thought of these women. When I got to the top, I saw a whole stunning landscape, my beautiful city. I am always proud to make part of this community, of this city.

(Interview, 2020)

This quotation illustrates the sense of pride and belonging is very strong. When interviewers were asked to choose a photo that for them represents the heritage and the urban landscape, they always revealed their sense of affection and nostalgia. The personal perspective and the experience of the landscape implies a reflection on whether the cities have changed for the better or worse. It's not just merely a personal perspective, it concerns collective meanings and social relationships between the local community members, place, and time.

When expressing their feelings, interviewers do not focus on specific categories; instead, they blend and combine them. Through the tags in the photos, we also obtain important information regarding the attribute and its location, but also the city's history and how different layers are interconnected. The results show how key words differ from one area to another within the city. The interviewers use terms about the location and temporalities, but mostly also about feelings and emotions (e.g., #authentic, #happiness, #emotional, #beautiful).

The tags express the interaction between the interviewers, the environment, and the attributes that impact their landscape perception. These tags include users' own vocabulary and reflect daily life practices or expressions (e.g., "cityscape"; "daily life") and sometimes concern conflictual values in relation to the landscape, the social fabric, or the social and economic conditions (e.g., "the worst tour ever"; "multi-layer collage").

The tags, the images, and the quotations reveal how people relate urban heritage to their own lives and how individuals experience certain events and places. This experiential value (Van der Hoeven, 2020) captures the personal significance attached to urban landscape and heritage, through memories, emotions, and opinions.

Social, affective, and experiential values contribute to our understanding of how cities have evolved. Engaging with the urban landscape cannot be separated from the historical value. These values support filling knowledge and historical gaps, uncovering the multiple layers associated with the urban landscapes, and document emotions and affects.

Conclusion

Heritage practitioners and policymakers often regard social, affective, and experiential values expressed by contemporary communities as more ephemeral than historic, scientific, economic, and aesthetic values. Also, the means for evaluating historic, scientific, and aesthetic values have been established for a long time. Therefore, storytelling combined with lived experience and co-presence might be useful to reach a consensus on the identification of the heritage attributes and values to preserve. It is important to work closely with institutional and academic actors, recognising the need to diversify the criteria and to incorporate it into the digital inventories, databases, and master plans.

The methodology applied improves our understanding of people engagement and the context of exceptional and everyday urban landscape. Results highlighted areas where heritage boundaries are challenged and alternatives to the AHD can be articulated and complementary. Storytelling plays a significant role in the development of new tourist practices, combining urban walking, photography, and social media (Robinson and Picard, 2009). The heritage attributes identified reveal predominately affective, social, and experiential values. Further research is required to combine with the visitors' perspectives and to make comparisons between residents' and visitors' stories and representations.

Opening up heritage to new groups, restructuring the dynamics between actors, the possibility of a more democratic engagement with the past and history (Adair, Filene, and Koloski, 2011), and finally the possibility of creating more participatory heritage and sustainable tourist organisations (possibility of exchanging information in a more fluid way, creation of consultation spaces, etc.) constitute a way forward, that could be integrated into the broader heritage practice.

In this sense another form of engagement is possible by creating complementary pathways to heritage representation that move away from a binary opposition between "real objects" and their digital representations, but rather explores the possibilities of a model of urban landscape engagement.

Acknowledgements

We would like to thank the reviewers for their important comments and efforts towards improving our manuscript.

Funding

This paper was financed by Portuguese National Funds through the FCT – Foundation for Science and Technology, under the project UIDB/04059/2020.

Notes

1 https://it-it.facebook.com/carquejeirasdoporto (accessed 20 July 2021).
2 The Troika (2010) was constituted by the European Commission, the European Central Bank and the International Monetary Fund, being responsible for auditing the economic situation of Greece, Portugal, Ireland and Cyprus during and after the economic crisis of 2008.

References

Adair, B., Filene, B., and Koloski, L. (eds.) (2011). *Letting Go? Sharing Historical Authority in a User-generated World*. Walnut Creek: Left Coast Press.

Albuquerque, A. R. and Go, M. L. (2019). Repenser les frontières des paysages urbains historiques. Pratiques et discours sur la ville de Porto. *Culture and Musées. Muséologie et recherches sur la culture*, 33: 133–156.

Antunes, G. (2019). Política de habitação social em Portugal: de 1974 à actualidade. *Forum Sociológico. Série* II, 34: 7–17.

Bandarin, F. and Van Oers, R. (2012). *The Historic Urban Landscape: Managing Heritage in an Urban Century*. Hoboken: John Wiley and Sons.

Bandarin, F. and Van Oers, R. (eds.) (2014). *Reconnecting the City: The Historic Urban Landscape Approach and the Future of Urban Heritage*. Hoboken: John Wiley and Sons.

Boellstorff, T., Nardi, B., Pearce, C., and Taylor, T. L. (2012). *Ethnography and Virtual Worlds*. Princeton: Princeton University Press.

Burlingame, K. (2020). *Dead Landscapes – and How to Make Them Live* (Doctoral dissertation, Lund University).

Davis, D. K. (2011). Reading Landscapes and Telling Stories: Geography, the Humanities, and Environmental History. In S. Daniels, D. DeLyser, J. Nicholas Entrikin, and D. Richardson (eds.), *Envisioning Landscapes, Making Worlds: Geography and the Humanities*. Abingdon: Routledge, pp. 170–176.

De Certeau, M. (1990 [1980]). *L'invention du quotidien 1. Arts de faire*. Paris: Gallimard.

Ferreira, T. C. and Silva, A. T. (2019). Perspectives for a Historic Urban Landscape Approach in Porto, Portugal. In A. Pereira Roders and F. Bandarin (eds.), *Reshaping Urban Conservation*. Singapore: Springer, pp. 403–421.

Ginzarly, M., Pereira Roders, A., and Teller, J. (2019). Mapping Historic Urban Landscape Values through Social Media. *Journal of Cultural Heritage*, 36: 1–11.

Goldstein, B. E., Wessells, A. T., Lejano, R., and Butler, W. (2015). Narrating Resilience: Transforming Urban Systems Through Collaborative Storytelling. *Urban Studies*, 52(7): 1285–1303.

Hine, C. (2020). *Ethnography for the Internet: Embedded, Embodied and Everyday*. Abingdon: Routledge.

Hjorth, L., Horst, H., Galloway, A., and Bell, G. (eds.). (2017). *The Routledge Companion to Digital Ethnography*. Abingdon: Routledge.

ICOMOS. (2018). *Technical Evaluation Report on the Conservation State of the Site Inscribed in the World Heritage List of UNESCO. Historical Centre of Oporto, Luíz I Bridge and Monastery of Serra do Pilar*. Lisboa: ICOMOS Comissão Nacional Portuguesa.

INE. (2020). *Estatísticas do Turismo 2019*. Lisboa: INE, Instituto Nacional de Estatística.

Istasse, M. (2017). Facebook et les amateurs de patrimoine. *Reseaux*, 6: 193–218.

Jones, S. (2017). Wrestling with the Social Value of Heritage: Problems, Dilemmas and Opportunities. *Journal of Community Archaeology and Heritage*, 4: 21–37.

Lorimer, H. (2005). Cultural Geography: The Busyness of Being "More-than representational", *Progress in Human Geography*, 29(1): 83–94.

Loza, R. (2000). *Porto Património Mundial III. CRUARB–25 anos de Reabilitação Urbana*. Porto: Câmara Municipal do Porto.

Maitland, R. (2007). Culture, City Users and the Creation of New Tourism Areas in Cities. In M. Smith (ed.) *Tourism, Culture and Regeneration*. Wallingford: CABI, pp. 25–34.

Moscardo, G. (2020). The story Turn in Tourism: Forces and Futures. *Journal of Tourism Futures*, 7(2): 168–173.

Mossberg, L. (2008). Extraordinary Experiences Through Storytelling. *Scandinavian Journal of Hospitality and Tourism*, 8(3): 195–210.

Muzaini, H. and Minca, C. (2018). Rethinking Heritage, But "From Below". In H. Muzaini and C. Minca (eds.), *After Heritage: Critical Perspectives on Heritage from Below*. Cheltenham: Edward Elgar, pp. 1–21.

PDM Porto. (2021). *Revisão do Plano Diretor Municipal do Porto*. Porto: Câmara Municipal do Porto. Retrieved from: https://pdm.cm-porto.pt/.

Smith, L. (2006). The Uses of Heritage. *Labour*, 193(6): 195.

Rico, T. (2017). Technologies, Technocracy, and the Promise of "Alternative" Heritage Values. In H. Silverman, E. Waterton, and S. Watson (eds.), *Heritage in Action*. Cham: Springer, pp. 217–230.

Ricœur, P. (1983). *Temps et récit 1. L'intrigue et le récit historique*. Paris: Editions du Seuil.

Robertson, I. J. (ed.). (2016). *Heritage from Below*. Abingdon: Routledge.

Robinson, M. and Picard, D. (2009). Moments, Magic and Memories: Photographing Tourists, Tourist Photographs and Making Worlds. In D. Picard and M. Robinson (eds.), *The Framed World: Tourism, Tourists and Photography*. Abingdon: Routledge, pp. 1–37.

Távora, F. (1969). *Estudo de Renovação da Ribeira Barredo*. Porto: Câmara Municipal do Porto.

Thrift, N. (2008). *Non-representational Theory: Space, Politics, Affect*. Abingdon: Routledge.

UNESCO. (1972). World Heritage Convention: Convention Concerning the Protection of the World Cultural and Natural Heritage. Retrieved from: https://whc.unesco.org/en/convention/.

UNESCO. (1996). Historic Centre of Oporto, Luiz I Bridge and Monastery of Serra do Pilar. Retrieved from: https://whc.unesco.org/en/list/755/.

UNESCO. (2003). Convention for the Safeguarding of the Intangible Cultural Heritage. Retrieved from: https://ich.unesco.org/en/convention.

UNESCO (2005). Vienna Memorandum on World Heritage and Contemporary Architecture–Managing Historic Urban Landscape. Paris: UNESCO. Retrieved from: https://whc.unesco.org/en/documents/5965.

UNESCO. (2011). Recommendation on the Historic Urban Landscape, Including a Glossary of Definitions. Retrieved from: https://whc.unesco.org/en/hul/.

UNESCO. 2016 [1992, 1994, 2005]. The Operational Guidelines for the Implementation of the World Heritage Convention. Paris: UNESCO. Retrieved from: https://whc.unesco.org/en/news/2259.

UNESCO. (2016). Rapport des décisions adoptées lors de la 40e session du Comité du patrimoine mondial (Istanbul). Retrieved from: https://whc.unesco.org/fr/sessions/40COM.

Van der Hoeven, A. (2019). Historic Urban Landscapes on Social Media: The Contributions of Online Narrative Practices to Urban Heritage Conservation. *City, Culture and Society*, 17: 61–68.

Van der Hoeven, A. (2020). Valuing Urban Heritage Through Participatory Heritage Websites: Citizen Perceptions of Historic Urban Landscapes. *Space and Culture*, 23(2): 129–148.

Veldpaus, L. (2015). *Historic Urban Landscapes: Framing the Integration of Urban and Heritage Planning in Multilevel Governance*. Eindhoven: Eindhoven University of Technology.

Veschambre, V. (2007). Patrimoine: un objet révélateur des évolutions de la géographie et de sa place dans les sciences sociales. *Annales de géographie*, 4: 361–381.

Waterton, E. (2013). Landscape and Non-representational Theories. In P. Howard, I. Thompson, and E. Waterton (eds), *Routledge Companion to Landscape Studies*. Abingdon: Routledge, pp. 66–76.

Waterton, E. (2019). More-than-representational Landscapes. In P. Howard, I. Thompson, E. Waterton, and M. Atha (eds), *The Routledge Companion to Landscape Studies*. *2nd ed*. Abingdon: Routledge, pp. 91–101.

Winter, T. (2013). Clarifying the Critical in Critical Heritage Studies. *International Journal of Heritage Studies*, 19(6): 532–545.

7 From landscape as heritage to biocultural heritage in a landscape

The ecological and cultural legacy of millennial land use practices for future natures

Vincenza Ferrara, Anneli Ekblom and Anders Wästfelt

Introduction

Globally, a high proportion of biodiversity resides outside of protected areas, in landscapes where biodiversity and communities must continue to co-exist. The survival of agricultural landscapes with high nature value can be key to both biodiversity conservation and rural development. Nonetheless, we need tools and methods to better understand formation dynamics of such landscapes, especially where landscape elements may be very old and local practices are continuous. In these cases, the conceptualisation of landscape dynamics in terms of hierarchical relationships and patch dynamics (see for instance Wu and Loucks, 1995; Wu and David, 2002; Pickett and Cadenasso, 2013) has strong potential but, at the same time, does not fully explain the complexity of interacting human practices and natural dynamics working at different temporal and spatial scales (cf. Crumley and Marquardt, 1987, 1995, 2019; McGlade, 1995). With our contribution we explore the possibility to develop new conceptualisations of landscape as heritage, laying out a conceptual toolbox for viewing at spatial and time scales as heterarchically organised and from a more-than-human approach, using the example of an olive intercropping landscape in an inner area of rural Sicily. The approach can be applied also in other geographical areas, and we will end this chapter by discussing its wider potential to foster new forms of integration between different research fields and practice-based knowledge for biocultural heritage preservation, grounded on the acknowledgement of the ecological function played by place-based communities and the consequent need to re-think our engagement space. As we will argue, care for biocultural heritage is interlinked with and promotes ecological engagement.

Space–time heterarchies for a more-than-human relational ontology

The predominant dichotomous thinking on nature-culture and use of anthropocentric concepts is unable to capture all the dynamics and relationships among the

DOI: 10.4324/9781003195238-7

different participants of the more-than-human world (O'Gorman and Gaynor, 2020; Tsing Lowenhaupt, Mathews, and Bubandt, 2019; Stone-Jovicich, 2015). We build on the idea of biocultural heritage as the ecological and cultural legacy of millennial land use practices on present-day biological diversity (Maffi, 2001; Maffi and Woodley, 2012; Barthel, Crumley, and Svedin, 2013; Cevasco, Moreno, and, Hearn, 2015; Gavin et al., 2015; Swiderska and Argumedo, 2017; Eriksson, 2018; Lindholm and Ekblom, 2019). Biocultural heritage encompasses biological and cultural features, constantly developing and changing by direct and indirect reciprocal interrelatedness. Biocultural Heritage to us is fundamentally about co-constitution, the set of "changing material, social, and symbolic relations between and among human and nonhuman actors" (cf. O'Gorman and Gaynor, 2020: 715) from which it arises. The co-constitution and relations have primacy here over discrete entities ("human" and "nonhuman") – similar to related perspectives in hybrid geography, as well as non-representational theories and some materiality approaches (see Whatmore, 2002; Hinchliffe, 2007; Lorimer, 2012; Thrift, 2007; Waterton, 2013; Kerridge, 2018; and Bennett, 2010 to name just a few). Humans are, in this sense, participants in manifold ecologies, a series of becomings with nonhuman beings. In our approach such relational perspectives are enriched by the dimension of history and temporal depth, at the interface between historical ecology (Crumley, 2019) and critical geospatial ontology (Harvey, 2018; Sundberg, 2014; Schuurman, 2008). Geographical spaces are the place where non-linear, multidirectional, and multi-scalar historical processes, expressions of diverse voices and their legacies, ecologi-cally materialise themselves, and where both space and time have their own agency (Barker and Pickerill, 2020; Reid, Sieber, and Blacknd, 2020). Biocultural Heritage is, in other words, the living non-discursive archive of ecological diversity emerging, mostly unintentionally, from the multiple intra-acting performances of beings (material entities – nature, where humans are not the only actors in the play) (cf. Abbott, 2021; Rackham, 2015; Barker and Pickerill, 2020) and meanings (discursive practices – culture) (Hunt, 2014) at any single place (Wästfelt et al., 2012: 1173). Landscapes are the endless result of different biophysical and socio-cultural processes, operating simultaneously at *multiscalar* and *transtemporal* levels. These processes are entangled in a non-linear way, in the sense that their spatial and temporal patterns do not respond to a hierarchical order (i.e. from larger to smaller, or from older to younger), but follow various relational pathways where they have the potential to be ranked in a number of different ways (Crumley, 1995: 3). In such a framework, biocultural heritage emerges as the accumulation of heterarchical processes through space-time: the result of complex interactions between more-than-human processes, agents, and actors at different, both nested and unranked, spatio-temporal scales which can never be regarded as independent.

To capture and show how these space-time heterarchies unfold, we look at different but interwoven timescales, both rapid variables of landscape change, but also slower variables with less visible features (see similar discussion in Crumley, 2019; Sinclair, Moen, and Crumley, 2017; Lane, 2019). In other words, it is the biocultural heritage that continually forms and re-shapes (both spatially and temporally) a landscape, while creating future natures in terms of heterogeneity and biodiversity (Crumley and Marquardt, 1987; Benton, Vickery, and Wilson, 2003; Barthel, Crumley, and Svedin, 2013). In our example, we will show how the spatial configurations of past land use practices have an agency of their own, influencing the composition and patterns of other species and their communities, including also human practices and interactions, and where the temporal is both influencing and influenced by such contextual relationships.

Space-time heterarchies in a rural area of Sicily

As in other Mediterranean agroecosystems (Meeus, 1995; Agnoletti and Emanueli, 2016), on the island of Sicily it is still possible today to find remnants of ancient olive trees (*Olea europaea var. sativa*). These are woody plants capable of living for millennia and still providing fruits, while playing a crucial ecological role for soil stability and the surrounding ecosystems (Rühl et al., 2011). These long-lasting trees can be seen as stabilities in a spatially and temporally changing landscape, and as expressions of local practices which convey heritage and identity in the form of non–discursive ecological knowledge. They represent different spatial scales of tree cultivation arrangements, a result of distinct historical land uses and intentionalities, combined with ecological processes, climatic variations, and both local and global socio-economic dynamics (Ferrara, 2016).

Cozzo del Lampo is a hill in a rural area of inner Sicily, in the municipality of Villarosa (Enna province).

The hill has a top elevation of approximately 550 metres above sea level (a.s.l.) and the total area, covering also the surrounding "contrade" *Vigne Grandi, Quattro Aratate, Barone* (Italian medieval term used to indicate rural small districts), has an overall extension of nearly six square kilometres. At first sight Cozzo del Lampo could represent a marginal location. It does not have any known archaeological or historical site, and has not been officially listed of high natural value. Locally it is not regarded as a heritage place and it is geographically remote from core economic areas. Nonetheless, located in the middle of agricultural landscapes dominated by cereal crops, the hill is characterised by a great variety and heterogeneity of olive trees, particularly considering its relatively small area, which resembles a vegetation mosaic. These agroecosystems have an extraordinary ecological value since, made of very old trees (having large canopies and huge empty trunks), present a high diversity of flora and fauna, being rich in ecological niches and refuges for other species (Morgado et al., 2020; Pizzolotto et al., 2018).

Thanks to the identification of breaking points in time and spatial nodes of connection in the ecological and social history of these trees, we have been able to show how olive trees occur in a variety of spatial configurations, each of them directly related to a unique time period and a particular spatial arrangement of land use (see full detail in Ferrara, Ekblom, and Wästfelt, 2020): scattered olive trees could be dated back to the beginning of random olive grafting and domestication practices from wild olive, while more and more systematic forms of plantations (from terraces to semi-intense linear groves, passing through the intercropping systems of the "Mediterranean garden" model) are the results of the progressive agricultural specialisation over the centuries (Figure 7.1). Such different space-time configurations can all be identified in the landscape today. In many cases, as shown from Figure 7.1, they are even partially overlapping in the same field. The resulting landscape mosaic which can be observed at present embodies the combined spatial and temporal configurations of land use logics over time.

Conceptualising biocultural heritage in ontological terms, as we propose above, has direct implications for how to frame in a novel way the management of landscape as heritage. Below we will outline our perspective.

A new ontology for a new landscape management

The solutions for managing purposes of biocultural heritage (in landscapes) cannot be generalised, but they need to be tailored to different contexts and co-developed with locals. There is the need to develop new integrated approaches, based on the understanding and recognition of the ecological contributions of place-based communities along the history. This could pave the way for delineating a constructive way forward: a re-appropriation of our ecological engagement space, which means 1) being aware of past long-lasting legacies on today's ecological communities, 2) re-conceptualising such continuity in light of local needs and different time horizons, both over the short and the long term, and 3) taking into consideration that we are constantly creating and re-shaping future natures through our actions today.

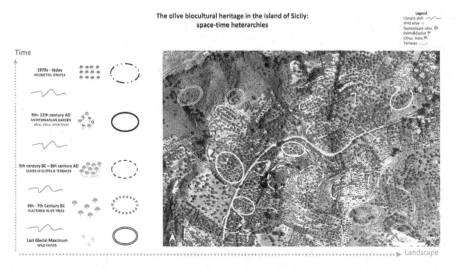

Figure 7.1. Space-time heterarchies in the olive biocultural heritage of Sicily. Location: Cozzo del Lampo, Villarosa (Enna), 37°35'09.7"N 14°11'28.1"E

Acknowledge the ecological function of place-based communities

From our work on the olive biocultural heritage of inner Sicily, it emerges that the locals' engagement with nature is part of a broader, more-than-human, long-term process that has generated one of the most biologically diverse agroecosystems in Europe. The recognition of the ecological function that place-based communities have played throughout history in a particular land-scape is thus crucial. In more-than-human biocultural systems, past habitat fragments and novel ecosystems need to be understood in their specific social and environmental contexts. As shown by the example of Cozzo del Lampo, long-term biological and cultural relationships between people and their sur-roundings have constantly shaped and reshaped complex and hybrid landscape mosaics, at a variety of time and spatial scales. It is in the very legacy of these ecological relationships where the motivation for today's conservation engage-ment lies (see also Grove et al. 2020). From the legacy of the ecology of interactions may emerge the engagement and initiative of local communities to combine preservation of biocultural heritage and landscape management, while also adapting and re-innovating agricultural practices (see also discussion in Kmoch et al., 2018; Kongsager, 2018; Schermer, et al. 2018).

As palaeoecological reconstructions (Mercuri and Sadori, 2014) and historical ecology (Grove and Rackham, 2001; Braje et al., 2017) have shown, rather than seeing a dichotomy between "protection" on one hand or "destruction" on the other, Mediterranean landscapes and their plant communities are continuously transformed by climatic variations, ecological processes through a network of socio-political and economic drivers (Squatriti, 2014; Renes et al., 2019). Accepting that Mediterranean landscapes are in a constant state of flux (Braje et al., 2017; Allen, 2003), new conceptualisations of co-management are possible, changing our approaches to future management.

Imagine the near future of olive agroecosystems in inner areas

The biocultural heritage embodied by the ancient olive trees surviving at Cozzo del Lampo, as in many other remote inner areas of Sicily, is today located in a place where there has been a massive out-migration during the last 50 years, resulting in a large-scale land abandonment. Only a few part-time and hobby-farmers have remained, while the young generations still living in rural areas are almost totally uninterested in agricultural work. A great volume of the olive orchards are today owned by people living in North Italy or abroad. Due to the strong cultural attachment that Sicilian people have with the olive tree, landowners still commission locals to manage their olive trees. Related man-agement practices are mainly focused on keeping the land "clean" with the primary reason to protect olive orchards from summer fires. Heavy machinery is thus used to guarantee a quick and good clearance, resulting in progressive soil impoverishment and ecosystem degradation (Figure 7.2). Paradoxically, by

Figure 7.2. Evident signs of soil erosion and habitat degradation, due to heavy tilling. Location: Cozzo del Lampo, Villarosa (Enna), 37°35'09.7"N 14°11'28.1"E

this practice it is precisely the people who continue to take care of their land, if even from a distance, who are contributing to the destruction of the very agroecosystems they are striving to preserve. At the same time, the very few elders who are carriers of traditional knowledge and ecological memory are progressively passing away, and it becomes more and more difficult to document and transfer the large entire body of non-discursive knowledge they hold.

Imagining the near future, there are two possible scenarios:

1   "New entrants" movements begin with people returning to inner areas and taking over small-scale agricultural activities (Sutherland et al., 2016). In this scenario the continuity in biocultural heritage preservation is guaranteed, albeit in new forms of landscape mosaics. This would probably be facilitated through new forms of mobilising labour, such as for instance eco-labelling, eco-tourism, and/or through multifunctional agriculture (cf. D'Auria et al., 2020).

2   Depopulation trends of rural areas continue or increase in magnitude, which will lead to the progressive degradation of biocultural heritage and serious marginalisation of the remaining rural population (Gennai-Schott et al., 2020; Martínez-Abraín et al., 2020; Biasi et al., 2017). This is a scenario in which a "new" landscape is formed by a discontinuity of management, with outcomes already observed in the past (Braje et al., 2017; Rühl et al., 2011).

In both scenarios, we have to consider that plants shift their ranges over time, in response to climatic fluctuations for instance, while diseases and animals' activity represent both opportunities and threats for plant communities (Squatriti, 2014). From this exercise of imagination, we wanted to illustrate the importance of place-based communities in shaping biocultural heritage and landscape. Within this context, we want to discuss what could be realistic, sound, and viable forms of re-appropriation of our ecological engagement space?

A re-appropriation of our ecological engagement space

First of all, such re-appropriation may be a full awareness of our more-than-human entanglements. Compared to the past, today we are better aware of the role we play in shaping future natures. When we position ourselves within co-constituted and more-than-human worlds, we realise that we are all embedded within particular sets of relationships that together shape our collective worlds, and this has entirely new political and ethical repercussions: looking at more-than-humans means giving equal importance to different relations and voices, overcoming the conceptual division between human and nonhuman, nature and culture, and to consider multispecies and multi-natural entanglements (O'Gorman and Gaynor, 2020).

Second, in a relational more-than-human system, such re-appropriation could mean being able to be *in-between* humans and non-humans, past and present. We have seen how biocultural heritage is the ecological and cultural legacy of millennial land use practices (millennial entanglements), affecting present-day biological diversity and landscape. The maintenance of biocultural heritage requires the local ecological engagement of place-based communities and the transmission of the ecological memory embodied in those practices (Moragues-Faus, 2014; Murray et al., 2019). However, for economic, cultural and social reasons it is not possible today to guarantee such continuity in many areas of southern Europe.

There is therefore the need to find alternative conceptualisations of our ecological engagement. These could be approaches that take advantage of the broader and more fluid engagement spaces in which we live today, exploiting the wider networks that sustain such "spaces". There are already very interesting initiatives in this direction, in which the wider connections that a local place has are seen as a strength and may be "exploited" in innovative ways, maintaining a stewardship continuity of the local biocultural heritage. One example are distance adoption initiatives (cf. Varotto and Lodatti, 2014) or the identification of research priorities and emerging issues through collaboration with local communities (i.e. the transdisciplinary research project "The Biocultural Heritage of Sicilian Olive Trees", funded by The Swedish Research Council and entirely co-designed and developed with locals). Indeed, a re-appropriation of our ecological engagement space means also positioning ourselves *in-between* different types of knowledge, with a new look at the entire body of non-discursive knowledge referring to biocultural heritage as constantly evolving, inevitably linked with the environmental and cultural context, as well as constantly re-adapting to changing circumstances and needs of its holders.

With our contribution, we have tried to lay out an alternative way to look at the landscape as biocultural heritage, to offer a diverse way forward for researchers and communities in landscape management, which is hopefully only the beginning of a constructive dialogue. Many landscapes are simply not considered as heritage because of the loss (more or less intentional) of cultural memory (Eriksson, 2018; Braje et al., 2017). This may remind us that the value we assign to material manifestations of heritage is directly linked to what we choose to keep "alive" through our daily work. However, through this selective engagement, we risk losing both biological and cultural heritage and the knowledge associated. Maybe, with a new ontology, informed by a deep-time history and a sincere openness to new and other forms of knowledge, we will learn other stories. And we may also see how our daily activities, in terms of landscape management, can easily encompass more species and other forms of knowledge, so to help us better preserve what we most cherish – such as ancient olive trees.

Acknowledgements

This work was supported by Vetenskapsrådet under the project "*The Biocultural Heritage of Sicilian Olive Trees*", 2020–02625. The authors would like to thank the anonymous reviewers and the Editor-in-Chief for their very helpful comments on an earlier version of this manuscript. Any and all errors are the responsibility of the authors.

References

Abbott, S. (2021). Approaching Nonhuman Ontologies: Trees, Communication, and Qualitative Inquiry. *Qualitative Inquiry*, 27(8–9):1059–1071.

Agnoletti, M. and Emanueli, F. (eds.) (2016). *Biocultural Diversity in Europe*. Cham: Springer International Publishing.

Allen, H. D. (2003). Response of Past and Present Mediterranean Ecosystems to Environmental Change. *Progress in Physical Geography: Earth and Environment*, 27(3), 359–377.

Barker, A. J. and Pickerill, J. (2020). Doings with the Land and Sea: Decolonising Geographies, Indigeneity, and Enacting Place-agency. *Progress in Human Geography*, 44(4): 640–662.

Barthel, S., Crumley, C. L., and Svedin, U. (2013). Bio-cultural Refugia – Safeguarding Diversity of Practices for Food Security and Biodiversity. *Global Environ. Change* 23: 1142–1152.

Bennett, J. (2010). *Vibrant Matter: A Political Ecology of Things*. Durham: Duke University Press.

Benton, T. G., Vickery, J. A., and Wilson, J. D. (2003). Farmland Biodiversity: Is Habitat Heterogeneity the Key? *Trends in Ecology and Evolution* 18(4): 182–188.

Biasi, R., Brunori, E., Ferrara, C., and Salvati, L. (2017). Towards Sustainable Rural Landscapes? A Multivariate Analysis of the Structure of Traditional Tree Cropping Systems Along a Human Pressure Gradient in a Mediterranean Region. *Agroforestry Systems*, 91: 1199–1217.

Braje, T., Leppard, T., Fitzpatrick, S., and Erlandson, J. (2017). Archaeology, Historical Ecology and Anthropogenic Island Ecosystems. *Environmental Conservation*, 44 (3): 286–297.

Cevasco, R., Moreno, D., and Hearn, R. (2015). Biodiversification as an Historical Process: An Appeal for the Application of Historical Ecology to Bio-cultural Diversity Research. *Biodiversity Conservation*, 24: 3167–3183.

Crumley, C. L. and Marquardt, W. H. (eds.) (1987). *Regional Dynamics: Burgundian Landscapes in Historical Perspective*. San Diego, CA: Academic Press.

Crumley, C. L. (1995). Heterarchy and the Analysis of Complex Societies. *Archeological Papers of the American Anthropological Association*, 6(1): 1–5.

Crumley, C. (2019). Integrating Time and Space in Dynamic Systems. In C. Ray and M. Fernández-Götz (eds.), *Historical Ecologies, Heterarchies and Transtemporal Landscapes*. New York: Routledge, pp. 287–297.

D'Auria, A., Marano-Marcolini, C., Čehić, A., and Tregua, M. (2020). Oleotourism: A Comparison of Three Mediterranean Countries. *Sustainability*, 12: 8995.

Ekblom, A. (2019). Archaeology, Historical Sciences, and Environmental Conservation. In Isendahl, C. and D. Stump (eds.), *The Oxford Handbook of Applied Archaeology*. Oxford: Oxford University Press.

Eriksson, O. (2018). What Is Biological Cultural Heritage and Why Should We Care About It? An Example from Swedish Rural Landscapes and Forests. *Nature Conservation* 28: 1–32.

Ferrara, V. (2016). *Olive Trees of Sicily: A Historical Ecology* (Dissertation). Department of Archaeology and Ancient History, Uppsala University.

Ferrara, V., Ekblom, A., and Wästfelt, A. (2020). Biocultural Heritage in Sicilian Olive Groves: The Importance of Heterogeneous Landscapes over the Long Term. In M. I. Goldstein and D. A. DellaSala (eds.), *Encyclopedia of the World's Biomes*, vol. 5. Amsterdam: Elsevier, pp. 135–145.

Gavin, M. C., McCarter, J., Mead, A., Berkes, F., Stepp, J. R., et al. (2015). Defining Biocultural Approaches to Conservation. *Trends in Ecology & Evolution*, 30 (3): 140–145.

Gennai-Schott, S., Sabbatini, T., Rizzo, D., and Marraccini, E. (2020). Who Remains When Professional Farmers Give up? Some Insights on Hobby Farming in an Olive Groves-Oriented Terraced Mediterranean Area. *Land*, 9: 168.

Grove, A.T. and Rackham, O. (2001). *The Nature of Mediterranean Europe: An Ecological History*. New Haven, CT: Yale University Press.

Grove, R., Evans Pim, J., Serrano, M., Cidrás, D., Viles, H., and Sanmartín, P. (2020). Pastoral Stone Enclosures as Biological Cultural Heritage: Galician and Cornish Examples of Community Conservation. *Land*, 9: 9.

Harvey, F. (2018). Critical GIS: Distinguishing Critical Theory from Critical Thinking. *The Canadian Geographer / Le Géographe Canadien*, 62: 35–39.

Hinchliffe, S. (2007). *Geographies of Nature: Societies, Environments, Ecologies*. Los Angeles: Sage.

Hunt, S. (2014). Ontologies of Indigeneity: The Politics of Embodying a Concept. *Cultural Geographies*, 21(1): 27–32.

Kerridge, R. (2018). New Directions in the Literary Representation of Landscape. In P. Howard, I. Thompson, E. Waterton, and M. Atha (eds.), *The Routledge Companion to Landscape Studies*. Abingdon: Routledge, pp. 253–263.

Kmoch, L., Pagella, T., Palm, M., and Sinclair, F. (2018). Using Local Agroecological Knowledge in Climate Change Adaptation: A Study of Tree-Based Options in Northern Morocco. *Sustainability*, 10: 3719.

Kongsager, R. (2018). Linking Climate Change Adaptation and Mitigation: A Review with Evidence from the Land-Use Sectors. *Land*, 7: 158.

Lane, P. J. (2019). Just How Long Does "Long-Term" Have to Be? Matters of Temporal Scale as Impediments to Interdisciplinary Understanding in Historical Ecology. In C. Isendahl and D. Stump (eds.), *The Oxford Handbook of Applied Archaeology*, Oxford: Oxford University Press.

Lindholm, K. J. and Ekblom, A. (2019). A Framework for Exploring and Managing Biocultural Heritage. *Anthropocene*, 25: 100–195.

Lorimer, J. (2012). Multinatural Geographies for the Anthropocene. *Progress in Human Geography*, 36(5): 593–612.

Maffi, L. (2001). *On Biocultural Diversity. Linking Language, Knowledge and the Environment.* Washington London: Smithsonian Institution.

Maffi, L. and Woodley, E. (2012). *Biocultural Diversity Conservation: A Global Sourcebook.* Abingdon: Routledge.

Martínez-Abraín, A., Iménez, J., Ferrer, X., Llaneza, L., Ferrer, M., et al. (2020). Ecological Consequences of Human Depopulation of Rural Areas on Wildlife: A Unifying Perspective. *Biological Conservation*, 252: 108860.

McGlade, J. (1995). Archaeology and the Ecodynamics of Human-modified Landscapes. *Antiquity*, 69(262): 113–132.

Meeus, J. H. A. (1995). Pan-European Landscapes. *Landscape and Urban Planning*, 31(1–3): 57–79.

Mercuri, A. M. and Sadori, L. (2014). Mediterranean Culture and Climatic Change: Past Patterns and Future Trends. In S. Goffredo and Z. Dubinsky (eds.), *The Mediterranean Sea*. Dordrecht: Springer.

Moragues-Faus, A. (2014). How Is Agriculture Reproduced? Unfolding Farmers' Interdependencies in Small-scale Mediterranean Olive Oil Production. *Journal of Rural Studies*, 34: 139–151.

Morgado, R., Santana, J., Porto, M., Sánchez-Oliver, J. S., Reino, L., et al. (2020). A Mediterranean Silent Spring? The Effects of Olive Farming Intensification on Breeding Bird Communities. *Agriculture, Ecosystems and Environment*, 288: 106694.

Murray, I., Jover-Avellà, G., Fullana, O., and Tello, E. (2019). Biocultural Heritages in Mallorca: Explaining the Resilience of Peasant Landscapes within a Mediterranean Tourist Hotspot, 1870–2016. *Sustainability*, 11: 1926.

O'Gorman, E. and Gaynor, A. (2020). More-Than-Human Histories. *Environmental History*, 25: 711–735.

Pickett, S. T. A. and Cadenasso, M. L. (2013). Chapter 10 – Ecosystems in a Heterogeneous World. In K. C. Weathers, D. L. Strayer, and G. E. Likens (eds.), *Fundamentals of Ecosystem Science*. New York: Academic Press, pp. 191–213.

Pizzolotto, R., Mazzei, A., Bonacci, T., Scalercio, S., Iannotta, N., et al. (2018). Ground Beetles in Mediterranean Olive Agroecosystems: Their Significance and Functional Role as Bioindicators (Coleoptera, Carabidae). *PLoS ONE* 13(3): e0194551.

Rackham, O. (2015). *Woodlands*. London: William Collins.

Reid, G., Sieber, R., and Blackned, S. (2020). Visions of Time in Geospatial Ontologies from Indigenous Peoples: A Case Study with the Eastern Cree in Northern Quebec. *International Journal of Geographical Information Science*, 34(12): 2335–2360.

Renes, H., Centeri, C., Kruse, A., and Kučera, Z. (2019). The Future of Traditional Landscapes: Discussions and Visions. *Land*, 8: 98.

Rühl, J., Caruso, T., Giucastro, M., and La Mantia, T. (2011). Olive Agroforestry Systems in Sicily: Cultivated Typologies and Secondary Succession Processes After Abandonment. *Plant Biosystems*, 145(1): 120–130.

Schermer, M., Stotten, R., Strasser, U., Meißl, G., Marke, T. et al. (2018). The Role of Transdisciplinary Research for Agricultural Climate Change Adaptation Strategies. *Agronomy*, 8: 237.

Schuurman, N. (2008). Database Ethnographies Using Social Science Methodologies to Enhance Data Analysis and Interpretation. *Geography Compass*, 2: 1529–1548.

Sinclair, P., Moen, J., and Crumley, C. (2017). Historical Ecology and the Longue Durée. In C. Crumley, T. Lennartsson, and A. Westin (eds.), *Issues and Concepts in*

Historical Ecology: The Past and Future of Landscapes and Regions. Cambridge: Cambridge University Press, pp. 13–40.

Squatriti, P. (2014). The Vegetative Mediterranean. In P. Horden and S. Kinoshita (eds.), *A Companion to Mediterranean History*, Oxford: Wiley-Blackwell.

Stone-Jovicich, S. (2015). Probing the Interfaces Between the Social Sciences and Social-ecological Resilience: Insights from Integrative and Hybrid Perspectives in the Social Sciences. *Ecology and Society*, 20(2): 25.

Sundberg, J. (2014). Decolonizing Posthumanist Geographies. *Cultural Geographies*, 21 (1): 33–47.

Sutherland, L.A., Visser, A., Pinto-Correia, T., Lorleberg, W., Monllor, N., et al. (2016). *EIP-AGRI Focus Group "New Entrants into Farming: Lessons to Foster Innovation and Entrepreneurship" Final Report.* European Commission.

Swiderska, K. and Argumedo, A. (2017). What is Biocultural Heritage? Retrieved from: http://pubs.iied.org/pdfs/G04151.pdf.

Thrift, N. (2007). *Non-Representational Theory: Space, Politics, Affect.* New York: Routledge.

Tsing Lowenhaupt, A., Mathews, A. S., and Bubandt, N. (2019). Patchy Anthropocene: Landscape Structure, Multispecies History, and the Retooling of Anthropology. *Current Anthropology*, 60: 186197.

Varotto, M. and Lodatti, L. (2014). New Family Farmers for Abandoned Lands. *Mountain Research and Development*, 34(4): 315–325.

Waterton, E. (2013). Landscape and Non-representational Theories. In P. Howard, I. Thompson, and E. Waterton (eds.), *The Routledge Companion to Landscape Studies*, Abingdon: Routledge, pp. 66–75.

Whatmore, S. (2002). *Hybrid Geographies: Natures, Cultures and Spaces.* London: Sage.

Wästfelt, A. (2021). Landscape as Filter – Farm Adaptation to Changing Contexts. *Journal of Land Use Science*, 16(2): 142–158.

Wästfelt, A., Saltzman, K., Berg, E. G., and Dahlberg, A. (2012). Landscape Care Paradoxes: Swedish Landscape Care Arrangements in a European Context. *Geoforum*, 43(6): 1171–1181.

Wu, J. and David, J. L. (2002). A Spatially Explicit Hierarchical Approach to Modelling Complex Ecological Systems: Theory and Applications. *Ecological Modelling*, 153: 7–26.

Wu, J. and Loucks, O. (1995). From Balance of Nature to Hierarchical Patch Dynamics: A Paradigm Shift in Ecology. *The Quarterly Review of Biology*, 70: 439–466.

8 Heritigizing traditional adaptations to natural hazards

A critical perspective

Pavel Raška and Rory Walshe

Introduction

Traditional adaptations to environmental stressors and natural hazards are increasingly valorized as offering climate change adaptation options (Nakashima, Krupnik, and Rubis, 2018) or the potential to mitigate the impacts of extreme events in disaster risk reduction (DRR) (Kelman, Mercer, and Gaillard, 2012). Much of this attention has been focused on traditional ecological knowledge (TEK) which, for the sake of this chapter, is defined as sets of beliefs, norms, and practices held by different groups representing long-term direct human interaction with the environment (Berkes, 2018). The academic examination of TEK can be traced back to anthropological research on folk knowledge at the turn of 1970s. Recent decades have seen its further divergence to various domains including environmental management and conservation, whereas investigation of TEK as a way to mitigate natural hazards (NH) within DRR has been relatively less addressed (Dekens, 2007; Kelman, Mercer, and Gaillard, 2012). In addition, the conceptual nexus of TEK and NH offers important implications for landscape management, as both of the related processes contribute to the evolution of cultural landscapes. This mutual contribution goes beyond the physical and social dichotomy (Wylie, 2006), however, as it denotes the reflective and dynamic nature of landscape evolution (Wu, 2010) and poses questions on what is considered as a natural hazard and as an adaptation practice in certain environments and by certain cultures. This finally raises the question of how TEK can be valued and preserved as a landscape heritage. Particularly since specific adaptive landforms and structures should be understood as materialized social practices that are linked to the time and purpose of their origin and alteration. Similarly, historical accounts such as flood maps, in turn, are socialized materialities of hazardous processes. We therefore argue that the designation of landscape features as "artifacts" may be an act of decontextualizing heritagization (Dolejš et al., 2018) creating a functional and interpretative disconnect that undermines the justification of integrative landscape management efforts aimed at such features (Freeman, Duguma, and Minang, 2015).

DOI: 10.4324/9781003195238-8

This chapter will present and discuss TEK adaptations to NH in selected written and oral cultures and will detail the critical discussion on efforts to record, classify, and apply TEK adaptations to mitigate contemporary NH. For the purpose of this chapter, natural hazards are understood as phenomena (both events and processes) with a potentially adverse impact on society, ranging from rapid events (e.g., flash floods, rockfalls) to slow-onset events and environmental stressors (e.g., water erosion, droughts). The second section will present a critical analysis of TEK, its definition and surrounding discourses including those related to heritagization. The third section delivers a broad typology and diverse examples of TEK as pertains to adaptations to natural hazard-related disasters. By comparing studies which are both historical and cross-cultural, this chapter provides a framework for understanding the spatio-temporal and environmental contexts in which TEK developed, has been sustained or transformed, and in some cases was lost or forgotten. Finally, based on the evidence presented in this chapter, we reconsider the role of heritagized historical knowledge in DRR and identify key future challenges.

Traditional ecological knowledge and heritage discourses

Within TEK, the term ecological is broadly used to denote knowledge developed to understand, explain, and sustain human interaction with the environment, as well as to recognize and mitigate forces of nature perceived as adverse (Folke, 2004; Berkes, 2018). The designation of knowledge as "traditional" is problematic and shares certain characteristics with the process of heritagization, in that this process is often led by outside individuals, groups, or institutions, the implications of which are mostly overlooked (Briggs, 2005). This being said, there is also a role for local communities in transmitting TEK and codifying it, thereby heritagizing it (including for DRR or climate change adaptation) and therefore the situation is complex. To unpack the complexity of conceptual sources for the heritagization of TEK and its consequences, we provide three central arguments.

As a backdrop to these arguments and debates, there is a persistent barrier to the full acknowledgement and understanding of TEK, which results from its ambiguous relationship with overlapping terms (local-, lay-, or indigenous knowledge) and their inconsistent use across disciplines. This vagueness makes it difficult to find common ground across different fields, but also obscures which of the historically, regionally, and functionally diverse beliefs, norms, and practices are considered as TEK (Dekens, 2007) and which might offer pathways of adaptation to NH in a climate change context. The most commonly cited characteristics of traditional (and particularly of indigenous) knowledge systems include their holistic nature, lengthy acquisition, culture-specific embeddedness, the use of local skills, resources and materials, informality, explanations based on examples and parables (often using religious examples), experiential familiarity, and close relation to survival and subsistence (e.g., Dekens, 2007; Shaw, Sharma, and Takeuchi, 2009; Kelman, Mercer, and Gaillard, 2012). Although semantic boundaries among these terms will always remain partially blurred, they must be explored, especially in terms of spatial and temporal dynamics of these knowledge systems (Folke, 2004).

Our first argument concerns the issues surrounding the performative power of authorized heritage discourses (see Neumann, 2011) that apply in DRR, with multiple central formative discourses determining research agendas. Such discourses also include key policy processes like the UNDRR Sendai framework that sets targets and priorities to prevent and reduce disaster risks. These discourses are unavoidably reductionist, as they seek to constrain research to certain topics, when examining TEK as a component of DRR. The authorized discourses resulting in further separation of codification of TEK between external researchers and internal community members, and the definition of TEK itself, has encouraged an artificial insider/outsider division. While local communities play an active role in valuing and transmitting TEK, and are therefore heritigizing it, it is more often outsiders who treat TEK as heritage, when it comes to its application in DRR due to the ownership of these discourses primarily resting in policy spheres.

Second, we suggest that the complex positive and negative feedbacks of TEK over the long term (referred to as the *longue durée*, Adamson, Hannaford, and Rohland, 2018) are overlooked. These feedbacks should be understood within the process of the origination, codification, persistence, and transformation of TEK in changing environments (due to natural- and human-induced feedbacks), across space (due to migration and mobility), as well as under evolving socioeconomic patterns (resulting from the previous). Considering these transforming contexts, certain TEK that proved effective at one time, and in one place, may later become ineffective or even induce adverse environmental changes posing new NH.

Third, the above also creates a false optimism surrounding the use of TEK in DRR. While much of the literature investigates the value of TEK, the notion of traditional communities being inherently environmentally responsible has been also criticized as being simplistic (Dekens, 2007). Diamond (1987) concluded that the idea of environmental ethics in pre-modern civilizations is a naïve concept drawing from noble savage myth. This has been polemized as selective, leading to an erroneous conclusion that "sound environmental practices were absent in such civilizations" (Johannes, 1987; McAnany and Yoffee, 2010). Thus, there have been growing calls to challenge the problematic assumption of either environmental stewardship or neglect (Fairhead and Leach, 1995) and Johannes (1989: 8) cautioned that some traditional management systems "cannot be expected to solve today's problems where demands on resources exceed their productive limits".

Typology and global empirical cases

In this section, we propose a tentative typology of TEK related to NH. This aims to provide an exploratory framework to understand the nature, development, and use of TEK in various cultural and environmental contexts and to stress the similar solutions and their functional equivalents that may be revealed across cultures (Lewis in Williams and Baines, 1993) and over long periods of time (Walshe and Argumedo, 2016). Based on a global literature review and our previous empirical research on DRR (e.g., Raška et al., 2014), the typology introduces four main TEK domains: (i) the use of NH-related environments, (ii) names for NH-related features and processes; (iii) explanations and reporting of NH-related features and processes; (iv) practices and measures to cope with NH-related features and processes. Since TEK develops as a complex and intertwined set of beliefs, norms, and practices, clear links exist among and between the individual domains.

The use of NH-related environments

In many cultures, specific natural features and environmental processes have been used to secure subsidiary needs. Among such examples, the periodical floods in Near and Far East civilizations are commonly known and the knowledge of these environments enabled the development of norms and practices to keep populations safe from flooding (e.g., Viollet, 2007). In the Pacific islands, despite the potential risk, sea transportation proved essential for migration and trade (Campbell, 2009), and from volcanic islands worldwide many cultures have profited from improved biochemical properties of soils episodically enriched by tephra fallout (Reid, 2019).

Names for NH-related features and processes

Among the fundamental manifestations of human understanding of the environment are the terms used for specific features in the landscape; yet these have received relatively little attention in the literature. Examples which have become used globally include volcanic features, such as *lahar* for volcanic flows (Indonesia) or Pahoehoe (*pāhoehoe*) and aa (*'a'ā*) for different types of lava (Hawaii), but also *dagala* (Italy) and *kīpukas* (Hawaii), denoting small, often vegetated patches that escaped the destruction by lava flows (del Moral and Walker, 2007). These terms indicate the ability of local populations to observe differences in the origin of features and processes, such as distinguishing chan-nellized recurrent debris flows (*Áar-skriðulop*) from rapid non–channellized debris slides (*Brekkuskriðulop*) on the Faroe Islands (Dahl et al., 2012). Specific ter-minologies may also refer to distinctive areas, events or periods of time, such as the Aboriginal *Yanyuwa* concepts of seasons characterized by specific weather patterns (Baker in Williams and Baines, 1993).

Explanations and reporting of NH-related features and processes

Societies typically developed rationalizations of NH and disaster events. Various beliefs and mythologies provide explanations for causes of NH. They also helped to define the risk zones as the sites where gods or spirits reside (e.g., *kami* ghosts in Japanese volcanoes; see Section 3.4), or allowed for blaming those who were believed to cause the event (e.g., Pfister, 2006). The impact of mythologies and beliefs on behaviour are still subject to discussion among historians (Hoffmann, 2014) and as Donovan, Suryanto, and Utami (2012) notes for Indonesia, some beliefs have previously resulted in unnecessary loss of life.

More recent records come from historical documents, reflecting a tendency for societies to try to quickly understand the causes of disasters (Janku, Schenk, and Mauelshagen, 2012). The strict distinction between the mythological, esoteric, and scientific ways of understanding are defective, as these represent continual complexities rather than different modes of thought. More specific approaches can be seen in the ways NH and their impacts are recorded and described (e.g. flood maps in Saxony) (Poliwoda, 2007), or reported by storytelling (Pfister, 2015).

Practices and measures to cope with NH-related features and processes

This includes defining zones of high risk, specific nature-based or artificial interventions, approaches to environmental management, and codes for behaviours and actions during NH-related disasters. Historical toponyms are known to define risk zones in many cultures. Sousa et al. (2010) listed a variety of local names from Spain associated with hydronyms for wetland features and Sweeney, Jurek, and Bednář (2007) attempted a floodplain reconstruction analysing the occurrence of the term *blato* (mire). Tropeano and Turconi (2004) illustrates the use of the term *rovine* (remains) for the location of two villages buried by debris flows in Northern Italy in the 19th century. Similarly, Cain, Goff, and McFadgen (2019) suggests the village name of *Namu* (translates as 'bad smell') in the Duff Islands (South Pacific) encapsulates cultural memory of tsunamis and a hastily dug mass burial site.

Further examples include marks for recurrent NH affecting community wellbeing. Typical examples are flood marks in Central European river channels (Brázdil, Kundzewicz, and Benito, 2006) or so-called hunger stones that became visible at the bottom of channels during low discharges. Similarly, for tsunami risk, carved stones or trees can denote historical run-up height in Vanuatu (Walshe and Nunn, 2012).

Many historical societies used natural features to adapt to settings where security and food provision were balanced by trade-offs with NH. Medieval Frisians settled in treeless salt marshes with dunes protecting them from storm surges and tides (Meier, 2004). *Manawa* (*Avicennia resinifera* mangroves) have been used by Maori in New Zealand for acquiring food, timber and dyed flax, but also as protection from storm surges and tides (del Moral and Walker, 2007). In high-altitude 'nivographic' societies, settlements were frequently protected from avalanches by stone walls and forests with restricted timber harvesting (Pfister, 2015).

Protective alterations were made to buildings, displaying analogies across cultures. For floods, most adaptations are based on elevated houses (e.g., *Mizuya* houses in Japan; Takeuchi and Shaw in Shaw, Sharma, and Takeuchi,

2009), elevated floors, or by designating safe places within houses (*chakka* shelfs; Dekens in Shaw, Sharma, and Takeuchi, 2009). Complex construction measures exist to mitigate impacts of earthquakes, including timber framed walls (e.g., Cruz et al., 2015), load-bearing trapezoidal-shaped doors and windows (Oliver-Smith, 1999), or pedestal foundations reducing earthquake force (e.g., *sandi* in Indonesia, Pribadi in Shaw et al., 2009). The Polynesia *Fale* design is adapted to a range of environmental risks including cyclones thanks to its open sided construction, deep buried posts and reinforced lashed frame (Campbell, 2009). Further interventions include bamboo constructions to prevent the collapse of dykes during heavy rains in Bangladesh (*Chikon Thok*, Bose et al., 1998) and loose boulders to reduce the cutting effect of streams in Nepal (*Bhakari*, Verma, 1998). In coastal and river inundation areas, mounds and elevated islands were built to avoid floods, such as islands surrounded by *Waju* dykes in Japan (Takeuchi and Shaw in Shaw, Sharma, and Takeuchi, 2009). In steep terrain, terraced fields and dry-stone walls and levees were used worldwide to acquire land and reduce risk of erosion (Inbar and Llerena, 2000).

Alterations were also used to cope with environmental constraints and slow-onset hazards, such as droughts. These vary from wooden troughs and sophisticated channel and dyke systems in mountain environments, to irrigated pond field *taro* systems in Vanuatu (Spriggs, 1989) which reduce surface runoff and gully erosion. Food preservation burial pits have existed in the South Pacific to plan for NH (Campbell, 2006).

Such alterations were often supported with management practices. Vertical transhumance has been identified since ancient times (e.g., Walshe and Argumedo, 2016) and maintained for centuries (Oteros-Rozas et al., 2013). In Medieval England, the risk of droughts was reduced as a side effect of *ridge and furrow* ploughing patterns that enabled control of the moisture levels in the fields (Hoffmann, 2014). Increased occurrence of river ice during the Little Ice Age resulted in the establishment of a practice of *ice breaking* in European towns (de Kraker, 2017).

During the onset of a hazard event, warning signs may prove essential for mitigating the impacts. An example is the orally transmitted word *Smong*, denoting "*the ocean coming onto the land*" on Simeulue island in Indonesia to warn against the 2004 tsunami (McAdoo et al., 2006). Some early warning practices were institutionalized – in the 18th century Upper Engadin in Switzerland guards were responsible for monitoring river conditions and for warning messages (Pfister, 2009).

Along with rationalizations of NH, religious beliefs have also been transformed into practices of defining risk zones and the deployment of symbols perceived to be protective, such as amulets or prayers. The role of such practices cannot be strictly evaluated in a risk mitigation context, but rather exist as a cultural framing of disasters. In an early European Christian example, St. Florian was believed to protect people from floods and Hoffmann (2014: 95) reports a treatise written by Martin of Braga (ca. 520–580 AD), who describes sacrifices to trees, rivers, and springs to "placate the powers that resides within".

During the emergency and recovery phase of a disaster, culturally-based moral obligations may denote demands to secure the sustainability of populations within given environmental conditions (e.g., the *Chanincha* concept in Quechua Peruvian communities, Walshe and Argumedo, 2016). Moral obligations were also used to collect and allocate resources for relief and recovery, for example by voluntary financial collections after flash floods in early 20th-century Central Europe (Raška and Brázdil, 2015).

Finally, learning and remembering may be considered fundamental TEK. Historical periods with a lower-than-normal frequency of extreme events may represent gaps in acquisition of experiential knowledge (Dekens, 2007; Pfister, 2015), giving impetus for cross-generational knowledge transfer. Storytelling is a fundamental medium to communicate histories and cultural information across generations. In more spatially mobile or transient communities, various kinds of *memoria* are used to support cross-generational transitions, such as flood marks, chapels, monuments, folk songs, poems, and relics of past events.

Discussion and conclusions

In this section we use the broad typology and empirical examples presented above to address the three main challenges resulting from heritagization of TEK.

First, some authorized heritage discourses surrounding TEK lead to understandings of past adaptations as being rigidly employed over time and space (e.g., elevated constructions to avoid flooding), which tends to accentuate adaptations that present either physical interventions (e.g., seismic-proof constructions) or codified practices (e.g., using the names *rovine* or *blato* for hazardous environments). To the contrary, we argue that the term "traditional" in TEK should denote (i) any long-term evolved and transformed knowledge without strictly relating its long-term evolution to particular locations, and (ii) knowledge that may be held both in oral and written sources, representing physical interventions as well as cultural practices (such as warning signs – *Smong* in Indonesia, or post-disaster community help). While some level of TEK can be portrayed as inherent to local conditions and societal formations controlling its contents, it is also often a product of long-term adaptation to changing environments or shifting societal needs and expectations.

In this respect, just as "traditional" knowledge does not originate from or apply to single discourses, topics, or silos, neither can it be materialized in a formally bounded DRR adaptive intervention or practice. This also means that relics of landscape features denoting past adaptations cannot be simply restored and replicated with a promise to effectively reduce current risks, because they are currently situated in the realms of a different environment and social practice. Rather, TEK develops as a culturally derived interrelated system of mental models and practical behaviours (Krüger et al., 2015). To better understand

TEK in detail requires a narrowing of explorations to focus on certain paths, but any focus (including on NH) must bear in mind that the related mental models and behaviours would not have been developed without a deep connection to other matters of daily life (Kelman et al., 2016). Consequently, the labelling of certain knowledge as stable and able to be safeguarded, as occurs in heritagization, is somewhat illusionary, given the inherently dynamic and changing nature of knowledge.

Second, it is increasingly appreciated that TEK is as diverse and heterogeneous as communities themselves. Both knowledge and culture regarding NH are constantly evolving and dynamic (Kelman et al., 2012). We argue that a lack of diachronic depth in dealing with TEK as a heritage discourse results in neglected considerations about the long-term positive and negative feedbacks of adaptations and hinders a full understanding of how TEK can or should be utilized in DRR (Degroot et al., 2021). Instead, TEK is often presented as having developed during an unspecified "past" or alternatively the result of a single stressor, event, or period, rather than its long-term development. Using the example of medieval Frisia, it can be shown that adaptations used to protect communities from storm surges and tides in salt marshes finally resulted in vegetation depletion and increased soil erosion.

Finally, we argue that reporting on TEK practices is often disconnected from any preceding catastrophic events. While past communities are perceived by some authors as environmentally responsible, some TEK developed to transform the environment for expanding social and provisional demands in unfavourable environments. Terracing field systems on steep slopes, irrigation, or dyking to cope with water scarcity are just a few examples. TEK may have also evolved to cope with NH amplified by societal actions, such as elevated mounds and constructions in human-altered floodplains. Along with challenges raised by focusing on TEK dynamics and its positive and negative effects, this finally contrasts with the rather optimistic expectation of the transferability of TEK and calls for further research of TEK as reflective knowledge.

In this chapter, we discussed the traditional ecological knowledge developed and used to cope with natural hazards. We emphasized the fallacy of considering TEK as a rigid set of knowledge that can be easily stored and transposed to other regions and periods of time. Instead, we pointed to the reflective nature of TEK, that evolves across the long-term in changing cultural contexts. Accordingly, future research should explore the paths of specific TEK and its feedbacks with environmental conditions and cultural mental models. This can assist in disentangling the contribution of TEK and NH to the evolution of cultural landscapes and the evaluation of relevant management practices aimed to reduce disaster risk.

Acknowledgements

Authors would like to thank G. Adamson for his comments on the early draft of this chapter. R. Walshe received funding from the ERC [grant no. 804162] which supported the development of this chapter.

References

Adámson, G. C. D., Hannaford, M. J., and Rohland, E. J. (2018). Re-thinking the Present: The Role of a Historical Focus in Climate Change Adaptation Research. *Global Environmental Change* 48: 195–205.

Berkes, F. (2018). *Sacred Ecology*. London: Routledge.

Bose, S. K., Ghani, O., Emdad Hossain, A. T. M., Mridha, N. N., and Muhammad, T. (1998). *A Compilation of Indigenous Technology Knowledge for Upland Watershed Management in Bangladesh*. Dhaka: Forest Department, Rome: Food and Agriculture Organization.

Brázdil, R., Kundzewicz, Z. W., and Benito, G. (2006). Historical Hydrology for Studying Flood Risk in Europe. *Hydrological Sciences Journal* 51(5): 739–764.

Briggs, J. (2005). The Use of Indigenous Knowledge in development: Problems and Challenges. *Progress in Development Studies* 5(2): 99–114.

Cain, G., Goff, J., and McFadgen, B. (2019). Prehistoric Coastal Mass Burials: Did Death Come in Waves? *Journal of Archaeological Method and Theory* 26: 714–754.

Campbell, J. (2009). Islandness: Vulnerability and Resilience in Oceania. *The International Journal of Research into Island Cultures* 3(1): 2009–2085.

Campbell, J. R. (2006). *Traditional Disaster Reduction in Pacific Island Communities*. GNS Science Report 2006/038, Lower Hutt.

Cruz, H., Saporiti Machado, J., Campos Costa, A., Xavier Candeias, P., Ruggieri, N., Manuel, and Catarino, J. (eds.) (2015). *Historical Earthquake-resistant Timber Framing in the Mediterranean Area*. Cham: Springer.

Dahl, M-P. J., Mortensen, L. E., Jensen, N. H., Veihe, A., and de Neergaard, M. (2012). Classification of Debris Flow Phenomena in the Faroe Islands. *Geografisk Tidsskrift* 112: 27–39.

de Kraker, A. M. J. (2017). Ice and Water: The Removal of Ice on Waterways in the Low Countries, 1330–1800. *Water History* 9(2): 109–128.

Degroot, D., Anchukaitis, K., Bauch, M.et al. (2021). Towards a Rigorous Understanding of Societal Responses to Climate Change. *Nature* 591: 539–550.

Dekens, J. (2007). *Local Knowledge for Disaster Preparedness: A Literature Review*. Kathmandu: International Commission for Mountain Development (ICIMOD).

del Moral, R. and Walker, L. R. (2007). *Environmental Disasters, Natural Recovery and Human Responses*. Cambridge: Cambridge University Press.

Diamond, J. M. (1987). Archaeology: The Environmentalist Myth. *Nature* 324: 19–20.

Dolejš, M., Nádvorník, J., Raška, P., and Riezner, J. (2018). Frozen Histories or Narratives of Change? Contextualizing Land-use Dynamics for Conservation of Historical Rural Landscapes. *Environmental Management* 63(3): 352–365.

Donovan, K., Suryanto, A., and Utami, P. (2012). Mapping Cultural Vulnerability in Volcanic Regions: The Practical Application of Social Volcanology at Mt Merapi, Indonesia. *Environmental Hazards* 11(4): 303–323.

Fairhead, J. and Leach, M. (1995). False Forest History, Complicit Social Analysis: Rethinking Some West African Environmental Narratives. *World Development* 23(6): 1023–1035.

Folke, C. (2004). Traditional Knowledge in Social-ecological Systems. *Ecology and Society* 9(3): 7.

Freeman, O. E., Duguma, L. A., and Minang, P. A. (2015). Operationalizing the Integrated Landscape Approach in Practice. *Ecology and Society* 20(1): 24.

Hoffmann, R. C. (2014). *An Environmental History of Medieval Europe*. Cambridge: Cambridge University Press.

Inbar, M. and Llerena, C. A. (2000). Erosion Processes in High Mountain Agricultural Terraces in Peru. *Mountain Research and Development* 20(1): 72–79.

Janku, A., Schenk, G. J., and Mauelshagen, F. (2012). *Historical Disasters in Context: Science, Religion, and Politics*. London: Routledge.

Johannes, R. E. (1987). Primitive Myth. *Nature* 325: 478.

Johannes, R. E. (1989, Ed.). *Traditional Ecological Knowledge: A Collection of Essays*. Gland and Cambridge: IUCN.

Kelman, I., Mercer, J., and Gaillard, J. C. (2012). Indigenous Knowledge and Disaster Risk Reduction. *Geography* 97(Part 1): 12–21.

Kelman, I., Gaillard, J. C., Lewis, J., and Mercer, J. (2016). Learning from the History of Disaster Vulnerability and Resilience Research and Practice for Climate Change. *Natural Hazards* 82: S129–S143.

Krüger, F., Bankoff, G., Cannon, T., Orlowski, B., and Schipper, E. L. F. (eds.) (2015). *Cultures and Disasters*. London: Routledge.

McAdoo, B. G., Dengler, L., Prasetya, G., and Titov, V. (2006). Smong: How an Oral History Saved Thousands on Indonesia's Simeulue Island during the December 2004 and March 2005 tsunamis. *Earthquake Spectra* 22(S3): 661–669.

McAnany, P. A. and Yoffee, N. (eds.) (2010). *Questioning Collapse: Human Resilience, Ecological Vulnerability, and the Aftermath of Empire*. Cambridge: Cambridge University.

Meier, D. (2004). Man and Environment in the Marsh Area of Schleswig–Holstein from Roman Until Late Medieval Times. *Quaternary International* 112(1): 55–69.

Nakashima, D., Krupnik, I., and Rubis, J. T. (2018). *Indigenous Knowledge for Climate Change Assessment and Adaptation*. Cambridge: Cambridge University Press.

Neumann, R. P. (2011). Political Ecology III: Theorizing Landscape. *Progress in Human Geography* 35(6): 843–850.

Oliver-Smith, A. (1999). Peru's Five-hundred-year Earthquake: Vulnerability in Historical Context. In A. Oliver-Smith and S. M. Hoffman (eds.), *The Angry Earth: Disaster in Anthropological Perspective*. London: Routledge, pp. 74–88.

Oteros-Rozas, E., Ontillera-Sánchez, R., Sanosa, P., Gómez-Baggethun, E., Reyes-García, V., and González J. A. (2013). Traditional Ecological Knowledge Among Transhumant Pastoralists in Mediterranean Spain. *Ecology and Society* 18(3): 33.

Pfister, C. (2006). Climatic Extremes, Recurrent Crises and Witch Hunts: Strategies of European Societies in Coping with Exogenous Shocks in the Late Sixteenth and Early Seventeenth Centuries. *The Medieval History Journal* 10(1–2):33–73.

Pfister, C. (2009). Learning from Nature-induced Disasters: Theoretical Considerations and Case Studies from Western Europe. In C. Mauch and C. Pfister (eds.), *Natural Disasters, Cultural Responses: Case Studies Toward a Global Environmental History*. Lanham: Rowman and Littlefield, pp. 17–40.

Pfister, C. (2015). "The Monster Swallows You" Disaster Memory and Risk Culture in Western Europe, 1500–2000. In H. Egner, M. Schorch, and M. Voss (eds.) *Learning and Calamities*. London: Routledge, pp. 77–93.

Poliwoda, G. (2007). Learning from Disasters: Saxony Fight the Floods of the River Elbe 1784–1845. *Historical Social Research* 32: 169–199.

Raška, P., Zábranský, V., Dubišar, J., Kadlec, A., Hrbáčová, A., and Strnad, T. (2014). Documentary Proxies and Interdisciplinary Research on Historic Geomorphologic Hazards: A Discussion of the Current State from a Central European Perspective. *Natural Hazards* 70: 705–732.

Raška, P. and Brázdil, R. (2015). Participatory Responses to Historical Flash Floods and Their Relevance for Current Risk Reduction: A View from a Post-communist Country. *Area* 47 (2): 166–178.

Reid, F. (2019). Doing Paleo-social Volcanology: Developing a Framework for Systematically Investigating the Impacts of Past Volcanic Eruptions on Human Societies Using Archaeological Datasets. *Quaternary International* 499: 266–277.

Shaw, R., Sharma, A., and Takeuchi, Y. (eds.) (2009). *Indigenous Knowledge and Disaster Risk Reduction: From Practice to Policy*. New York: Nova Science Publishers.

Sousa, A., García-Murillo, P., Sahin, S., Morales, J., and García-Barrón, L. (2010). Wetland Place Names as Indicators of Manifestations of Recent Climate Change in SW Spain (Doñana Natural Park). *Climatic Change* 100: 525–557.

Spriggs, M. J. T. (1989). *The Past, Present and the Future of Traditional Irrigation in the Pacific: An Example of Traditional Ecological Knowledge*. SPREP Occasional Paper Series, No. 3. Noumea.

Sweeney, S., Jurek, M., and Bednář, M. (2007). Using Place Names to Interpret Former Floodplain Connectivity in the Morava River, Czech Republic. *Landscape Ecology* 2: 1007–1018.

Tropeano, D. and Turconi, L. (2004). Using Historical Documents for Landslide, Debris Flow and Stream Flood Prevention. Applications in Northern Italy. *Natural Hazards* 31: 663–679.

Van Aalst, M. K., Cannon, T., and Burton, I. (2008). Community Level Adaptation to Climate Change: The Potential Role of Participatory Community Risk Assessment. *Global Environmental Change* 18(1): 165–179.

Verma, L. R. (1998). *A Glimpse of Indigenous Technology Knowledge for Watershed Management in Upper North-West Himalayas of India*. PWMTA Field document no. 15, Kathmandu.

Viollet, P-L. (2007). *Water Engineering in Ancient Civilizations 5,000 Years of History*. London: CRC Press.

Walshe, R. and Nunn, P. (2012). Integration of Indigenous Knowledge and Disaster Risk Reduction: A Case Study from Baie Martelli, Pentecost Island, Vanuatu. *International Journal of Disaster Risk Science* 3(4): 185–194.

Walshe, R. and Argumedo, A. (2016). Ayni, Ayllu, Yanantin and Chanincha: The Cultural Values Enabling Adaptation to Climate Change in Communities of the Potato Park, in the Peruvian Andes. *GAIA* 25(3): 166–173.

Williams, N. M. and Baines, G. (eds.) (1993). *Traditional Ecological Knowledge: Wisdom for Sustainable Development*. Canberra: Australian National University, pp. 126–143.

Wu, J. (2010). Landscape of Culture and Culture of Landscape: Does Landscape Ecology Need Culture? *Landscape Ecology* 25, 1147–1150. doi:10.1007/s10980-010-9524-8.

Wylie, J. (2006). *Landscape*. Abingdon: Routledge.

9 Establishing nationhood through heritage landscapes

Bear biopolitics in the Catalan Pyrenees

Guillem Rubio-Ramon and Karen Lykke Syse

Introduction

In the summer of 2018, there were a series of bear attacks on livestock animals in the small mountainous region in Catalonia called Pallars Sobirà (Spain) (Figure 9.1). The culprit was a brown bear (*Ursus arctos*) that had recently been reintroduced to the Pyrenees. The attacks were widely covered by both local and national media, and unveiled a multi-layered conflict which culminated with the unusual death of two bears in the mountain range during the spring of 2020 (Willsher 2020; France 24 2020). The controversy transcended the mere presence of the bear in the Pyrenees, because local and national identity politics also played essential roles. A bear soon became a symbol of resistance in a landscape in which livestock farmers and crofters had their livelihood. The bear was the manifestation of the unwanted, reintroduced wild animals in the Catalan Pyrenees, and symbolized a general feeling of discontent with a far-off public administration. The Catalan case we shall explore in this chapter does not stand alone – parallel cases of conflict and contestation can be found in other parts of the world in which rural development involves tensions between focussing on biodiversity and intrinsic landscape values or agriculture (Syse 2010). In this chapter, we analyse an environmental conflict in Catalonia while also examining the intersections between nature politics and national identity in the heritage landscape of Pallars Sobirà. This region has struggled to maintain a steady human population in recent decades. We ask whether the opposition to the reintroduced bear is simply a case of environmental Nimbyism,[1] or if there is more at stake.

The entanglement of ideas of nature, development, and nationhood have been thoroughly studied by geographers and scholars from related disciplines. This work covers topics such as the social and cultural construction of more-than-human nature (Zimmer 1998; Smith 2011), the intersections between nationalist and environmentalist political agendas and discourse (Dawson 1996; Fowler and Jones 2005; Hamilton 2002), and the state (and counter-state) discourses of ownership, control, and identity of natural resources (Arbatli 2018; Childs 2016; Wilson 2015; Todd 2018). Syse (2009, 2013) has studied issues of Scottish nationalism within Scottish National Heritage's landscape management strategy,

DOI: 10.4324/9781003195238-9

Figure 9.1. Pallars Sobirà (grey) in Catalonia
Source: Servitje, CC BY-SA 4.0, https://creativecommons.org/licenses/by-sa/4.0/deed.en

and in the following, we would like to pay further attention to how stateless nations have used biophysical landscapes and nonhuman nature to naturalize and reinforce their discourses on nationhood. Catalonia is a case overlooked in scholarly research in which regional nationalism shapes practice and policy relating to the management of nonhuman nature (for exceptions see: Darier and Tàbara 2006; Marshall 1996; Nogué and Vicente 2004; Roma i Casanovas 2004). Therefore, the overarching objective of this chapter is twofold: first, to explore the intersections between rural development, nature politics, heritage landscapes, and broader ideas on Catalan national identity in Pallars Sobirà. Next, to identify the ways in which selected ideas of nationhood and agendas implement or contradict contemporary nature and animal protection discourses in the Catalan Pyrenees. By doing this, we also aim to understand the recent historical development of these intersections.

Methodology

This project's methodology is inspired by recent work in the field of animal geographies (Buller 2015; Gibbs 2019; Seymour and Wolch 2010) and cemented in a constructivist approach to grounded theory (Charmaz 2006, 2012). We have analysed reports from the government, NGOs, stakeholders, media articles, and environmental education material. However this chapter's main empirical sources are 22 qualitative interviews conducted during fieldwork in Pallars Sobirà between July and September 2018 – a "muddy boots" approach to research (Syse 2001, 2009). Most of the interviews started with a short informal conversation followed by a recorded interview (Charmaz 2006; Glaser and Strauss 2017). A further inspiration for this methodology is the work of the anthropologist Tim Ingold (1993). He uses the term "temporality" to define landscape, emphasising the ongoing processes herein (Ingold 1993: 153). Such a processual methodology has allowed us to study the past "as well as the emerging present ... engag[ing] critically with the future" (Harvey 2015: 920).

The big, bad bear

The brown bear was brought back from the brink of extinction in the Pyrenees by the French authorities in 1996 (Palazón 1996: 143). In 1993 the French and Spanish governments signed an agreement to reinforce the populations of the brown bear, the wild goat, and the bearded vulture in the Pyrenees under the umbrella of an EU LIFE wildlife conservation project (Muntané i Puig 2017: 9). After that, three Slovenian bears were introduced in 1996 and 1997 to boost genetic diversity. All of these translocations were conducted in an increasingly tense environment (Palazón 1996: 146) and were met with protests from some farmers who saw their livelihoods potentially affected and with no voice in the decision-making process. Further reintroductions from the same Slovenian population were conducted during the early 2000s and the 2010s, making up today's thriving population of more than 50 individuals (Generalitat de Catalunya 2020). However, the conflict which started more than 25 years ago still persists. In 2016 the Catalan Government instigated a new translocation to add more genetic material to the Pyrenean population. This was the first addition of a brown bear to the Pyrenees fully coordinated by the Catalan regional administration. A dominant male, Goiat, was introduced to Pallars Sobirà. Goiat's presence was almost without conflict until the summer of that year, when he started killing large animals such as horses, abandoning their carcasses uneaten. This gave Goiat a reputation for being a "sadistic" animal and reinforced the idea that brown bears were deceitful and evil (Casanova 1997). Goiat's actions, thus, reignited a latent conflict in the Catalan Pyrenees not only concerning the brown bear but also the role of institutions and their political ideologies and epistemologies. For some livestock farmers, the Pyrenees mountain range had exceeded its wildlife "carrying capacity" and this had grown into a chronic "wildlife problem". Moreover, ideas of human and nonhuman belonging, and the development of top-down models applied to these mountainous zones, also played an essential role (Vaccaro and Beltran 2007).

Scholars like Vaccaro and Beltran (2009: 501) affirm that the application of conservation policies in the Catalan Pyrenees has become an alibi to many public institutions, who have regulated and managed rural landscapes for "white and green" tourism (i.e. skiing and ecotourism). This contrasts with a model based on a combination of subsistence agriculture and an extractivist industry that dominated the region for most of the 20th century. This ranges from several hydropower stations to iron mining and industrial logging to satisfy urban demands (Vaccaro and Beltran 2007: 147). Considering these priority changes in rural development, wildlife management becomes a multidimensional issue that privileges the idea of a certain kind of nature. Such a nature offers an apparent win-win solution to both local economic development and the green legitimacy gained by applying certain measures. This has led scholars to describe Pallars Sobirà as an authentic ecological engineering "larger-than-life laboratory in which public agency reworks the whole concept of biodiversity" (Vaccaro and Beltran 2009: 503).

Reworking of the concept of biodiversity in this manner can be understood both culturally and politically: the morphological characteristics we value in landscapes and nonhuman natures are always embedded in history and culture (Deary and Warren 2017; Cronon 1996). Landscape values are never neutral, and they usually contain certain power mechanisms hidden under the appearance of scientific objectivity. According to Olwig (1984, 2003) ecological restoration can be extremely political, and can both shape and be shaped by certain socioeconomic worldviews. Such an approach can even be problematic, particularly when authenticity requires humans to be absent (Cronon 1996: 14) or if certain peoples and their historic role are not taken into consideration (Shelton 2004: 7).

The "wildlife problem" in the Pyrenees can also be understood from a perspective in which both biodiversity and conservation policies are viewed as culture-laden endeavours. In this sense, the Foucauldian concept of biopower, defined as the power "to foster life or disallow it to the point of death" (cit. in Rabinow 1984: 261) provides a productive theoretical lens to understand the place of nonhuman nature within broader human socioeconomic systems ranging from the individual scale to populations (Srinivasan 2017a; Asdal, Druglitro, and Hinchliffe 2016). Accordingly, Biermann and Mansfield (2014: 262) characterize conservation biology as a biopolitical and "crisis-oriented discipline" with the objective "to foster and protect the diversity of nonhuman life, taking as their object not individuals … but populations, communities, and species".

Because most of the pressures relating to the brown bear population stem from social unrest towards its reintroduction, the EU LIFE conservation project allows substantial funding to enable the co-existence of this predator with other land uses such as extensive livestock farming. From a biopolitical perspective, today's efforts to foster bears' lives cut across human and nonhuman divides: current measures are less focused on the brown bears' ecological or biological aspects, and more on applying specific social and cultural policies to mitigate a social tension which could burst into these plantigrades being poached by the local population. Few species are as well protected as the bear, and the re-emergence of the figure of the shepherd today goes hand-in-hand with the reintroduction of the brown bear. Although the bear and the shepherd are historically linked, their relationship has been altered, as we will explain below.

Shepherds of wildlife

Shepherding is a traditional occupation in Catalonia with a strong symbolic meaning, both religiously and socially. Along with the shepherd's obvious Christian symbolism, shepherds represented hard work and modesty and, for centuries, their role had been to protect the flock from predators during the grazing season. As a result of the disappearance of the bear in the Pyrenees, and in addition to other socioeconomic factors, the need for shepherds gradually disappeared. However, this changed in 1996 with the reintroduction of the brown bear. In 2007, the Catalan Government decided to initiate a programme to provide livestock farmers with a shepherd and a herding dog that looked after their animals over the summer season. In this particular case, the role of the government ceased to be a central, negative power, which could take or give life at the individual level; instead, it transformed into one that, "exerts a positive influence of life, that endeavours to administrate, optimise and multiply it, subjecting it to precise controls and comprehensive regulations" (Foucault, 1998: 137). The function of shepherding was radically subverted: its primary function was not to protect sheep or goats from bears anymore but to protect bears from certain humans' harmful actions. Shepherds working for the natural park quickly became wildlife shepherds, with similar objectives to park rangers: keepers of a recreational landscape containing the iconic bear. These wildlife shepherds – although similar in their roles from yesteryear – reinforce a radically different hierarchy of life in which the farmed animals they are looking after have less political value than the wild animals that they are protecting them from. The idea of hierarchy is not new neither to cultural historians, with Thomas' (1991) approach on "privileged species", nor animal geographers, with Lorimer's (2016) work on nonhuman charisma and Hovorka's (2019) critical analysis of human-made hierarchical models of animals. Within the animal hierarchy examined here, the bear is an *endangered species* with high political value while the sheep and goats are lively commodities (Collard and Dempsey 2013) sold for their meat. The shepherd thus preserves both the economic and instrumental value of farmed animals while the bear's political value remains intact. These co-existence strategies remind us how projects determined to preserve biodiversity can also be led by values other than conservation itself, such as fostering economic development (Srinivasan 2017b: 23) or creating new leisure and tourism areas (Vaccaro and Beltran 2009: 505). While environmental protection might be considered its main driver, the chosen approach to preserve the brown bear attempts to foster synergies between conservation, livestock farming, and a tourist economy to achieve a win-win solution that both protects wildlife, preserves tradition, and promotes local economic growth. In a similar vein, Srinivasan (2017b), when analysing the multiple discourses on the conservation of Olive Ridley turtles in Odisha (India), characterized a win-win approach much like this, as a part of a *sustainability episteme*. In her article, Srinivasan (2017b: 1472) argues that win-win approaches are essential traits of this sustainability episteme: a set of organizing principles that are presented as addressing opposed normative objectives regarding socioeconomic development and more-than-human wellbeing to satisfy the needs of both people and the environment. Nevertheless, the win-win outcomes of this approach are superficial, since when closely analysed, they fail to address the radical tensions it declared to overcome.

For your own good: green permissible harm

Even when the hegemonic political discourse in the current debate remains conservation-oriented and targeting a pro-wildlife audience, during the peak of the social conflict that coincided with our study, the Catalan Government affirmed in multiple occasions that they were willing to remove Goiat from the Pyrenees. This removal, of course, would have only raised new ethical questions to the government's approach considering that the 2018 bear intervention protocol described this removal as either elimination, captivity, or replacement (Grupo de trabajo del oso pardo en Pirineos 2018). In case one or multiple bears had been removed to a sanctuary, they might have suffered from the stress-related health-impacts resulting from the relocation (Teixeira et al. 2007). Furthermore, Goiat's questionable classification as an intrinsically flawed and problematic animal for his disruption of human economic interests would create a dangerous precedent for other conservation programmes. In Biermann and Mansfield terms (2014: 263), a version of biopower would then be applied to preserve certain non-conflictive visions of nature while allowing abnormal individuals such as Goiat to die off. Ultimately, the willingness from the government to remove Goiat reminds us how bears do not have a political life as individuals but only as genes at worst or as part of a population at best.

In line with Srinivasan's (2014: 511) analysis on Olive Ridley turtle conservation, because the win–win outcomes of the bear's presence did not appear, the bear lost its individual value and was regarded as a homogeneous collective. The government operated under a "sacrificial logic of population" involving biopolitical calculations concerning "how individuals can be best deployed, intervened upon, or sacrificed so as to ensure the flourishing of the population" (Srinivasan 2014: 507). It was considered beneficial for the bear population as a whole that the conflictive bear was either disciplined through deterrent measures or removed from the population. In this sense, it was the level of political tension and the constitutive tensions of win–win approaches that moduled the acceptability of harm inflicted to individual bears. The government's discourse, therefore, depicted the brown bear as an interchangeable part of a collective which could be harmed in exchange for local political and social stability when the win–win social contract was at risk. It is the moral and ontological consideration of the bear as a collective rather than as an individual which mitigates the conflict between opposing livestock farmers and the reintroduction programme. The bear population's existence in the Pyrenees can only be ensured by inflicting harm to some of its individuals.

Getting back to the nation's nature

The government's discourse employs a set of ideological resources, such as a focus on the local level, and a defence of Catalonia's "right to implement its own territorial model" (Nogué 1991: 69). The figure of the wildlife shepherd is used to avoid a social conflict and as a symbol that cements the win–win duality in their own politics of nature. The shepherd makes compatible a deemed-as-outsider conservationist agenda with a ruralist discourse praising the value of living off the land, agropastoral traditions, and the right to farm. This ruralist discourse claims to be autochthonous – rooted in the rural areas and communities – in contrast to a mainstream green discourse from beyond the cultural boundaries of the region.

In 1975, Tom Nairn (1975) characterised nationalism as "the modern Janus", the Roman god of change and time, known for having to see its future, precisely, by looking into its past (Jonathan 2006: 118). Similarly, today, the wildlife shepherd acts as a rediscovered symbol sustaining a social order based on the win-win triad of conservation, tourism, and livestock farming, while producing the image of a bucolic rurality. This view is materialized as a pre-industrial pastoral landscape, where both tourism, livestock farming, and bears can spatially coexist. In contrast with other contexts, where a pristine and untouched image is fostered in natural parks (Cronon 1996), this landscape corresponds to one of the most celebrated ideas of nature in Catalonia, often situating the Pyrenees as the cradle of the Catalan nation (Nogué 1993: 197, 2016: 30–31; Sala 2017). This pre-industrial landscape is associated to small-town goodness, idealised ruralism and agrarianism (Marshall 1996: 545) and coupled with the admiration for green mountainous areas fostered by romantic and cultural revivalist nationalist movements (Nogué and Vicente 2004: 122). The government, therefore, is not only choosing a conservation approach that revitalizes a cultural tradition but also promoting a vision of heritage landscapes and nature shaped by predominant Catalan national imaginaries. In this sense, a particular notion of heritage is used in order to legitimate a "national consciousness" or a communal memory akin to a nearly "nation state" (D. C. Harvey 2001: 328). Nature and cultural restoration – both "heritigised" (Vaccaro and Beltran 2009) – are, therefore, co-constitutive of one another and developed through a prism privileging a specific version of the nature of the nation. This is done partly by reworking political participation and land ownership as stewardship and by transforming the work of farmers into cultural heritage, considering them "gardeners" of an esteemed national landscape (Estrada, Nadal, and Iglesias 2007; Olwig 1997, 24). The outcomes of this stretch beyond the local population ultimately aiming to "generate a sense of national attachment by having visitors identify with particular natural landscapes as stand-ins for the country and its territory" (Stinson and Lunstrum, 2021: 12)

In Pallars Sobirà, the wildlife shepherd can be identified as a figure which not only preserves an agropastoral past but also becomes a key element in the production of a pre-industrial national heritage landscape fit to these ruralist ideals. At the same time, the figure of the wildlife shepherd makes these ruralist ideals compatible with the public administration implementation of an agenda in Pallars Sobirà based on green and white tourism and mainstream conservation, with the brown bear being its iconic component. Both these discourses are influenced by concepts of what a national nature ought to be. It allows bears to be protected as a population but, at the same time, the removal of those "problematic" individuals that do not share the desired non-conflictive characteristics needed in a harmonic landscape where opposed interests are obliged to coexist.

This idyllic landscape used as a reference state or restoration baseline (Marris, 2011), as we have seen, is inspired by ideas of what a Catalan nature is thought to be. The cultural revitalisation of the shepherd – synchronous with the reintroduction of the bear – becomes a crucial process in a landscape which, in Zimmer's terms, is "put at use in such a way as to reflect alleged national characteristics … and an image of national authenticity" (1998: 644).

Concluding thoughts

By focussing on the reintroduction of the brown bear in the Catalan Pyrenees, we have examined how past and present ideas of Catalan identity and belonging still play an important role in conditioning nature conservation and rural development policymaking in Pallars Sobirà. We consider the reintroduction of the brown bear a paradigmatic case of these cultural, social, and ecological entanglements. As we have described, whilst reintroducing the brown bear, the Catalan Government also revitalized the historical figure of the shepherd metamorphosed into a wildlife shepherd. In this case, nature restoration cannot be understood without a parallel process of cultural heritage revitalisation. Simultaneously, the wildlife shepherd becomes a central figure in the reconfiguration of the Pyrenees as a harmonious landscape taking the shape of "the physical dimension of the national past" (Zimmer 1998: 644). In that sense, our study contributes to previous work studying nonhuman animals as an active sociocultural and geographical force shaping both more-than-human landscapes and imagined communities (see Syse 2014; Franklin 2006; H. Lorimer 2006; Smith 2011).

Moreover, we have reviewed the reintroduction programme as a biopolitical endeavour in line with similar work bringing Foucault's conception of biopower to the study of human-nonhuman relations. We have analysed how the cultural revitalisation of shepherding reinforces existing hierarchies of nonhuman life: by protecting the economic value of local farmed animals, the bear's political value is protected. Yet these hierarchies of life are far from independent of context: while the bear is usually protected at an individual level, this radically changed during the peak of the conflict in 2018. In this year, the collective animal (bears as a population) was privileged over the individual: a win–win solution on the surface solely adopted to appease an infuriated public opinion and local economic interests. We have further argued the problems of this approach, considering how a compliant vision of nonhuman life was promoted while a noncompliant one was disciplined or disallowed almost to the point of death.

In sum, most human stakeholders in the region involved in the conflict appear to neglect the ethical stance and consequences for animals themselves of the aforementioned development and conservation strategies. This omission compromises past, present, and future solutions as ethically devoid at worst and incomplete at best. To bridge the gaps between different concerned constituencies in the Pyrenees and around the world such as wildlife activists, farmers and protected areas' administrators, the perspectives of both humans with legitimate needs and the individuality of nonhuman animals must be recognised. Re-imagining landscapes in which the rightful presence of nonhuman animals of all species – including those whose interests' conflict directly with our own – is acknowledged, would be a first step towards truly inclusive conservation.

Note

1 NIMBY is the acronym for "Not-In-My-Backyard", "an attitude adopted by individuals resisting the sitting of a source of perceived negative externalities ... close to their homes, and campaigning for it to be located elsewhere" (Gregory 2009: 501).

References

Arbatli, E. (2018). Resource Nationalism Revisited: A New Conceptualization in Light of Changing Actors and Strategies in the Oil Industry. *Energy Research and Social Science* 40: 101–108.

Asdal, K., Tone, D., and Hinchliffe, S. (2016). Introduction: The "More-than-human" Condition: Sentient Creatures and Versions of Biopolitics. In K. Asdal, D. Tone, and S. Hinchliffe (eds.), *Humans, Animals and Biopolitics: The More-than-human Condition*, Abingdon: Routledge, pp. 1–29.

Biermann, C. and Mansfield, B. (2014). Biodiversity, Purity, and Death: Conservation Biology as Biopolitics. *Environment and Planning D: Society and Space* 32(2): 257–273.

Buller, H. (2015). Animal Geographies II: Methods. *Progress in Human Geography* 39(3): 374–384.

Casanova, E. (1997). *L'ós Del Pirineu, Crònica d'un Extermini*. Lleida: Pagès Editors.

Charmaz, K. (2006). *Constructing Grounded Theory: A Practical Guide through Qualitative Analysis*. London: SAGE.

Charmaz, K. (2012). The Power and Potential of Grounded Theory. *Medical Sociology Online* 6(3): 2–15.

Childs, J. (2016). Geography and Resource Nationalism: A Critical Review and Reframing. *Extractive Industries and Society* 3(2): 539–546.

Collard, R. and Dempsey, J. (2013). Life for Sale? The Politics of Lively Commodities. *Environment and Planning A* 45(11): 2682–2699.

Cronon, W. (1996). The Trouble with Wilderness. *Environmental History* 1(1): 7–28.

Darier, E. and Tàbara J.D. (2006). Els Objectes Naturals i La Identitat Nacional. Les Muntanyes a Catalunya i al Quebec. *Papers* 82: 37–55.

Dawson, J. (1996). *Eco-Nationalism: Anti-Nuclear Activism and National Identity in Russia, Lithuania, and Ukraine*. Durham: Duke University Press.

Deary, H., and Warren C. R. (2017). Divergent Visions of Wildness and Naturalness in a Storied Landscape: Practices and Discourses of Rewilding in Scotland's Wild Places. *Journal of Rural Studies* 54: 211–222.

Estrada, F., Nadal E., and Iglesias J. R. (2007). Transhumantes Del Siglo XXI. La Transhumancia En El Contexto de Las Transformaciones Socioeconómicas de La Alta Ribagorça. In I. Vaccaro and O. Beltran (eds.), *Ecología Política de Los Pirineos*. Tremp: Garsineu Edicions, pp. 117–138.

Foucault, M. (1998). *The Will to Knowledge: The History of Sexuality*. London. Penguin.

Fowler, C. and Jones, R. (2005). Environmentalism and Nationalism in the UK. *Environmental Politics* 14(4): 541–545.

France 24. (2020). 'Third Bear Killed in Pyrenees This Year', 30 November 2020. Retrieved: www.france24.com/en/live-news/20201130-third-bear-killed-in-pyre nees-this-year.

Franklin, A. (2006). *Animal Nation: The True Story of Animals and Australia.* Sydney: University of New South Wales Press.

Generalitat de Catalunya. (2020). La Població d'ossos Als Pirineus Arriba Als 52 Exemplars. Barcelona: Oficina de Comunicació i Premsa. Departament de Territori i Sostenibilitat de la Generalitat de Catalunya. Retrieved: https://depana.org/wp-content/uploads/2020/11/ 20200421-La-poblaci%C3%B3-ursina-del-Pirineu-arrriba-a-52-exemplars-al-2019.pdf.

Gibbs, L. (2019). Animal Geographies I: Hearing the Cry and Extending Beyond. *Progress in Human Geography* 44(4): 769–777.

Glaser, B. G. and Strauss A. L. (2017). *The Discovery of Grounded Theory: Strategies for Qualitative Research.* New York: Routledge.

Gregory, D., Johnston R., Pratt, G., Watts, M. J., and Whatmore, S. (2009). *The Dictionary of Human Geography.* 5th edition. Chichester: Wiley-Blackwell.

Grupo de trabajo del oso pardo en Pirineos. (2018). *Protocolo de Intervención En Osos En Los Pirineos'.* Comisión Estatal para el Patrimonio Natural y la Biodiversidad. Retrieved from: http://mediambient.gencat.cat/web/.content/home/ambits_dactua cio/patrimoni_natural/fauna_salvatge_autoctona/gestio-especies/mamifers/ursus_a rctos_os_bru/protocolo_intervencion_osos.pdf.

Hamilton, P. (2002). The Greening of Nationalism. *Environmental Politics* 11(2): 27–48.

Harvey, D. (2015). Landscape and Heritage: Trajectories and Consequences. *Landscape Research* 40(8): 911–924.

Harvey, D. C. (2001). Heritage Pasts and Heritage Presents: Temporality, Meaning and the Scope of Heritage Studies. *International Journal of Heritage Studies* 7(4): 319–338.

Jonathan, H. (2006). *Rethinking Nationalism: A Critical Introduction.* New York: Palgrave Macmillan.

Lorimer, H. (2006). Herding Memories of Humans and Animals. *Environment and Planning D: Society and Space* 24(4): 497–518.

Lorimer, J. (2016). Nonhuman Charisma. *Environment and Planning D: Society and Space* 25(5): 911–932.

Marris, E. (2011). *Rambunctious Garden: Saving Nature in a Post-Wild World.* London: Bloomsbury.

Marshall, T. (1996). Catalan Nationalism, the Catalan Government and the Environment. *Environmental Politics* 5(3): 542–550.

Muntané i Puig, J. (2017). *Rere El Conflicte Amb l'ós Bru. Percepció Social de La Convivència Amb Ursus Arctos al Pirineu Català.* Master Thesis, Environmental Science, Universitat Autònoma de Barcelona.

Nairn, T. (1975). The Modern Janus. *New Left Review* 94: 3–29.

Nogué, J. (1991). *Els Nacionalismes i El Territori.* Barcelona: El Llamp.

Nogué, J. (1993). La Dimensió Territorial Del Nacionalisme. *Treballs de La Societat Catalana de Geografía* 8(35): 193–201.

Nogué, J. (2016). La Génesis y La Evolución de La Valoración Moderna Del Paisaje En Cataluña. *Cuadernos Geográficos* 55(2): 28–45.

Nogué, J. and Vicente, J. (2004). Landscape and National Identity in Catalonia. *Political Geography* 23(2): 113–132.

Olwig, K. (1984). *Nature's Ideological Landscape.* Boston: George Allen and Unwin.

Olwig, K. (1997). The "Natural" Landscape and Agricultural Values. In J. Brendalsmo, M. Jones, K. Olwig, and M. Widgren (eds.), *NIKU Temahefte 4, Landskapet Som Historie*. Oslo: Norsk institutt for kulturminneforskning, pp. 24–31.

Olwig, K. (2003). Natives and Aliens in the National Landscape. *Landscape Research* 28 (1): 61–74.

Palazón, S. (1996). Situació Actual de l'ós Bru Als Pirineus Centrals. *Ripacurtia* 4: 141–149.

Rabinow, P. (ed.) (1984) *The Foucault Reader*. New York: Pantheon Books.

Roma i Casanovas, F. (2004). *Del Paradís a La Nació. La Muntanya a Catalunya. Segles XV–XX*. Barcelona: Cossetània Edicions.

Sala, T. M. (2017). *Visions Dels Pirineus. Entre La Renaixeça i El Modernisme*. Barcelona: Edicions de la Universitat de Barcelona.

Seymour, M. and Wolch , J. (2010). "A Little Bird Told Me …": Approaching Animals Through Qualitative Methods. In D. De Lyser, S. Herbert, S. Aitken, M. Crang, and L. McDowell (eds.), *The SAGE Handbook of Qualitative Geography*. London: SAGE, pp. 305–320.

Shelton, J. A. (2004). Killing Animals That Don't Fit In: Moral Dimensions of Habitat Restoration. *Between the Species* 4: 1–16.

Smith, N. (2011). Blood and Soil: Nature, Native and Nation in the Australian Imaginary. *Journal of Australian Studies* 35(1): 1–18.

Srinivasan, K. (2014). Caring for the Collective: Biopower and Agential Subjectification in Wildlife Conservation. *Environment and Planning D: Society and Space* 32(3): 501–517.

Srinivasan, K. (2017a). Biopower. InD. Richardson, N. Castree, M. Goodchild, A. Kobayashi, W. Liu, and R. Marston (eds.), *International Encyclopedia of Geography: People, the Earth, Environment and Technology*. Hoboken: Wiley.

Srinivasan, K. (2017b). Conservation Biopolitics and the Sustainability Episteme. *Environment and Planning A* 49(7): 1458–1476.

Syse, K. L. (2001). Ethics in the Woods. *Ethics, Place and Environment* 4(3): 226–234.

Syse, K. L. (2009). *From Land Use to Landscape. A Cultural History of Conflict and Consensus in Argyll 1945–2005*. PhD Thesis, University of Oslo.

Syse, K. L. (2010). Expert Systems, Local Knowledge and Power in Argyll, Scotland. *Landscape Research* 35(4): 469–484.

Syse, K. L. (2013). The Ebb and Flow of Trees and Farmland: Symbols of Nationhood in Scotland and Norway. *Journal of the North Atlantic* 4: 219–228.

Syse, K. L. (2014). Stumbling Over Animals in the Landscape: Methodological Accidents and Anecdotes. *Nordic Journal of Science and Technology Studies* 2(2): 20–26.

Teixeira, C. P., Schetini de Azevedo, C., Mendl, M., Cipreste, C., and Young, R. (2007). Revisiting Translocation and Reintroduction Programmes: The Importance of Considering Stress. *Animal Behaviour* 73(1): 1–13.

Thomas, K. (1991). *Man and the Natural World: Changing Attitudes in England 1500–1800*. Harmondsworth: Penguin Books.

Todd, Z. (2018). Refracting the State Through Human-Fish Relations. *Decolonization: Indigeneity, Education and Society* 7(1): 60–75.

Vaccaro, I. and Beltran O. (2007). El Paisaje Del Pallars Sobirà: Pastores, Centrales Hidroeléctricas y Estaciones de Esquí. In I. Vaccaro and O. Beltran (eds.), *Ecología Política de Los Pirineos*. Tremp: Garsineu Edicions, pp. 139–156.

Vaccaro, I. and Beltran O. (2009). Livestock versus "Wild Beasts": Contradictions in the Natural Patrimonialization of the Pyrenees. *Geographical Review* 99(4): 499–516.

Willsher, K. (2020). French Government to Launch Legal Action against Bear Killers. *The Guardian*, 10 June 2020, sec. World news. Retrieved from: www.theguardian.com/world/2020/jun/10/french-government-to-launch-legal-action-against-bear-killers.

Wilson, J. D. (2015). Understanding Resource Nationalism: Economic Dynamics and Political Institutions. *Contemporary Politics* 21(4): 399–416.

Zimmer, O. (1998). In Search of Natural Identity: Alpine Landscape and the Reconstruction of the Swiss Nation. *Comparative Studies in Society and History* 40(4): 637–665.

10 The Intimate Place

Towards a Decolonising Approach to Protect and Maintain the Territory and Cultural Heritage of the Kamëntšá People

Marcelo Marques Miranda, Jully Acuña Suárez, Silvia Jamioy Juajibioy and Milena Aguillón Chindoy

Introduction

Suppose the reader has ever heard of the Kamëntšá people, it was probably because of their famous traditional medicine, the research and photographs of Richard Evan Schultes or, perhaps, their numerous *mingas* against extractive industries and neocolonial projects. The Kamëntšá people are native to the region nowadays known as Sibundoy Valley, Putumayo, Colombia. The Kamëntšá language, which has no connection with any other, attests to the development of this culture over millennia in a region identified as *Uaman Tabanok*.

When the Capuchins of Catalonia arrived in the Putumayo region and established a prefecture in the late 19th century, *Uaman Tabanok*, at the intersection of the Andean highlands and the Amazon rainforest, was a very isolated area. Their mission was to evangelise the Kamëntšá and Inga peoples – who also inhabit this region since the 15th century – by transforming and destroying their cultures to impose a new lifestyle and economic system based on agriculture, livestock, and land tenure. This objective was achieved in part by resorting to extreme and constant physical and psychological violence and resulted in the appropriation of territories and the repression and exploitation of Indigenous Peoples.

Although the colonisation of *Uaman Tabanok* and the Kamëntšá people began in 1535 with the arrival of the first Spanish invaders, it was only in the 20th century when a more effective step was taken with the work of the Capuchin missionaries, who imposed the most effective and violent acts that definitively stripped the Kamëntšá people of their territorial and human rights. As the Kamëntšá philosopher Juan Alejandro Chindoy states (2020: 16), the 20th century "marked the most critical form of colonisation under which my ancestors lived."

This chapter addresses the process and impacts of colonialism on the Kamëntšá people and on *Uaman Tabanok*. On the other hand, we address how coloniality persists to this day and leads to injustices, human suffering, and the

DOI: 10.4324/9781003195238-10

destruction of the environment. Furthermore, we also emphasise the importance of understanding cultural continuity and the interrelationships between heritage and territory to protect and maintain Kamëntšá culture.

This contribution is the result of five years of collaborative work between researchers from Leiden University (Jully and Marcelo) and members of the Kamëntšá people, more closely with *Colectivo Ayentš* (of which Silvia and Milena are representatives). This work with and for the Kamëntšá people is based on creating conditions in which people can have a decisive voice in all matters that concern them. This approach implies an informed, empowered, and active participation of the Kamëntšá people throughout the entire research process.

The Territory as an Intimate Place

What do we mean by *Uaman Tabanok*? As Willian Mavisoy (2018: 241), a Kamëntšá anthropologist, explains, the term "territory" can be problematic because it is related to the State and official history and, moreover, it weakens the possibility of a close connection with the environment. Likewise, only recently Anglophone geographers have started to approach the concept of territory beyond a Eurocentric perspective (Halvorsen, 2019; Dang, 2021). Therefore, Mavisoy developed an understanding of *Uaman Tabanok* as an "intimate place" based on the Kamëntšá knowledge and worldview, in which there is a reciprocal relationship between people and nature. For the Kamëntšá people, the territory is understood as "parent". This is evidenced by the term *tsabatsana mamá*, generally translated as "Mother Earth". Such an understanding implies that human beings depend on the environment to live and a sense of belonging, responsibility, and care for it. Therefore, the Kamëntšá people see the maintenance and protection of the environment as an obligation, rooted in sustainability, collectivity, and relationality principles (Mavisoy, 2008: 225–226). Hence our use of the term *Uaman Tabanok*, which is widely applied by the community.

Uaman Tabanok then refers to the place of origin and harmonious coexistence of the Kamëntšá people since time immemorial. In general, the term is used today by the Kamëntšá people to refer to their ancestral lands, which includes what is known as Sibundoy Valley and the surrounding regions that cross other Colombian departments. *Uaman Tabanok* is a place where human beings, nature, time, and space make up a single body in which all the elements are in constant dialogue (Mavisoy, 2018). This intimate connection with, or feeling of personal belonging to place is also evidenced in the Kamëntšá surnames, which all have the locative suffix *oy* (Chindoy, 2020: XVI). The way in which the Kamëntšá identify themselves as *kamuentsa kabëng kamëntšá biya*, that is, "people from here [*Uaman Tabanok*] with their own worldview and language" (Jamioy, 2010: 23), is demonstrative of a feeling of belonging to place.

This understanding contrasts with the predominant and imposing Western worldview that focuses on the exploitation of natural elements and in which the environment is seen as something external to human beings (Ingold, 2002: 63).

Figure 10.1. "Bengbe Fshantš". Part of an artistic intervention and performance on a touristic sign in the main square of Sibundoy. Artists' statement: "In memory of our sacred place of origin and the spirits of our ancestors. With the advent of colonisation, it became a 'public square' but, for our people, a place of torture and suffering. Recently, it has undergone structural changes and was renamed as 'Park of Interculturality', a place where all sorts of events and shows are held, which profoundly disrespect the memory of the Kamëntšá people."

Source: © Colectivo Ayentš, July 2021

As described ahead, *Uaman Tabanok*'s colonial conceptualisation was based on the idea that "not only was America's nature envisaged as a discrete set of resources to be possessed, categorised and exploited; the New World as such was imagined and objectified as nature" (Coletta and Raftopoulos, 2016: 1–2). Therefore, at present, there is a coexistence between a dominant Western idea of territory, which can be easily seen on maps, place names and national history, and *Uaman Tabanok*, a "hidden" territory but very much alive in the spirituality, language, art, resilience, and daily life of the Kamëntšá people. Hence, in this chapter, we do not speak of landscape or territory in an aesthetic sense or as a backdrop, but rather as a place of sociopolitical crossroads. Our intention is not to replace the colonial notion with the Kamëntšá one, but to examine the coexistence of ideas and practices structured by violent colonial power relations that create hierarchies of knowing and being (Halvorsen, 2019).

The Territory as Wilderness

The history of the colonisation of *Uaman Tabanok* could be divided into two general aspects: 1) the transformation of the landscape aimed at the exploitation of natural resources for a capitalist market-based economic system and the consequent depredation of the environment; and 2) the evangelisation of the

Kamëntšá people and their insertion into the aforementioned economic system through the elimination or transformation of their worldview, language, traditions, history, and knowledge, which have been reshaping the landscape for millennia and are deeply associated with the care for the environment.

The colonial process was centred on the idea that Europeans were genetically, culturally, and technologically superior (Blaut, 1993). As we will see, these practices were developed and imposed in *Uaman Tabanok* by missionaries, mainly since the beginning of the 20th century, something already well researched (see, for example, Bonilla, 2006), but this type of discourse was also shared and applied by academics and scientists. For instance, Triana, a Colombian engineer and archaeologist, portrayed the Valley and the Kamëntšá people with these words:

> Looking at the beautiful valley, in which the sibundoyes [Kamëntšás] are an insurmountable obstacle to civilisation and cultivation, and in consideration of these terrifying energies of the barbarians, one is to ask to what extent the testament of Don Carlos Tamabioy can be valid, given the interests of public utility.
>
> (1907: 322 [translated by the authors])

Likewise, Hardenburg, an engineer who arrived in the Putumayo region from the USA, on his way to participate in extractivist projects in Brazil, referred to the region as:

> A part of the Valley is low and swampy, but the rest is good, rich soil, quite suitable for agricultural purposes, and covered with a thick, short grass. Although all the encircling mountains are clad with forests, the Valley is, at present, cleared and ready for cultivation.
>
> (1912: 55)

These writings demonstrate an idea of nature related to domination and extraction, and that land and its control are the most essential aspects of colonialism (Dang, 2021). They are also evidence of the use of concepts of nature, race, and culture to establish power relations and legitimise European colonisation. As Demos points out (2016: 14), these ideas emerged from the Enlightenment principles of Cartesian dualism between human and nonhuman worlds, which situated the nonhuman world as objectified, passive, and separate. This understanding allowed the development and rationalisation of an extractive, destructive and dissociative perspective of the environment. In this sense, nature was to be colonised both in concept and in practice.

Within this understanding, Indigenous Peoples who did not exploit their lands, not at least in a Western understanding, were "below all social levels" (Triana, 1907: 231). Besides, this idea of nature was directly associated with economic wealth, which would lead people to be civilised, cultured, and patriotic (Triana, 1907: 224). This discourse, based on the "natural order" and the "will of God", served to legitimise power and justify the colonisation, destruction and appropriation of Indigenous People's lands and cultures (Jansen and Pérez Jiménez, 2017: 28).

Since the beginning of the 20th century, the environmental destruction of *Uaman Tabanok* was facilitated by the Colombian State's concessions to the Capuchin missionaries (Marques and Acuña, in press) The result was the appropriation of territories because these were considered "wilderness" and the repression and exploitation of Indigenous Peoples to integrate them into "civilisation". Some of these measures included the construction of roads that used not only slave labour but also disturbed ecosystems and, consequently, opened the way for the (illegal) exploitation of minerals, particularly gold, and deforestation in the region. One of the most shocking measures that the missionaries took was the drainage of the Sibundoy lake and wetlands to extend the agricultural frontier. This work ignored both the economic and cultural connection that the Kamëntšá people had with the lake and wetlands to impose a new meaning on the landscape and transform the local economic system by intensifying livestock and single-crop farming. Later, in

Figure 10.2. Page of a 2nd-grade reading and teaching book used in Colombian schools (Charry, 1948). It represents a notion of national territory related to extractivism, agriculture, and livestock, which Indigenous Peoples should accommodate to in order to become citizens of the nation

1962, the drainage works would be continued by a State institution, the Colombian Agrarian Reform Institute, which also modified the course of the Putumayo River. These works led to greater and irreparable social, economic and environmental damage, such as the disappearance of autochthonous fauna (Mavisoy, 2008: 224).

Uaman Tabanok in the 21st Century

Nowadays colonialism is perpetuated in different ways, including corporate colonialism and its acts of accumulation by dispossession (Demos, 2016: 16–17), which result in illegal mining and logging, oil exploitation, single-crop farming, and GMOs, but also in drug trafficking, narcopolitics, and the endless Colombian armed conflict. Connected to these are other projects with profound impacts on the environment, such as the construction of a new road from the Sibundoy Valley to the city of Mocoa to facilitate the exploitation and transportation of natural resources (Lizcano, 2020). The growing militarisation, disguised as protection for the community and a solution to climate change instead, appears to be related to recent extractivist and neocolonial projects associated with the so-called "green capitalism" or "ecofascism" (Betencourt, 2021), such as the plans for the construction of a hydroelectric dam (Calle, 2019) and a REDD+ project that since 2019 some attempt to forcefully advance in *Uaman Tabanok* under suspicious principles of free, prior, and informed consent, and for the supposed benefit of local communities. However, other experiences in this area have shown problematic outcomes (Kill, 2015). This summarises, as Dang states (2021: 1006–1007), that the colonial enterprise is focused on the conversion of endogenous ecosystems for single-crop agriculture, on the development of infrastructure, and on a capitalist market in which the political and economic powers are concentrated in the cities, and the exploitation of resources is done on the peripheries of the country. The relationship between territory and colonialism, with the multiple forms of violence and inequality that it generates, together with the cultural, economic, political, and environmental problems that are transversal to it, make up what Betencourt calls "territorial coloniality" (2021) and contribute to the progressive extinction of Indigenous Peoples of Colombia and a territorial disorder of life.

Thus, the sustainable livelihoods of the Kamëntšá people are affected by the direct threat to the environment. These impacts are both environmental and sociocultural since the lack of access to land and the destruction of the environment endanger food sovereignty, self-determination, and the culture and spirituality of the Kamëntšá people. Therefore, we cannot approach the conservation of cultural heritage from a Western perspective, which treats the natural and the cultural as ontologically distinct categories (Marques, 2019a). The right of Indigenous Peoples to land, the use of natural resources and the conservation of their cultures requires the understanding that there are deep spiritual roots with their territories, that these have a communal character and are related to environmental conservation (see Jansen and Raffa, 2015; May Castillo and Strecker, 2017).

Heritage and Colonisation

In the beginning of the 20th century the Kamëntšá people were settled in the mountains of *Uaman Tabanok*, while their most sacred place was in the centre of what is now the town of Sibundoy. The historical records of missionaries and travelers also refer that the majority of around 1500 Kamëntšás lived in the mountains, and only a few families lived in the "rectilinear" town of Sibundoy (Triana, 1907: 327; Hardenburg, 1912: 61). Consequently, one of the missionaries' first steps to colonise and evangelise the Kamëntšá people was to gather the population in a village and displace them from their traditional lifestyle in the mountains. According to the Capuchin missionaries, the Kamëntšá people needed to live in connection and closely with the settlers to learn the "civilised manners" and lose their "disgusting customs". The missionaries understood that a more efficient colonisation could be achieved by transforming the Kamëntšá culture from its roots. This work intensified with the arrival of Marcelino de Castellví and the creation of the Centre for Linguistic and Ethnographic Research of the Colombian Amazon (CILEAC, in Spanish) in 1933. This Centre was described by its founder as a place, with its library and museum, to educate religiously, physically and intellectually the "indigenous races" through modern and scientific methods that would facilitate their colonisation and integration into Western culture (Castellví, 1938). Linguistic studies served, for example, to replace Kamëntšá narratives with European myths and tales, which led to the loss of relationality, knowledge about fauna and flora and traditional environmental conservation practices, since these are deeply interconnected (Hart, 2010: 3). Another step was the resignification of the concepts of sacredness and spirituality that began with constructing a church, today a landmark of the Valley, precisely on top of the most sacred place of the Kamëntšá people. This process also attests to the symbolic power of monuments and that Western concepts of cultural heritage are intrinsically connected with the maintenance of colonial perceptions of territory and nationalist and elitist conceptions of culture (Smith, 2006). For example, Castellví (1938: 1) associated the Renaissance architecture of the CILEAC with its evangelising and civilising mission. Coloniality is thus expressed not only through the representation of the land, but can also be inscribed on the land itself. Architecture, urbanism, and memorials have the power to embed colonial metanarratives in the landscape (Dang, 2021). The monuments in Sibundoy's central plaza, for instance, not only commemorate troubled histories of land-grabbing, but the very ground on which they sit reflects a topography of violent colonial dispossession.

The Capuchin missionaries researched extensivelly and developed strategies to transform the Kamëntšá culture from within (Serra de Manresa, 2011), which allowed them to replace Indigenous knowledge, practices and livelihoods with Christian notions of evil and salvation, of a "single truth", to impose Western culture and to open the doors of *Uaman Tabanok* to extractivism. With these transformations, the missionaries were able to resignify the "sacred", turning different Indigenous cultural elements into "evil things" or "superstitions", as was done in general, for example, with pre-Catholic tombs and ritual objects (Gnecco and Hernandez, 2010). This process was fundamental to exercise dominance and control of the population and because aversion to life in the "wilderness" is a paradigm of the Western worldview (Ingold, 2002: 63).For instance, narratives that are an obvious imposition of the Catholic faith, such as "The Lord of Sibundoy" (Friede, 1945), were introduced to naturalise the slave labour performed by the Kamëntšás to build the roads to nearby cities and to justify the construction of a church over the pre-colonial Kamëntšá burials due to the "divine will" and not as a violent imposition. This completely contradicts the stories of the Kamëntšá elders who went through the scourge and violence perpetrated by the missionaries in those works. Despite all this, the Kamëntšá people have the central area of Sibundoy as a sacred place, as an essential part of *Uaman Tabanok*.

Archaeology also worked from its beginnings side-by-side with the State and the Church in the colonisation of Indigenous Peoples and their territories through the denial of coevalness (Jansen and Pérez Jiménez, 2017: 34), that is, in creating a discontinuity between "pre-Colombian" cultures and contemporary Indigenous Peoples. This is evident in the research by Herrera (2020: 115), who refers to the Incas as the "civilised pre-Christian people of the high Andes" but their descendants, the Inga people of Sibundoy Valley, as mere quechua speakers (2020: 120). Archaeology then acts in the landscape by extracting Indigenous Peoples' objects, disrupting sacred sites, and by resignifying these as "national heritage", now exhibited in museums or part of national parks, for the supposed common good of all humanity – but far from or barring access to the communities to whom they really matter. This process has colonial origins because the subsistence of Indigenous Peoples' religious practices was a potential focus of resistance against cultural domination (Gnecco and Hernandez, 2010: 109). In practice, this implies imposing Western systems of property and custody, as well as Western notions of time and space (Jansen and Pérez Jiménez, 2017).

Heritagisation processes maintain and perpetuate coloniality because archaeologists, anthropologists and others who work to advance the interests of the State and multinational companies, now under multicultural ideas and false inclusion (see Gnecco, 2016), carry out their tasks without free, prior and informed consent, and violate the rights of Indigenous Peoples established in the *Declaration on the Rights of Indigenous Peoples* (UN, 2007). All these processes demonstrate the complicity of academics and museums with colonialist and racist discourses and attitudes and a total lack of humanity and disconnection of their work with the reality and struggles of Indigenous Peoples. Recently, external agents and newcomers to *Uaman Tabanok* are using problematic claims by archaeologists about the alleged "foreign origins" of the Kamëntšá people to claim and access lands and property in the region in order to exploit its natural resources, thus exacerbating a wave of multiple sociopolitical and territorial problems. The main issue we address here is that these claims, based on academic knowledge and a supposed national heritage, not only ignore Kamëntšá history, but were initially used to legitimise the appropriation of *Uaman Tabanok* by the missionaries and, today, legitimise its appropriation by the Colombian State and others.

. Many researchers have shown the impact that the Western idea of heritage conservation has on Indigenous Peoples and their direct relationship with their ancestral territories (see, for instance, Marques, 2019b and Apaydin, 2020, Part III). Consequently, we can no longer ignore that colonialism in its different forms – including heritage conservation – is directly related to the destruction of the environment and climate change (Betencourt, 2021; Ferdinand, 2022)

Decolonising Heritage and Territory

Decolonisation implies undoing and deconstructing coloniality, that is, the colonial matrix of power, being and knowledge that became a central dimension of the hegemonic and civilising project of the West. Decolonisation refers to the restoration of humanity in all orders of existence, social relationships, symbols and thoughts. Likewise, this process implies action on the part of the colonised (Maldonado-Torres, 2018). Decolonisation then requires conducting research in such a way that the worldviews of those who have suffered a long history of oppression and marginalisation have space to communicate from their frames of reference. This includes a critical analysis of mainstream academic practice to expose the problematic influence of the West (Chilisa, 2019: 11–12). The main political agenda of decolonisation is both the return of colonised lands to Indigenous sovereignty and a radically transformed appreciation of non-colonial ways of relating to the land. In the context of landscape studies, decolonisation requires a long process of dismantling the colonial structures on which the vast majority of contemporary and historical landscapes are based (Dang, 2021: 1011–1012).

In this sense, the idea of cultural heritage should not be confused with the Western conception, which is connected to monuments, objects or landscapes of aesthetic and historic significance that, in turn, are related to nationalist, colonialist and elitist ideas of culture (Smith, 2006). This conception also emphasises nature/culture and tangible/intangible divides that are foreign to the Kamëntšá worldview (Marques, 2019a). Consequently, cultural heritage cannot be understood in such categorisations. As we have seen, the Kamëntšá notions of territory and heritage, as is the case with Indigenous Peoples in general, are deeply interrelated (Jansen and Raffa, 2015; May Castillo and Strecker, 2017). We can thus define the cultural heritage of the Kamëntšá people as the knowledge, memory, spirituality, language, and environment (in the sense of *Uaman Tabanok*), which has been developed, created, maintained, and transmitted from generation to generation since time immemorial, and which is reflected and materialised in different artistic and narrative forms. In this process, the Kamëntšá ancestors, who are "protagonists of ethically important narratives that are played out in religiously charged and ritual landscapes (memory sites)" (Jansen and Pérez Jiménez, 2017: 36), play a fundamental role.

Consequently, the conservation of this cultural heritage cannot be done by creating lists and safeguarding plans, nor by commodifying and hierarchising knowledge by disconnecting communities from their places, objects and rituals through the bureaucratic systems of the State, its experts, and their nationalist and universalist principles. Rather, it is essential to maintain an integrated understanding of cultural heritage as reflected in the Kamëntšá concept of *jua-beman*, that is, the action of cultivating and maintaining knowledge and the teachings of *tsabatsana mamá* in order to endure as a people (Mavisoy, 2008: 228). This spiritual relationship with the land is directly related to a sense of responsibility in which the rituals, ceremonies, and ordinary activities that are carried out are mainly based on respect for the environment, biodiversity, and society, all condensed in the notion of *Uaman Tabanok* as an intimate place.

As Mavisoy refers (2018: 245), faced with the nightmare of extractivism, it is urgent to apply a decolonial pedagogy that restores and revitalises the human-culture-nature balance as a single integral being. The decolonisation of the territory requires exposing colonial hierarchies and also valuing the "local" as a powerful scale of thought and practice (Halvorsen, 2019: 802) In addition, decolonising implies a radical reorientation of academic practices, including who and what we quote, from whom we learn, from where we theorise and with whom, how we work with colleagues from the Global South, develop long-term commitments with these colleagues, and how we respond to colonial hierarchies within our institutions (Halvorsen, 2019: 804).

This is a process that, in recent years, we have advanced in a collaborative manner on different fronts with the Kamëntšá people. Particularly, our process addresses various but interconnected areas such as the recovery and documentation of Kamëntšá knowledge and language and its insertion in spaces such as the museum (Marques, Acuña, and Ayentš, 2022), the digital world or the traditional Kamëntšá vegetable garden, in order to deconstruct colonial imaginaries about the Kamëntšá people and seeking to undo the social injustices that are a consequence of colonialism (see https://en.ayents.com/). In this process, we establish reciprocal relationships with the environment, strengthen community bonds, and reinforce cultural continuity. As academics, artists, and activists, we also develop this process by decolonising young people's mindsets using Indigenous Methodologies (Chilisa, 2019). A fundamental part of our process is to legitimate Kamëntšá knowledge, history and territory, as Indigenous Peoples cannot continue to be used as mere objects of scientific curiosity or seen as primitive beings that impede neocolonial extractivism.

Conclusion

We contend that the colonisation of *Uaman Tabanok* generated a catastrophic environmental impact and aimed at transforming the culture and worldview of the Kamëntšá people to impose a new meaning on the landscape and transform the local economic system. This proves that colonialism is directly linked with environmental destruction and climate change. In this process, academics and heritage-related institutions have also played their role in protecting the colonisers' interests and maintaining the status quo.

Although the State and missionaries partially failed their goals, the consequences of colonialism are enduring and have paved the way for the contemporary environmental and cultural depredation of *Uaman Tabanok*. As Chindoy puts it (2020: 16), "with the arrival of the Spaniards, the once sacred place of origin, the home of the Kamëntšás, gradually became a place of struggle for land property, human dignity, and cultural survival".

Despite this, the Kamëntšá people have maintained a perception of the environment and ancestral territory as an intimate place. However, the colonial mindset has partially disintegrated cultural continuity, and contemporary issues are increasing the disconnection between younger generations of Kamëntšás and their native language, history and worldview. Based on this, we are putting forward new rights-based and decolonising strategies to recover, protect and maintain the cultural heritage of the Kamëntšá people.

Acknowledgements

We would like to all thank those who have participated in some way in this research process, especially Kamëntšá elders. Some of them have already left us, but part of their knowledge will continue to be passed on to new generations.

Jully and Marcelo appreciate the support of their supervisors Maarten Jansen and Aurora Pérez Jiménez, and colleagues Fernanda Kaingáng, Rocio Vera Flores, and Osíris González Romero in the writing of this article.

This research process has been possible thanks to two PhD grants (Jully: AZ 25/BE/19; Marcelo: AZ 12/BE/21) of the Patrimonies funding initiative of the Gerda Henkel Foundation, and the support of the Santo Domingo Centre of Excellence for Latin American Research, British Museum.

Marcelo also acknowledges the support of the German Academic Exchange Service (DAAD) for a short-term research grant (57507441) for a stay at the Rachel Carson Center for Environment and Society, LMU, during which this chapter was initially developed as an article.

References

Apaydin, V. (2020). *Critical Perspectives on Cultural Memory and Heritage. Construction, Transformation and Destruction.* London: UCL Press.

Blaut, J. M. (1993). *The Coloniser's Model of the World: Geographical Diffusionism and Eurocentric History.* New York: The Guilford Press.

Betencourt Santiago, M. (2021). Colonialidad territorial, relaciones sociedades-naturaleza y violencias a escala global-local: desafíos para la paz territorial en Colombia (y el mundo). In P. López and M. Betencourt Santiago (eds.), *Conflictos territoriales y territorialidades en disputa: Re-existencias y horizontes societales frente al capital en América Latina.* Buenos Aires: CLACSO, pp. 145–173.

Bonilla, V. D. (2006). *Siervos de Dios y Amos de Indios. El Estado y la misión capuchina en el Putumayo.* Popayan: Universidad de Cauca.

Calle, H. (2019). La 'pequeña' hidroeléctrica que alerta a indígenas de Putumayo. *El Espectador.* Retrieved from: www.elespectador.com/noticias/medio-ambiente/la-pequena-hidroelectrica-que-alerta-a-indigenas-de-putumayo/.

Castellví, M. (1938). Centro de Investigaciones Lingüisticas y Etnográficas de la Amazonia Colombiana. *Boletín de la Sociedad Geográfica de Colombia,* 2 (V).

Charry, J. V. (1948). *Cartilla Charry Enseñanza Simultánea de Lectura y Escritura.* Bogotá: Talleres Editoriales de Librería Voluntad.

Chilisa, B. (2019). *Indigenous Research Methodologies.* London: SAGE.

Chindoy Chindoy, J. A. (2020). *A Decolonial Philosophy of Indigenous Colombia. Time, Beauty, and Spirit in Kamëntšá Culture.* Lanham: Rowman and Littlefield.

Coletta, M. and Raftopoulos, M. (2016). Whose Natures? Whose Knowledges? An Introduction to Epistemic Politics and Eco-ontologies in Latin America. In M. Coletta and M. Raftopoulos (eds.), *Provincialising Nature: Multidisciplinary Approaches to the Politics of the Environment in Latin America.* London: Institute of Latin American Studies, School of Advanced Study, University of London, pp. 1–18.

Dang, T. K. (2021). Decolonizing Landscape. *Landscape Research,* 46(7): 1004–1016.

Demos, T. J. (2016). *Decolonizing Nature: Contemporary Art and the Politics of Ecology.* London: Sternberg Press.

Ferdinand, M. (2022). *A Decolonial Ecology: Thinking from the Caribbean World.* Cambridge: Polity Press.

Friede, J. (1945). Leyendas de Nuestro Señor de Sibundoy y El Santo Carlos Tamabioy. *Boletin de Arqueologia,* 1(4): 315–318.

General Assembly of the United Nations (2007). *Declaration on the Rights of Indigenous Peoples.* UN.

Gnecco, C. and Hernandez, C. (2010). La historia y sus descontentos: estatuas de piedra, historias nativas y arqueólogos. In C. Gnecco and P. Ayala Rocabado (eds.), *Pueblos Indígenas Y Arqueología En América Latina.* Bogotá: Fundación de Investigaciones Arqueológicas Nacionales, pp. 85–136.

Gnecco, C. (2016). Dos Epocas de la Arqueología. In J. Tocancipá-Falla (ed.), *Antropologías en Colombia: Tendencias y Debates.* Popayán: Universidad del Cauca, pp. 85–98.

Halvorsen, S. (2019). Decolonising Territory: Dialogues with Latin American Knowledges and Grassroots Strategies. *Progress in Human Geography,* 43(5): 790–814.

Hardenburg, W. E. (1912). *The Putumayo: The Devil's Paradise* London: T. Fisher Unwin.

Hart, M. A. (2010). Indigenous Worldviews, Knowledge, and Research: The Development of an Indigenous Research Paradigm. *Journal of Indigenous Voices in Social Work* 1(1): 1–16.

Herrera Wassilowsky, A. (2020). Changing Andes–Amazonia Dynamics: El Chuncho Meets El Inca at the End of the Marañón Corridor. In A. J. Pearce, D. G. Beresford-Jones, and P. Heggarty (eds.), *Rethinking the Andes–Amazonia Divide. A Cross-disciplinary Exploration.* London: UCL Press, pp. 115–126.

Ingold, T. (2002). *The Perception of the Environment. Essays on Livelihood, Dwelling and Skill.* Abingdon: Routledge.

Jamioy Juagibioy, H (2010). *Danzantes del viento: Bínÿbe Oboyejuayëng.* Bogotá: Ministerio de Cultura.

Jansen, M. E. R. G. N. and Pérez Jiménez, G. A. (2017). *Time and the Ancestors: Aztec and Mixtec Ritual Art.* Leiden: Brill.

Jansen, M. E. R. G. N. and Raffa, V. (2015). *Tiempo y Comunidad. Herencias e Interacciones Socioculturales en Mesoamérica y Occidente.* Leiden: Leiden University Press.

Kill, J. (2015). *REDD: una colección de conflictos, contradicciones y mentiras.* Montevideo: World Rainforest Movement.

Lizcano, M. F. (2020). Un elefante blanco oculto en la selva de Putumayo. *Mongabay Series: ESPECIAL.* Retrieved from: https://es.mongabay.com/series/especial-un-elefante-blanco-oculto-en-la-selva-de-putumayo/.

Maldonado-Torres, N. (2018). The Decolonial Turn. In J. Poblete (ed.), *New Approaches to Latin American Studies. Culture and Power.* Abingdon: Routledge, pp. 111–127.

Marques Miranda, M. (2019a). Gestão do patrimônio e povos indígenas: a necessidade de uma abordagem inclusiva e intercultural. *Espaço Ameríndio* 13(1): 9–38.

Marques Miranda, M. (2019b). The Resurgence of the Heritage of Indigenous Peoples of Thailand in the Aftermath of Development. *Journal of Heritage Management* 4(1): 73–84.

Marques Miranda, M. and Acuña Suárez, J. (*in press*). Putting Indigenous Heritage on the Map. A Counter-mapping Experience with the Camëntsá People. *Proceedings of the 6th International Conference on Heritage Conservation and Site Management.* Cottbus and Berlin, Germany. Retrieved from: www.researchgate.net/publication/338390551_Putting_indigenous_heritage_on_the_map_A_counter-mapping_experience_with_the_Camentsa_people.

Marques Miranda, M., Acuña Suárez, J., and Colectivo, A. (2022). Decolonising the Representation of the Camëntsá People at the Museum. Developments in the Bëngbe Benacheng project. In J. Cooper and L. Osorio Sunnucks (eds.), *Mapping a New Museum. Politics and Practice of Latin American Research with the British Museum.* Abingdon: Routledge, pp. 271–280.

Mavisoy Muchavisoy, W. J. (2008). Kabëngbe Lware "Nuestro Territorio". El Reflejo del Cambio Espacial en la Tradición Oral Kamentsa del Valle de Sibundoy, Putumayo. In C. E.López and G. A.Ospina (eds.), *Ecología Histórica. Interacciones Sociedad- Ambiente a Distintas Escalas Socio-Temporales.* Pereira: Tecnológica de Pereira, pp. 219–228.

Mavisoy Muchavisoy, W. J. (2018). El conocimiento indígena para descolonizar el territorio. La experiencia Kamëntsá (Colombia). *NÓMADAS* 48: 240–248.

May Castillo, M. and Strecker, A. (2017). *Heritage and Rights of Indigenous Peoples. Patrimonio y Derechos de los Pueblos Indígenas.* Leiden: Leiden University Press.

Serra de Manresa, V. (2011). El Repte D'Inculturar la Fe en les Missions Ad Gentes dels Caputxins Catalans. *Revista Catalana de Teología* 36(2): 535–573.

Smith, L. (2006). *Uses of Heritage.* Abingdon: Routledge.

Triana, M. (1907). *Por el sur de Colombia. Excursion Pintoresca y Científica al Putumayo.* Paris: Garnier Hermanos.

11 Remains of privileged spaces

Moral landscapes in Delfland, the Netherlands

Maurits W. Ertsen

Introduction

Water may be the most popular natural resource for scholars studying human societies, wellbeing and suffering. Water is closely associated with emerging civilizations in Mesopotamia, the Nile, ancient India, China, Mexico, and Peru (see Mithen, 2012, for a very good overview). This close relation between water and the societal elites actually controlling it has stimulated several powerful, yet problematic ideas on water and power. One of the more famous contributions is Wittfogel's idea of hydraulic civilizations (Wittfogel, 1957). According to Wittfogel, water could be mobilized by a central state through labour control in the construction of large irrigation systems that produced the food surpluses that fed the non-peasant population. His claims have been heavily criticized for being too simple, too political, or simply wrong (see Harrower, 2009 for a useful discussion). Nevertheless, even when Wittfogel did not provide a convincing analysis, water and power are closely linked. As I showed in my own work on irrigation in Gezira (20th-century colonial Sudan), water-related power relations are literally channelled through infrastructures of different kinds (canals, roads, banks, etc.) (Ertsen, 2016a, 2016b). Gezira was shaped by many efforts by many agents, who did not necessarily agree with the outcomes of those same efforts. However, (dis)agreements were not negotiated on a level, open playing field. Many of the properties of the field "within which we may find ourselves, and the advantages or disadvantages they imply, pre-date our arrival" (Cudworth and Hobden, 2013: 440). Buildings, bank accounts, pipe lines, material components, and infrastructure are vital to allow power relations to be sustained over time. Power would have a hard time surviving without any material components (Strum and Latour, 1987; see Latour and Strum, 1986). Power and hierarchies may need continuous re-enactment, but this becomes easier with the material as a supporting agent. Building on the observation that matter and power are closely linked to our past, I will develop the argument that we are confronted with the morality of our ancestors in our built environment. I argue that although we may have the desire to transform our own (built) environment, we are actually constrained in doing so by the same environment that we want to change. Our built heritage

DOI: 10.4324/9781003195238-11

resists our desire for change, or at least engages with and transforms it. This chapter tests the proposition that many of the material remains in the Dutch coastal landscape—canals, sluices, harbours, etc.—represent "morality".

1   When landscapes are created and changed, artefacts and infrastructure co-shape the relationship between humans and their world. In these emerging landscapes, artefacts and infrastructure helped to shape relations between different social groups. Today, we encounter these two landscape elements as material remains of those relations.

2   We can trace through the material remains how groups of stakeholders managed to realize what they considered "right". As such, we encounter the privilege of groups to realize what is morally justified.

3   The material expressions of moral decisions of access and control continue to be present in the landscape and are appreciated today as heritage. This raises the issue of which landscape elements are considered worth preserving and which are not. What is the "right" decision to preserve these landscapes and elements?

Two examples from the Dutch landscape close to the city of my university, Delft, within the management area of Delfland, one of the oldest water managing agencies (water boards) in the Netherlands, allow the discovery of how material remains in that landscape—canals, sluices, embankments, and so on—represent historical ideas of what was seen as valuable at the time—by certain groups or stakeholders. The first one, the Orange Sluice, symbolizes how the practical need for managing water in this part of the Netherlands coincides with issues of power, control, and payment. It also symbolizes how history is built into the water infrastructure and continues to be of relevance for current discussions. My second example is a polder area east of Delft, Polder Berkel. Its history shows how a landscape of peat was transformed into a lake. Later, the lake was drained and turned into a polder. Apart from local drainage issues, the inherited water infrastructure has recently been transformed to fulfil new goals. We encounter new connections between local landscape and the larger Delfland area. The local landscape was mobilized to solve water-related problems elsewhere. Both cases are based on extremely limited source material, which I would think is allowed given the explorative nature of this text on the issue of privileged positions to decide what is right in the past in relation to heritage discussions in the present.[1]

This chapter builds on my work on colonial irrigation in Sudan (Ertsen 2016a, 2016b) and on early irrigation in Mesopotamia (2016c). Without going into as much empirical depth as this work and without suggesting that the Dutch developments I engage with were a continuous violent struggle between stakeholders, I do think that it is important to stress that the water-rich history of the Netherlands and its heritage need to be understood in terms of power relations created by actor-networks of human and non-human agencies. Too often, popular Dutch water history is written as a general story of humans against nature (for two recent examples, see Van der List (2019) and Vink (2019)). Such simplifications are problematic for at least two reasons. First, the categories of "humans" and "nature" suggest too much agreement within those same groups and hide issues of power and interest. Second, the division between the two categories ignores that they continuously co-shape(d) landscapes together, blurring the distinction between the human and the natural.

My two examples show how Dutch water infrastructure shaped social relations—such as who could access certain land or control certain infrastructure—through physical landscapes. We will encounter morality in the making through water infrastructure, suggesting that the preservation of historical elements and landscapes—heritage—is as closely related to issues of power, identity and access as building the original infrastructure used to be. Heritage is inherently moral.

The Orange Sluice

Those that drive along the Maasdijk today may not realize that it was constructed as early in 1238 to protect the area to its north from threats by the river Meuse.[2] The Maasdijk was paid for by Countess Machteld and her son Willem—providing my first example of power and infrastructure being closely related. After her son Willem had become the main family powerhouse, Machteld retreated to her possessions in the protected area of the Maasdijk. In financing the Maasdijk, Machteld paid for her own protection. In return for the safety that was initially paid for by Machteld, those who happened to live in the same area had to provide support as well. Each inhabitant was expected to maintain some 200 meters of the river defence structure. Much later, in 1676, at the order of the Delfland Water Board—established in 1289—the Orange Sluice was constructed.[3] It was paid for by Willem III of Orange—the same Willem that became King of England, Ireland and Scotland in 1689. We see here that another important person is engaging in realizing key infrastructure.

The act of building the sluice is an example that power is not something "out there" on its own, but is realized through the material—as I already mentioned in the Introduction. The sluice included a sluice controller's house, which also served as a guest house for friends of Willem and as a resting place during hunting parties. Originally, the sluice brought water to the gardens of castle Honselaarsdijk (owned by Willem III). Soon, however, the water became too salty for the precious plants of the ruler. When changes were made in the larger Delfland water system, the Orange sluice turned out to be useful to drain part of the Delfland area; instead of bringing water in, the sluice diverted water away. The sluice turned out to be rather small compared to the amount of water to drain. When a pumping station powered by steam was realized elsewhere in the Delfland area in 1865, the drainage situation in the larger Orange area did improve. The sluice continued to be used but was no longer the only means to drain the territory.

Today, when still driving along the Maasdijk, it is difficult to miss a building with an octagonal roof construction. Nowadays, the casual observer's eyes focus automatically on this striking building close to the road and a national monument, but only few realize that what is underneath the building deserves our attention as well. The actual Orange Sluice is a very important water-control device, connecting the Orange drainage area with the Orange Canal that brings water to a main pumping station. In 2006, Delfland proposed to enlarge the drainage capacity of both the sluice and canal. The canal capacity was enlarged earlier than the sluice that had to deliver the water to the canal. Changing the sluices was much more difficult, as two (moral) perspectives were confronted with each other. First, as the sluice is a monument under Dutch law, one is not allowed to change its structure. Second, Delfland does not allow other societal actors to build something in an embankment that has to protect an area from flooding.

In 2006, Delfland—responsible for sufficient drainage and flood protection and as such responsible for building permits concerning embankments—had to follow its own strict rules to obtain permission to reconstruct the Orange sluice. The water board was confronted with a choice between changing an artefact with heritage status or creating a new artefact that would increase safety, but would change the historical embankment. Additional drainage capacity was found by the water board in building a new sluice through the embankment, but Delfland could only start building the new structure next to the existing sluices once long and tedious procedures had been completed. Today, the Maasdijk is no longer a flood protection structure, as recently its status as a secondary flood defence has been removed. With regulations on keeping the Maasdijk intact loosened, municipalities around it immediately saw options for building new residential areas. In addition, discussions on the value of the embankment itself came up. Given the history of the structure, would it be useful and valuable to keep it as intact as possible?

Polder Berkel

Similar discussions on what to keep in the process of creating a new water infrastructure have taken place in my second example within Delfland.[4] Polder Berkel is a drainage area, which used to have its own, separate water board within the larger Delfland institution. The name "Berkel" is encountered for the first time in 1161 in the archives; in 1471 the polder area of that name had been created (De Wilt, 2015). A polder board was responsible for managing its own water affairs within the polder. As soon as the water entered the main Delfland water system, it became Delfland's task. Since medieval times, peat digging in the area provided the cities with fuel, but created artificial lakes. The loss of land caused by peat digging increased the need to protect the remaining land from the water and its waves. We encounter individual decisions that create collective problems, which on their turn do not influence all individuals equally. In the 18th century, many officials, including those responsible for the

Berkel area, agreed that draining the lakes was a suitable answer to the safety issues. Lake Berkel became Polder Berkel (again). Because of this diverse history of peat digging and draining, Polder Berkel includes 12 separate units, each with its own water levels. Rain water that enters and excess groundwater from the polder is stored in the ditches. A set of pumping stations brings this polder water to a set of canals that connect the different polder sub-units. This internal belt canal collects the water from all the smaller units; it is the central plumbing facility. From the internal belt canal, a single larger pumping station pumps the water up to the next level, to the central belt canal system of Delfland.

Through this canal system, which also flows through the city of Delft, water is drained or pumped to the sea. One additional facility could be found in the area: the belt canal storage. This storage would store water in case there was more water entering the internal belt canal than could be pumped out. More importantly, it would store water from the internal polder system in case the central belt canal system of Delfland was full. It is at such moments that the authorities of the polder and Delfland would directly meet. Berkel decided on its own polder, but Delfland decided on the central belt system. One action that Delfland could take was to block polders from draining into the Delfland canals. Each polder would have to find a solution for its excess water. Berkel used the storage area. As soon as the central belt system could receive additional water, the Berkel area would pump its water to the main system. The storage area was dry for most of the year and was used for cattle grazing. Once a year, the grass in the area was harvested for winter fodder.

In the 1970s, daily water management in the polder became Delfland's responsibility. Before that shift (and unrelated to it, as far as I can see), the polder authorities sold the land in the emergency storage area to the farmers in the 1970s. The main reason for the sale was that the storage had not been used after 1945, mainly because of improved pumping facilities. The storage area remained officially operational, but was not used as such, until some extreme events in the early 21st century made Delfland rethink its water infrastructure. In the same project that drafted the changes to the Orange sluice that we just discussed, the Berkel storage area was redesigned. New infrastructure and new arrangements with the farmers were drafted. The Berkel storage area may have been legally designated as an emergency storage area, but the many years of not using it as such had changed the practical meaning of the facility. For farmers, their land did not represent storage options at all. In moral terms, the decision whether using local storage in Berkel to protect the larger Delfland water system from flooding was right had to be negotiated with the farmers. These new arrangements include how farmers will be warned, how damage is dealt with and who is responsible for drowning cows and sheep.

In the entire operation to redesign the meaning and the shape of the historical water storage facility, the position of the storage area within Delfland changed as well. Originally, the Berkel area would store its own water to ensure that the Delfland water system would not be overloaded. The new design changed that: in addition to storing its own water, Berkel is now able to receive water from the central Delfland canal system. The infrastructure is adapted for this: a pipe line with pumps ensures that water can flow both ways. The pipe line can bring water from the Berkel area into the Delfland canal system, which is in line with the original setup of the storage system in the area. However, as water can also be brought into the Berkel area from the canal system, the regional water manager Delfland has the option to store excess water from other regions within Delfland in Berkel. When the canal system is full, but an area that is considered more important than Berkel would still need to be drained, Delfland has the option to create storage capacity in the canal system by flooding the Berkel emergency storage space. As such, through a local adaptation in terms of water flow control—with a pipe and pump that allow two-directional flow—the local area of Berkel is now subject to moral decisions that concern a much larger area.

Revisiting the argument: moral landscapes and heritage

I have argued that engagements between humans and artefacts on the Orange sluice or the Berkel polder are key in understanding how decisions about correct water management (the "morality" of water management) is shaped and transformed in the landscape of Delfland. The water management structures that I mentioned were supposed to facilitate certain distribution of flows—either removing water or bringing water. These distributions were and are not neutral: some agents gain(ed), some agents lose (lost). Some gained access to water, some were flooded. In both cases, "the question [was] how to act, and technologies appear to give material answers to this question" (Verbeek, 2006: 369). In a "progressive construction of reality" (Latour, 1991: 117) of the Orange Sluice and Polder Berkel, morality was produced along the way—in terms of actual values that seemed worthwhile pursuing, in terms of values that could be pursued by some, and in terms of material shapes that allowed values to be realized.

Matter and objects have an active role to play in landscape shaping. Both Orange Sluice and Polder Berkel were continuously reshaped, which changed their relations with other agents in the Delfland landscape. The Maasdijk used to be a major flood defence, but changed into a secondary defence ring and may soon no longer be an official flood protection embankment—not so much because the Maasdijk itself changed, but because flood defences elsewhere have taken over its tasks. One of the consequences is, however, that the Maasdijk may be less interesting to preserve for local municipalities. Polder Berkel was connected to the larger Delfland area for a long time, as the option to hold its water back would potentially save areas and communities elsewhere in Delfland. Now that the Berkel storage area is again capable of storing water from elsewhere, similar solidarity has been created. At the same time, the function of storage may be very similar to what was there before, but its shape and management are quite different.

The Delfland examples show (again) that entities like a "state" or "water board" need material engagements to exist (Schouten, 2013). Expanding infrastructure enables some to organize other agents across larger temporal and spatial scales. Canals, sluices, and embankments stabilize relations between agents (Strum and Latour, 1987; see Ertsen, 2016a, 2016c). My argument is not necessarily that judgements of "good" and "bad" were incorporated intentionally. Many discussions on water infrastructure would have shown arguments based on "functions" or "economics". However, as the success with which agents build new networks "determines the success of their designs" (Van de Poel and Verbeek, 2006: 228), those functional or economic solutions that managed to remain became "good" solutions. In the process of becoming "good", it was matter that helped shape morality, as matter provided temporal and spatial links between human agents. Matter allowed those same agents to pursue certain political, economic, or cultural agendas. In the process of becoming "good", matter showed persistency—in infrastructure, in institutions, and in policies.

In order to become persistent or allow relations between agents to become stable, arrangements within landscapes of power needed to be confirmed continuously. Without such confirmation—through maintenance, mobilizing labour and other resources—the "material underpinnings of rule" (Schouten, 2013: 21) could not continue to be successful. Building infrastructure and landscapes is a process within which (historical and modern) actors are continuously (re)shaping relevant networks. These networks confirm and change the relations between themselves and other (non-human and human) agents. Infrastructure is the "materialization of ongoing communication, in which there are often conflicts among different constituents to achieve consensus" (Smith, 2016: 164). Precisely, therefore, it is impossible for power relations to simply "be stored in a bank" (Latour, 1991: 118; see also Hodder, 2012, 2014). Power relations are produced in a process "of 'thinging' entities together" with only a promise of "the possibility of holding society together as a durable whole" (Latour, 2007: 140). Relations need continuous confirmation, reconstruction, and adaptation; maintaining stability is hard work for all human agents, precisely because other human agents and their non-human colleagues strike back.

Water heritage

An important—although not exclusive—focus of the heritage field is preserving buildings and landscapes. After what I tried to argue above, we may need to reconsider what these "material manifestations" stand for. They are not neutral travelers from the past, nor are they exclusively material remains. As I suggested, Dutch water heritage is a narrative of power—and therefore of winners and others—and shifts in power over time. What we encounter today as (potential) water-related heritage is the result of a certain persistency—a continuous confirmation of and change in power relations. Heritage discussions confront us with the continuous presence of former human and non-human others, as much as our successors will encounter us and our choices in the future—assuming there is a future. In society, artefacts helped and help "to shape what counts as 'real'" and as such "the moral decisions human beings make" (Verbeek, 2006: 366). Artefacts are crucial to articulate, create, and maintain power.

Studying morality in action through actor-networks consisting of humans and infrastructure also allows reflection on one's own perceptions of what is "correct" or "wrong"—or "fair" or "unfair" for that matter. The meaning of Dutch water heritage is as much a moral issue as the production of that heritage would have been. In order to understand our own heritage dilemma's and appreciate the many issues that our predecessors dealt with, it is key to understand heritage as negotiations between (humans and non-human) agents that shape morality through historical practices. We should realize that our appreciation of water heritage engages with both its material shapes and its moral implications. To repeat myself, heritage is inherently moral.

Notes

1 For a very instructive general introduction to Dutch water history, see Van de Ven (2004).
2 https://nl.wikipedia.org/wiki/Oranjesluis, visited on May 25, 2017; see also De Wilt (2015).
3 https://nl.wikipedia.org/wiki/Oranjesluis, visited on May 25, 2017.
4 This section is based on Van Leeuwen-Canneman and Vrolijk (1996) and https://nl.wikipedia.org/wiki/Polder_Berkel.

References

Cudworth, E. and Hobden, S. (2013). Of Parts and Wholes: International Relations Beyond the Human. *Millennium: Journal of International Studies* 41(3): 430–450.
De Wilt, C. (2015). *Landlieden en Hoogheemraden*. Hilversum: Uitgeverij Verloren.
Ertsen, M.W. (2016a). A Matter of Relationships: Actor-Networks of Colonial Rule in the Gezira Irrigation System, Sudan. *Water Alternatives* 9(2): 203–221.
Ertsen, M.W. (2016b). *Improvising Planned Development on the Gezira Plain, Sudan, 1900–1980*. New York: Palgrave MacMillan.
Ertsen, M.W. (2016c). Friendship is a Slow Ripening Fruit: An Agency Perspective on Water, Values, and Infrastructure. *World Archaeology* 48(4): 500–516.
Harrower, M.J. (2009). Is the Hydraulic Hypothesis Dead Yet? Irrigation and Social Change in Ancient Yemen. *World Archaeology* 41(1): 58–72.
Hodder, I. (2014). The Entanglements of Humans and Things: A Long-Term View. *New Literary History* 45(1): 19–36.
Hodder, I. (2012). *Entangled: An Archaeology of the Relationships between Humans and Things*. Chichester: Wiley-Blackwell.
Latour, B. (2007). Can We Get Our Materialism Back, Please? *Isis* 98: 138–142.
Latour, B. (2000). When Things Strike Back: a Possible Contribution of 'Science Studies' to the Social Sciences. *British Journal of Sociology* 51(1):107–123.

Latour, B. (1996). On Interobjectivity. *Mind, Culture, and Activity* 3(4): 228–245.

Latour, B. (1991). Technology is Society Made Durable. *The Sociological Review*, 38(S1): 103–132.

Latour, B. and Strum, S.C. (1986). Human Social Origins: Oh Please, Tell Us Another Story. *Journal of Sociological and Biological Structures* 9: 169–187.

Mithen, S. (2012). *Thirst: Water and Power in the Ancient World*. London: Weidenfeld and Nicolson.

Schouten, P. (2013). The Materiality of State Failure: Social Contract Theory, Infrastructure and Governmental Power in Congo. *Millennium—Journal of International Studies* 41(3): 553–574.

Smith, M.L. (2016). Urban Infrastructure as Materialized Consensus. *World Archaeology* 48(1): 164–178.

Strum, S.S. and Latour, B. (1987). Redefining the Social Link: from Baboons to Humans. *Social Science Information* 26 (4): 783–802.

Van de Poel, I. and Van Gorp, A.C., (2006). The Need for Ethical Reflection in Engineering Design. The Relevance of Type of Design and Design Hierarchy. *Science, Technology, and Human Values* 31 (3): 333–360.

Van de Poel, I. and Verbeek, P., (2006). Ethics and Engineering Design. *Science, Technology, and Human Values* 31(3): 223–236.

Van der List, B. (2019). Water Experts for the World. *Strategy and Business*, Retrieved from: www.strategy-business.com/article/Water-Experts-for-the-World?gko=37810.

Van de Ven, G.P. (2004) *Man-Made Lowlands. History of Water Management and Land Reclamation in the Netherlands*. Utrecht: Matrijs.

Van Leeuwen-Canneman, M.C. and Vrolijk, P.F.A., (1996). *Inventaris archief polder Berkel*. Delft: Hoogheemraadschap van Delfland.

Verbeek, P. (2006). Materializing Morality: Design Ethics and Technological Mediation. *Science, Technology, and Human Values* 31(3): 361–380.

Vink, J. (2019). Woedend water smeekt om ingenieurs. *NRC*, Retrieved from: www.nrc.nl/nieuws/2019/02/08/woedend-water-smeekt-om-ingenieurs-a3653473.

Wittfogel, K. (1957). *Oriental Despotism: A Comparative Study of Total Power*. New Haven: Yale University Press.

12 Cross-border landscape as heritage?

Insights from Slovenian borderlands

Marjeta Pisk and Špela Ledinek Lozej

Introduction

Heritagization of landscape is a multi-folded (and not necessarily intentional) process that might be initiated by various triggers and can have different aims. It involves diverse actors and stakeholders and has several (also unforeseen) outcomes. These processes and outcomes are anchored in politics of power and are at the same time also a result of the contingency of events, actors, and opportunities. After the political changes in the late 1980s and the intensification of European integration and territorial cooperation, borders, and borderlands became a contested site of representations and policy-making. Thus, cross-border landscape heritagization is of special interest, as a tool of overcoming past and present boundaries and creating possibilities of heritage beyond its nation-building perspective.

This chapter presents four different cross-border initiatives from the borderlands of Slovenia, Italy, Austria, and Hungary that are constituent and are at the same time producing and representing the landscape and heritage discourse and involve several heritage-making practices in cross-border territories. Drawing on various sources, from planning documents, institutional and media reports, to the ethnography of border sites by employing (participant) observation, informal conversations, and more or less structured interviews with various actors, and by using a comparative perspective on involved actors, their roles, competencies, agendas, and scales, we try to reflect on how cross-border heritage landscape is produced, appropriated and eventually internalized.

Borderlands' landscapes of heritage and heritage landscapes

Borders[1] are often perceived as "a tool that consolidates the power of a certain social and/or ethnic group over a territory and show its ability to exercise economic, cultural, ideological and political control over it, and a form of this control" (Sebentsov and Kolosov, 2012; Kolosov, 2020: 12). In our scrutiny we move away from approaches in which borders are mere delimitations of sovereignty, presented as naturalized and static territorial lines, and built on the concept of *borderscape*, as it was presented and employed by Chiara Brambilla

DOI: 10.4324/9781003195238-12

(2015),[2] as dynamic social processes and practices of spatial differentiation. The concept of borderscape thus enables "a productive understanding of the processual, de-territorialized and dispersed nature of borders and their ensuing regimes and ensembles of practices" (Brambilla, 2015: 22).

Borderscapes and borders in particular are thus sites of (re)appropriation of dominant national discourses and places where different national policies and interests of bordering countries collide. Since today's borders are a tangible expression of the past (O'Dowd and Wilson, 2002), borderscapes are the result of past and present actions, but also harbingers of possible future conflicts.

The landscape – in its synthesized diaphoric meaning, as domain or land inhabited, and as a scenery perceived (Tuan, 1978; Olwig, 2007) – is hence at the same time the backdrop for human and non-human agencies and an active foreground in borderlands' agencies and institutional development. The landscape, its management, protection, and enhancement are situated in an orbit of governmental duty as a means through which governance ambitions can be instrumentalized (Harvey and Waterton, 2015: 905). Despite being (usually) far from the centres of power, the governance ambitions on the borderlands' landscape, as the presented case studies in the chapter show, are evident at several scales, and even at the cross-border local/regional level. These transboundary ambitions and administrative practices are embraced and codified by the Council of Europe's European Landscape Convention (ELC, adopted by the Committee of Ministers of the Council of Europe in 2000) (Olwig, 2007), that puts "ordinary" as well as "special" landscapes onto government agendas. Shifting from the idea of "outstanding" landscapes, it potentially covers the entire territory (Toce and Dourou, 2020: 11). A specific provision of ELC covers cross-border ("trans-frontier") landscapes; Article 9 encourages parties to engage in cross-border cooperation at local and regional levels in order to identify, evaluate, protect, manage and plan landscapes which straddle borders.[3] ELC signatory states are asked to rely, as far as possible, on local and regional authorities (Toce and Dourou, 2020: 12). The *Recommendations on the implementation of the ELC* even mention that the

> transfrontier cooperation may result in joint landscape protection, management and planning programmes and take the form of instruments and measures agreed between the authorities (different administrative levels and general and sectoral competences) and relevant stakeholders on both sides of the border.[4]

The landscapes and borderscapes are in continuous interplay with heritage, forming and reconstituting each other (Harvey, 2015; Katić, Gregorič Bon, and Eade, 2017). Borders in a particular way influence understandings of heritage and are undeniably crucial for heritage production (Balogh, 2019: 30). And vice versa, the concept of heritage creates material, mental, and monumental boundaries "between past and present, between us and them, between what is worth preserving and what is not" (Källén, 2019: 8–9). When trapped in national narratives, heritage can be (mis)used to construct and reinforce borders (Källén, 2019: 7–8) and boundaries among different communities living in the borderlands (Mészáros, 2019). Both heritage and borders define and demarcate an identity, culture, or experience against the Other. Borders, in turn, influence the understanding of heritage and define categorizations of heritage on national, regional, and local level (Källén, 2019: 8–9).

Presented cross-border initiatives addressing landscape and heritage arguably "participate in the symbolic and networked de-bordering of the EU" (Niklasson, 2019: 118–119), but, on the other hand, the state still constantly struggles to control heritage landscapes and landscapes of heritage on the border. We follow these processes in four case studies of the Slovenian-Italian and Slovenian-Austrian-Hungarian borderland landscapes under scrutiny and present different modalities of heritagization implied.

Trilateral Park Goričko–Raab–Örség

The Trilateral Park Goričko–Raab–Örség is a cross-border initiative of the three parks in the Slovenian-Austrian-Hungarian border area.[5] This territory was an organic and administrative unit until the division between the three states after the implementation of the Treaty of Trianon in 1920. The separation deepened after World War II, followed by the establishment of the Iron Curtain and the introduction of special legal and military regulations that restricted free movement in the border area (Pisk, 2020). The idea to establish

Figure 12.1. Location of the presented case studies
Author: Špela Ledinek Lozej; Source of the map: https://commons.wikimedia.org/wiki/File:Slovenes_distribution_map.png

the Trilateral Park thus intertwined the tendencies to create new cross-border relations after the fall of the Iron Curtain and to recognize the value of the exceptional biodiversity of these until then isolated territories along it. The rise of highlighted ecological awareness spurred the internationally recognized European Green Belt (EGB) initiative,[6] a movement for nature conservation and sustainable development under the patronage of the International Union for Conservation of Nature (IUCN) which connects protected areas around the former Iron Curtain. As an ecological network connecting high-value natural and cultural landscapes, it serves to harmonize human activities with the natural environment and to increase the opportunities for the socio-economic development of local communities (Jesel, 2011: vii). Moreover, the territories involved in EGB initiative are, after the organization's representative, memorial landscapes and their outstanding natural and cultural values qualify them to be nominated as a World Heritage site.[7]

Closer cooperation in the Slovenian-Austrian-Hungarian cross-border territory was initiated in 1992, resulting in an agreement on co-financing the establishment of a trilateral nature park, which was signed in Vienna in 1995. Subsequently, the until then Landscape Park of Örség (Hungary) was recategorized into Nature Park in 1995 and into a National Park in 2002. On the Austrian side of the border, the nature reserve Raab was proclaimed in 1998. As there was no counterpart on the Slovenian side, one of the first Phare Cross-Border Cooperation bilateral projects between Slovenia and Hungary[8] was to support the creation of a park on the Slovenian side, which would form a part of the proposed Trilateral Park Goričko-Örség-Raab,[9] dedicated to the coordination of nature preservation as well as sustainable development in the borderlands (Dešnik and Domanjko, 2011). In 2003, Goričko Landscape Park, the second largest protected area in Slovenia was proclaimed.

In a *Memorandum of Understanding* signed by all three parks in 2006 in Windisch-Minihof (Austria), all three parties, following IUCN regulations, "identified the preservation and presentation of the region's natural values and cultural heritage as common interest" (Hesz, 2016: 13). The three parks involved are categorized differently according to IUCN protected area management categories and their primary aim ranges from cultivating and protecting natural habitats (Örség) to heritage tourism (Raab), and to a declarative merging of both goals in the Goričko park. All three are heavily dependent on national policy and the founders' politics: Örség and Goričko are state-funded organizations within the state park systems, while Raab is founded and managed by the board of trustees. These factors prevent the Trilateral Park from functioning fully as a cross-border entity. So far, the planned joint institutional structures of Trilateral Park with an equal share of involved authorities and experts between Slovenia, Hungary, and Austria have not been established and stable funding has not been achieved. Co-management, as one of the essential conditions for the area to be considered transboundary (Vasilijević and Pezold, 2011: 5), has not been realized, but parks continuously participate in joint bilateral partnerships in EU founded cross-border projects.

Julian Alps UNESCO Biosphere Reserve

Compared to the Trilateral Park cross-border heritage landscape pretensions that have not been institutionalized yet, the strivings of the two parks from the northern Italian-Slovenian borderlands for the cross-border protected area seem more promising. The Slovenian Triglav National Park, established in 1961 and enlarged to its present borders in 1981,[10] and the Italian Regional Park of the Julian Prealps, established in 1996,[11] have been gradually realizing the intention for the Transboundary Biosphere Reserve Julian Alps. Biosphere Reserves have been designated by the UNESCO's Man and Biosphere Programme (MAB) since 1971.[12] The Julian Alps in Slovenia were included in the MAB Reserve network in 2003 and in Italy in 2019.[13] At the moment, the two parks, supported by state and regional government, and to a different extent also by local municipalities, are striving for a transboundary ecoregion. The two parks have a long history of cross-border cooperation, as over the years, various EU projects have supported interactions and joint initiatives. The already close collaboration between them expanded when the idea of a cross-border park was born in 2007.[14] In 2019, UNESCO's recognition of the National Park of the Julian Prealps as Biosphere Reserve paved the way for a joint recognition of the two parks as transboundary Biosphere Reserve aimed in the following years. While the transboundary EUROPARK, established in 2016, encompasses the area of the two parks, is the area of the Biosphere Reserves more extensive and includes the buffer and transition areas outside the parks. If the motivation behind the establishment of parks is predominantly nature preservation (culture and cultural heritage are mentioned only in more recent documents), are biosphere reserves intended as "learning places for sustainable development",[15] referring and building on heritage (discourse) only indirectly. While nature preservation, ecological cohesion, as well as environmental education, sustainable tourism, and opportunities for joint promotion of local products of the whole Julian Alps area are invoked, the official discourse does not address directly the cross-border landscape and heritage. Even though the two institutions collaborate in the long term, awareness of the institutional cross-border initiatives and ecoregion in the public and among the local population is very low.

Brda/Collio/Cuei transboundary terraced cultural landscape

While the borderlands of the Julian Alps are already part of the UNESCO MAB Programme, the cross-border Brda/Collio/Cuei region is still seeking recognition through inclusion in the UNESCO World Heritage List. In comparison to the previously mentioned protected areas, that address cross-border landscape heritage indirectly, are intentions for building the cross-border landscape heritage/heritage landscape with the joint cross-border nomination for the inscription of the cultural landscape of Brda/Collio/Cuei[16] on the UNESCO World Heritage List more straightforward. The idea was initiated by the mayors of the Brda/Collio municipalities along the central part of the Slo-venian-Italian borderlands. Initially, the agricultural landscape with innovative land management systems was the focus of the nomination. The pre-dossier was prepared by the local municipalities with the assistance of the authorities of the Province of Gorizia, the Friuli Venezia Giulia Region (FVG), and the regional UNESCO clubs and ICOMOS (all in Italy). In 2019, it received a negative opinion from the Ministry of Culture of Slovenia due to insufficient compliance with the UNESCO norms for the assessment of Outstanding Universal Value, which was also partly caused by the non-involvement of the representatives of the Slovenian expert institution (i.e. the Nova Gorica regio-nal unit of the Institute for the Protection of Cultural Heritage of Slovenia) in the previous phases of the preparation of the proposal.[17] The assistance of the Ministry of Culture of Slovenia in continuing the nomination process was crucial, as it was agreed that the proposal should be officially submitted to UNESCO by Slovenia (even though there was only one partner from Slove-nia, i.e. Municipality of Brda). It was supposed that it would be easier to gain national support in Slovenia due to the generally smaller number of nomina-tions. But the formally allowed quota of proposals for 2019 and 2020 had already been reached at the time of the submission of the Brda candidacy.

Since November 2020 the Italian Temporary Association of Purpose[18] and the Slovenian Municipality of Brda have been working intensively together to prepare an elaborated dossier on the terraced cultural landscape. The so-called technical-scientific committee has been preparing the proposal, which focuses on terraces as the main feature of the landscape in the region. Only individual parts of the landscape would be included in the list, so this would impose only minor restrictions on land use. Thus, the acquisition of the UNESCO heritage label is thus envisaged mainly to accelerate (heritage) tourism and the broader recognition of the cross-border landscape and its wine production.[19] Brda/Collio cross-border heritage landscape is much more notorious among locals as the more coordinated, straightforward, and institutionalized actions of the two parks in the Julian Alps, partly also because of the sometimes contradictory claims between the protection of past agricultural practices and today's intensive agriculture and tourism.

Walk of Peace

Different aspects of cross-border cooperation – operational or institutional – and their territorialization in the form of a cross-border park, ecoregion, and an UNESCO site have been at the core of the initiatives presented so far. On the other hand, the last endeavour from the Slovenian-Italian borderlands, the Walk of Peace, was ideated and developed in Slovenia and has only lately applied a transboundary perspective. It is not a territorialized protected area, but a trail, a heritage landscape or a network that (inter)connects military ceme-teries, caves, trenches, charnel houses, chapels, monuments, outdoor museum, crosses, tombstones, memorial tablets, and other memorials of the First World

War along the present Slovenian-Italian border and onetime Isonzo Front from the middle of the Julian Alps to Trieste at the Adriatic Sea.[20] The Walk of Peace was ideated by the versatile locals in the Upper Soča Valley in Slovenia, who have been promoting the heritage of the Isonzo Front since the 1980s. It has been developing since 2000 by the eponymous foundation, the Walks of Peace in the Soča Region Foundation through several projects, local, national, and European funds and self-motivated collaboration of several institutions, local communities and individuals. In 2007, the outdoor museums, major monuments, and memorials of the Isonzo Front, natural points of interest, two museums, some private museum collections, and tourist information centres were connected to form the Walk of Peace in the Upper Soča Region trail, that has been since 2010 progressively connected with similar endeavours in southern parts of the Isonzo Front, either in Slovenia or in Italy. The Walk of Peace became Slovenia's flagship contribution to the pan-European formal remembrance of the First World War's centenary (Fikfak and Jezernik, 2018: 120). Besides, in 2016, the nomination *The Walk of Peace from the Alps to the Adriatic – Heritage of the First World War* was listed on the UNESCO World Heritage Tentative List.[21]

Since 2000 the Foundation has managed to get support and to involve actors at various scales and from different spheres. Besides the Government of the Republic of Slovenia, its founder, it has been financially and expertly supported by three Slovenian ministries, by the Institute for the Protection of Cultural Heritage of Slovenia, and the Research Centre of the Slovenian Academy of Sciences and Arts. At the local level, it cooperates intensively with the municipalities and the regional development centre, as well as with Kobarid Museum, the associations gathering the (re)interpreters of the events and collectors of the remains of the Isonzo Front, the local tourist societies and tourist information centres, and private collectors. It has also gained support from the different actors in the southern part of the former Isonzo Front in Slovenia and Italy. These networks of stakeholders and (memorial) sites enabled simultaneous cooperation at local, regional, and national scale, in cross-border actions, as well as in the commemorations of the centenary of the First World War and in actions aiming at the inscription of the Walk of Peace on the UNESCO list also at supranational level.

The germinal motivations and aims of the Walk of Peace initiative were renovation and preservation of the Isonzo Front remnants, establishment of a study centre for the First World War, and development of tourism. In the last decades, the Walk of Peace initiative has outgrown its initial goals, and has also become a promoter of coexistence and reconciliation between formerly hostile nations, and, by representing Slovenia at the supranational commemoration of the centenary of the First World War, it has also become a recognizable brand, not only in the Soča Valley and in Slovenia, but also in Europe and, through its inclusion on the UNESCO World Heritage Tentative List also on a global level. Even though the Walk of Peace is not a territorialized initiative as parks and terraced landscape, but a meshwork of paths, sites, memorials, and actors, its heritage-making endeavours seem promising in making cross-border and even transnational heritage landscape, and, by this memory-work, enabling new landscapes of heritage.

Conclusions

The four presented cross-border initiatives referring to heritage (and) landscape differ regarding the scale, the actors and stakeholders involved, as well as their motivations, aims, and perspectives. All of the described case studies of heritage landscape share a cross-border perspective, that was motivated either by environmental and nature protection, culture preservation or economic (especially tourism) development since the late 1980s, and intensively since the late 1990s, after Austria had joined the EU in 1995, and after Hungary's and Slovenia's accession in 2004. Three of them were extensively supported by the European Regional Development Fund, especially Phare Pre-Accession and Interreg Cross-Border Cooperation Programmes. Cross-border cooperation was initiated and implemented at different scales – from the (predominantly) local and regional scale (Trilateral Park, Brda/Collio initiative and the Walk of Peace), with differently intensified up-scaling, to regional and national ones (cf. the Julian Alps UNESCO Biosphere Reserve).

The embeddedness of the initiatives in the territory and social network(s) as well as the thickness of the connections varies. While the establishment of the transboundary Biosphere Reserve between the two parks is a bilateral intertwining, the transboundary park at the Austrian-Hungarian-Slovenian tripoint trilateral is the Walk of Peace, a meshwork of actions, actors, and sites at local, regional, national, and supranational levels.

The Trilateral Park cross-border protection of the (predominantly natural) landscape was motivated by mutually supportive pan-European Green Belt and regional initiatives after the fall of the Iron Curtain. Despite the ambition for a joint authority, a common cross-border management structure has not been established. Although it cannot be considered as a transboundary protected area, the activities have had an impact on biodiversity, and different habitats, as the three separate parks have cleverly exploited the situation to obtain EU funds through several projects in the framework of the cross-border cooperation programmes, thus being involved in the environmental, sustainable development, and heritage discourses (Tiran et al., 2008; Mód, 2019; Bajuk Senčar, 2019; Pisk, 2020).

While the Trilateral Park was conceived from scratch in the atmosphere of the late 1990s that fancied Europeanization and de-bordering, the idea of a transboundary ecoregion in the Julian Alps was growing gradually out of actual common nature protection actions and projects after the establishment of the Park of the Julian Prealps on the Italian side of the border. It is an exemplary and effective institutional cooperation between management structures, regional and national ministries aiming at joint long-term transboundary activities. Whereas cross-border collaboration at regional and national level is impressive, it has no substantial impact on the daily lives and life-worlds of the parks' inhabitants.

On the contrary, Brda/Collio strivings for the UNESCO cross-border nomination of the (terraced) cultural landscape operate mainly at the local governmental level. Non-recognition by national administrative and expert institutions has – until now – prevented the realization of the ambitions of the local municipalities. Only recently have local governments managed to scale up their endeavours to the national level, which is necessary for further proceeding towards the listing on the UNESCO Tentative List. The future will show their capabilities in realizing it.

The Walk of Peace heritage work seems to be the most balanced: it is a grassroots initiative that is recognized and supported in the wider region and by the state government, and they have managed to involve different ministries and other actors at various scales. The meshwork of (cross-border) trails, heritage sites, and stakeholders has, since 2000, been orchestrated by the eponymous foundation. Although the Walk of Peace is not territorialized as a protected area or terraced landscape, its landscape heritage-work is evident: not in making a (cross-border) heritage landscape, but in creating (cross-border) landscapes of heritage on the phenomena of the First World War by emphasizing coexistence and reconciliation between formerly hostile nations, and by transcending past and present boundaries and creating possibilities of heritage beyond the national. And, following Brambilla (2015: 24), by encouraging the transition from a "politics of being" to a "politics of becoming."

Notes

1 The heading of the subsection is inspired by the editorial to a special issue of the journal *Landscape Research* by David Harvey and Emma Waterton (2015).
2 See also dell'Agnese and Amilhat Szary (2015) and Kricher (2019).
3 "The Parties shall encourage transfrontier co-operation on local and regional level and, wherever necessary, prepare and implement joint landscape programmes" (see *European Landscape Convention*, https://rm.coe.int/CoERMPublicCommonSea rchServices/DisplayDCTMContent?documentId=09000016802f80c6).
4 *Recommendation CM/Rec(2008)3 of the Committee of Ministers to member states on the guidelines for the implementation of the European Landscape Convention*, Appendix I, http s://search.coe.int/cm/Pages/result_details.aspx?ObjectID=09000016805d3e6c.
5 For more see www.park-goricko.org/go/1149/Partnerstvo-Tridezelnega-parka -Goricko-Raab-rs-g.
6 For more see www.europeangreenbelt.org/.
7 "The European Green Belt is an exceptional symbol of European history. This living memorial reminds us of the peaceful overcoming of the Cold War and the Iron Curtain. It is a physical reminder in the landscape of the turbulent and often tragic history of the 20th century": www.europeangreenbelt.org/initiative/history/.
8 Standard Summary Project Fiche SI.00.08.01: https://ec.europa.eu/neighbourhoo d-enlargement/sites/default/files/pdf/fiche-projet/slovenia/other/2000/ si0008-01-fichproj-natureparkdev.pdf.
9 A bilateral cross-programme between Slovenia and Hungary (from 2000 to 2003) partly replaced the Phare Trilateral Cross-border Programme between Hungary, Austria, and Slovenia (from 1995 to 1996).
10 Actually, the first proposal for establishing the park dates back to 1908, but the idea was not realized, however, in 1924 the Alpine Conservation Park was established in

the smaller area of the Triglav Lakes Valley, which was promulgated as the Triglav national Park in 1961. For more see Bajuk Senčar (2013) and www.tnp.si/sl/spozna jte/podatki-o-parku-2/.

11 For more see www.parcoprealpigiulie.it/it/principale/parco#.

12 For more see https://en.unesco.org/mab.

13 For more see www.unesco.org/new/en/natural-sciences/environment/ecologica l-sciences/biosphere-reserves/europe-north-america/slovenia/julian-alps/ and https:// en.unesco.org/biosphere/eu-na/julian-alps-italy.

· 14 In 2009, the two parks were recognized as the Julian Alps Transboundary Ecoregion by EUROPARC, the Federation of European protected areas and "the representative body of Europe's Protected Areas". In 2016 EUROPARC recognized the two parks as members of the European Charter for Sustainable Tourism in Protected Areas as the first transboundary protected areas in Europe to be granted this status (see www.europarc.org/about-us/europarc-federation/). In 2014, the Alpine Convention designated the two protected areas as an official Alpine pilot region for eco-connectivity to recognize their efforts in sustainable development and nature conservation cooperation (see www.tnp.si/en/javni-zavod/mednarodna-priznanja/).

15 See https://en.unesco.org/mab.

16 In the title of the proposal three names of the region are used: Brda on the Slovenian side of the border and the Italian name Collio as well as the Friulian name Cuei for the Italian part of the territory. For ease of readability and respect of the cross-border nature of nomination, we use in the text only "Brda/Collio".

17 It is therefore surprising that despite the non-involvement of the conservators of the regional expert institution, the initiative was already in 2016 recognized by the Institute for the Protection of Cultural Heritage of Slovenia, ICOMOS Slovenia and Office of the Slovenian National Commission for UNESCO as one of the Slovenian initiatives awaiting the inscription on the UNESCO Tentative List (Stokin, 2016: 70–73).

18 The Temporary Association of Purpose was established in January 2020 in order to manage the various participating entities and the necessary funds in a more coordinated way. It is led by Venezia Giulia Chamber of Commerce and members of the Municipalities of Gorizia, Cormons, San Floriano del Collio, Mossa, Capriva del Friuli, Dolegna del Collio, Farra d'Isonzo, San Lorenzo Isontino, the Banca di Cividale and the Collio Wines Consortium, and with support of the FVG.

19 Several other actions have been taken with this aim: for example, in 2021, the Brda/Collio region was presented as an example of a potential transboundary site of Globally Important Agricultural Heritage Systems (GIAHS) at the 2nd Regional Dialogue on GIAHS in Europe and Central Asia organized by Food and Agriculture Organisation of United Nations (see www.fao.org/europe/events/detail-events/zh/ c/1395148/). Moreover, in 2021, Municipality of Brda was awarded the Special Mention of the Landscape Award of the ELC for "Brda tourist destination development" as part of the Landscape Award Alliance of the Committee of Ministers of the Council of Europe, as a source of inspiration: https://rm.coe.int/10th-plena ry-session-of-the-cdcpp-18-june-2021-7th-session-of-the-land/1680a2c350.

20 For more see Likar and Klavora (2015), Klavora (2016), Koren (2015), Testen and Koren (2015), and www.potmiru.si/eng/publications-and-articles.

21 See the UNESCO World Heritage Tentative List at https://whc.unesco.org/en/ tentativelists/6077/. After listing the nomination came to a halt because UNESCO formed an expert body that re-considered the nominations of so-called difficult heritage, based on wars and conflicts. See *ICOMOS Discussion Paper Evaluations of World Heritage Nominations related to Sites Associated with Memories of Recent Conflicts* (2018): www.icomos.org/images/DOCUMENTS/World_Heritage/ICOMOS_Dis cussion_paper_Sites_associated_with_Memories_of_Recent_Conflicts.pdf.

Acknowledgement

The authors acknowledge the financial support from the Slovenian Research Agency (research core funding Heritage on the Margins, No. P5–0408, and research project Protected areas along the Slovenian-Hungarian Border, No. J6–8254).

References

Bajuk Senčar, T. (2013). Načrt upravljanja Triglavskega narodnega parka in kultura dediščinskih praks. *Traditiones*, 42(2): 9–25.

Bajuk Senčar, T. (2019). Cross-border Cooperation and the Europeanization of the Slovenian-Hungarian Border Region. *Traditiones*, 48(1): 213–231.

Balogh, P. (2019). The Revival of Cultural Heritage and Borders: A Literature Review with Some Explanatory Remarks. In A. Källén (ed.), *Heritage and Borders*. Stockholm: Kungl. Vitterhets Historie och Antikvitets Akademien, pp. 13–35.

Brambilla, C. (2015). Exploring the Critical Potential of the Borderscapes Concept. *Geopolitics*, 20(1): 14–34.

Dell'Agnese, E. and Amilhat Szary, A. L. (2015). Borderscapes: From Border Landscapes to Border Aesthetics. *Geopolitics*, 20(1): 4–13.

Dešnik, S. and Domanjko, G. (2011). Goričko-Raab-Örség – Developing with Nature in a Trilateral Park. In M. Vasilijević and T. Pezold (eds.), *Crossing Borders for Nature. European Examples of Transboundary Conservation*. Gland, Switzerland and Belgrade, Serbia: IUCN Programme Office for South-Eastern Europe, pp. 39–42.

Fikfak, J. and Jezernik, B. (2018). Introduction: The Cultural Heritage of the Isonzo Front. *Folklore*, 73: 7–18.

Harvey, D. (2015). Landscape and Heritage: Trajectories and Consequences. *Landscape Research*, 40(8): 911–924.

Harvey, D. C. and Waterton, E. (2015). Editorial: Landscapes of Heritage and Heritage Landscapes. *Landscape Research*, 40(8): 905–910.

Hesz, R. (2016). *Crossing the Borders. Studies on Cross-Border Cooperation within the Danube Region: Case Study of the Örség-Goričko Cooperation*. Budapest: Central European Service for Cross-Border Initiatives.

Jessel, B. (2011). Foreword. In M. Vasilijević and T. Pezold (eds.), *Crossing Borders for Nature. European Examples of Transboundary Conservation*. Gland, Switzerland and Belgrade, Serbia: IUCN Programme Office for South-Eastern Europe, p. vii.

Källén, A. (2019). An Introduction. In A. Källén (ed.), *Heritage and Borders*. Stockholm: Kungl, Vitterhets Historie och Antikvitets Akademien (KVHAA), pp. 7–12.

Katić, M., Gregorič Bon, N., and Eade, J. (2017). Landscape and Heritage Interplay: Spatial and Temporal Explorations. *Anthropological Notebooks*, 23(3): 5–18.

Klavora, M. (2016). Pot miru od Alp do Jadrana in dediščina soške fronte. *Glasnik Slovenskega etnološkega društva*, 56(3–4):134–136.

Kolosov, V. (2020). Phantom Borders: The Role in Territorial Identity and the Impact on Society. *Belgeo*, 2, online. Retrieved: https://journals.openedition.org/belgeo/38812.

Koren, T. (2015). *The Walk of Peace from the Alps to the Adriatic: A Guide Along the Isonzo Front*. Kobarid: Ustanova Fundacija Poti miru v Posočju.

Krichker, D. (2019). Making Sense of Borderscapes: Space, Imagination and Experience. *Geopolitics*, 26(4): 1224–1242.

Likar, Z. and Klavora, M. (2015). WWI and the Possibilities for Developing Historical Tourism – The Case of the Walk of Peace from the Alps to the Adriatic. In A. Gosar, M. Koderman, and M. Rodela (eds.), *Dark Tourism: Post-WWI Destinations of Human Tragedies and Opportunities for Tourism Development.* Koper: University of Primorska, pp. 97–106.

Mészáros, C. (2019). Flexible Boundaries at the Slovenian Raba Region: The Story of two Infrastructure Developments. *Traditiones,* 48(1): 233–250.

Mód, L. B. (2019). "A Border that Divides and Connects": Monuments and Commemorations on the Slovenian-Hungarian Border. *Traditiones,* 48(1): 101–116.

Niklasson, E. (2019). Borders of Belonging in the European Heritage Label. In A. Källén (ed.), *Heritage and Borders.* Stockholm: Kungl. Vitterhets Historie och Antikvitets Akademien, pp. 105–126.

O'Dowd L. and Wilson, T. (2002). Frontiers of Sovereignty in the New Europe. In N. Alkan (ed.), *Borders of Europe.* Bonn: Universität Bonn, pp. 7–30.

Olwig, K. R. (2007). The Practice of Landscape "Conventions" and the Just Landscape: The Case of the European Landscape Convention. *Landscape Research,* 32(5): 579–594.

Pisk, M. (2020). Challenges of Cross-border Cooperation: The Initiative of Trilateral Goričko-Raab-Örség Nature Park. *Acta Ethnographica Hungarica,* 65(2): 415–432.

Stokin, M. (2016). Slovenian Cultural Monuments and Sites Awaiting Inscription on the Tentative List. In M. Stokin (ed.), *Heritage in Slovenia and UNESCO.* Ljubljana: Institute for the Protection of Cultural Heritage of Slovenia, ICOMOS Slovenia and Office of the Slovenian National Commission for UNESCO, pp. 59–77.

Testen, P. and Koren, T. (2015). Učilnica na prostem – primer Poti miru. *Prispevki za novejšo zgodovino,* 55(2): 183–198.

Tiran, J., Kozina, J., Gostinčar P., and Pirjevec E. (2008). Razvojni potenciali zavarovanih območij. *Dela,* 29: 177–192.

Toce, B. and Dourou, E. (2020). Culture Without Borders: Cultural Heritage Management for Local and Regional Development. *CG/CUR* (2020)15–3. Retrieved from: https://rm.coe.int/cg-cur-2020-15-03-en-cultural-heritage/16809f9fbd.

Tuan, Y.-F. (1978). Sign and Metaphor. *Annals of the Association of American Geographers,* 68(3): 363–372.

Vasilijević, M. and Pezold, T. (eds.) (2011). *Crossing Borders for Nature: European Examples of Transboundary Conservation.* Gland, Switzerland and Belgrade: IUCN Programme Office for South-Eastern Europe.

13 Remaking a landscape after the trauma

The Brumadinho dam catastrophe and the Memorial for the victims

Edilson Pereira and Leonardo Vilaça Dupin

Introduction

In 2019, Brazil experienced one of the most devastating socio-environmental disasters and the largest work accident in the country's history: the rupture of a dam holding mineral extraction tailings owned by the multinational Vale S.A., in the city of Brumadinho, Minas Gerais. Millions of tons of toxic sludge buried workers and residents, causing 272 deaths and 11 disappearances, while leaving a trail of destruction in surrounding areas, spread by rivers in the region. A year later, while the victims were still fighting for the right to reparation, the construction of the "Brumadinho Memorial" was announced, in reference to the catastrophic event.

The memorial project will occupy 1,200 square metres of built area. According to those responsible for its proposal, visits to the memorial that depicts the lives of the fatal victims will follow a route that passes through exhibition rooms and culminates in an outdoor overlook directly facing the

Figure 13.1. Overlook, perspective
Source: Gustavo Penna Architects and Associates

DOI: 10.4324/9781003195238-13

epicentre of the catastrophe.[1] The site of the dam rupture, which was once a valley formed by surrounding mountains and has become a collective trauma, materialised by the enormous volume of displaced earth and devastated human and non-human lives, will become a place of contemplation of the catastrophic landscape in order to produce a type of memory. This memory is to be mediated by the mining company responsible for the immense tragedy, which plans to finance the construction of the memorial as part of the reparative policy for the crime committed.

In this chapter, beginning with this emblematic case, we reflect on the relationships between landscape, heritage and memory. Initially, we present the historical and geographic context that encompasses the memorial project and the socio-environmental crime that justifies its proposal. Then, we analyse the narrative that the memorial triggers concerning this territory and the extent to which it supports a specific perspective on the traumatic landscape and its past. In addition to the recent history and massive socio-environmental destruction linked to the spill that occurred in Brumadinho, this case study is also interesting for its exemplary nature: the region where the city is located was one of the first territories to be explored in Brazil by the mining industry, some 300 years ago.

Within this extensive history, we highlight some historical and social effects of this practice on the landscape and its agents, human and non-human. On the one hand, the extraction of minerals in the eighteenth century was accompanied by the concentration of material wealth and the creation of a Portuguese-Brazilian aesthetic culture that is crystallised in colonial architecture of a civil and religious character. At the time, Minas Gerais became the most important captaincy of the Portuguese empire. Two centuries later, in the first half of the twentieth century, this same colonial architecture and urbanism became the ultimate example of "Brazilian historical and artistic heritage", encompassing cities located in the geographical surroundings of Brumadinho, which were representative historic areas to be observed in conjunction with the mountainous landscape.

On the other hand, the history of material and aesthetic wealth is composed of an underground face marked by oppression and havoc caused by intensive mining (Aguiar, 2013). The economic activity in question developed as a process of slow violence that, for centuries, eroded geological and human elements simultaneously. Large-scale mining creates a dystopian horizon composed of huge asymmetries in the economic and political process[2] and, on the physical plane, giant holes in the soil and toxic deposits that strongly contrast with the historical areas that have become part of the collective heritage. Acting in these territories, the Brazilian state facilitates the process of indiscriminate exploitation by transforming them into commodity exporting locations – a condition for large-scale exploration, which culminates in the destruction and reconstruction of landscapes, as has happened in Brumadinho and the surrounding areas.[3] Considering the past and present, we observe that colonialism and peripheral capitalism feed a dynamic that fatally affects biomes, interrelationships (human and non-human), and subjectivities, extinguishing ways of life and modifying landscapes established by traditional and ethnic populations.

In view of these factors, the proposal to construct a memorial that honours the victims of one of the most serious socio-environmental crimes in the world highlights the current strategies for reconstituting the landscape and collective memory. The memorial could become a device for narrating and remembering Brumadinho's tragedy from a particular point of view that does not necessarily represent the interests of the families of those who were buried and thousands of other actors from this territory. We seek to analyse the memorial the mining company plans to install, in front of the site devastated by the toxic wave of mud, to contemplate what public memory is being proposed in the midst of the catastrophe and how this case elucidates certain aspects of the historical relationship maintained between landscape and heritage in Brazil.

This work was based on a methodology consolidated in the human sciences, which endorses fieldwork and ethnographic encounter, in their various forms. It is an empirical research method used recurrently in anthropology, according to which, as stated by Roberto Cardoso de Oliveira, we begin from rites to arrive at the meanings of these rites, expressed by those who participate in them, to finally construct the meaning, that which results from the researcher's ethnographic interpretation (Oliveira, 2000: 22). Through the experience of one of the authors, who has been working for over a year advising a group of affected families, much of the stored data described is organised here. However, in this proposal, empiricism goes beyond "face to face" encounters and is also shaped by communications mediated by artifacts. Thus here, the ethnographic meeting and its questionings were also guiding the documents, in their virtual and material forms, including the monuments. For some time, this mode of research has gained prominence in the social sciences, with anthropologists turning to documents and archives as places of interest, which are seen not only as material sources of the events, but devices of localised knowledge and power practices, which perform tasks, communicate, and generate consequences. In short, they are artifacts that form a living corpus and produce realities "as something that must remain and last, given, above all, their character as 'documents'" (Vianna, 2014: 47).

Mining: the landscape between heritage and ruin

In Portuguese and English, the word *mineiro* (miner) refers to the worker who excavates the soil with the intention of extracting ores and geological riches. The *minas* (mines) produce a commodity. In Brazil, the same terms designate the name of a political region in the country (Minas) and those born there (*mineiros*). The State of Minas Gerais is located in a region far from the coast and has a larger territory than that of Spain ($586,528 \text{ km}^2$). In common use in Brazilian speech, the most accepted meaning of the word *mineiro* refers to the inhabitants and customs of the state, as a qualifier. *Mineiros* are known as those who embody "*mineiro* traditions", their history, and "Minas heritage" as an important part of Brazilian national heritage (Pereira, 2014, 2017; Dupin, 2017, 2019).

Minas Gerais is a prominent region in the historical narratives concerning Brazil's colonial and modern past. Up to the mid-seventeenth century, the springs that made up the countless rivers of sinuous topography in the central region of the state, characterised by areas of rocky and mountainous formations, were part of the ecosystem inhabited by indigenous populations. Progressive colonial occupation began in the seventeenth century, with rapid growth in the beginning of the eighteenth century. The fever for gold, silver, and precious stones led to a demographic explosion in the region over a short period of time. Geological exploration marked the history of the first cities in Minas Gerais, making them the largest gold-producing centre of the Portuguese colonial empire. At the same time that this wealth was produced by continuous exploitation of slave labour and the existing biome, the region became the scene of several conflicts between local and Portuguese explorers, creating the symbolic basis for subsequent discourses on national independence. At the turn of the twentieth century, after the institution of the first Republic in Brazil, the economic and political history of Minas Gerais became an important part of the narratives that enabled the construction of an image of the Brazilian nation, chronicling a history of national identity.

This process culminated in the 1930s with the creation of the federal agency for the study and defence of the *Serviço do Patrimônio Histórico e Artístico Nacional* (SPHAN) (National Historical and Artistic Heritage Service). This was a modern project defended by historians, artists, politicians, and architects – many of whom were born in Minas Gerais, including *mineiro* Rodrigo Melo Franco de Andrade, SPHAN's first director. As Françoise Choay observed, "The cult of the past monument coexists with that, soon nominated, of 'modernity'"[4] (1996: 107), and modernism also played a key role in understanding the national past in Brazil. The architectures and landscapes of the past became a substratum of the history of "Brazilian civilisation" that sought political validity.

Several of the cities born together with the first consolidated gold mining fields in eighteenth century Minas Gerais, in the twentieth century, came to be seen as being in danger of disappearance and ruin (Gonçalves, 1996). The threat, in this case, was represented by the relative impoverishment of the population and the action of time on the colonial architecture. The mountains and urban architecture were then combined in their classification as the country's cultural and environmental heritage. This is the case, for example, of the 12 soapstone prophets sculpted by the baroque artisan Antônio Francisco Lisboa (Aleijadinho) in the municipality of Congonhas, in the Sanctuary of Bom Jesus de Matozinhos, for which the backdrop is a serra that was seen by the sculptor as the frame for sculptures that replicate figures from the Bible.

Over the decades, these national treasures have achieved international recognition, including World Heritage titles awarded to the city of Ouro Preto in 1980 and to the Sanctuary of Bom Jesus de Matozinhos as a whole in 1985, located approximately 100 km from Brumadinho. In this and other urban heritage sites, the anthropic and natural landscapes were associated with an image of national history, since they produced a unique and picturesque atmosphere (Choay, 1996; Simmel, 1996: 16). In these towns, the view and the heritage turn to the visible surface that represent something valued from the past. Visiting these places informs tourists from the rest of the country about an important part of national history and culture.

The valuing of Brazilian historical and landscape heritage coexists, however, with the continuous alterations and suppression of territory in the regions that border these listed perimeters. There is an underground history, historically associated with the economic model adopted by Brazil, that remains to be known. It was ore extraction, from the end of the seventeenth century, that within the colonial process and modernity, integrated Minas Gerais as a source of raw material aimed at foreign markets. In 1942, under the dictatorial government of Getúlio Vargas, the same president who authorised the creation of the national heritage institutions, the Brazilian state created the state company Companhia Vale do Rio Doce.[5] The company's headquarters and main operating area are located in the so-called Quadrilátero Ferrífero (Iron Quadrangle), in the southern central region of the state, with a territorial extension of approximately 7,000 km^2, which occupies the position of the largest producer of iron ore in Brazil, encompassing cities like Brumadinho, Ouro Preto, Congonhas, and Mariana. The region where several of the "historic cities" that form part of this heritage are located is the very region that currently concentrates 72.5 per cent of Brazil's ore reserves (Gomide et al., 2018: 189). This industry turns mineral masses, which surround and conform the geology and landscape of heritage sites in the country, into a commodity that yields high profits for foreign corporations. Through countless socio-technical processes, what was once a constituent part of the landscape becomes the object of a long history of expropriation of natural resources. In 2018 alone, the Paraopeba Complex, which encompasses a set of dams located in and around Brumadinho (including the one that ruptured) produced 27.3 million tons of iron ore to serve the European market (Ragazzi and Rocha, 2019).

The wealth of the mining industry is maintained to the extent that it produces an irreversible transformation of the environment and the territory. In many places in the Quadrilátero Ferrífero, what could be classified as part of the natural landscape heritage is converted into gigantic holes and toxic waste deposits. The advance of economic exploitation produces a device of continuous destruction that, in times of great tragedy, holds the national media spotlight, as in the monumental case of Brumadinho. However, in general, multinationals like Vale S.A., through strong lobbying power, obtain the support of government officials to continue producing a wide trail of destruction of native biomes and ways of life, like a machine that transforms the existing landscape into ruins and advances the trail of destruction that characterises the Anthropocene. Their actions reveal that infrastructure and ruins are interconnected, parts of the same process that must be considered together: "Ruination calls attention to both the constructive and destructive nature of infrastructure. Ruins remind us that infrastructures have the potential to offer numerous benefits but that they are also ultimately incapable of forever satisfying the tasks they are meant to carry out" (Howe et al., 2016: 7).

The context in which the city of Brumadinho is inserted – a political and symbolic territory in which heritage, economic exploitation and the active production of ruins are articulated – shows us that the landscape should not be seen as a scenario that is external, pre-existing, and independent of people. More than a place to contemplate or visit occasionally, the landscape results from several processes of creation, transformation, and destruction over time. Therefore, it must be analysed as a set of relationships in continuous transformation that combine human and non-human forces (Ingold, 2000; Latour, 1994; Simmel, 1996). Thus, like "heritage", the landscape is collectively constructed and signified at the same time that it acts as an agent in the constitution of its collective identities, guiding specific forms of relationship between human beings and the existing terrain, including its devices for memory.

Catastrophic landscape and the Memorial

The rupture of the dam in Brumadinho, containing waste from the Córrego do Feijão mine, has been considered by analysts and social entities to be the most serious socio-environmental disaster, in terms of loss of human life, and the largest work accident ever recorded in Brazil. In the moments following the collapse of the 86-metre-high dam, underpinned by an embankment of grass-covered earth, 13 million cubic metres of iron ore tailings descended in the form of a terrifying wave. It reached a height of 30 metres, flowing at 120 kilometres per hour, destroying everything in its wake. The spill caused devastation that began in the company's administrative and operational structure, then swamped and buried houses, farms, communities, and local assets.

The tragedy immediately claimed more than 270 lives, including many mine workers and surrounding residents. Over the following days, in a chain reaction, the ore tailings – which float on water and cannot be diluted – travelled about 300 kilometres from the Paraopeba River and affected the entire hydrographic basin, annihilating life where it passed. In total, about 20 municipalities bathed by the river were impacted, causing interruptions in life projects, economic projects, impoverishment, property devaluation, future uncertainties, psychological disorders, and the stigmatisation of food products from the region and their producers.

This catastrophic crime scene, consisting of the destructive revelation of tons of tailings that were supposed to remain hidden under the earth, reversed the usual order attributed to the human and natural elements that composed the landscape from top to bottom. It is not by chance, while still under the effects of the terror experienced following the immense toxic spill, that the firefighters, police, family members, and volunteers who came together to search for the disappeared after the disaster named these people "jewels", like a precious asset that is historically sought through mining activity, through underground work. In this case, however, the jewels do not correspond to economic heritage, but family and friends, human beings. The relatives, friends, and neighbours of the disappeared came to represent it in the form of a central symbol of the narratives that make up the initial identity of Minas Gerais, linked to its heritage cities.

A year after the tragedy, while the victims still fought for the reparation of rights, several communication channels reported the construction of the "Brumadinho Memorial", in reference to these buried "jewels" and the location of the traumatic event. In March 2020, the site and the project were chosen, in which the members of an association of people affected by the tragedy – the *Associação dos Familiares de Vítimas e Atingidos pelo Rompimento da Barragem Mina Córrego do Feijão Brumadinho* (AVABRUM) "Association of Family Members of Victims and those Affected by the Córrego do Feijão Mine Brumadinho Dam Rupture) – chose between two different architectural proposals presented by Vale S.A. The winning proposal was prepared by the offices of architect Gustavo Penna, a well-known professional in Minas Gerais, who was responsible for the construction of a museum dedicated to Aleijadinho's work in the "historic city" of Congonhas, which, as mentioned above, also forms part of the Quadrilátero Ferrífero.

In contrast to the historical heritage recognised by the oldest cities in Minas Gerais, the Brumadinho Memorial does not aim to safeguard material elements of value to antiquity, which play a positive cultural role in nationalist discourses and local identity. In fact, the project includes the registration and exhibition of the names and portraits of each of the fatal victims, serving as a space for visiting and expressing collective mourning for family members, friends, neighbours, and tourists. It is, therefore, a memorial guided by emotion and grief, which raises important questions regarding the type of political and architectural strategy that must be adopted to deal with the negative memory of a trauma. According to the company, which treats the construction of the memorial as part of the reparative policy put into action in the territory, the memorial should favour the future political recognition of the area as a "sensitive" or "emotional memory site" (Fabre, 2013; Castriota, 2019) – a notion approaching that of "difficult heritage" (Logan and Reeves, 2009) triggered in other cases of catastrophic losses involving suffering, whether in Brazil or other parts of the world.

The terrain intended for the construction of the new memorial, in a five-hectare area acquired by the mining company, is located in the vicinity of the rupture, followed by the enormous wave of toxic waste. By including the construction of a lookout, the project proposes to establish a new point of observation and relationship to the catastrophic landscape – in the exact location where the mountain and the mine previously existed.[6]

The construction will be made of exposed concrete mixed with red earth, creating a sense of continuity between the colour of the turned earth and the memorial itself. In addition, the new memory space (Nora, 1993) was designed as a long crack in the ground – in reference to the idea of cracking – complemented by exhibition rooms that produce a play of light and shadows, including spaces with low lighting that precede access to open and sunny areas. When the works are completed, the visitors will cover over 230 metres, within the built terrain, until they reach the lookout that leads to the dam's rupture site. The path will be complemented on both sides by a grove of yellow ipe trees; the number of trees will correspond to the number of fatal victims of the incident. According to the architect responsible for the project, the ipe is a "tree symbolic of Brazil" and its periodic flowering cycles refer to the cyclical movements of life.

Another fundamental premise of the memorial is that it is designed as *arquitetura de caráter público* (public architecture) – as the terms of reference issued by the mining company dictate to orient projects presented by the architectural offices pre-selected by it.[7] In this aspect, the memorial for Brumadinho reflects a key dimension of several other international memorials and monuments that question the meanings associated with the notion of "public" – tacitly associated with democratic contexts – and the idea of "participation" (Deutsche, 1992; Young, 1992). As with so-called "public art" (Felshin, 1995), the memorial architecture is justified to the extent that Vale S.A. encompasses the relatives of the fatal victims and others affected by this socio-environmental crime as part of the agents that define the destinies of the project. Participation, however, is modulated by a position of evident asymmetry between the victims and the mining company.

First, only those belonging to an association of victims' relatives (AVABRUM) were listened to. Their choice, moreover, results from conditions predefined by the company responsible for the disaster: Vale summoned four engineering offices at its discretion and chose, among their projects, two to be put forward for an online vote on a website. The remote, non-face-to-face nature of the procedure accentuates the feeling of deterritorialisation, of continuous loss of cultural referents and spatial landmarks for local identity, that was initiated by the toxic waste spill that barely a year earlier had destroyed houses, gardens, land, and the pre-existing affective and anthropic landscape. Once the winning office hired by the company was announced, the "participation" of the victims' "families" was ensured by "listening carefully" to their expectations.

At this point, however, the discourse of a good relationship with the "community" as a way of legitimising the memorial project itself, as a type of reparative activity in terms of collective memory, contrasts with the reality experienced by many residents, who have yet to receive compensation, drinking water, food for their animals, among other violations, due to the continuous losses generated by Vale. In June 2020, a judge in Brumadinho county issued an injunction prohibiting protests by family members and those affected. Strategically, the victims concentrated at the entrance to the city and in front of the company's gates to publicly manifest the demand for reparations. The request for justice was then transformed into a misdemeanour subject to a fine.[8] Eleven people affected by the mining spill have become defendants in court for continuing to protest. In contrast, on 4 February 2021, the company concluded a financial agreement with the state and institutions of justice, without the participation of the affected families; the entire process was held in secret. With this settlement, the widespread collective damage that the company caused was resolved in court and, as a consequence, it can continue operating in the international commodities market without further problems with the Brazilian justice system.

Furthermore, the "public" character projected for the new memorial is again called into question when we consider that the land on which it is located is not part of the local public heritage, rather it is privately owned by the company, which will control the access to and use of the built space. The new place of memory designed as a place to remember the traumatic event and its fatal victims plays on evocation and a collective feeling, a "loss for us all", and thus avoids addressing the long history of social manifestations and struggles for rights of those affected by dams and mining companies active in Minas Gerais. By using mourning to generate a diffuse sense of solidarity for the victims of socio-environmental crime, the construction of the memorial materialises a specific way of perceiving the landscape and its relationship with the passage of time. Although remembering the fatal victims is an important step in the reparations demanded by their families and friends, the memorial financed by the mining company presents a narrative of the catastrophic events that minimises the continuous conflicts generated by the exploitation and ruination of the landscape as previously perceived and experienced by the local communities. Rather than observing the landscape as a marker of the passage of time and the effects of mining in general, the memorial focuses on a specific time-event in order to singularise it, isolating it from the chain of events and changes in the environment caused by centuries of mining.

Notes

1 The proposed design of the Memorial is available at: www.gustavopenna.com.br/memorialbrumadinho

2 Despite receiving financial assistance as compensation for mineral exploration, the cities in which this activity is located generally show comparatively low indicators of social development. In these places, situations of inequality and dependence on the mineral extraction industry feed on each other. On the one hand, poverty facilitates the establishment of extractive activities and the acceptance of their impacts, while on the other, the operations of the mining industry hinder the establishment of other economic activities, thus contributing to a reduction in the diversity of economic structure, such that dependence on the activity is created and reinforced by public and private investments (Milanez et al., 2016).

3 Since 1986, at least seven tailings dam ruptures have been recorded in Minas Gerais, leaving hundreds of people dead and thousands of people homeless, as well as causing serious water supply problems.

4 "Le culte du monument passé coexiste avec celui, bientôt nommé, de 'la modernité'." *L'allégorie du patrimoine* by Choay (1996).

5 Following privatisation, the mining company Vale do Rio Doce changed its name to Vale S.A. in 2008, becoming a publicly traded multinational. Sadly, and ironically, the Doce River, which gave the company its name for almost half a century, was destroyed by another tragedy caused by Vale in 2015.

6 Information concerning the memorial is based on the description provided by the architectural office responsible for the works: www.gustavopenna.com.br/memoria lbrumadinho (Portuguese only) and the site of Vale S.A.: www.vale.com/brasil/PT/a boutvale/news/Paginas/memorial-em-homenagem-as-vitimas-do-rompimento-da-barragem-sera-erguido.aspx (Portuguese only) Retrieved on: 10/2/2021.

7 Term of reference used by Vale S.A. www.vale.com/brasil/pt/aboutvale/news/ documents/versaofinal_valecom_tr_espaço%20de%20memória_brumadinho_homena gem%20às%20vítimas_vf%20_rev_case%20comunicação.pdf (Portuguese only) Retrieved on: 10/2/2021.

8 A report from one news outlet on this issue: https://recordtv.r7.com/balanco-geral/ videos/vitimas-de-brumadinho-viram-res-apos-juiza-proibir-protestos-de-moradores-11062020 (Portuguese only) Retrieved on: 10/2/2021.

References

Aguiar, L.B. (2013). Cidade morta, cidade documento, cidade turística: a construção de memórias sobre Ouro Preto. In C. Castro, A. Magalhães, and V. Salgueiro (eds.), *História do Turismo no Brasil*. Rio de Janeiro: FGV, pp. 180–193.

Castriota, L. (2019). Lidando com um patrimônio sensível. O caso de Bento Rodrigues, Mariana MG. *Arquitextos*, 20, online. Retrieved from: https://vitruvius.com.br/revista s/read/arquitextos/20.230/7423.

Choay, F. (1996). *L'allégorie du patrimoine*. Paris: Éditions du Seuil.

Deutsche, R. (1992). *Public Art and Its Uses*. In H. Senie and S. Webster (eds.), *Critical Issues in Public Art*. New York: Harper Collins, pp. 158–170.

Dupin, L.V. (2017). Les réseaux qui affinent: la conversion symbolique des fromages artisanaux à Minas Gerais, Brésil. *Vibrant*, 14(1).

Dupin, L.V. (2019). *A vida dos queijos mineiros: uma etnografia multiespécie*. Tese (doutorado) Campinas: Universidade Estadual de Campinas, Instituto de Filosofia e Ciências Humanas.

Fabre, D. (ed.) (2013). *Émotions patrimoniales*. Paris: Éditions MSH.

Felshin, N. (1995). *But Is It Art? The Spirit of Art as Activism*. Seattle: Bay Press.

Gomide, C.P., Coelho, T., Trocate, C., Milanez, B., and Wanderley, L. (eds.) (2018). *Dicionário crítico de mineração*. Marabá, PA: iGuana.

Gonçalves, R. (1996). *A retórica da perda: os discursos do patrimônio cultural no Brasil*. Rio de Janeiro: Editora UFRJ/IPHAN.

Howe, C., Lockrem, J., Appel, H., Hackett, E., Boyer, D., Hall, R., Schneider-Mayerson, M., Pope, A., Gupta, A., Rodwell, E., Ballestero, A., Durbin, T., el-Dahdah, F., Long, E., and Mody, C. (2016). Paradoxical Infrastructures: Ruins, Retrofit, and Risk. *Science, Technology, and Human Values*, 3(41): 1–19.

Ingold, T. (2000). *The Perception of the Environment*. Abingdon: Routledge.

Latour, B. (1994). *Jamais fomos modernos: ensaio de antropologia simétrica*. Rio de Janeiro: Editora 34.

Logan, W. and Reeves, K. (ed.). (2009). *Places of Pain and Shame*. Abingdon: Routledge.

Nora P. (1993). Entre Memória e História: a problemática dos lugares. *Proj. História*, (10): 7–28.

Oliveira, R. (2000). *O trabalho do antropólogo*. São Paulo: UNESP.

Pereira, E. (2014). *O Teatro da Religião*. Tese de doutorado em Antropologia Social. Rio de Janeiro: PPGAS/Museu Nacional/Universidade Federal do Rio de Janeiro.

Pereira, E. (2017). The Bodies of Christ: Performances and Agencies of Passion in Ouro Preto. *Vibrant*, 14(1).

Ragazzi, L. and Rocha, M. (2019). *Brumadinho: a engenharia de um crime*. Belo Horizonte: Editora Letramento.

Ruckys, Ú. A. and Machado, M. M. (2013). Patrimônio geológico e mineiro do Quadrilátero Ferrífero, Minas Gerais - caracterização e iniciativas de uso para educação e geoturismo. *Boletim Paranaense de Geociências*, 70: 120–136.

Simmel, G. (1996). A filosofia da paisagem. *Revista de Ciências Sociais: Política e Trabalho*, 12: 15–24.

Vianna, A. (2014). Etnografando documentos: uma antropóloga em meio a processos judiciais. In S. Castilho, A. de Souza Lima, and C. Teixeira (eds.), *Antropologia das Práticas de Poder: reflexões etnográficas sobre burocratas, elites e corporações*. Rio de Janeiro: ContraCapa/LACED, pp. 43–70.

Young, J. E. (1992). The Counter-Monument: Memory Against Itself in Germany Today. *Critical Inquiry* 18(2): 267–296.

Zonta, M. and Trocate, C.(eds.) (2016). *Antes fosse mais leve a carga: reflexões sobre o desastre da Samarco/Vale/BHP Billiton*. Iguana: Nova Marabà.

14 Damming the past

Interplay between landscape heritage and water management

Mesut Dinler and Özgün Özçakır

Introduction

The 1963 Turkish movie *Dry Summer* (Susuz Yaz)[1] is a rural story that takes place in the western Turkish village of Urla in the İzmir province. The main narrative of the film centres around the problem of distributing water to the fields of the villagers. This problem soon triggers both cascading conflicts among the villagers, who gradually turn into criminals because of dysfunctional legal sanctions, and family disputes, in which a young woman becomes a victim of violence. In the dramatic story of *Dry Summer*, economic and societal dynamics centre around water and landscape management, which is a theme that is shaped by the political underpinnings of the Cold War, especially through managing river basins with the realisation of large dam projects. The close alliance between the United States (US) and Turkey in the post-war context has led to US-supported dam-based economic development projects throughout the 1960s and 1970s. These projects did not only trigger immense changes in the landscape, but also in the community experiences. This theme is significant to the notion of "landscape heritage" as well, because the development of the term underlines the role of community and brings into focus the way that communities interact with and perceive the landscape.

Dam projects have, historically, played an immense role in completely transforming (terminating, in most cases) the relationship between communities and their environment. The development goal that dam projects promise, and their underlying political dynamics, have a profound impact that still shapes current landscape management regimes to this day. As will be shown with the case study of the Ilısu Dam, although the main premise of such dam projects is "development", the lived experience of the communities is usually dislocation; the term development is limited to the financial gain of a limited community of local and global elites. Within this context, the main aim of this chapter is both to show how the Ilısu Dam exemplifies the impact of dam projects on landscape heritage, and to provide a framework in which the current heritage management scheme in Turkey, particularly the cultural landscape heritage around the city of Hasankeyf that has already been destroyed by the Ilısu Dam construction, is understood, not as a standalone case, but within an almost century-long historical continuum.

DOI: 10.4324/9781003195238-14

In the post-war rearrangement of the world order, technology exports (especially by the US to other countries) functioned as a reinforcement of the US perception of what civilisation and society should be (Adas, 2006; Ekbladh, 2010). Dams have been perceived as potential generators of global development, and responses to the need for food production. However, as technological instruments, dam projects were also the products of political dynamics (Sneddon, 2015).

Despite the domination of large dams on the landscape, at least since 2000, when the World Commission on Dams – WCD[2] published its well-known report *Dams and development: A new framework for decision-making*, dam construction is now internationally questioned. In the report, the WCD acknowledges the past benefits of dams to human development, yet it also states that "an unacceptable and often unnecessary price has been paid to secure those benefits, especially in social and environmental terms, by people displaced, by communities downstream, by taxpayers and by the natural environment". Although the report makes no reference to landscape heritage, the negative impact of dam construction on heritage is evident, at least since the 1960s. One of the most emblematic cases that highlights the complex dynamics between global techno-politics of dam construction and landscape heritage is the construction of the Aswan High Dam, in Egypt and Sudan, in the 1960s.[3] A UNESCO-led international campaign was launched to rescue the to-be-submerged Pharaonic temples and has been a milestone in the emergence of the idea of "international cultural property" (Meskell, 2018).[4]

In Turkey, in 2020, a half-century-long debate concluded with the construction of the Ilısu Dam. As will be discussed further, due to the internationally acknowledged significance of the landscape heritage of Hasankeyf, the main controversy was centred around heritage discussions, as well as the socio-economic aspects of the project and environmental consequences have also been the subject of various scholarly studies.

Constructing the dam or preserving the heritage?

The above-mentioned UNESCO rescue campaign of the 1960s, as Meskell (2018, p.57) notes, "united, on a grand stage, development and large-scale infrastructures with international economics and politics while playing off former colonial and Cold War tensions within a peopled landscape where the past held ambivalent connotations". This historical moment, in fact, was a continuum of a landscape management experiment from the 1930s in Southern USA, that lead to the construction of the Ilısu Dam in the late 2010s and early 2020s.

The 1933 Tennessee Valley Authority (TVA) in the US, as one of the flagship programs of President Roosevelt, was designed as a government initiative acting as a private company to construct dams in the southern US lands[5] that are cut through by the Tennessee River (covering portions of seven states: Tennessee, Alabama, Mississippi, Kentucky, Georgia, North Carolina, and

Virginia). In addition, the US Bureau of Reclamation, which oversaw water development projects in the US in the 1930s, acted as an agency that fought against communism in other countries through the export of technical know-how and capacity from the post-war era to the 1970s (Sneddon, 2015, p.4).[6] Not only in Turkey, but in many countries in Asia, Africa, South America, and the Middle East, the bureau continued to construct dams and built capacity through training local engineers and providing technical assistance. In the 1950s, the bureau became deeply involved in water projects in Turkey, in close collaboration with technicians from the DSİ (Devlet Su İşleri – State Hydraulic Works) which was modelled after the Bureau of Reclamation (Sneddon, 2015, p.82; Luke, 2019, pp.102–104).

One of the most important Turkish political figures of the 1960s and 1970s, Süleyman Demirel (who was the on/off prime minister of this period), was one of the engineers at DSİ who had visited the US Bureau of Reclamation in 1949, benefiting from an Eisenhower Fellowship, where he learnt about the activities of TVA. He became the Director-General of DSİ from its establishment in 1955 to 1960, launching many dam projects all over Turkey, enough to be called the "King of Dams" (Akbulut et al., 2018). In the 1960s, the first ideas to realise GAP (Güneydoğu Anadolu Projesi – Southeastern Anatolia Project) also took shape. GAP is still the largest and most expensive project in the Republic of Turkey's history to date. Covering nine provinces in the Euphrates-Tigris Basin and Upper Mesopotamia plains (Adıyaman, Batman, Diyarbakır, Gaziantep, Kilis, Mardin, Siirt, Şanlıurfa, and Şırnak), GAP was conceived in the 1970s as a program aimed at expanding the region's water and land resources. The plans were to build 22 dams, 19 hydraulic power plants, and irrigation projects encompassing 1.8 million hectares of land (GAP Regional Development Administration, no date).

It is noteworthy that, simultaneously, heritage experts could enact a strong heritage movement that aligned Turkish preservation standards with international (especially European) developments (Dinler, 2022). Therefore, the pressure for development and the heritage movement coalesced to historically form the complex dynamics of landscape heritage at Hasankeyf, starting from the first attempts to construct Ilısu Dam, which was initially designed within the GAP Project. GAP has undoubtedly generated several benefits, in terms of agricultural and energy production, but its impact on the landscape, cultural heritage, and socio-economic structure of the inhabitants living within the dam construction areas is rather disruptive. Eberlein et al. (2010) analysed the impact of GAP and underlined that several disadvantaged communities (particularly the landless and the poor) were confronted with vulnerabilities and substantial losses. Moreover, many cultural, religious, and archaeological sites were flooded (Harris, 2002), in addition to various unsolved ecological problems such as erosion, sedimentation, salinisation, and problems with water quality (Sahan et al., 2001).[7] The historically significant landscape of Hasankeyf has already been lost, that is, the traditional vernacular architecture and other significant, intangible characteristics because of the Ilısu Dam.

Landscape as heritage and Hasankeyf as landscape heritage

According to the Council of Europe, the term "landscape" "means an area, as perceived by people, whose character is the result of the actions and interaction of natural and/or human factors" (CoE, 2000). Drafted throughout the 1990s and finally published in Florence in 2000, this document locates the role of people, citizens, and communities at the core of landscape.[8] The role of human interaction in the definition of landscape is underlined by many scholars. For instance, Eugenio Turri frames the landscape as "the reflection of our actions, the measure of our living and working in the territory" (Turri, 1998) and Salvatore Settis sees it as a representation of the territory, arguing that its preservation is a civic duty since its degradation is interlinked with social degradation (Settis, 2010, pp.252–253). This representational power of landscape inevitably enacts social dynamics when we talk about the heritagisation of landscapes. Scholars of critical heritage studies have already shown that conflict and contestation are embedded in the very nature of heritage (Ashworth, Graham, and Snippe, 2007) and the case of Hasankeyf shows how these dynamics become visible through heritagisation and deheritagization.

Hasankeyf is a prehistoric settlement and its oldest surviving elements date back to the Middle Ages. It had later been the centre of the Silk Road in the Tigris valley that reaches the Gulf of Basra. Hasankeyf was mentioned in historic sources since Assyrian times under different names (such as Kepa, Kipani, Cepha, Hesna de Cepha, Hısn-ı Kayfa), all of which are variations of the word cepha, which means rock in Sumerian (Arık, 2004). The villages constructed on the dolomite and limestone mountains[9] and the Medieval monuments constructed in the Dicle Valley (as well as the castle and now-submerged rock caves) are the elements that define the landscape heritage characteristics of Hasankeyf (Ahunbay and Balkiz, 2009) (Figure 14.1). Hasankeyf was registered as a national heritage property on 14 April 1978 and became a "natural protection area" in 1981.

Two years after its registration in 1978, the plans for Ilısu Dam were being drafted to make way for the dam. It may seem ironic that Hasankeyf was granted official protection status in a period when plans to destroy it with a dam was on the state agenda, however, as explained above, this bipolar approach between expert-led historic preservation and economic development was a definitive essence of the 1970s (Dinler, 2021). The 1980 coup d'etàt did not only reinitialise the power dynamics with a neoliberal state structure but also defined a key momentum point for accelerating the realisation process of GAP through private investments. As presented in Figure 14.1, in more than half a century, GAP never lost its importance despite the drawbacks of dam-based development.

Constructing the Ilısu Dam in Hasankeyf: processes and actors

The destruction of cultural heritage in favour of dam construction is not a rare practice in Turkey. Ilısu Dam in Hasankeyf, the dam projects at Zeugma (a

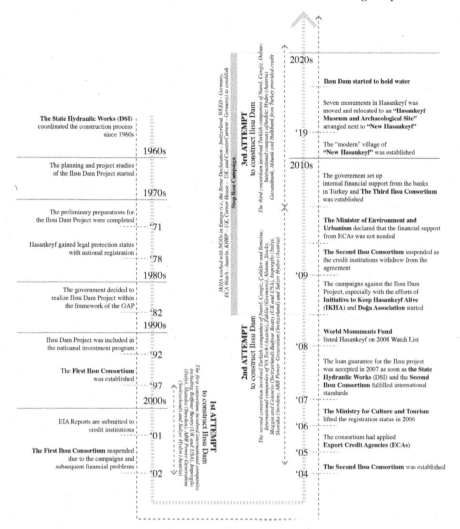

Figure 14.1. Project development process of the Ilısu Dam and the actors involved
Source: Produced by the authors

Roman garrison city near Gaziantep, in Southeastern Turkey) and Allianoi (an ancient spa centre near Pergamon, in Western Turkey) sparked widespread public and scholarly interest over the inundation of cultural heritage of global significance. These are examples of the conflict between water management and heritage preservation. As such, a brief overview of the history of the Ilısu Dam is important, to both underline the complexity of managing/preserving landscape heritage and demonstrate the diversity of the actors involved in these processes.

Following the feasibility studies for the construction of the Ilısu Dam over the Tigris River in the 1960s (Sami, 2010), in 1971 the preliminary preparations were completed and in 1982, the government ratified the project, reframing its future realisation within the framework of the above-mentioned GAP. The first attempt to build the dam through the state-designed Build-Operate-Transfer (BOT)[10] model had failed due to a lack of investors (Hildyard et al., 2000). The First Ilısu Consortium was established in 1997 by the government, to initiate the project involving various international companies (Nelson, 2000).[11] However, due to the protests against the Ilısu Dam, the First Ilısu Consortium was suspended in 2002 and, thus, the project stopped (Hasankeyfi, 2019).

In 2004, under the Justice and Development Party (AKP) government that still runs the country (as at 2021), the Second Ilısu Consortium was established.[12] At that stage, the project became a transnational and international, political and financial decision, rather than a national one (Warner, 2008). In 2005, the consortium had applied to ECAs (Export Credit Agencies) in Germany, Austria, and Sweden and ECAs asked for the satisfaction of 153 prerequisites to guarantee the loan.[13] The loan for the Ilısu project was provisionally guaranteed in 2007, as soon as DSİ and the Second Ilısu Consortium fulfilled the prerequisites (Aykaç and Kaya, 2020).[14]

With these developments, the fight to defend the protection of the Hasankeyf landscape heritage, especially with the efforts of "Initiative to Keep Hasankeyf Alive (IKHA)"[15] and the "Doğa (Nature) Association",[16] started in 2007, aiming to increase awareness about the possible catastrophic natural, social, and cultural consequences of the project. The IKHA worked with NGOs in Europe which especially focus on certain aspects of Hasankeyf, such as human rights, poverty reduction, environmental protection, and environmental and social justice, to form "the Stop Ilısu" campaign which has publicized the brutish project and its looming cultural, human rights, and environmental abuses. ICOMOS Austria, ICOMOS Germany and ICOMOS Switzerland also highlighted the destructive impact of Ilısu Dam to the government authorities responsible for the loan guarantees for the Second Ilısu Consortium. Besides, ICOMOS Turkey worked with several other NGOs and local people to stop the construction of the dam (Machat, Ziesemer, and Petzet, 2008). As such, there is no doubt that the international and national heritage community was united against the construction of Ilısu Dam and advocated the preservation of Hasankeyf.

After it was revealed by the Ilısu Committee of Experts (established to assess whether Turkey fulfilled the requirement of 153 prerequisites) that the project did not satisfy international standards for resettlement, ecology, riparian states, and protection of cultural heritage (Eberlein et al., 2010), the credit institutions withdrew from the agreement in 2009 (Hasankeyf'i, 2019). At that point, the Minister of Forestry and Environment at that time (Veysel Eroğlu) declared that the ECAs' financial support was not needed to build the dam (Bakan, 2009), as the Turkish Government set up internal financial support from the Turkish banks for the Ilısu Project's completion.

It is noteworthy that 2010 marked a sharp change in the environmental policies of the AKP government, in terms of both increasing the central power limiting the capabilities of local authorities (Kuyucu, 2018) and encouraging state-led private sector-managed gentrification projects in historic urban areas (Özçakır, Bilgin Altınöz, and Mignosa, 2018). The Ilısu Dam construction in Hasankeyf then gained pace. In 2010, the state-built "modern" village of "New Hasankeyf" was established and at the first stage, 45 families who once lived in old Hasankeyf moved there. The seven monuments in old Hasankeyf were moved and relocated to an "open-air museum" arranged next to "New Hasankeyf" to "save" the cultural heritage from being submerged by the summer of 2019,

Afterwards, on the morning of 23 July 2019, Ilısu Dam started to hold water and, today, old Hasankeyf is almost submerged; its landscape heritage is almost totally lost (Hasankeyfi, 2019). With a half-century in between, the rescue campaign for the Nubian Temples from the High Aswan Dam is replicated on a smaller scale in Hasankeyf, using the very same methods.

Aftermath of Ilısu Dam in Hasankeyf

Initially, there were ten different alternatives for the location of the dam, and the current one was thought to be the best option by the Turkish Government (Su Hakkı, 2010). However, as evidenced by Yalçın and Tigrek (2016), it was possible to save Hasankeyf and its heritage with the five-dam system instead of one mega-dam at approximately the same cost. Besides, Akkaya et al. (2009) and Tüzün (2010) emphasised that the Ilısu Dam is not a remedy for the rising energy demand in Turkey and questions remain, in terms of its efficiency, considering the damage that it may inflict on the cultural heritage, natural landscape, biological environment, and inhabitants.

Dajani (2013) reflected on her observations on the disparities caused by the Ilısu Dam by highlighting that multi-national corporations and elitists benefited from the project, while all the negative consequences were experienced by the local communities who are more prone to poverty. The locals had been making their living mostly on fishing, and as they are separated from the natural resources due the rising water levels resulting from the dam, their incomes were drastically reduced. Bimay (2021) also highlighted the decline in the inhabitants' socio-economic status after the construction of Ilısu Dam, as tourism activities are not as vibrant before. Yoksu (2021) provided evidence of the inequalities between the ağas[17] and the villagers based on his interview with one of villagers, who declared that the government had first made the houses of ağas but the villagers were left alone. However, Hasankeyf's District Governor had said that "Hasankeyf will be transformed into a very modern city in the new settlement site. With restaurants, accommodation facilities, and so forth, it will have much better opportunities than it has today" (Harte, 2013).

Conclusion

The involved stakeholders of the project are threefold: (i) Governments for their lack of strategic planning, as well as their prioritisation of political and economic criteria above environmental parameters in policy planning; (ii) large multi-national companies for their insufficient environmental and socio-cultural awareness and profit-driven practices; and (iii) non-governmental organisations for their campaigns against the Ilısu Dam, protecting villagers' interests and striving to save Hasankeyf's landscape heritage.

In a setting with the multiple stakeholders, the construction of a large hydropower project like Ilısu Dam is not only a technical venture but also involves a complex governance process and complicated financial organisation. Ilısu Dam is also a historic extension of the imagination of the US in a post-war world. With an ambitious agricultural reprogramming project (that was mainly managed by the US Bureau of Reclamation based on the TVA model), the US exported technical knowledge on dams through diplomatic encounters and raised politicians/officials in the countries of investment with a future vision of forming loyal alliances. On the other hand, it was not just a dam but a living thing that constantly changed and evolved depending on the power dynamics. Despite the well-acknowledged negative impacts of dam-based development (which is evident in WCD's report) and the national and international cultural activist campaigns, Ilısu Dam was constructed, the landscape heritage of Hasankeyf submerged, and people were displaced.

In the movie *Dry Summer*, Osman Ağa, the eldest of a two-brother family, constructs a small reservoir in his field, blocking the downfall of water to other fields. When he kills one of the villagers, he convinces his younger brother Hasan to take the blame and go to prison, then abuses Hasan's young wife Bahar with lies and abuse. Based on the memoirs and stories of the eminent Turkish author, Necati Cumali, these mid-century stories describe the Anatolian rural landscape and depict how the control of water activates social violence. Yet, at the end of the movie, this violence turns back to Osman. In Hasankeyf, it may seem like a decades-long debate has been concluded with the displacement of people and loss of landscape heritage. However, as Dry Summer narrates, once activated, power dynamics do not stop and also damage the powerholders, as long as the equal distribution of resources and consensual management of the processes are not granted.

Notes

1 Directed by Metin Erksan and based on the short story by Necati Cumalı, *Dry Summer* is representative of Turkish neorealism in cinema. It won the grand prize Golden Bear in the 1963 Berlin Film Festival and was restored in 2008 by Martin Scorsese's World Cinema Project initiative.

2 The WCD was established by the World Bank and IUCN in 1998, due to the worldwide opposition against large dams. In its main findings, the report also stated that "large dams have been a long–time favourite of politicians, government officials, dam building companies and development banks. They have provided opportunities for corruption and favouritism and have skewed decision–making away from cheaper and more effective options". The reception of the report has been contradictory and people in the dam business even condemned it (Sneddon, 2015, pp.2–3).

3 The first Aswan Dam was constructed at the turn of the twentieth century, strengthened and raised in height in 1907–12, and raised again in 1929–33. In the 1960s, the construction of the High Dam was triggered with Cold War politics and the interest of countries over the Suez Canal, see Laron (2013).

4 In addition to UNESCO's rescue campaign, the contemporary heritagization process of the renowned Egyptian architect Hasan Fathy's New Gourna Village project (designed with local materials and vernacular architectural inspirations) and the recent UNESCO campaign for the safeguarding of Fathy's village show how certain heritage dynamics are centred around the construction of the High Aswan Dam, not only in terms of submerging ancient temples but also producing new heritage items. For Fathy's design, see Fathy (1973). For a critique of the relationship between Egypt's changing political milieu and Fathy's architectural response, see Rabbat (2003). For a post-colonial approach to the political background of heritage dynamics in Egypt, see Mitchell (2002, pp.179–205).

5 The power of the TVA model in social engineering and economic development did not only impress Julian S. Huxley, who was the first Director-General of UNESCO but also had an influence on the members of CIAM (the Congrès Internationaux d'Architecture Moderne), including the most famous CIAM member Le Corbusier, in terms of "decentralization and the potential of mechanized agriculture to revive family" (Luke, 2019, pp.79–81).

6 One of the most emblematic instances to demonstrate how the technical knowledge of dam construction relates to Cold War politics, as well as regional nation-making dynamics, is the design process of the Pa Mong dam on the Mekong River throughout the 1960s (Sneddon, 2012).

7 International rescue archaeology projects supplanted the Keban and Atatürk dams constructed across the Euphrates River in the 1960s and 1980s, but only a small portion of the cultural heritage in the dam reservoir areas was salvaged.

8 Although the UNESCO World Heritage Convention of 1972 (Convention concerning the Protection of the World Cultural and Natural Heritage) also refers to the integrity of culture and nature, the role of communities has remained rather undervalued until the 2013 Recommendation on the Historic Urban Landscape. Therefore, the interest of the heritage community on the social dynamics activated by the landscape heritage is relatively recent.

9 The Tigris River is one of the main rivers that flow through Mesopotamia and contributes to the formation of a cave-like landscape heritage. For over 10,000 years, it served as the primary source of freshwater for humans and other ecosystems. The river flows through a variety of ecosystems, including dense canyons, humid gallery forests, semi-desert sandbanks, and calcareous steppes (Biricik and Karakaş, 2012).

10 A Build-Operate-Transfer (BOT) contract is a project delivery mechanism that is commonly employed for big "Public-Private Partnerships (PPP)" projects. The term PPP refers to a wide range of collaborations between the public and commercial sectors that benefit both parties (Açıkgöz, 2020).

A BOT contract is one in which a private company agrees to complete a project, i.e. an infrastructure project such as Ilısu Dam in Hasankeyf, in exchange for a concession from a public sector partner, usually a government department, to finance and build it. The private organisation is then given the right to operate the project for a set amount of time, in exchange for a financial benefit.

11 Balfour Beatty (UK and USA), Impregilo (Italy), Skanska (Sweden), ABB Power Generation (Switzerland), and Sulzer Hydro (Austria).

12 The consortium involved four companies from Turkey and six companies from Europe: Nurol, Cengiz, Çelikler, Temelsu International from Turkey; VA Tech from Austria; Züblin from Germany; Alstom, Stucky, Maggia and Colencio from Switzerland.

13 153 prerequisites are related to environmental and social principles of the World Bank, World Dams Commission and the United Nations, aiming to minimise the impact of the infrastructure projects on society and the environment.

14 At that time, as the possibility of realisation of the Ilısu Dam project increased, an international reaction also emerged against the possible loss of Hasankeyf landscape heritage. One instance of this reaction is the World Monument Fund's listing Hasankeyf in its 2008 Watch List of the World's 100 Most Endangered Sites (World Monuments Fund, n.d.).

15 In January 2006, the Initiative to Keep Hasankeyf Alive (Hasankeyf'i Yaşatma Girişimi) was created by 20 human rights and environmental organisations from Diyarbakıir, Batman, Hasankeyf, and Ilıısu. One year later, the campaign had brought together 73 independent organisations, including the concerned municipalities, local and international NGOs (like the Berne Declaration [today known as Public Eye] – Switzerland, WEED – Germany, ECA Watch – Austria, KHRP – UK, Corner House – UK, and Counter Current – Germany), associations, and unions – something unprecedented in Turkey (Eberlein et al., 2010).

16 The work of the Doğa Association (Doğa Derneği) is motivated by the need to take steps to save biodiversity. Their goal is to protect the rights of nature in all of its ways, including the processes that are needed for the survival of life on Earth (Who we are, n.d.).

17 A powerful person who has vast lands suitable for agriculture in the rural areas' feudal and patriarchal traditions, whose word is law where he has the authority.

References

Açıkgöz, B. (2020). Public-Private Partnership – The Case of Turkey. In H. Kiral and T. Akdemir (eds.), *Public Financial Management Reforms in Turkey: Progress and Challenges, Volume 1*. Springer, Singapore, pp. 105–118.

Adas, M. (2006). *Dominance by Design: Technological Imperatives and America's Civilizing Mission*. Cambridge: Belknap Press.

Ahunbay Z. and Balkız Ö. (2009). *Outstanding Universal Value of Hasankeyf and the Tigris Valley, Doğa Derneği*. Online. Retrieved from: www.dogadernegi.org/wp-content/up loads/2015/10/Outstanding-universal-value-of-hasankeyf-and-the-tigris-valley.pdf.

Akbulut, B., Adaman, F., and Arsel, M. (2018). Troubled Waters of Hegemony Consent and Contestation in Turkey's Hydropower Landscapes. In Menga, F. and Swyngedouw, E. (eds.), *Water, Technology and the Nation-state*. Abingdon: Routledge, pp. 96–114.

Akkaya, U., Gultekin, A.B., Dikmen, and C.B, Durmus, G. (2009). *The Analysis of Environmental Impacts of Dams and Hydroelectric Power Plants (HEPP): Sample of Ilısu Dam*, 5th International Advanced Technologies Symposium (IATS'09), 13–15 May 2009, Karabük, Türkiye, 2212–2218.

Arık, M.O. (2004). *Hasankeyf: üç dünyanın buluştuğu kent [Hasankeyf: the town where three worlds meet]*. Istanbul: Türkiye İş Bankası Kültür.

Ashworth, G., Graham, B., and Snippe, J.T. (2007). *Pluralising Pasts: Heritage, Identity and Place in Multicultural Societies*. London: Pluto Press.

Aykaç, P. and Kaya, B. (2020). Hasankeyf'te Sona Yaklaşırken: Korumada İnsan Odaklı Yaklaşımlar ve İnsan Hakkı Olarak Kültürel Miras [Toward the End in Hasankeyf: People-Centred Approaches in Conservation and Cultural Heritage as Human Rights], *Mimarlık* 411: 12–17.

Bakan kararlı konuştu (2009) Ilısu'da desteğe ihtiyaç yok. (8 July2009) Retrieved from: www.cnnturk.com/2009/turkiye/07/08/bakan.kararli.konustu.Ilısuda.destege.ihtiyac. yok/534107.0/index.html.

Bimay, M. (2021) Spatial, Social and Environmental Effects of Forced Displacement due to Dam Construction: The Case of Hasankeyf. *Econharran*, 5(7): 49–83.

Biricik, M. and Karakas, R. (2012). Birds of Hasankeyf (South-Eastern Anatolia, Turkey) Under the Threat of a Big Dam Project. *Natural Areas Journal*, 32(1): 96–105.

CoE, Council of Europe Landscape Convention, Bruxelles, 2000. Retrieved from: www.coe.int/en/web/landscape.

Dajani, M. (2013). *Environmental Activism: The Case of Hasankeyf and the Ilısu Dam.* Berlin: Heinrich Böll Stiftung.

Dinler, M. (2022). A Political Framework for Understanding Heritage Dynamics in Turkey (1950–1980). *Urban History*, 49(2), 364–382.

Dinler, M. (2021). Formulation of Historic Residential Architecture as a Background to Urban Conservation, *Journal of Cultural Heritage Management and Sustainable Development*, 11(1): 1–17.

Eberlein, C., Drillisch, H., Ayboga, E., and Wenidoppler, T. (2010). The Ilısu Dam in Turkey and the Role of the Export Credit Agencies and NGO Networks. *Water Alternatives*, 3(2): 291.

Ekbladh, D. (2010). *The Great American Mission: Modernization and the Construction of an American World Order.* Princeton: Princeton University Press.

Fathy, H. (1973). *Architecture for the Poor.* Chicago: University of Chicago Press.

Gambino, R. (2011). *Il paesaggio tra coesione e competitività.* Trento: Forum Osservatorio del Paesaggio.

GAP Regional Development Administration. (n.d.). Retrieved from: www.gap.gov.tr/en/what-s-gap-page-1.html.

Harris, L.M. (2002). Water and Conflict Geographies of the South-eastern Anatolia Project. *Society and Natural Resources*, 15(8): 743–759.

Harte, J. (2013) Rare Footage of Ilısu: The Dam That Will Flood Homes and History Across Southern Turkey. Retrieved from: https://blog.nationalgeographic.org/2013/08/22/rare-footage-of-Ilısu-the-dam-that-will-flood-homes-and-history-across-southern-turkey/.

Hasankeyf'i Yaşatma Girişimi. (2019). Retrieved from: www.hasankeyfgirisimi.net/turk ce-Ilısu-baraji-ve-hidroelektrik-santrali-projesi-elestiri-raporu/?lang=tr.

Hildyard, N., Tricarico, A., Eberhard, S., Drillisch, H., and Norlen, D. (2000). *If the River Were a Pen … The Ilisu Dam, the World Commission on Dams and Export Credit Reform.* London: The Corner House.

Kuyucu, T. (2018). Politics of Urban Regeneration in Turkey: Possibilities and Limits of Municipal Regeneration Initiatives in a Highly Centralized Country, *Urban Geography* 39(8): 1152–1176.

Laron, G. (2013). *Origins of the Suez Crisis: Post-war Development Diplomacy and the Struggle over Third World Industrialization, 1945–1956.* Baltimore: Johns Hopkins University Press.

Luke, C. (2019). *A Pearl in Peril Heritage: Heritage and Diplomacy in Turkey.* New York: Oxford University Press.

Machat, C., Ziesemer, J., and Petzet, M. (2008). *Heritage at Risk: ICOMOS World Report 2006–2007 on Monuments and Sites in Danger.* Berlin: hendrik Bäßler verlag.

Meskell, L. (2018). *A Future in Ruins: UNESCO, World Heritage, and the Dream of Peace.* New York: Oxford University Press.

Mitchell, T. (2002). *Rule of Experts: Egypt, Techno-politics, Modernity.* Berkeley: University of California Press.

Nelson, J. (2000). *The Business of Peace: The Private Sector as a Partner in Conflict Prevention and Resolution.* London: Prince of Wales Business Leaders Forum. Retrieved from:

https://media.business-humanrights.org/media/documents/files/reports-and-materials/Ilısu-Dam.htm.

Özçakır, Ö., Bilgin Altınöz, G., and Mignosa, A. (2018). Political Economy of Renewal of Heritage Places in Turkey, *METU Journal of Faculty of Architecture*, 35(2): 221–250.

Rabbat, N. (2003). Hassan Fathy and the Identity Debate. In G. Tawadros and S. Campbell, (eds.), *Fault Lines: Contemporary African Art and Shifting Landscapes*. London: Institute of International Visual Art, pp. 196–203.

Sahan, E., Zogg, A., Mason, S.A., and Gilli, A. (2001). *Case-study: South-eastern Anatolia Project in Turkey – GAP*. Zurich: Swiss Federal Institute of Technology.

Sami, K. (2010). ILISU BARAJI: Sürdürülebilir Toplumsal Hayata "Ket Vurma" ve Su Toplama Havzasında Sivil (Kırsal) Mimari Yerleşimlerin Serencamı [ILISU DAM: "Inhibition" of Sustainable Social Life and Aftermath of the Architectural Civic (Rural) Settlements in the Water Basins], *Mimarlık*, 353.

Settis, S. (2010). *Paesaggio. Costituzione. Cemento. La battaglia per l'ambiente contro il degrado civile [Landscape, Constitution, Cement: The battle for the ambient against the civil degradation]*. Torino: Einaudi.

Sneddon, C. (2012). The "Sinew of Development": Cold War Geopolitics, Technical Expertise, and Water Resource Development in Southeast Asia, 1954–1975. *Social Studies of Science*, 42(4): 564–590.

Sneddon, C. (2015). *Concrete Revolution: Large Dams, Cold War Geopolitics, and the US Bureau of Reclamation*. Chicago: University of Chicago Press.

Su Hakkı. (2010). Ilısu Barajı ve Hidroelektrik Santralı Projesinin insan, kültür ve çevre üzerindeki etkileri. Retrieved from: www.suhakki.org/2010/03/Ilısu-baraji-ve-hidroelektrik-santrali-projesinin-insan-kultur-ve-cevre-uzerindeki-etkileri/.

Turri, E. (1998). *Il paesaggio come teatro. Dal territorio vissuto al territorio rappresentato [The landscape as a theatre: From the lived territory to the represented territory]*. Venezia: Marsilio.

Tüzün, N.M. (2010). Ilısu-Hasankeyf-Enerji. Ne Uğruna? Kimin İçin? [Isilu-Hasankeyf-Energy: For What? For Whom?]. *Diyarch Mimarlık Bülteni*, 44–47.

Warner, J. (2008). Contested Hydrohegemony: Hydraulic Control and Security in Turkey. *Water Alternatives*, 1(2): 271–288.

World Commission on Dams (WDC) (2000). *Dams and Development: A New Framework for Decision-Making. A Report of the World Commission on Dams*. London: Earthscan.

Yalçın, E. and Tigrek, S. (2016). Hydropower production Without Sacrificing Environment: A Case Study of Ilısu Dam and Hasankeyf, *International Journal of Water Resources Development*, 32(2): 247–266.

Yoksu, M.Ö. (2021). Suya gömülen Hasankeyf'ten sonrası: Elektriksiz, susuz derme çatma yaşamlar [After the submerged Hasankeyf: Without electricity, without water, flimsy lives]. Retrieved from: https://yesilgazete.org/suya-gomulen-hasankeyften-sonrasi-elektriksiz-susuz-derme-catma-yasamlar/.

15 Heritage landscapes and cues to care

Exploring the concepts of guardianship and care within a forgotten rural New Zealand cemetery

Shannon Davis and Jacky Bowring

Introduction

As an overgrown site within a mundane and perfunctory agricultural landscape, the cemetery at Ashley Dene Farm (formally known as the Burnham Cemetery) could be read as insignificant. However, through the lens of critical landscape heritage, the cemetery and its setting are recognized as important, evolving, relational elements. This chapter reveals how an emphasis on care and a novel use of a theory from landscape ecology can be applied to the cemetery site to support its continued state of becoming and ensure its protection from the possibility of erasure through neglect.

The cemetery at Ashley Dene Farm slips through the net of conventional, formal heritage recognition. In Aotearoa New Zealand, the criteria for formal heritage recognition are set out in the Heritage New Zealand Pouhere Taonga Act 2014, section 66(3), with the overarching proviso for satisfying the requirement that "the place reflects important or representative aspects of New Zealand history" (Heritage New Zealand Pouhere Taonga Act 2014). The criteria include providing knowledge of New Zealand history, importance to tangata whenua (people of the land), public esteem, community association, public education, technical or design aspects, symbolic or commemorative value, rare and very early examples, and being part of an extensive complex of historic elements. Further criteria relate specifically to Māori (indigenous peoples of Aotearoa New Zealand) cultural heritage, and the importance of sites to iwi (tribes) and hapū (sub-tribes). The cemetery at Ashley Dene Farm falls outside these criteria, as even despite it being the earliest European cemetery on the Canterbury Plains, this is a provincial rather than national context. Further, the cemetery's integrity was eroded with the removal of the chapel, as explained further below.

It is within the framing of critical landscape heritage that a site like the cemetery at Ashley Dene Farm registers as an integral part of the cultural landscape. Critical landscape heritage parallels critical heritage in the shift from conventional and traditional views of heritage, but in a landscape setting. Landscape heritage is an

DOI: 10.4324/9781003195238-15

aspect of heritage which is challenged by dimensions of scale and temporal change. While conventional heritage was typically concerned with buildings and artefacts, landscape heritage focuses on valued environmental settings. As MacKenzie and Saniga explain, the evolution of landscape heritage was accelerated through Australia's Burra Charter (1979) "which was in part a rejection of the architectural emphasis of European charters [and] significant cultural landscapes – both designed and organically evolved – have been identified and protected" (MacKenzie and Saniga, 2015: 2).

However, the concept of landscape as heritage implies that there is value ascribed to the site, that it is something that can be inherited. As Goodchild notes, such landscapes can include cultivated rural landscapes, that are "settled by humans and where arable cultivation (i.e. ploughing, or having the surface broken up) and the growing of non-local plants are a main feature of the local economy and way of life" (Goodchild, 2008: 196). Goodchild adds that heritage landscapes include a mix of both natural and cultural heritage (Goodchild, 2008: 197). In the case of Ashley Dene Farm cemetery there is a tension between the practical values associated with farming and production and the spiritual, cultural, and aesthetic values of the cemetery. The farm is now owned by Lincoln University and is managed in two parts, as a dryland research farm and as an irrigated research and development station. Although the cemetery is part of lands that fall under the management of the Anglican Property Trust, because it is landlocked within the farm it appears to have become a forgotten landscape. There are also tensions between natural and cultural dimensions of the landscape, as the abandoned cemetery has become an untended enclave within the farmed landscape, therefore undergoing its own natural processes of colonisation by plants. Resolving these tensions are intertwined with research on the history of the farm and its cemetery, and with consideration of its potential future from a heritage perspective.

Landscape is challenging in the context of heritage. While buildings and artefacts are relatively stable over time, landscapes are constantly changing. These temporal and ephemeral shifts raise questions over the condition that is of value, what is the actual "heritage landscape"? The protection of object-based heritage is, from a logistical point of view, straightforward. Through being placed in a controlled context like a museum, or by the use of rules and regulations to prevent alteration or demolition, artefacts' and buildings' heritage values can be captured. While there are aspects of heritage that are inevitably in flux, such as changing cultural and political perspectives on heritage, the objects themselves can remain unchanging. Landscapes, however, cannot be removed into protected and controlled settings, and directing that they remain unchanged is not viable in the context of environmental processes. Such a principle of "control" is in tension with the landscape's temporality. Geographer Edward Relph, drawing on the work of philosopher Martin Heidegger, suggests the concept of "environmental humility", which as he says, "promotes guardianship rather than control of environments and communities" (Relph, 2015: 8).

While guardianship is adopted as an ethos of care, the operationalization of this requires a language of landscape – a "vocabulary" of landscape elements and a "syntax" for putting them together so they make sense (Spirn, 1998). This landscape language could provide an aesthetic frame that will support the practice of caring. We propose the use of a theory of landscape architecture that comes not from the realm of heritage, but from ecology. Through adopting the "cues to care" theory (Nassauer, 1995), we offer a further layer of critical landscape heritage, through critiquing the ways in which heritage is perceived and framed in design terms, and through this how it can be interpreted and understood.

Method

A qualitative case study methodology was selected to deepen understanding of the cemetery at Ashley Dene Farm, where the concepts of care and guardianship are explored within this forgotten and neglected agricultural landscape. Using a descriptive critique method, this research sets out to enhance the understanding of the concepts of guardianship and care within a heritage landscape and explore the application of the landscape ecology theory "cues to care", within a heritage setting.

Descriptive critique is a method which complements the case study approach, and involves developing understandings of context in a range of ways, including how a work "came about, how it relates to the designer's *oeuvre*, and the political and social conditions that contributed to its development" (Bowring, 2020: 32). Methodologically, descriptive critique focuses on techniques of documentation and description, with a particular emphasis on temporal aspects and how a site has changed over time. Through identifying the dynamic elements of change, including social and political influences as well as ecological processes, the cultural landscape is recognized as a dynamic rather than static entity. Descriptive critique has parallels with the concept of "thick description" in contrast to "thin description", as described by Bernadette Blanchon and Kamni Gill, quoting anthropologist Clifford Geertz:

> He suggests, that "thin description" is an unadorned, first-order account of behaviour. But, "thick description" adds many layers of cultural significance; "it confronts a multiplicity of complex conceptual structures, many of them superimposed upon or knotted into one another, which a researcher must contrive somehow to grasp and then to render".
>
> (Geertz, 1973, in Blanchon and Gill, 2014: 4)

The cemetery at Ashley Dene Farm

The central Canterbury landscape of Aotearoa New Zealand had been occupied by Māori for 600 years prior to European settlement during the 1800s. A vast, flat landscape stretching from the abundant coastline of the South Island's east coast, to the towering mountains of the Southern Alps, the Ashley Dene Farm sits within the Canterbury Plains Ngā Pākihi Whakatekateka o Waitaha.

In 1851, with the colonization of New Zealand by Britain, immigrants began to settle in the central Canterbury area. Reverend Henry Harper, the first vicar of the district, based himself in the area now known as Burnham. In 1861 the first Christian church and cemetery on the Canterbury Plains was developed on land where the Lincoln University-owned Ashley Dene Farm now sits.

The church was located on 15 acres of land donated by Richard Bethell, one of the early colonial settlers in the area, approximately 3 km from the small settlement of Burnham. The church grounds included a cemetery, vicarage and glebe (Collins, n.d.: 3) (Figure 15.1), and was a key part of Bethell's vision to create an "English village" on his extensive landholding, including farm, church and grounds, school, and cottages. Completing the All Saints' Church and churchyard in 1864, the "village" envisioned by Bethell and Reverend Harper did not eventuate, and early accounts of the landscape in which the church and cemetery sat was described as a bleak and lonely setting (Collins, n.d.: 5). Other writings describe the All Saints' Church as "standing on its low knoll with miles of dry tussock undulating to the mountains… Only matagouri, occasional cabbage trees and manuka broke the monotony of the wind-swept plains" (Collins, n.d.: 5). The first church service held in the All Saints' Church was on 17 April 1864, and it was formally consecrated in 1866. Despite its bleak setting, with an increase in settlers to the district, the church and parish flourished during the late 1860s and early 1870s. Unusually for a church, All Saints' was constructed with a cross at one end of the roof and a flagpole at the other. A flag was hoisted on the flagpole several days before the next service was to be held to enable passing travellers to notify other worshippers of the news, emphasising the remote and sparse landscape within which the church and cemetery sat.

By the late 1870s, however, the railway and a main coach "road" though the province had been constructed through the settlement of Burnham, 3 km from the All Saints' Church, which ultimately saw the centre of community move away from Bethell's farm to the growing Burnham settlement, where the railway station, hotel, and school had been established. Between 1868 and 1878 seven other Anglican Churches were built within a 16 km radius of Burnham, to service the district originally served by All Saints' (Collins, n.d.) With this growth in the establishment of other churches closer to Burnham, and the hard farming years that typified the 1880s and 1890s in the region, the parish of All Saints' declined. In 1901, the Anglican Synod offered the church to the government for use as a chapel at the Burnham Industrial School, and the Church was moved from its position within the "dreary, desolate, broom-grown churchyard" in 1909 (unknown author in Burtt et al., 2012: 11), to the grounds of the Industrial School in Burnham, which became the New Zealand Burnham Military Camp. Today the Church is non-denominational and has been renamed the All Saints' Garrison Church (Burtt et al., 2012).

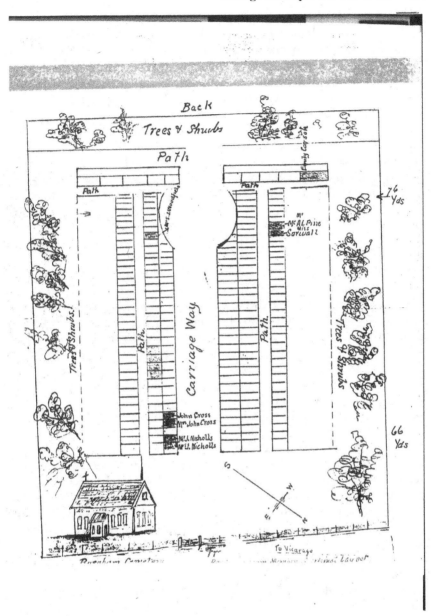

Figure 15.1. Burnham Cemetery. Historic Plan of the Cemetery at Ashley Dene Farm
Source: Image provided by Records Management, Selwyn District Council, New
Zealand, Achieve Box 362 "Burnham Cemetery – History", and Box 307 "C1/13".
(Personal communication, 25 March 2021.)

The removal of the chapel arguably subtracted a key signal of the cemetery as a heritage site in conventional terms, leaving it physically insubstantial and also reduced in importance as a site for formal religious practice. As an active cemetery with a chapel, there would have been a sense of continuity and reassurance of the cemetery's future. With the religious presence came practices of care and an accepted aesthetic convention for a tended rural cemetery. Without such a presence there is an ethical and aesthetic void. Absence and silence in terms of heritage can be a powerful force, as Harvey notes of Jay Winter's work on the Spanish Civil War, where the silence was intentional and was about actively "throwing history into oblivion" (Harvey, 2015: 919). For the Burnham Cemetery at Ashley Dene Farm the decades of silence are less the product of an active silencing, and perhaps more of a slippage and sense of forgetting.

Fifty-three people had been laid to rest in the windswept Burnham Cemetery between 1865 and 1895. Of these, 33 were children aged below 10 years, including 27 infants aged two years and under (Collins, n.d.; Burtt et al. 2012). Since 1895 only four burials were recorded, with the last internment recorded in 1937 (Collins, n.d.). It was, however, noted by the Ellesmere County Council (now the Selwyn District Council) that the record of burials is by no means complete, as it is understood that there may be several unrecorded burials of children from the former Burnham Industrial School within the confines of the cemetery or burials which took place following the removal of the Church and the closure of its records (Anonymous, 1987)

The combination of scarce evidence on site to show the cemetery layout and the presence of burials, together with the existence of several versions of plans of the church grounds (including cemetery, vicarage, and glebe), mean that "reading" the cemetery is difficult.

In 1909, approximately 13 of the 15 acres originally donated by Richard Bethell to the Anglican Church of New Zealand were sold by the Church Property Trustees to the Canterbury Agricultural College (subsequently Lincoln College, now Lincoln University), and amalgamated into Ashley Dene Farm, leaving approximately 1–2 acres of cemetery sitting isolated, surrounded on all sides by privately-owned farmland. With no internments occurring since 1937, the cemetery closed, and, seldom visited, the cemetery fell into disrepair, overtaken by grass and tussock-land, occasionally grazed by the University's sheep flock.

The site within the farm where the cemetery lays, not visible from the road, 800 meters down a "right of way", its existence not known by most, is today known simply as paddock C8, within the Cemetery Block at Ashley Dene Farm (Lucas et al., 2012: 9). Very few headstones are now left to record the burial sites of the 57 souls laid to rest within the cemetery. Today, with its seven remaining headstones, a corrugated iron-roofed hay shed, and surrounded by a circle of wind-damaged oak trees, the cemetery at Ashley Dene Farm is all but forgotten. "Like many of our old cemeteries its history, like its headstones, will gradually become lost" (Anonymous, 1987). Burtt et al.

explain that "Although not owned by Lincoln University, the cemetery remains in the University's care to this day with a guaranteed right of way to visitors" (Burtt et al., 2012). Today, however, the cemetery is isolated within the heart of the Farm (Figure 15.2.), and aspects of care and access are not clear. Lost within a landscape where production values of efficiency and functionality reign, this small landscape of memory, with intangible values associated with family, community, and faith, sits quietly enclosed by a circle of historic English oak trees, within the vast flat, dry, windswept Canterbury Plains.

With the movement of time, the farm and cemetery, once part of the same "vision" and governance, have moved at different speeds. The university-owned Ashley Dene Farm has, at times, led the world in pastoral innovation and animal biology. The cemetery, sitting still, expressing the passing of time in its weathered and "un-kept" state, shows signs of forgotten-ness. With no clear "guardian", the site has become invisible from outside the farm gates. And within, the cemetery, slowly folding back into the land, being reclaimed by nature, sits in visual contrast to the regimentation of the surrounding farmscape, both in space and time. This research explores the disconnection between landscape values – both ethical and aesthetic – visible within this landscape. Drawing on the concept of guardianship as a possible approach to "caring" for this site from an ethical perspective, and the landscape ecology theory of "cues to care" is investigated from the perspective of mediating aesthetic values.

Guardianship and caring for the cemetery landscape

Guardianship is a term which embraces the idea of caring for something. Often applied in formal arrangements in the care of people, this same ethos can be used in the care of the landscape. In the United Kingdom, guardianship has a specific definition in relation to heritage, where an ancient monument is in private ownership but is under the guardianship of a public authority. So-called "guardianship monuments" are managed and maintained by a public authority, such as English Heritage, but the authority does not take over ownership of the site (United Kingdom Government, 1979). This formalization of guardianship illustrates a "care-taking" role, one that is particularly relevant to heritage landscapes. As noted earlier, landscapes undergo constant change, and for landscapes whose heritage value is related to a particular function, design or aesthetic, this can be problematic. Further, where those landscapes are threatened by other land uses, the concept of guardianship embodies the practices of taking care and protecting. As in the UK's formalisation of the role of guardianship, there is a sense of transcending aspects of ownership for the sake of the wider cultural value of that site. Alongside this is Relph's concept of environmental humility which draws on principles of guardianship and custodianship, and the practices of care which are entwined within these principles (Relph, 2015).

One of the challenges of the cemetery's future is how ethical conceptions of guardianship and custodianship translate into an aesthetic expression of care. In its current state the cemetery can read as "messy" in aesthetic terms, and this is part of its vulnerability. Caring for the site does not necessitate changing the wild vegetation cover over the cemetery itself, but of protecting it so that there is a clear expression of value, significance, and heritage. This contradictory scenario – of messiness and signals of care – has been theorised in landscape architecture in the approach of "messy ecosystems and orderly frames", and it is proposed that this offers a model for navigating a future for the cemetery at Ashley Dene Farm.

Cues to care

The recognition of value within this quotidian landscape resonates with Yi-Fu Tuan's concept of "fields of care", those places in the landscape which are not the grand civic spaces, but are where there are strong connections and a sense of dwelling (Tuan, 1974). Edward Relph echoes this sense of care for the landscape, including both sparing and caring, where sparing is

> letting things, or in this context places, be the way they are; it is a toler-
> ance for them in their own essence; it is taking care of them through
> building or cultivating without trying to subordinate them to human will.
> (Relph, 1976: 38–39)

Care-taking underpins an approach to the cemetery as heritage in its own right. And sparing signals that it does not need to be wrestled into an alternative landscape type. Yet, as overgrown and abandoned it is out of step with the agricultural landscape (Figure 15.2.). Leaving it in this overgrown state with no intervention is ethically and aesthetically problematic. Landscapes can be seen as kinds of texts, symbolic arrays that are intentionally or unwittingly broadcasting values and meaning to observers (Cosgrove and Daniels, 1988; Egoz and Bowring, 2004). Tidying the cemetery itself is a possibility, although the vegetation that has developed offers biodiversity in a landscape sometimes described as a green desert. Earlier research on farms on the Canterbury Plains revealed how for "conventional" farmers, the sight of unmanicured vegetation was a sign of laziness and neglect (Egoz, 2000; Nassauer, 1995). Maintaining a closed cemetery to a manicured level is problematic in a range of ways. At present the extent of burials is not certain, and work at the surface level to maintain the landscape could damage the soil substrate below. Further, with the cemetery no longer in active use, what sense of history and the passage of time would a heavily manicured landscape convey? Yet, allowing the cemetery to remain a "messy" element in the farmed landscape is a challenge.

The theory of "cues to care" was developed within the discipline of land-scape ecology as a means of signally apparently messy ecologically healthy landscapes as intentional. Because these ecologically-rich landscapes can read as untended, Joan Nassauer developed the concept of clearly expressing that they are cared for through introducing "orderly frames" (Nassauer, 1995). Orderly

Figure 15.2. The "messy" cemetery, bounded by oak trees, and sitting within the orderly fields of Ashley Dene Farm
Source: credit: Shannon Davis, 2020

frames include elements of the cultural landscape that signal care, such as mown verges, fences, and other familiar dimensions of local settings. Transposing this theory of cues to care from landscape ecology to heritage landscapes provides a means of framing apparently untended, and by implication unvalued, sites with clear indications of attention and guardianship.

Adopting a theory from landscape ecology also prompts reflection on the abandoned cemetery from an ecological perspective. Aggressively maintained cemeteries, as in lawn cemeteries that are common in many Western countries, are limited in their biodiversity (Clayden et al., 2018; Watson et al., 2020). Could the cemetery at Ashley Dene Farm transition to an ecologically and culturally rich enclave within the wider agricultural landscape? Ecologically enriching the cemetery can offer a further stepping stone to species navigating the Canterbury landscape, and support a range of fauna (Greer, Bowie, and Doscher, 2017). In this sense, the cemetery in turn becomes a kind of ecological guardian of the farm, recognising how, as Goodchild explained, landscape heritage is both natural and cultural (Goodchild, 2008). Harvey and Wilkinson suggest "the question is less about what heritage is, and more about what it *does*" (Harvey and Wilkinson, 2013: 177). The potential of abandoned cemeteries as ecological sites has been explored in places such as the UK, where cemeteries have been closed for quite some time and have evolved into hybrid landscapes.

Applying the concept of cues to care, and of potentially ecologically enriching the site as a supplementary outcome, embraces the idea that the cemetery needs to matter to those who encounter it and to manifest the care of those from the past. Critical Heritage Studies suggest that "the discourses that frame our understanding of heritage are a performance in which the meaning of the past is continuously negotiated in the context of the needs of the present" (Gentry and Smith, 2019: 1149). Further, "This process is then used in a wide range of ways to stabilise or destabilise issues of identity, memory and sense of place – all of which have consequence for individual and collective well-being, equity and social justice" (Gentry and Smith, 2019: 1149). This process of heritage being negotiated in the context of the present depends on the framing of it – and this is where cues to care can provide the signals to connect to the familiar landscape of care.

An orderly frame for messy heritage provides a potential strategy for the cemetery to be clearly signalled, yet for it not to be necessarily tidied into a high-maintenance regime. The orderly frames also represent a liminal zone, a passage between the two landscapes which are moving at different speeds – the constantly evolving farm, and the temporally marooned cemetery. Catherine Heatherington expresses the sense of landscape components moving at different paces with the concept of "time edges" (Heatherington, 2021). Heatherington defines time edges as "abrupt juxtapositions between different time layers: ruined structures contrast with successional vegetation or new material interventions are juxtaposed with remnants from the past" (Heatherington, 2021: 29). Maintaining these time edges at Ashley Dene Farm could help the legibility of the cemetery, signalled and visually supported through the introduction of "orderly frames".

Orderly frames and time edges are also means to help make the invisible visible. Laurajane Smith emphasized how "heritage" is not a "thing" or a "site", or an object or a building, but

> Rather, heritage is what goes on at these sites, and while this does not mean that a sense of physical space is not important for these activities or plays some role in them, the physical place or "site" is not the full story of what heritage may be.
>
> (Smith, 2006: 44)

Intangibility is a significant part of the constellation of elements that makes up the heritage of the cemetery, beyond the pragmatic landscape of the farm, and the cemetery as a "record" of deaths, there is a fugitive and ephemeral layer of memory and spirit that needs attending to. As Smith further explains, "Whether we are dealing with traditional definitions of 'tangible' or 'intangible' representations of heritage, we are actually engaging with a set of values and meanings, including such elements as emotion, memory and cultural knowledge and experiences" (Smith, 2006: 56).

Conclusion

Critical reactions to the overlooking of the heritage value of landscapes which fall outside the purview of conventional and formal processes of patrimonialization often come from groups whose identity is embedded in those locations. The cemetery at Ashley Dene Farm, however, has no such voice. The farm's pragmatic, perfunctory landscape is at odds with the historic and emotional content of the cemetery. Over time, its landlocked situation within the farm, not visible to passers-by, has meant that it has been forgotten. The passage of time between the last burial (eight decades) and its obscuring through being landlocked inside the farm, mean that it has become all but invisible in the local cultural landscape. David Harvey observes that, "Heritage and landscape do not move as parallel lines but are constantly folded into each other: no linearity and no stability" (Harvey, 2015: 921).

Practices of caring have the potential to signal the guardianship of the cemetery. Emphasizing the practice of caring for landscape offers a potential direction for the cemetery to have a meaningful long-term presence. Expressing care on the site is an ethical and aesthetic issue. Ethically, the cemetery as a site of death and memory necessitates practices that respect the internments on the site, and provide protection for the historical narratives tied up in the landscape. The ethic of landscape guardianship which identifies deep layers of ecological, temporal and spiritual connection offers a meaningful frame for the care of the cemetery. Aesthetically, the challenge is to navigate the messiness of the cemetery's overgrown vegetation within the manicured agricultural landscape. Cues to care and time edges provide tools for finding design forms for framing the cemetery.

In the context of Aotearoa New Zealand, heritage landscapes have other important dimensions that relate to the bicultural partnership instilled in the Te Tiriti o Waitangi/The Treaty of Waitangi (1840). The cemetery sits within a landscape that has long and deep connections to mana whenua, Māori who have jurisdiction over a specific area of land. In contrast with this expansive frame of indigenous history, the cemetery is relatively recent, and is a colonial imprint on the land. The connection with Indigenous Knowledge within the scholarship of critical heritage landscapes of Aotearoa has the potential to further explore the ethics of guardianship and care holistically, across spatial, temporal and spiritual boundaries.

References

Anonymous. (1987). *Burnham Cemetery*. Unpublished document.

Blanchon, B. and Gill, K. (2014). Editorial: Critical Invention. *Journal of Landscape Architecture*, 9(1): 2.

Bowring, J. (2020). *Landscape Architecture Criticism*. London: Routledge.

Burtt, E., Clark, V., Whatman, T., and Collins, W. S. (2012). The Cemetery. In R. J. Lucas, N. G. Gow, and A. M. Nicol (eds.), *Ashley Dene: Lincoln University Farm: The First 100 Years*. Lincoln, NZ: Lincoln University, pp. 10–12.

Clayden, A., Green, T., Hockey, J., and Powell, M. (2018). Cutting the Lawn – Natural Burial and its Contribution to the Delivery of Ecosystem Services in Urban Cemeteries. *Urban Forestry and Urban Greening*, 33: 99–106.

Collins, W. S. (n.d.). *First Church on the Plains: A Centennial History of All Saints Garrison Church 1864–1964, Burnham Military Camp*. Burnham, NZ: Burnham Regional Support Centre.

Cosgrove, D. E. and Daniels, S. (1988). *The Iconography of Landscape: Essays on the Symbolic Representation, Design, and Use of Past Environments*. Cambridge: Cambridge University Press.

Egoz, S. and Bowring, J. (2004). Beyond the Romantic and naive: the Search for a Complex Ecological Aesthetic Design Language for Landscape Architecture in New Zealand. *Landscape Research*, 29(1): 57–73.

Egoz, Y. S. (2000). Clean and Green But Messy: The Contested Landscape of New Zealand's Organic Farms. *Oral History*, 28(1): 63–74.

Geertz, C. (1973). *The Interpretation of Cultures: Selected Essays*. New York: Basic Books.

Gentry, K. and Smith, L. (2019). Critical Heritage Studies and the Legacies of the Late-twentieth Century Heritage Canon. *International Journal of Heritage Studies*, 25(11): 1148–1168.

Goodchild, P. H. (2008). Landscape Heritage, Biosphere Change, Climate Change and Conservation A General Approach and an Agenda. In M. Petzet and J. Ziesemer (eds.), *Heritage at Risk 2006/7 (ICOMOS)*. Altenburg: E. Reinhold-Verlag, pp. 196–199.

Greer, P., Bowie, M. H., and Doscher, C. (2017). Mapping Restoration Plantings in Selwyn: The Stepping Stones of a Wildlife Corridor. Lincoln: Lincoln University Wildlife Management Report No. 64.

Harvey, D. (2015). Landscape and Heritage: Trajectories and Consequences. *Landscape Research*, 40(8): 911–924.

Harvey D. and Wilkinson T. (2013). Landscape and Heritage: Emerging Landscapes of Heritage. In P. Howard, I. Thompson, E. Waterton, and M. Atha (eds.), *The Routledge Companion to Landscape Studies*. Abingdon: Routledge, pp. 176–191.

Heatherington, C. (2021). *Revealing Change in Cultural Landscapes: Material, Spatial and Ecological Considerations*. Abingdon: Routledge.

Heritage New Zealand Pouhere Taonga Act 2014. Retrieved from: https://legislation. govt.nz/act/public/2014/0026/latest/whole.html#DLM5034914.

Lucas, R. J., Gow, N. G., Nicol, A. M., and Lincoln, U. (2012). *Ashley Dene: Lincoln University Farm: The First 100 Years*. Lincoln, NZ: Lincoln University.

MacKenzie, A. and Saniga, A. (2015). Guest Editorial – Introduction: New Directions in Landscape Heritage. *Landscape Review*, 16(1): 2–5.

Nassauer, J. I. (1995). Messy Ecosystems, Orderly Frames. *Landscape Journal*, 14(2): 161–170.

Relph, E. (2015). *Rational Landscapes and Humanistic Geography*. Abingdon: Routledge.

Relph, E. C. (1976). *Place and Placelessness*. London: Pion.

Smith, L. (2006). *Uses of Heritage*. Abingdon: Routledge.

Spirn, A. W. (1998). *The Language of Landscape*. New Haven: Yale University Press.

Tuan, Y.-F. (1974). Space and Place: Humanistic Perspective. In R. J. C. C. Board, P. Haggett, and D. R. Stoddard (ed.), *Progress in Human Geography – Vol. 6*. London: Edward Arnold, pp. 211–252.

United Kingdom Government. (1979). Ancient Monuments and Archaeological Areas Act: Guardianship of Ancient Monuments. London.

Watson, C. J., Carignan-Guillemette, L., Turcotte, C., Maire, V., Proulx, R., and Ming Lee, T. (2020). Ecological and Economic Benefits of Low-intensity Urban Lawn Management. *The Journal of Applied Ecology*, 57(2): 436–446.

16 "Institutionalized landscapes, who cares!"

The young people of Gernika and their criticism of the urban landscape heritage discourse

Juan Sebastián Granada-Cardona

Introduction

The bombing of Gernika – an emblematic place of Basque freedoms – is the keystone of the horrors inflicted on the population during the Spanish Civil War (1936–39). Linked to the process of democratization and the establishment of Autonomous Communities in Spain, during the last 30 years Gernika has been the object of a large project of space redevelopment intended to promote the ideas of memory, peace, and reconciliation.

The city and, more concretely, some key spaces of its urban landscape – like the Place des Fors, the historic building of the Council, the Pasileku, and the former ASTRA arms factory – have become places of heritage because of the Basque, Spanish, and European authorities' intervention.[1]

However, this heritage process has led to some controversies. First, because it has been part of a hegemonic agreement (Smith, 2006) resulting from the Spanish transition to democracy (1975–82), in which strategies trying to erase the contentious subjects of the Civil War were implemented; second, because since then authorities have chosen to make a heritage of ruins that no longer exist: it is the absence that bears witness.

On the other hand, for the younger generations, ASTRA and the Gaztetxe in Pasileku acquired major importance at the end of the 20th century and during the first decade of the 21st century and during its first decade (Granada-Cardona, 2017). But the ideas they form of these cityscapes are not always the same as their parents and grandparents.

How do the young Gernikarras, who did not directly experience the violence of the Spanish Civil War, relate to the heritage processes of the Civil War landscapes that take place in their city in the second decade of the 21st century? The impressions that young people have gained of their city are not always the same: war, violence, and childhood are the images that emerge most often when one refers to the civil war in the city. On the other hand, as we will present in this chapter, these constitute the parts from which singular discourses are constructed.

DOI: 10.4324/9781003195238-16

The aim of this chapter is to identify the ways in which different groups of young people participating during the 2010s in the community life of the city of Gernika through self-run projects challenged: a) the institutionalized way of remembering and b) the development of landscape heritage of their own space. The interviews and the observation reports that serve as material for the central argument are the result of a two-year exercise of ethnographic work carried out in the city of Gernika specifically with young people linked to the ASTRA and Gaztetxe organizations.

We must not forget that youth is a concept which hides subjective experience and well-defined social conditions. Both as an age group and as a social group, youth is variable. At the time of the ethnographic research (2011–13), the young people participating in the Gaztetxe varied between 12 and 30 years old. Indeed, faced with the ambiguity of the notions of youth and adolescence, we have chosen to use a youth cohort because it seems to us more appropriate when it comes to expressing this social involvement in heritage projects that we intend to emphasize (Bucholltz 2002).

We were introduced to the Gaztetxe group by the members of two Gernika associations: Gernika Gogoratuz and Ideas Sur. In our view, this fostered – to a certain extent – the freedom of speech and the trust that the young people of ASTRA and Gaztetxe gave to us. Nevertheless, the latter were always rather reserved, especially regarding the Basque political subject.

Through our reflection, we want to highlight the link between landscape and memory, pointing out that this relationship does not obey a logic of truth, but a logic of construction of intelligibility (Marie, 2004), produced from local identity paths and stories, and therefore partial (Cosgrove, 1998). Space and memory relate here to the subject of identity, which is always in motion and always subject to debate and reinterpretation (Hirsch, 2012; Dwyer and Alderman, 2008).

On this subject, the empirical work that we analyse here could be metaphorically read from a performative understanding of the landscape, in the sense of the work of the synthesis carried out by Dwyer and Alderman (2008), because we especially want to underline the importance of the social investment of the place by new generations as a key aspect of the renewal and challenge of political meanings.

On the bombing of Gernika

The bombing of Gernika is the keystone of the horrors inflicted on the population during the Spanish Civil War. With the support of the German and Italian fascists, the Francoist rebels did not come to bomb classic military objectives. It was necessary to destroy a symbol in order to sow fear among the Basques rebels:[2] they wanted to suppress the whole city of Gernika, an emblematic place of Basque freedoms, and to destroy its civilian population (Cava, 1996).

Regarding this last point, there is no agreement about the number of dead: the Basque government has always claimed that there were 1,500 victims, while historians close to Francoism only mention 200. On this controversial subject – which constitutes one of the subjects of dispute over the memory of the violence experienced by the Gernika's citizens – we cannot close the debate. Even if one may think that a work of memory is essential, there is no point in asking the question, because now, in accordance with the decisions approved by the political authorities who led the process of democratic transition in Spain, there is an explicit agreement that they will not come back to this subject.

As the dead are the real body of the crime and lie at the heart of a silent controversy, the evidence of this crime – and the narrative that forms with it – lie in the ruins. Therefore, paradoxically, there is an absence that testifies: it is the city that no longer exists.

The heritage development process in Gernika is based on the idea that buildings can also be witnesses of a past whose memory is still fragile; the presence of places reaffirms memory and prevents it from withering until it disappears.

How did it happen? During the Franco's Spain (1939–75) remembering the vanquished wase prohibited. The influence of Francoism can be identified in the time lag between the start of the heritage development processes in Europe – in the 1970s – and the start of similar initiatives in Spain, towards the end of the 1980s to the early 1990s.

Members of the Peace Museum, the Civil War Documentation Center, and the Gernika Gogoratuz Association – with whom we discussed separately on memory and war – have informed us that after the bombardment, everything was set in motion for the rebirth of Gernika. The Francoists themselves led the reconstruction work.

The dictatorship thus prevented any memorial expression. As people returned to rebuild their city and live there, Francoism imposed a normalization that sought to completely hide the events. Likewise, as in a strict sense it was not a battlefield, the Francoist authorities did not erect a monument about it. And, as the controversy over the number of dead and over the responsibility for the act arose the day after the bombing, from the outset it was not possible to build an ossuary to commemorate the dead civilians.

So, if during Francoism there was repression that silenced all testimony, from the transition to democracy, these hidden voices which probably only circulated in a very intimate environment, could and should speak publicly.

Young people keep hearing the siren

For a community to exist, you need ideas that cross the collective, both intergenerational and intra-generational. As Wydra (2018) has argued, there are, on the one hand, inherited ideas that pass from one age group to another and thus become traditional; and on the other, there are the strictly current ideas that circulate within a group and serve to point out the difference between them and the others.

Since the beginning of democratization, the city has been bursting with symbolic elements and activities where memories of events and people linked to the Basque Country and the Spanish Civil War take centre stage. This almost obsessive identification and control of traces is very characteristic of the notion of memory thought of as a political tool.

Public discourse on the memory of the bombing then began to take place and manifest itself in several ways. In fact, it has changed so much during the last 20 years that now these places of memory saturate the town of Gernika, where previously any mention of war and bombing posed serious risks for the population (Cava, 1996: 142).

Among the reconciliation projects encouraged by the Basque Autonomous Government after the end of Franco's Spain period, we have identified:

–Reading stories about the civil war in schools
–Carrying out workshops about civil war memory in the museum
–The liberation of the word that circulates in and out of intimate spaces
–The installation of several commemorative sculptures
–The development of a heritage development process for buildings that survived the bombardment
–Solemn commemorations.

We can group these projects into three privileged axes of memorialization in Gernika. First, the City Museum, which was founded to preserve and show a historical memory. Second, witness accounts, which have been recorded to ensure their preservation and repetition. And what interests us here, third, the buildings – almost by their mere presence – which testify to the veracity of the stories.

Places thus participate in the unification of memories. If people do not necessarily agree with the stories, memories around the places become the symbol of a community which uses them as irrefutable traces.

Indeed, the involvement of municipal, provincial, and national governments is central to the support of most of the associative activities linked to the duty of remembrance; with those which promote the dominant vision of the public memory of the city – repeated and stabilized through the buildings of the various memorials, for example. As analysed in other cases by Monk (1992) and Peet (1996), this support of dominant versions normally excludes alternative interpretations and remembrances and makes them marginal versions.

Besides the Peace Museum and the House of Juntes which deal respectively with the memory of the bombardment and the Oak of Gernika (*Gernikako arbola*),[3] other groups participating in the cultural life of the city and dealing with the subject of memory are: the House of Culture, the Gernika Gogoratuz organization, the Gernikazarra History Group, and ASTRA and Gaztetxe. The latter are the ones that interest us the most, since they are the places that have been occupied and developed by the initiatives of the city's youth groups.

ASTRA had been built in 1916 and its outbuildings had survived the bombings of 26 April 1937. The factory had been abandoned since 1998 and by that reason was used by squatters in 2005, with the support of the local community. One of the participants of told us that the reason for occupying the factory was the lack of socio-cultural infrastructures in the city, the factory – a place that survived the bombing, but which was ignored by the institutional authorities – being the most convenient place to be transformed in a cultural centre (Granada-Cardona, 2017).

As the spaces of ASTRA had to be enabled for the new uses, the youth of ASTRA organized themselves into a Gaztetxe or House of Youth. Linked to the ASTRA project, it was not really an autonomous space, but – like the factory – it was a space that survived the bombing and had not been used by the municipality: the abandoned public schools of Gernika (Granada-Cardona, 2017).

ASTRA and Gaztetxe have been established in part as a reaction to other Gernika organizations. Stifled by the cultural environment dominated by these associations, young people also have advocated the need for a new freedom. They did not want to feel influenced, even if they were.

Indeed, in the work *Memoria colectiva del bombardeo de Gernika* carried out by the Gernika Gogoratuz organization in the late 1980s, researchers had already spotted the contempt of the city's youth for stories linked to the civil war.

This, of course, may be due to the proliferation of memory as a topic that permeated all Gernika. Obviously, all the members of the community who were born between 1982 and 1998 (who were therefore between 14 and 30 years old in the time of the ethnographic research) had to experience the blossoming of this public memory and did not know the limitations that previous generations had to experience during the dictatorship. Those last are part of the Generation of Postmemory (Hirsch, 2012).

Memory saturation is experienced by young people as a massive invasion. Thus, this reality which they did not experience, and which their fathers and grandparents so badly need to tell, does not ignite a genuine interest in them. These young people of the first decade of the 21st century were the first generations after the dictatorship; they were born and raised in post-Franco Spain and, as a result, the content of the stories that repeatedly circulated around them did not hold the same value for them as for older generations.

Cava (1996) points out that their fathers wanted to explain to them how the war happened, and in this war how they experienced this famous bombardment that so much silence and ambiguity had distorted. The members of this first generation wanted to tell who had been the real attackers of the city and the reasons which prompted them. In short, they wanted to pass on their experiences of life during the war and the dictatorship.

Nevertheless, the young people were bored, especially with the details of the stories (Cava, 1996). Why did they have to be interested in these stories that were not anchored in their everyday experiences? Young people do not always understand why in Gernika we keep talking about the same subject in this way over and over.

Official commemorations have only been done since 1995. For young people this means a lifetime, while previous generations had to wait over 50 years for this to happen. For them, the commemorations are the result of a great struggle. This is why, for the city's elders, it is so important that the institutions recognize the need for a "correct" memory on the war.

The exercise of memory has changed dramatically since then. It has moved from intimate narratives to official narratives which, moreover, rely on the support of the development of historic monuments and landscape heritage.

Common places, suspicious heritage

These official stories are subject to a process of standardization which makes them socially usable, because they carry a collective message. Because they are shared by public authorities who act as authorized spokespersons and take place during annual commemorations which are representative spaces, these stories become iconic and attain general approval (Stern, 2000).

Young people not only complained about the saturation of the memory of the civil war. In fact, they complained about all the symbolism in the city, because it is highly institutionalized. It is not just about the Civil War, but also about the symbolism of the Oak of Gernika. We could say that the criticism is directed especially towards the latter.

In this regard, several young people we met in various situations told us about the famous hundred-year-old Oak of Gernika with both indifference and indignation. In Gaztetxe, they told us, the activities on offer really incorporate the community. On the other hand, the House of Juntes with the famous *Gernikako arbola* and the other monuments which were built in the Parque de los Pueblos de Europa were, from their point of view, constructions which could offer nothing to them. Those places express a symbolism linked to the outdated discourse of the formation of the Basque nation (on landscape and modernity cf. Cosgrove, 1998).

For them, the *Gernikako arbola*, the statue *Gure Aitaren Etxea* by Eduardo Chillida, and *Large Figure in a Shelter*, by British sculptor Henry Moore in the Parque de los Pueblos de Europa, as well as that of George Steer and the reproduction of Picasso's Gernika, are only a "bureaucratic" response from political institutions – Basque, Spanish, and international – to the faults they themselves have committed before.

But young people were not convinced – nor even touched – by these efforts of memorialization that settle in their urban landscape. For them, these symbols are devoid of content. At best, they can only interest tourists. The attachment to this symbolism lacks the vitality and especially the effectiveness that it can find in other activities. As we have discussed elsewhere (cf. Granada-Cardona 2017, 2018), young people show their pride in a different way; for example, through their relationship to traditional and contemporary music.

Disappointed with the institutions they inherited, but also aware of the impossibility of taking the path of radical violence that has marked the struggle of young people since the mid-20th century with ETA (Zulaika, 2005), in Gernika the young people with whom we have conducted our research were constantly debating and wanting to find a new way to act.

The moment of the commemoration of the bombardment clearly shows the criticisms formulated by the young people of the city. Normally, the commemorations involve the celebration of a mass, the bringing of a community floral offering which is deposited at the ossuary and finally one or more speeches, held by one of the members of the municipality and by one of the survivors of the bombing.

As a result of the ASTRA redevelopment project, since 2012 the factory siren – which had been repaired shortly before – has also been triggered at 4.30 p.m. According to most of the people we interviewed, it is around the siren and not the factory that memories of the bombing are concentrated. It is the main place of memory in this moment of commemoration. Indeed, having announced the warplanes in 1937, the siren helps to remember the bombardment. This is an achievement that can be attributed to the proposals made by the youth project organized in ASTRA. It could be read as a sign of dialogue with the other commemorative projects and as a link of continuity amid a discourse of rupture and change.

As ASTRA is associated with a social function recognized by the community, the group of young people leading the collective were also trying to reposition ASTRA as a central place in the memory of the city. However, they never wanted to deprive the siren of its value. They advocated for the building's inclusion on the list of heritage sites.

For young people, the commemorations of the bombing were, in principle, the precise moment to participate in this duty of remembrance. Yet, as they were not the only ones attending commemorations, and as they certainly did not hold the lead role, they saw their words suppressed in this uproar of speeches in which other, better-known groups have benefited from a wide circulation.

But there are also other more appropriate occasions, in which the intentions, ideas and objectives of young people can be listened to with greater attention in the community. However, as they had to persuade their fellow citizens of the value of the ASTRA project to the whole city, joining the memory projects was an ingenious option. Also, using these historic buildings to attract attention will always be part of their strategic approach.

Institutional urban landscapes, who cares!

As we have shown, the heritage of Gernika urban landscape has been a long and polemic process crossed by the challenges of institutional change, the emergence of new European institutions, the reformulation of the discourse on Spanish democratization, and, finally, the confrontation between generations.

Although we may suppose that confrontations and misunderstandings are commonplace in relations between different generations, what is striking here is the way in which spaces are placed at the centre of the ideological debate and of the questioning of practical uses (cf. introduction on this volume and Harvey and Waterton, 2015).

As buildings surviving the bombardment, Gaztetxe and ASTRA were subjected to the process of patrimonialization: they were, in a certain way, sacred, as central spaces of the city. But, when young people took hold of them, the debate on their meaning and their uses began.

For young people, for example, the Gaztetxe remains above all a very important symbol of their social and political commitment, which began in 2005. As a space for squatters, the Gaztetxe itself expresses the protest spirit of young people who have mobilized to conquer a place in their city. Here we see how places express, above all, a singular meaning that emerges from a situated, changing, and personal experience (Marie, 2004).

Previously the building housed the public schools, and now the Gaztetxe occupies several lounges; the largest room houses the bar. In another, ten computers donated by members of the community were installed. In the other, the young people set up a stage for concerts and for theatrical performances. In one of the smaller ones, a radio studio has been set up. The last is a storage room.

Contrary to the commemorative spirit which – according to the young people – only uses heritage spaces for major festivities, at the Gaztetxe they offered various activities to community members: documentary film screenings, public temporary exhibitions of drawings and caricatures, historical and political commemorations on the Basque Country, concerts by local groups, plays they wrote themselves, computer lessons, artistic workshops, and so on. This diversity of the activities offered reflects the flexibility, imagination, and plurality of the young members of the community who have been involved in the organization of the place.

The Gaztetxe is a place where the private and the public worlds merge. It is difficult to distinguish the border. But, as Marcel Roncayolo (2005) says, spatial planning expresses in a very particular way this relationship between private space and social space. The demand for a space for young people and its subsequent conquest reflects this relationship, because from the moment they squatted in the place, young people have a space for themselves; but, at the same time, it's a space which does not isolate them. Thus, the Gaztetxe seems to have served primarily to create an identity and make young people visible, which is ultimately useful for projecting them socially and for participating in the community.

The same goes for ASTRA, which was used for squatting because there was no socio-cultural infrastructure in the city, according to the young people. In this alleged lack of facilities, the young people omitted the existence of another heritage place in the city: the House of Culture, which for years has been a central space in the socio-cultural life of Gernika.

Because they are linked to the critical and politically engaged spirit of young people organized around ASTRA, there was a much more elaborate critical discourse in ASTRA activities. For instance, they pointed out the risks that can be engendered in our societies and in their relationship to power. Among the most alarming and formidable risks, they fear the control of all information under the watchful eye of the state.

For these committed young people, the panorama was as follows: information and knowledge are monopolized by companies which are allied to the political system which only seeks to monitor them, alienate them, and push them to consume. To combat this at the level of computer technologies, in the workshops hold at ASTRA they learned to reprogram computers with free software. Linux, PostgreSQL, GNOME, and Apache are some of the software they learn to install to "detox" their machines.

From the examples we have just proposed, we can see the distance that is worsened between the vision of heritage expressed by the municipality and that of the young people organized around these two places.

The activities proposed by the young people, as well as their relationship with the two buildings responded, above all, to an understanding of social life as an experience that requires horizontal links and, to this extent, their organization was based on community principles inspired by sources of anarchism.

Conclusions

From the moment of hidden remembrance of events until official commemorations, there has been a shift in collective psychology in Gernika. Indeed, this is not so strange, for no memory is truly imperturbable. Passing from generation to generation, all memories can experience a transformation: they are culturally translated. Around the same spaces we find a duplication of experiences that seek to take their legitimization from the spaces themselves. Yet it seems clear that the interpretation produced as well as the use made of it differ widely.

The young people accustomed to ASTRA and Gaztetxe did not care about the institutional value of the place. As such, it would only be representative of concepts far removed from their interests or even contested from their ideological position, close to anarchism. To place ASTRA as the emblem of the war and of the violence suffered would only extinguish the vitality of their activities, which were rather centered on the questioning of institutional memories "prêt-a-porter".

This does not mean, however, that they did not place any value on heritage places. On the contrary, they were at the heart of these process, because they had been directly influenced by and benefited from the city's redevelopment projects. Moreover, we can say that they had known how to use it to undertake their own ideas and activities.

Anchored in their own preoccupations, they took the issue of the heritage of the city to explicitly express the challenges that affect them at the present time. Thus, they upset a very rigid institutional process and whose established motivations had more conservative features, such as the rehabilitation of a democratic discourse delivered from the Basque and Spanish government centres. Against this flat discourse and practices, young people of ASTRA proposed 1) to question their fellow citizens, 2) to disturb their comfortable way of commemorating, and 3) to integrate them into new use of spaces, more linked to everyday life.

Heritage sites can be thought of as empty seashells that are always filled with very concrete actions. The nature and the goals that define its actions, as well as the participating public, will ultimately define the way in which one understands these places and the (in)coherence which is woven between them.

Notes

1 These kinds of interventions have spread in Europe since the end of the 1990s and intensified during the last ten years (Macdonald, 2013); this is especially the case in places marked by violent experiences, either from the beginning of the 20th century (cf. Saunders (2020) or Filippucci (2020) on the first war), or more recently (cf. Otrishchenko (2018) on the Balkan wars Urban landscape).
2 Specifically, the Francoists wanted to wrest the symbolism of the city from the Basques – therefore, their meaning, even normative (Harvey: 1979; Schein: 2003), as a cultural landscape of their socio-political world – and thus be able to rewrite its past and control its future.
3 It is an oak tree that symbolizes the Basques' liberties (royal assurances of fueros) from the Middle Ages. There is the nationalist memory par excellence.

References

Bucholltz, M. (2002). Youth and Cultural Practice. *Annual Review of Anthropology* 31: 525–552.

Cava, M.J. (1996). *Memoria colectiva del bombardeo de Gernika*. Gernika: Bakeaz y Gernika Gogoratuz.

Cosgrove, D. (1998). *Social Formation and Symbolic Landscape*. Madison: University of Wisconsin Press.

Dwyer, O. and Alderman, D. (2008). Memorial Landscapes: Analytic Questions and Metaphors. *GeoJournal* 73(3): 165–168.

Filippucci, P. (2020). 'These Battered Hills': Landscape and Memory at Verdun (France). In C. Horn et al. (eds.), *Places of Memory: Spatialised Practices of Remembrance from Prehistory to Today*. Oxford: Archaeopress, pp. 82–96.

Granada-Cardona, J.S. (2017). "Para vivir y crecer". Los jóvenes de Guernica y la organización social de los espacios urbanos: notas etnográficas". In R.M. Lince Campillo and F. Ayala Blanco (eds.), *Algunas formas políticas y socioculturales de habitar espacios*. México City: Universidad Nacional Autónoma de México (UNAM), pp. 101–116.

Granada-Cardona, J.S. (2018). Convivir en la música: Rock vasco y Bertsolarismo entre los jóvenes de Guernica. In R.M. Lince Campillo and F. Ayala Blanco (eds.), *Algunas formas políticas y socioculturales de habitar espacios*. México City: Universidad Nacional Autónoma de México (UNAM), pp. 171–192.

Harvey, D. and Waterton, E. (2015). Landscapes of Heritage and Heritage Landscapes. *Landscape Research*, 40(8): 905–910.

Harvey, D. (1979). Monument and Myth. *Annals of the Association of American Geographers*, 69: 362–381.

Hirsch, M. (2012). *The Generation of Postmemory: Writing and Visual Culture After the Holocaust.* New York: Columbia University Press.

Macdonald, S. (2013). *Memorylands: Heritage and Identity in Europe Today.* Abingdon: Routledge.

Marie, M. (2004). L'anthropologue et ses territoires. *Ethnologie française,* 1(34): 89–96.

Monk, J. (1992). Gender in the Landscape: Expressions of Power and Meaning. In K. Anderson and F. Gale (eds.), *Inventing Places: Studies in Cultural Geography.* Melbourne: Longman Cheshire, pp. 123–138.

Otrishchenko, N. (2018). Visible Traces: The Presence of the Recent Past in the Urban Landscape of Sarajevo. *City History, Culture, Society,* 5: 235–244.

Peet, R. (1996). A Sign Taken for History: Daniel Shay's Memorial in Petersham, Massachusetts. *Annals of the Association of American Geographers,* 86: 21–43.

Roncayolo, M. (2005). *La ville et ses territoires.* Mesnil-sur-l'Estrée: Gallimard.

Saunders, N. (2020). *Matter and Memory in the Landscapes of Conflict: The Western Front 1914–1999.* In B. Bender and M. Winer (eds.), *Contested Landscape.* Abingdon: Routledge, pp. 37–53.

Schein, R. (2003). Normative Dimensions of Landscape. In C. Wilson and P. Groth (eds.), *Everyday America: Cultural landscape studies after J.B. Jackson.* Berkeley: University of California Press, pp. 199–218.

Smith, L. (2006). *The Uses of Heritage.* Abingdon: Routledge.

Stern, S. (2000). De la memoria suelta a la memoria emblemática: Hacia el recordar y el olvidar como proceso histórico. In M. Garcés, P. Milos, M. Olguín, J. Pinto, M.T. Rojas, and M. Urrutia (eds.), *Memoria para un nuevo siglo: Chile, miradas a la segunda mitad del siglo XX.* Santiago:LOM, pp. 11–33.

Wydra, H. (2018). Generations of Memory: Elements of a Conceptual Framework. *Comparative Studies in Society and History,* 60(1): 5–34.

Zulaika, J. (2005). La tragedia de Carlos. Los vericuetos de la violencia vasca. In F. Ferrándiz and C. Feixa (eds.), *Jóvenes sin tregua. Culturas y políticas de la violencia.* Barcelona: Anthropos, pp. 95–111.

17 Moving Dolomites

The heritage value of an ordinary mountain landscape

Sara Luchetta, Benedetta Castiglioni and Mauro Varotto

Introduction

In 2019, in the frame of an Interreg transboundary territorial cooperation project, we, as professors and researcher of the University of Padova, were invited to reflect on the revitalisation of the landscape of Vallesina, a small village in the Venetian Dolomite mountains (Northeast Italy). Aside from the material restoration of an abandoned path—which was at the core of the traditional economic activities—we were invited to analyse and interpret the landscape of the whole village, searching for the sense of place to disclose, to care for and to share with both the inhabitants and the potential visitors. Vallesina had a relevant role in the socio-economic life of the area up until World War II, but nowadays it is a place where depopulation and abandonment are the prevalent driving forces. In a constantly rushing and changing world, Vallesina is apparently immobile, stuck with population decline and activities delocalisation. Nevertheless, listening to the multivocality of the landscape and exploring its tangible and intangible dimensions, mobility emerged as a key category that has contributed to moulding it. As a set of past and current materialities, practices, and meanings, a constellation of mobilities (Cresswell, 2010) started to inform our gaze on the landscape of Vallesina, which began to disclose its heritage potential. Ancient streets and artefacts, human and nonhuman movements framing everyday past and present life, and collective and individual memories have intertwined in time, shaping a multifunctional landscape to nurture.

In this chapter we take mobility as a category able to question the heritage potential of everyday landscapes in an alpine environment. Starting from the case study of Vallesina, we put into play the relationship between immobility and mobility in the identification of and care for alpine heritages, with particular attention to the contrast with the outstanding Dolomites UNESCO World Heritage Site (WHS) near Vallesina. This case study guides us to look at the relationship between ordinary and extraordinary landscapes. With the mobility of Vallesina, we aim to "move" the debate on landscape as heritage in the Alps.

DOI: 10.4324/9781003195238-17

Landscape, heritage, and mobility

Landscape and heritage are two widely explored concepts within a wide spectrum of disciplines. When explored together, many common points, or "parallel lines" (Harvey, 2013) emerge, such as the compresence of nature and culture, the tangible and the intangible, the constant state of becoming, the contingency of the value attributions, the collective dimension and political implications, and the open questions of authenticity, conservation and restoration (ibid). Considering landscape as heritage goes beyond the mere consideration of outstanding landscapes to be preserved, as often happens in the traditional institutional processes; the landscape-as-heritage perspective highlights the plurality of landscape values and the limits of a strict, detached definition of what is heritage and what is not. Both the Conventions proposed in 2000 and 2005 by the Council of Europe (European Landscape Convention and Faro Convention on the Value of Cultural Heritage for Society) on the one hand underline the importance of not only outstanding settings, but also everyday and ordinary ones; on the other hand, they ask for the involvement of non-expert people in the definition of landscape and heritage and in the design of actions, due to the relevance of these entities for people's well-being.

The landscape-mobility nexus has recently been observed from different points of view in the context of the mobility turn in social sciences and humanities (Sheller and Urry, 2006). The categories of materiality, representations, and practices that concern mobility studies in a political perspective (Cresswell, 2010) can be usefully applied in landscape studies, analysing how landscape features are impacted by or impact mobility in its different facets: "embodied movement plays an important role as the landscape continually changes depending on our movement through and experience with it" (Kokalis and Goetsch, 2018, p. 2). "How we encounter, apprehend, inhabit and move through landscapes" (Merriman et al., 2008, p. 191) are crucial topics of reflection, especially in a more-than-representational approach to landscape (Waterton, 2019). Mobility is viewed as "an important concept for exploring how landscapes are produced, lived, experienced and moved through in dynamic, embodied and highly politicised ways" (Merriman et al., 2008, p. 209).

Given these relevant debates on both the landscape–heritage and landscape–mobility associations, the heritage–mobility pair emerges as a key nexus and needs to be deepened, yet a comparable theoretical systematisation seems to be lacking. In the wide spectrum of perspectives that consider this pair, tourism is one of the main fields concerned, often including landscape issues and analysing topics like accessibility to heritage sites (considering both difficulties and excesses) and tourism traffic impacts (Scuttari, Orsi and Bassani, 2019), slow mobility for sustainable tourism (Maltese et al., 2017), cultural routes and pilgrimages (Moscarelli, Lopez, and Lois González, 2020), heritage authenticity in fragile communities affected by tourism mobility (Conway, 2014), mobility infrastructures (like old railways) acquiring heritage values becoming greenways

(Rovelli et al., 2020), and mobile and digital heritage representations (Hernández-Lamaset al., 2021). Research approaches in this case also include and often intertwine the three categories of materiality, representations and practices.

Focussing on the Dolomites, and in general on the Alps, mobility in relation to the landscape and heritage is addressed in migration studies, where landscape changes are strongly connected with depopulation and abandonment, and with a consequent loss of heritage values (Varotto, 2020). The importance of routes and paths as structural components of landscapes in an historical perspective (Franzolin, 2012) as well as the debate on traffic impacts on natural heritage are other related topics (Scuttari, Orsi, and Bassani, 2019). At an overall glance, however, mountain landscapes are mostly considered static, never changing and immobile; precisely for this reason, they acquire official heritage value.

Immobility, mobility and the Dolomites heritage

Mount Antelao, overlooking the small village of Vallesina, belongs to one of the nine mountain groups included by UNESCO in 2009 in the WHS of the Dolomites, according to criteria VII and VIII ("exceptional natural beauty" and "outstanding examples of earth's history": UNESCO, 2009). The border of the nine groups of the site includes the upper parts of forested slopes and dolomite rock walls and peaks, but excludes the lower part of the slopes and the valley bottoms with the villages and the human-made landscape. The UNESCO inclusion in the "natural heritage" list risks producing a double effect: in the name of its preservation, the Nomination has highlighted the values of natural heritage "immobility", overlooking the values of the relationships that linked the Alpine communities with their mountains (with many different forms of local mobilities), instead forging a closer relationship with tourist mobility. In this way, the Nomination implicitly emphasises trends already underway in the Alpine mountains, towards the "habitat's extremization" (Bätzing, 2005) or, more generally, to a clear demarcation between spaces for nature and spaces for humans, between human mobility and natural (geological) immobility.

Conceiving of the landscape of the Dolomites only as a natural space concentrates the efforts of preservation and protection inside the "fence". In opposition, beyond the perimeter of "protection areas" and "buffer zones" (and thus outside the UNESCO observation area), this indirectly risks stimulating the opposite effects of urbanization, tourist mobility, and anthropic impact as a function of valorization triggered by the same Nomination.

The UNESCO Nomination therefore risks also emphasising the dichotomy between mobility and immobility: on the one hand by favouring the paroxysmal, "hit and run" mobility of the tourists that increases anthropic stress on protected areas, on the other hand by further crushing the marginal areas around the "natural heritage" in a rhetoric of conservation and immobility. Moving the Dolomites, in this case, therefore means conceiving the same natural "good" in a dynamic and relational way, grasping the dialogue among other mobilities (of elements, animals, plants, and local population) that constitute the pivot of the Alpine cultural heritage, in the shadow of the Dolomites' recognition process. The boundaries of the nine areas are almost totally (96 per cent) drawn on those of the already existing protection rules (protected areas such as the Dolomiti Bellunesi National Park or Natura 2000 areas). The presence of these tools led to the inclusion of some areas and the exclusion of others lacking tools for protection from human action. Very narrow buffer zones "designed to support conservation" (UNESCO, 2009) do not help in grasping the value of medietas, the "middle" landscapes produced by a laborious and centuries-old work, the mediation between ecological–environmental and socio-economic needs, and the combination of immobility and mobility in the same space (Varotto, 2020).

In the text of the Nomination, there is no reference to local populations, prefiguring a mountain without mountaineers and the sole destiny of a "tourist machine" (De Fino and Morelli, 2009, p. 15). The risk is therefore to convert this heritage into an open-air museum to be made more usable and a winning model in conservation policies. Guidelines like these have already been put in place in other UNESCO WHSs with serious problems caused by the exponential growth of visitors (De Fino and Morelli, 2009, p. 26). The absence of local communities in the official documents clashes with the fact that the legal ownership of parts of the assets belongs to the inhabitants themselves through civic use institutes; the historical role of local communities conserving the asset through the agro–silvo–pastoral economy (Guichonnet, 1986) is likely to be decreasingly felt, since the local society itself has embraced models of development and tourist behaviours (Salsa, 2007). The renaturalization process that has been underway for decades – a consequence of depopulation and abandonment of previous activities – is even positively evaluated in the nomination file, responding to the requests of an urban population eager for pure wilderness without humans. This trend neglects the human presence and its traditional mobility being intimately linked to the whole Dolomite landscape, generating a "manicured landscape" (Vannini, Vannini and Valentin, 2020), the abandonment of which produces a loss of landscape variety and cultivated biodiversity, which is stigmatised in many Italian mountain areas.

In short, the image of the Dolomites area that comes from the UNESCO WHS's perimeter is that of an immense nature reserve with heritage features stuck in their immobility and encouraging outsiders' mobility. Nevertheless, the challenge today is mostly around the metaphorical "fence", represented by the WHS border (Varotto, 2012), where, as in Vallesina, the relationships between natural and cultural heritage, the historical connections between areas inside and outside the perimeter, and the mobile dimension of a heritage that is only apparently immobile need to be re-signified.

This framework suggests that alternative heritage values emerge when looking at a local, everyday landscape of Vallesina – that is not officially considered "heritage" – through the key category of mobility, considering a wide spectrum of landscape elements and both human and nonhuman mobility, and the intertwining of materiality, representations, and practices. Looking at landscape "tensions" between nature and culture, materiality and immateriality, proximity and distance, and absence and presence generated by or generating movement helps in defining Vallesina's meaningful identity, as "it's precisely an inter-twining, a simultaneous gathering and unfurling, through which versions of self and world emerge as such" (Wylie, 2007).

Vallesina: the (im)mobile village

Vallesina (divided into the hamlets of Vallesina di Sopra and Vallesina di Sotto) developed in what we can call a "mobile" context. The area, like many others in the Alps, was characterised by multi-scalar exchanges and movements linked to the availability of resources and to natural infrastructures. This area was the geographical linkage between the two sides of the Alps, the Mediterranean and the German worlds: along its routes and rivers, people, objects, and goods have travelled for centuries, and are still travelling every day. Moreover, during the territorial influence of the Republic of Venice (from 1420 until 1797), and up until the beginning of the twentieth century, these valleys were crucial for the timber industry and trade. Starting from the mobile and interconnected context in which the village was founded, we aim to explore some important mobilities that have shaped its landscape over the years, contributing to defining its past and present identity.

Before presenting the mobilities of Vallesina, a brief introduction to the research methodologies is needed. Field and desk research combined in a mixed method approach integrating embodiment and distancing, landscape observa-tion and exploration, interviews, literature reading, and image interpretation. A crucial part of the research was conducted by interviewing almost all 16 inha-bitants of Vallesina. Other interviews were conducted with local history and anthropology experts. The embodied research was conducted by visiting the area's museums and walking through Vallesina and the surroundings at different times (in winter snow, in spring, and in summer). A constellation of mobilities (following Cresswell's notion of constellation, the mobilities of Vallesina can be read as "historically and geographically specific formations of movements, nar-ratives about mobility and mobile practices", 2010, p. 17) emerged from the exploration and the research conducted on the landscape of the village, ranging from the material and nonhuman mobility of water, stones, fire, animals, and plants to the meaningful human practices of migration, trade, religious rituals, commuting, and tourism. The following part of the chapter is a descriptive account of some parts of this constellation.

Mobilities of water

The foundation of Vallesina is closely linked to the mobility of water. As a proto-industrial site, the village was established close to the Vallesina stream, taking advantage of the power of water for economic development. In 1776, according to the Venetian civil registry, in the area (mainly in Vallesina) there were 27 wheat mills, one sawmill, five weaving mills and 22 grindstones. Nowadays, water mobility is no longer animating any economic activities, and only one restructured watermill producing hydropower for the nearby house in the upper part of the village is left. Despite the passing of time, the social and economic relationship with water mobility is embedded into the landscape: it can be read in the position and the shape of the houses and in the vestiges of the mills along the abandoned route to be restored. It can also be read in the many millstones spread along the streets and in the gardens: they stand converted into strange planters and ornamental objects, material evidence of a past mobility.

Landscape not only discloses a specific economic and social relationship with water mobility; traces of another liquid mobility can be read in the materiality as well as in the memories of the village's inhabitants: flooding. Vallesina experienced two major floods in 1966 and 1994. Both the floods resulted in severe damage (luckily without physical damages to people); the flood in 1966 caused the final blow to the economic system based on water as a motor power, a system already exhausted by emigration and economic changes. The landscape of flooding can be read in the coexistence of presence and absence. A recently built bridge, a river cement cliff aimed at containing the flow and the inhabitants' memories, interrelate with the empty space left by the houses and mills wiped out by the stream.

Proximity to water, the core reason for the village, resulted in a landscape made up of the entanglement of two water ontologies (Yates, Harris, and Wilson, 2017) produced by two different relationships with water mobility: water as a resource and water as a threat. The complex connection with the flow of water has produced, and still produces, a set of infrastructures, practices, and intangible traces.

Nonhuman mobilities: animals (and plants)

In Vallesina, as in many alpine contexts, human and (domestic and wild) animals' lives intersect daily. The history of the village reminds us how animals and humans have shared mobilities for a long time. Domestic animals were used in the past for facilitating human movements: in Vallesina, mules were typically used for transporting the cereals and flour in and out the village. Moreover, some of the inhabitants still remember the two horses that used to drag the snowplough during the 1960s and 1970s, allowing people to move along the streets during the snowy winters. Domestic animals' mobilities can be read into the landscape of the ancient streets: up until 1828, Vallesina was crossed by the "royal street", an important infrastructure probably built on the track of the ancient Roman route that connected the plain with the Tyrol region. The width of this street (much more narrow than contemporary streets) was related to the width of the wagon carrying people and goods and being pulled by animals (horses or oxen).

Beyond the movements of domestic animals, nowadays the inhabitants of Vallesina must reckon with wild animals' mobility. From the second half of the twentieth century, with the population decline, people have ceased to hunt for food and have stopped cultivating wide spaces for sustenance: these changes in everyday spatialities have allowed animals to gain room and freedom of movement. The landscape of the wild can be read in the houses and their surroundings. A new relationship with what Ginn would call the "domestic wild" (Ginn, 2016, p. 2) has been set. A semi-domesticated fox returns every night to eat at the eldest inhabitant's doorstep, that becomes a stop-over along the fox's route. The air is moving, too: in spring, swallows return to their already-built nest under the roofs of the houses (both the uninhabited and the habited ones). Finally, routes of deer intertwine — and sometimes conflict — with human spaces. While exploring the area of the abandoned route to be restored, we came across three male deer at noon in wintertime. Such an unusual encounter made us reflect on the ongoing interconnection of human and animal spaces that can also be read in the enclosures of the vegetable gardens, built up to protect cultivations from deer's mobility and hunger.

As suggested above, mobility of wild animals and their daily interconnection with human spaces also depends upon the human relationship with space. After the abandonment of wide cultivations and mowing practices, the remaining inhabitants just cultivate small gardens close to the houses. This change in human spatiality fostered what we call the mobility of wild plants: the abandoned fields gave way to some plants, such as hazelnut trees and ashes, that are starting to become young woods: space for wild animals.

The mobilities of people

People have travelled along the streets of Vallesina and its surroundings for centuries. The village was crossed by the royal street: from the nearby villages as well as from Venice and Tirol, people, animals, and objects contributed to drawing the landscape. In 1828 a new street, called "Alemagna", was built uphill, replacing the former street and excluding Vallesina from everyday traffic. The Alemagna is now a route for trucks carrying goods from Austria to the plain and to eastern Europe, but it is also a route for many tourists going to Cortina d'Ampezzo and to the Dolomites UNESCO WHS.

People living in Vallesina unanimously claim the luck of staying downhill from Alemagna's traffic: the automobility of people and goods causes inconvenience to the inhabitants of the nearby villages crossed by the street. Most of the inhabitants of Vallesina chose to stay there for its peacefulness, and are willing to commute for work, even for long distances. The uncongested and "immobile" landscape, away from traffic, generates a new practice of daily mobility.

Vallesina went through another crucial phase of human mobility that can be found in the landscape and in the intangible value of individual and domestic memories: the mobility of emigration. As in many other valleys of the Alps, temporary and permanent emigration contributed to defining the identity of Vallesina (as well as of the entire province). The first important permanent migration from the village took place after a catastrophic fire in 1871 that left most of the people (117 is the number recorded in a coeval administrative document) homeless. This forced displacement corresponds to what is identified as the first period of the Italian great emigration (Audenino and Tirabassi, 2008). The destination was mainly South America (Brazil), but people also went to Austria and Switzerland. The other important emigration from Vallesina took place after World War II and had Peru and Argentina as the main destinations. Migration changed the face of Vallesina with regard to people's displacement, and the traces of this specific mobility can be partially read in terms of landscape absences: uninhabited houses and uncultivated fields depend in part on the small and great migrations of the last decades.

Conclusions

The mobilities presented, in terms of landscape materiality, past and present practices, and preserved meanings and memories, form what Cresswell (2010) suggests calling a constellation of mobilities. In the form of a constellation, the interrelation between past water uses, animal footsteps, old letters from Peru, commuters coming home, and so on, has heritage value: it produces the movable identity of Vallesina, its local distinctiveness. The diachronic and synchronic forces generating the constellation materialise in the everyday inhabited landscape, to be lived by the inhabitants, visited by tourists and studied by people interested in cultural heritage.

The value of the everyday landscape of Vallesina is different from the heritage values and management policies at the core of the Dolomites UNESCO recognition. With this chapter, our aim is to suggest an alternative way to think about and cope with heritage in mountain environments. We acknowledge the importance of rocks and peaks, the majesty of the Dolomites, their importance for the balance of a fragile ecosystem, as well as their key role in the construction of modern imaginaries and aesthetics; nevertheless, we propose building methodological and practical bridges overcoming the fence between nature and culture, the extraordinary and the ordinary, the uninhabited and the inhabited, and the (supposedly) immobile natural landscape and the mobile landscapes produced by centuries-old works at the crossroad of ecological–environmental and socio-economic needs. We claim the need to study and promote landscapes as heritage in contexts that are identified as marginal, but that have much to tell about the ongoing interrelation of past, present, and perhaps future times.

While interviewing the inhabitants of Vallesina, one of the final questions invited them to give a very short definition of the village (three words maximum). The definitions collected are all extremely positive: "happy island", "my home", "peace", and "a need" are a sample of the inhabitants' thoughts. For them, Vallesina already has heritage value. The challenge is to make this value recognisable, with the aim of generating policies—and new imaginaries—able to materially value this place. The meaningful constellation of mobilities already speaks to the inhabitants, and hopefully will speak to visitors interested in slow cultural tourism (a quite new type of tourism in the area) based on knowledge and awareness, as stated in the objectives of the project at the base of the research in Vallesina.

Finally, in our research, mobility is a key category able to put into play different reflections on the relationship between landscape and heritage. It is simultaneously the topic and perspective, material evidence and methodology. It allows us to understand Vallesina and to imagine the heritage value of its landscape. In the frame of the need to deepen the heritage–mobility nexus, we propose using this insightful category (including its antonym) to "mobilise" the analysis and interpretation of other landscapes beyond the alpine context as ongoing combinations of materiality, meanings, and practices.

Note

This chapter is the result of a reflection shared by the three authors. Nevertheless, the section "Vallesina: the (im)mobile village" and the Conclusions have been written by S. Luchetta; the Introduction and the section "Landscape, heritage, and mobility" have been written by B. Castiglioni; the section "Immobility, mobility and the Dolomites heritage" has been written by M. Varotto.

References

Audenino, P. and Tirabassi, M. (2008). *Migrazioni italiane. Storia e storie dall'Ancien régime a oggi.* Milano: Bruno Mondadori.

Bätzing, W. (2005). *Le Alpi. Una regione unica al centro dell'Europa.* Torino: Bollati Boringhieri.

Conway, F.J. (2014). Local and Public Heritage at a World Heritage Site. *Annals of Tourism Research*, 44: 143–155.

Cresswell, T. (2010). Towards a Politics of Mobility. *Environment and Planning D: Society and Space*, 28: 17–31.

De Fino, G. and Morelli, U. (eds.) (2009). *Dolomiti. Paesaggio e vivibilità in un bene Unesco.* Trento: TSM-STEP.

Franzolin, M. (2012). *Sulla strada regia di Alemagna.* Crocetta del Montello: Terra Ferma Edizioni.

Ginn, F. (2016). *Domestic Wild: Memory, Nature and Gardening in Suburbia.* Abingdon: Routledge.

Guichonnet, P. (ed.) (1986). *Storia e civilizzazione delle Alpi.* Milano: Jaca Book.

Harvey, D. (2013). Emerging Landscapes of Heritage. In P. Howard, I. Thompson, and E. Waterton (eds.), *The Routledge Companion to Landscape Studies*, Abingdon: Routledge, pp. 152–165.

Hernández-Lamas, P., Cabau-Anchuelo, B., de Castro-Cuartero Ó. and Bernabéu-Larena, J. (2021). Mobile Applications, Geolocation and Information Technologies for the Study and Communication of the Heritage Value of Public Works. *Sustainability*, 13: 2083.

Kakalis, C. and Goetsch, E. (2018). *Mountains, Mobilities and Movement*. London: Palgrave Macmillan.

Maltese, I., Mariotti, I., Oppio A., and Boscacci F. (2017). Assessing the Benefits of Slow Mobility Connecting a Cultural Heritage. *Journal of Cultural Heritage*, 26: 153–159.

Merriman, P., Revill, G., Cresswell, T., Lorimer, H., Matless, D., Rose, G., and Wylie, J. (2008). Landscape, Mobility, Practice. *Social and Cultural Geography*, 9: 191–212.

Moscarelli, R., Lopez, L., and Lois González, R.C. (2020). Who Is Interested in Developing the Way of Saint James? The Pilgrimage from Faith to Tourism. *Religions*, 11: 24.

Rovelli, R., Senes, G., Fumagalli, N., Sacco, J., and De Montis A. (2020). From Railways to Greenways: A Complex Index for Supporting Policymaking and Planning. A Case Study in Piedmont (Italy). *Land Use Policy*, 99, article no. 104835.

Salsa, A. (2007). *Il tramonto delle identità tradizionali. Spaesamento e disagio esistenziale nelle Alpi*, Torino: Priuli e Verlucca.

Scuttari, A., Orsi, F., and Bassani, R. (2019). Assessing the Tourism-traffic Paradox in mountain destinations. A stated preference survey on the Dolomites' Passes (Italy). *Journal of Sustainable Tourism*, 27: 241–257.

Sheller, M. and Urry, J. (2006). The New Mobilities Paradigm. *Environment and Planning A: Economy and Space*, 38: 207–226.

UNESCO. (2009). *IUCN Evaluation of Nominations of Natural and Mixed Properties to the World Heritage List – The Dolomites (Italy)*, WHC-09/33.COM/INF.8B2, IUCN Report, Sevilla.

Vannini, P., Vannini, A., and Valentin, E. (2020). Manicured Landscapes: A Video Exploration of the Dolomite Mountains as Memoryscapes. *Social and Cultural Geography*, 21: 114–134.

Varotto, M. (2012). Oltre il recinto Unesco: le sfide del territorio dolomitico, in M. Varotto and B. Castiglioni (eds.), *Whose Alps Are These? Governance, Ownerships and Belongings in Contemporary Alpine Regions*. Padova: Padova University Press, pp. 285–294.

Varotto, M. (2020). *Montagne di mezzo: Una nuova geografia*. Torino: Einaudi.

Waterton, E. (2019). More-than-representational Landscapes. In P. Howard, I. Thompson, E. Waterton, and M. Atha (eds.), *The Routledge Companion to Landscape Studies*. Abingdon: Routledge, pp. 91–101.

Wylie, J. (2007). *Landscape*. Abingdon: Routledge.

Yates, J.S., Harris, L.M., and Wilson, N.J. (2017). Multiple Ontologies of Water: Politics, Conflict and Implications for Governance. *Environment and Planning D: Society and Space*, 5: 797–815.

18 Waste Sits in Places

Post-Extractive Landscapes as Heritage

Melissa Baird

Introduction

In 2018, the American Anthropological Association held its annual conference in northern California, one week after a firestorm swept through the town of Paradise. The scene at the meeting was surreal: participants, some donning masks, shopped at upscale boutiques, and booked site-seeing tours while a toxic chemical fog blanketed the city. I arrived in California one day after the fire forced my daughter-in-law, a nurse at the Adventist Health Feather River Hospital, to evacuate with her patients and flee for their lives. While my decision to attend the conference was fraught, I rewrote my remarks to connect with the session theme – mining and extraction – and the apocalyptic event. I wanted to draw a line between northern California's post-extractive landscapes and the current firestorm. In this case, hydraulic gold mining transformed the landscape. In 1868 Samuel Bowles described the rush:

> Tornado, flood, earthquake, and volcano combined could hardly make greater havoc, spread wider ruin and wreck than are to be seen everywhere in the track of the larger gold-washing operations. None of the interior streams of California, though naturally pure as crystal, escape the change to a thick yellow mud from this cause ... Many of the streams are turned out of their original channels, either directly for mining purposes, or in consequence of the great masses of soil and gravel that come down from the gold-washing above. Thousands of acres of fine land along their banks are ruined forever by the deposits.
>
> (cited in Dawson and Brechin 2020: 35)

Bowles was describing a post-extractive landscape, a landscape transformed through extractive activities. Transformations can be physical, as in the northern California example, where nearly 150 years after the mining rush, the changes in the geomorphology and watersheds likely contributed to the path of the fire (see, e.g., Marcus, Grant, and Nimmo 2001). Transformations can also be cultural, psychological, or political. For example, the rush of hundreds of thousands of gold-seeking migrants and industries engendered

DOI: 10.4324/9781003195238-18

new political forces. These forces created what legal scholar Brenna Bhandar (2016) has termed a "culture of dispossession" whereby lands and resources are appropriated for capital projects, and new and violent modes of engagement, such as exclusion, removal, and surveillance, distinguish rights, access, and ways of life.

Extractive landscapes are often sites of heritage. In Northern Alberta, the home territories of First Nation communities, for example, made way for the world's largest industrial project, the Canadian Tar Sands. In their relentless promotion of the energy sector, the Albertan and Canadian governments pushed the narrative that extractive expansions were central to economic development and nation-building. Again, heritage played a pivotal role. At the Bitumount site, a historic oils sands mining and processing facility near Fort McMurray, environmental sociologists Mike Gismondi and Debra Davidson (2012) showed how the energy sector and provincial government worked together to promote oil expansion to legitimate public funding. Drawing on archival documents and photographs, the authors revealed how the energy sector drew heavily on heritage to promote a vision of the riches and energy potential locked within the boreal forested plains, bogs, and waterways. As their example shows, heritage works to shift the discussion away from the social and ecological trade-offs. It annexes the typical protocols around protection and presents the Tar Sands as a resource. Ultimately, it builds public support critical to industrialization and nation-building. Scrubbed from the promotion – and removed from the discussion – however, wase the incalculable destruction brought on by the waste stream created by the oil industry. If "wisdom sits in places", then waste does too (after Basso 1996).

The purpose of this article is twofold. The first is to examine post-industrial landscapes *as* heritage. The second is to draw attention to the most ubiquitous product of the post-extractive landscape: waste. Waste is more than a "thing" – something discarded, evidence of activity – it is connected through social, political, and economic spheres. Waste making, like placemaking, is layered with meaning (after Basso 1996: 7). Waste mediates how people interact with the world. Yet, waste, in post-industrial contexts, although ubiquitous, is often ignored. To understand this paradox, I begin this chapter with a brief discussion of the entanglements of waste in post-industrial contexts. I then provide a brief example of the Copper Country in northern Michigan, the treaty territories of the Anishinabe, and the location of the United States' first mineral rush. I argue that the region's robust heritage industry has missed an opportunity to address how historic waste menaces and impacts local and Indigenous communities. I discuss how the largely uncomplicated narrative cannot account for the effects of waste and that this has lived implications for regional and downstream communities. Finally, I argue that shifting our heritage stories to reckon with waste and providing a clear-eyed assessment of the post-extractive landscape could provide a cautionary tale relevant to communities grappling with proposed industrial projects.

Tailings are Forever

The story of the post-extractive landscape is the story of waste. From open-pit mining to chemical refining, extractive industries generate extraordinary amounts of waste. Each activity has its unique waste signature, and each alters the landscape. From overburden to dusts, tailings and sludge, rocks, rubble and debris, slags and solvents, the waste streams are extensive. Waste is not inert or dormant. It ebbs and flows, breaks down and builds up, and moves through processes and climactic events. Its deposition into a landfill or a tailings pond is not an endpoint in its "life". The Tar Sands industry provides one example. One industry expert estimates that at least one trillion liters of sludgy waste are stored in open and unlined tailings ponds (Berman 2017). The magnitude of Tar Sands waste is hard to imagine. The cumulative impact of this cocktail of arsenic, mercury, and other toxic chemicals and particulate matter on ecosystems is even harder to characterize. Waste creates new topographies of meaning, sculpting and carving the land and waters and leaving in its path unique waste formations.

Post-industrial communities adapt and innovate: they grade and recontour degraded landscapes and watersheds; rebuild and repurpose waste; restore the landscape; and shift narratives to avoid stigma. Waste also creates a social contract through consent. It is imbued with agency and purpose and challenges our central assumptions (Kohn 2013). Seeing beyond what "just is" to understand social relations is essential in complicating the stories we tell (see McKittrick 2006). Anthropologist Julie Cruikshank's innovative work with Tlingit and Athapaskan communities in present-day Mount Saint Elias ranges can provide a helpful analogy. Using historical records, oral histories, and contemporary interviews with community members, she found that people viewed glaciers as animate and sentient beings. Thus, like glaciers, waste is also sentient and animated, a part of a complex system of meaning. Waste is not an abstraction – something out there, but instead lived with and feared, and connected through complex webs of significance.

Living with waste means managing risk. Exposure to waste can have carcinogenic, neurological, and respiratory effects on health. Toxic wastes seep into the soils and waters, travel through wind-borne dusts, and are taken up into the bodies of fish. Risks also are social and cultural: disruptions in livelihoods, the loss of lands, forced displacement, or other unforeseen costs. Downstream communities, for instance, calculate the potential risk of waste debris fields or tailings ponds that could leach or shift, or worse, collapse. Managing risk is also complicated by a communities' spiritual and cultural connections: having to weigh eating a culturally important food source or risk exposure to chemicals embedded in the "fleshy bodies" of fish kin (see Todd 2017). And then there are the not-as-rare-as-you-think catastrophic risks. In 2011, for example, a mine tailings impoundment failed at the Mount Polley gold and copper mine in British Columbia. The release of over "24 billion liters of toxic mine waste and contaminated water into the surrounding salmon-rich habitat" is Canada's largest mining disaster to date (Berman 2017). Not only did the industry and government fail to protect communities (engineers had warned about a tailings failure for months before the accident), but the government also failed to deliver on post-spill promises to clean up the impacted lands and watersheds. When I visited the site in 2016, a local fishing guide shared his concerns. He feared that his community's livelihoods and the fish stocks were so severely impacted that they would never recover.

Learning to see waste beyond a static or material object can tell us many things. For example, we can investigate the labor of waste or its capitalist relations of production. We can also view waste as a social phenomenon and learn how it is normalized through language and practice; it can provide insights into power dynamics and how it is gendered and classed. That is, we can learn to see waste as historically contingent and embedded in a set of relations (see Kohn's 2013: 6.) Learning the stories *of* waste can reveal what people value or fear, about their vulnerabilities and strengths, as well as their anxieties. Do communities reuse or reimagine waste (e.g., landfill or road sand)? Do they hide waste or minimize its impact? Does waste hide a "sense of trauma" or "tales of everyday life" (Lepselter 2016)? Through these stories and connections of waste, we can think about social identities and community shame or stigma issues.

Learning to see waste also requires us to ask who profits from telling or suppressing waste stories. Waste is often separated in ways that prevent it from being viewed as a crime (i.e., dumping waste into watersheds; a mine that leaves a community in environmental collapse) – a shifting of responsibility. How far in the past do the stories of waste go? One compelling study by industrial heritage scholar John Baeten sought to locate long-forgotten "ghost" tailings ponds to understand how communities memorialize or forget waste. Environmental historians have done much to advance the study of mining and issues with the environment (see, e.g., Keeling and Sandlos 2015; McNeill and Vrtis 2017; Morse 2009; LeCain 2009; Robins 2011; Stiller 2000; Studnicki-Gizbert and Schecter 2010). They trace the engagements around what Studnicki-Gizbert (2017: 22) termed a mining ecology, a way to trace intersections between physical, socioeconomic, and biotic systems, as well as "energy and material flows". But, in heritage contexts, waste is more often dropped out of the story, neither a character nor a protagonist. The stories of the industrial past tend to follow a familiar script, the main character or dramatic situation, followed by a midpoint, plot point, and neat ending. In the telling of the industrial past, waste is uncomplicated, inert, and lifeless. And the shadow side of waste remains unremarked. These stories do not contend with how waste is contested. The story of waste is bracketed and untethered. The narratives of post-industrial landscapes tend to ignore – or at the very least, fail to grapple with current social impacts and consequences of waste.

Travel to any historic mining district in the western United States, Butte, Virginia City, Deadwood, or Bisbee, and you will see how waste hides in plain sight. The heritage narratives of these communities tend to follow a formula that talks of human ingenuity, technology, and ambition. The industrial tours celebrate the town's historic buildings, the mining infrastructure, and its colorful characters. Yet, waste is rarely discussed. A recent visit to Butte Montana's Historic Landmark District reminded me of this. Today the town is in an economic transition and is repurposing its mining history into an asset (see Leech 2011, 2018; see also Quivik 2017). The story of Butte is one of a vibrant and diverse mining city, one that built the nation's economy. Yet, these narratives comprise a discursive move that jettisons the more significant stories of disruptions and economic and environmental collapse. Butte is the site of the country's largest Superfund site, the Berkeley Pit, a 900-foot-deep dam filled with nearly seven trillion gallons of toxic sludge that must be continuously monitored to avoid overflow. Thus, the story of Butte is more than a story of industrial might or human ingenuity and innovation; it is also a story of legacy wastes. In the next section, I seek to show why understanding the complexities of industrial heritage matters. I present a brief example of one post-industrial landscape drowning in industrial waste, northern Michigan's Copper Country, a place where you can buy a smokestack for a dollar.[1]

The "Copper Country", Keweenaw Peninsula, Michigan

In the early 1840s, Michigan's Keweenaw Peninsula was the site of the United States' first mineral rush.[2] The story of the "Copper Country" is one of dramatic expansion, capitalist transformation, and nation-building through financial investments and speculation, and later exhaustion (after Studnicki-Gizbert 2017). Industrialists, speculators, and entrepreneurs set in motion political dynamics and cultural processes that industrialized the region. Intoxicated with the riches that the region held, the region became a puzzle of sorts – that required natural resources – timber and fuelwood and water, but also infrastructure, management, labor, and technologies. From railroads to timber operations, dredging and smelting the rush transformed the region. But there is an equally important story, the story of "Ojibwe Country".[3] Although the Keweenaw Penisula has today come to be defined around the mineral rush, these lands and waters are the treaty reserved lands and territories of the Anishinaabe people (see, e.g., Gagnon 2016; Keller 1986). The treaties were instruments of exclusion and erasure that primed capitalist expansion, at least in the eyes of the industrialists.[4] And, while it is true that the rush provided a model for future mineral expansions to follow, for Indigenous communities, treaties were not a giveaway. Instead they were a strategy, a way to protect their lands, sovereignty, and to assure continued access and lived connection to their lands and waters.

The laborers who migrated to the Keweenaw had to contend with an extreme climate, paternal management, and hazardous work (see, e.g., Lankton 1999). Liberating the copper from the bedrock formations required more than might. It required capital investments, labor, and technological innovations. It relied on uneven social and economic relationships and unfettered access to resources. Nevertheless, the copper extraction and processing technologies were crude, dispensing wastes across the landscape. The exhaustion of the land may have had different technologies, processes, or managerial techniques, but it laid the foundation for future mineral industrialization found in other mining districts (see, e.g., Moore 2007; 2003). That is, extracting value at whatever costs. Waste was not valued – and instead was something to dispose of. Yet, developing systems of production also meant pushing limits to increase productivity, and this included later phases, where mine managers revisited discarded waste streams to apply new technologies. For example, in the Keweenaw the once discarded mining wastes, were collected and restamped, to extract value. The result was that more waste entered into the environment. As Kerfoot et al. (2004) estimate, the "poor-rock piles ... lie scattered about the landscape, and at least 0.36 billion metric tons of copper-rich stamp sands were sluiced into streams, interior waterways, and along Lake Superior shorelines".

Today, communities struggle in the wake of these historic industrial copper mining activities that discharged toxic wastes into the air, land, and water. Not only in the billion tons of mine waste tailings that are distributed across the lands and watersheds of Lake Superior (Kerfoot et al. 2012; Kerfoot et al. 2020; Hayter et al. 2015), but also with legacy wastes and toxics that we cannot see. Today the Keweenaw Peninsula includes an active Area of Concern (formerly a Superfund site), with high concentrations of heavy metals and polychlorinated biphenyls (PCBs) (Perlinger et al. 2018). Clearly, industrialists and entrepreneurs did not account for the social and ecological values of waste or the impacts. For Great Lakes tribes, these contaminants present a profound challenge: resource areas have been destroyed and culturally important foods contaminated (Gagnon 2016).

The mine wastes impact traditional food sources and the geomorphology of nearshore and watersheds across the lake basin. Yet, ideas of what constitutes waste are often contested within the region: government agencies, scientists, tribal communities, and heritage organizations often have contradictory definitions of waste. As anthropologist Valoree Gagnon (2016) has shown, despite decades of coordinated and strategic efforts to remediate contamination and mining wastes, current policies and approaches (e.g., fish advisories, clean-up, and mine waste removal) have not found resolution.

Waste along the southern Lake Superior basin is relational and connected. It connects through histories, treaties, northern ecosystems, watersheds, animals, and fish. But it also connects through territorial expansions and capitalism. Yet, for communities of connection, the impacts of waste have cascading effects; waste impacts the fish stocks and wild foods, and other human and more-than-human communities (see, e.g., Langston 2017). Waste also transforms people's memories of place. For those who live and work or have ancestral connections to the region, mining wastes rupture connections; they have an "afterlife of destruction" (Gordillo 2014). One member working on a mining waste restoration project for the local community described the stamp sands as "cutting like a knife".[5] What they were referring to was how the stamp sands would cut and damage the plants. Much like Cruikshank's glaciers that "stalk people", mining waste is sentient and personified, and more importantly, menacing.

But what makes the "story of the Copper Country" so compelling is how waste has been promoted as an historical asset. Some industrial heritage scholars have narrated waste as central to heritage protections. That is, they advocate protecting industrial wastes as a cultural resource. They suggest that in some contexts, removing historic industrial waste constitutes a loss of history and memory. They argue that industrial waste has "historical significance" and should be recognized as a historical resource (Quivik 2007; see, also Gohman 2013; Quivik 2000). In summarizing the multiple and complex histories of waste and intricacies of industrial technologies, such as copper roasting, smelting, and conversion, they argue that waste has value. And, while removing waste from the landscape does remove its memory, it is hard to reconcile these views with how waste impacts contemporary communities; how waste distinguishes people's memories and connections; or how waste represents a form of state-santioned violence. While it is true that erasing waste from the landscape can limit current understandings of their impact, and that lessons are inherent to locating industrial waste streams, I am not entirely convinced that this approach to waste advocacy aligns with the nuances and lived experiences of communities on the frontlines of contamination. If waste is a cultural or historical asset, where do we draw the line? How does seeing waste as a historical asset shape public understanding? Do we risk overshadowing the realities of living with waste? Does it address how it secures the heritage industry's claims over contemporary communities' concerns (Baird 2017)?

Revisiting the specific language that we adopt to describe waste can tell us even more. In the Keweenaw, the term stamp sands refers to copper mine tailings waste. But it references the technology – the stamp – and not the material: mine waste. Copper mine tailings waste deposited in waterbodies has shifted and disrupts fish and benthic organism habitats. Referring to mining wastes as stamp sands provides an air of nostalgia and remove, and I believe helps to understate its impacts. Mining wastes are embedded throughout the community, used on recreational paths or for sanding our icy roads in the winter. As a resident of the Upper Peninsula – I see how mining waste is everywhere – including my property that includes a test mining trench. Learning to see waste as what it is – the material remains from extractive activities – could allow communities to understand how these wastes link to violent extractive processes. To see waste is evidence of violence and destruction; and to trace its afterlife within a post-industrial landscape (after Gordillo 2014). That is, how waste provides material evidence to understand the transformation of a region into capital or markets. To see waste as inseparable from the material conditions of social and cultural lives (Ingold 2012).

Conclusion

Extraction creates a political order that is constituted and valorized through a capitalist system. As Gavin Bridge (2009) asked: How do you account for its political nature? The histories of post-industrial landscapes are often stories about transforming landscapes for capital and industry. Waste is part of this transformation, not only in physical terms and topography but also in social inequality and poverty. We must account for waste's political nature. On the one hand, capitalist expropriation is the primitive accumulation that separates value from the land (Bhandar 2016). On the other hand, the states or local communities bear the clean-up of polluted lands and waters. Value is extracted from the land – and the costs are transferred to communities.

But the heritage stories we tell of waste are often romanticized or removed from the current realities. What if we shifted our stories to see waste, not as a cultural resource or historical asset, but as a teaching tool? One that sees waste as a byproduct of capital – a material that points us toward investigating its production. To understand waste beyond something removed or abandoned; instead seeing waste as the product of global capital at work (Ong 1999). Waste engenders risk – it has costs that are passed on to communities (see Appel 2012). The cleaving of waste works to remove responsibility – to shift these costs onto communities. Butte's Berkeley Pit is now in a state of dependency, of perpetual care. The state, as anthropologist Hannah Appel (2011) has noted, "consistently escapes consequential responsibility for local outcomes" (Appel 2011). Waste then is part of a state of impossible care. Yet, when we accept these terms, a social, ecological, and economic debt is produced.

The heritage of post-extractive landscapes has a unique opportunity to connect waste to current concerns (see, e.g., Kirsch 2018, Rogers 2015). The legacy of waste – and its contemporary impacts – are part of this approach. Understanding waste – what we can see (e.g., tailings, dust, overburden) and what we cannot (e.g., health risks, chemical contamination, radioactive waste) – is one step in moving heritage stories from nostalgia to repair. That is, a rapprochement with waste that shifts our stories of waste from nostalgia to one that directly ties waste to current social, economic, and environmental problems. Waste tells us more about the activity of mining and extraction; it can provide a conduit to connect the past to this moment and provides lessons on how to organize for the future. The proposed Palmer Project in the Alaska Panhandle in the Upper Chilkat Valley provides one recent example. Stakeholders who oppose the project argue that if built, the mine would generate unfathomable amounts of mine waste that would destroy the watershed, and the predictable salmon runs that the community relies on (Rushe 2021). Bringing in the histories and legacies of extractive landscapes could provide a way to understand the outcomes and impacts of new proposals often obscured in industry-speak of new jobs and economic growth. A reckoning with the complications and realities of industrial waste – not as heritage assets, but in real terms – would be essential to understanding the actual impacts of such projects. It would also reveal how the state and corporations often tap into the nostalgia of mining heritage to advance their interests (see Baird 2017).

What does a heritage of waste look like? Returning to the Camp Fire and the Feather River Canyon, a heritage of waste would interpret the post-industrial landscape in ways that make clear the materialities of waste. How mining wastes transformed the landscapes and watersheds, and how these changes linked to contemporary issues of water. We would learn how Lake Concow was not owned by the community, and how its water was diverted to Lake Oroville. We would learn about land regimes and water terrains that link to concerns of water management, fire control, and housing. We could try to think through the links to the mineral rush and how these connect to waste within the post-extractive landscape. In this way, the heritage industry becomes a site of social justice work and advocacy; of bringing historical accuracy together to address contemporary concerns; and to show why histories of waste matter.

Notes

1 www.mininggazette.com/news/2019/06/gay-smokestack-may-see-reprieve-local-citizens-grassroots-group-formed/
2 On the region's mining history, see Krause 1992; Lankton 1999; Reynolds and Dawson 2011.
3 J. Joundreau (2016), personal communication.
4 M. Richards (2021) and C. MacLennan (2018), personal communication.
5 V. Gagnon (2018), personal communication.

References

Appel, H. (2011). *Futures: Oil and the Making of Modularity in Equatorial Guinea*. Redwood City: Stanford University Press.

Appel, H. (2012). Walls and White Elephants: Oil extraction, Responsibility, and Infrastructural Violence in Equatorial Guinea. *Ethnography* 13(4): 439–465.

Baird, M. (2017). *Critical Theory and the Anthropology of Heritage Landscapes*. Gainesville: University Press of Florida.

Baeten, J. (2018). A Century of Red Water: Mine Waste, Legacy Contamination, and Institutional Amnesia in Minnesota's Mesabi Iron Range. *Water History* 10(4): 245–266.

Basso, K. H. (1996). *Wisdom Sits in Places: Landscape and Language among the Western Apache*. Albuquerque: NM Press.

Berman, T. (2017). Canada's Most Shameful Environmental Secret Must Not Remain Hidden. *The Guardian*. Retrieved from: www.theguardian.com/commentisfree/2017/nov/14/canadas-shameful-environmental-secret-tar-sands-tailings-ponds.

Bhandar, B. (2016). *Colonial Lives of Property*. Durham: Duke University Press.

Bridge, G. (2009). Material Worlds: Natural Resources, Resource Geography and the Material Economy. *Geography Compass* 3(3): 1217–1244.

Cater, T. and Arn, K. (2013). "That's Where our Future Came From": Mining, Landscape, and Memory in Rankin Inlet, Nunavut. *Études/Inuit/Studies* 37(2): 59–82.

Dawson, R. and Brechin, G. (2020). *Farewell, Promised Land*. Berkeley: University of California Press.

Gagnon, V. S. (2016). Ojibwe Gichigami ("Ojibwa's Great Sea"): An Intersecting History of Treaty Rights, Tribal Fish Harvesting, and Toxic Risk in Keweenaw Bay, United States. *Water History* 8(4): 365–384.

Gismondi, M. and Davidson, D. (2012). Imagining the Tar Sands 1880–1967 and Beyond. *Imaginations: Journal of Cross-Cultural Image Studies* 3(2): 68–103.

Gohman, S. M. (2013). It's Not Time to Be Wasted: Identifying, Evaluating, and Appreciating Mine Wastes in Michigan's Copper Country. *IA. The Journal of the Society for Industrial Archeology*, 39(1–2): 5–22.

Gordillo, G. R. (2014). *Rubble*. Durham: Duke University Press.

Hare, E. M. (2017). *Making Histories with Science: Paleoecology and Conservation in the Midwestern United States*. Unpublished dissertation. University of California, Santa Cruz.

Hayter, E. J., Chapman , R., Lin , L., Luong , P., Mausolf , G., Perkey , D., Mark , D., andGailani , J. (2015). *Modeling Sediment Transport in Grand Traverse Bay, Michigan to Determine Effectiveness of Proposed Revetment at Reducing Transport of Stamp Sands onto Buffalo Reef*. Vicksburg, MS: US Army Engineer Research and Development Center.

Ingold, T. (2012). Toward an Ecology of Materials. *Annual Review of Anthropology* 41: 427–442.

Jaebong, J., Urban, N., and Green, S. (1999). Release of Copper from Mine Tailings on the Keweenaw Peninsula. *Journal of Great Lakes Research* 25(4): 721–734.

Keeling, A. and Sandlos, J. (2015). *Mining and Communities in Northern Canada: History, Politics, and Memory*. Calgary: University of Calgary Press.

Keller, R. H. (1986). The Chippewa Treaties of 1826 and 1836. *American Indian Journal* 9: 27–32.

Kelley, R. L. (1954). Forgotten Giant: The Hydraulic Gold Mining Industry in California. *Pacific Historical Review* 23(4): 343–356.

Kerfoot, W. C., Harting S.L., Jeong J., Robbins J., and Rossmann R. (2004). Local, Regional, and Global Implications of Elemental Mercury in Metal (copper, silver, gold, and zinc) Ores: Insights from Lake Superior Sediments. *Journal of Great Lakes Research* 30: 162–184.

Kerfoot, W., Yousef, F., Green, S. A., Regis, R., Shuchman, R., Brooks, C. N., Sayers, M., Sabol, B., and Graves, M. (2012). Light Detection and Ranging (LiDAR) and Multispectral Studies of Disturbed Lake Superior Coastal Environments. *Limnology and Oceanography* 57(3): 749–771.

Kerfoot, W., Urban N., Jeong, J., MacLennan, C., and Ford, S. (2020). Copper-Rich "Halo" off Lake Superior's Keweenaw Peninsula and How Mass Mill Tailings Dispersed onto Tribal lands. *Journal of Great Lakes Research* 46(5): 1423–1443.

Kirsch, S. (2018). *Engaged Anthropology*. Berkeley: University of California Press.

Kohn, E. (2013). *How Forests Think*. Berkeley: University of California Press.

Krause, D.J. (1992). *The Making of a Mining District: Keweenaw Native Copper 1500–1870*. Detroit: Wayne State University Press.

Lankton, L. (1999). *Beyond the Boundaries: Life and Landscape at the Lake Superior Copper Mines, 1840–1875*. Oxford: Oxford University Press.

Langston, N. (2017). Iron Mines, Toxicity, and Indigenous Communities in the Lake Superior Basin. In J. R. McNeill and G. Vrtis (eds.), *Mining North America*. Berkeley: University of California Press, pp. 313–338.

Leech, B. (2011). Boom, Bust, and the Berkeley Pit: How Insiders and Outsiders Viewed the Mining Landscape of Butte, Montana. *IA The Journal of the Society for Industrial Archeology*, 37(1–2): 153–170.

Leech, B. (2018). *The City that Ate Itself: Butte, Montana and its Expanding Berkeley Pit*. Reno: University of Nevada Press.

LeCain, T. J. (2009). *Mass Destruction*. New Brunswick: Rutgers University Press.

Lepselter, S. (2016). *The Resonance of Unseen Things: Poetics, Power, Captivity, and UFOs in the American Uncanny*. Ann Arbor: University of Michigan Press.

Marcus, W. A., Meyer G., and DelWayne, R. N. (2001). Geomorphic Control of Persistent Mine impacts in a Yellowstone Park Stream and Implications for the Recovery of Fluvial Systems . *Geology* 29(4): 355–358.

McKittrick, K. (2006). *Demonic Grounds: Black Women and the Cartographies of Struggle.* Minneapolis: University of Minnesota Press.

McNeill, J. R. and Vrtis, G. (eds.) (2017). *Mining North America: An Environmental History since 1522.* Berkeley: University of California Press.

Morin, B. J. (2013). *The Legacy of American Copper Smelting: Industrial Heritage Versus Environmental Policy.* Knoxville: University of Tennessee Press.

Morin, B. J. (2011). *Reflection, Refraction, and Rejection: Copper Smelting Heritage and the Execution of Environmental Policy.* Houghton: Michigan Technological University.

Moore, J. W. (2007). Silver, Ecology, and the Origins of the Modern World, 1450–1640. In A. Hornborg, J. R. McNeill, and J. Martinez-Alier (eds.), *Rethinking Environmental History: World-System History and Global Environmental Change.* Lanham: Rowman & Littlefield, pp. 123–142.

Morse, K. (2009). *The Nature of Gold: An Environmental History of the Klondike Gold Rush.* Seattle: University of Washington Press.

Ong, A. (1999). *Flexible Citizenship: The Cultural Logics of Transnationality.* Durham: Duke University Press.

Perlinger, J. A., Urban, N. R., Giang, A., Selin, N. E., Hendricks, A. N., Zhang, H., Kumar, A., Wu, S., Gagnon, V. S., Gorman, H. S., and Norman, E. S. (2018). Responses of Deposition and Bioaccumulation in the Great Lakes Region to Policy and other Large-scale Drivers of Mercury Emissions. *Environmental Science: Processes and Impacts* 20(1): 195–209.

Poswa, T. and Clavell Davies, T. (2017). The Nature and Articulation of Ethical Codes on Tailings Management in South Africa. *Geosciences* 7(4): 101.

Quivik, F. L. (2000). Landscapes as Industrial Artifacts: Lessons from Environmental History. *IA. The Journal of the Society for Industrial Archeology* 26(2): 55–64.

Quivik, F. L. (2007). The Historical Significance of Tailings and Slag: Industrial Waste as Cultural Resource. *IA. The Journal of the Society for Industrial Archeology* 33 (2): 35–52.

Quivik, F. L. (2017). Butte and Anaconda, Montana: Preserving and Interpreting a Vast Landscape of Extraction. *Change Over Time* 7(1) 6–28.

Reynolds, T. S. and. Dawson V. (2011). *Iron Will: Cleveland-Cliffs and the Mining of Iron Ore, 1847–2006.* Detroit: Wayne State University Press.

Robins, N. A. (2011). *Mercury, Mining, and Empire: The Human and Ecological Cost of Colonial Silver Mining in the Andes.* Bloomington: Indiana University Press.

Rogers, D. (2015). Oil and Anthropology. *Annual Review of Anthropology* 44: 365–380.

Rushe, D. (2021). A Tiny Alaska Town is Split over a Goldmine. At Stake is a Way of Life. *The Guardian.* Retrieved from: www.theguardian.com/us-news/2021/jun/22/alaska-haines-village-salmon-fishing-gold-mine.

Stiller, D. (2000). *Wounding the West: Montana, Mining, and the Environment.* Lincoln: University of Nebraska Press.

Studnicki-Gizbert, D. (2017). Exhausting the Sierra Madre: Mining Ecologies in Mexico over the Longue Durée. In J. R. McNeill and G. Vrtis (eds.), *Mining North America: An Environmental History since 1522.* Berkeley: University of California Press, pp. 19–46.

Studnicki-Gizbert, D. and Schecter, D. (2010). The Environmental Dynamics of a Colonial Fuel-Rush: Silver Mining and Deforestation in New Spain, 1522 to 1810. *Environmental History* 15(1): 94–119.

Todd, Z. (2017). Fish, Kin and Hope: Tending to Water Violations in Amiskwaci-wâskahikan and Treaty Six Territory. *Afterall: A Journal of Art, Context and Enquiry* 43(1): 102–107.

White, R. (1996). *The Organic Machine: The Remaking of the Columbia River*. London: Macmillan.

19 Handling Change in Historic Urban Landscapes

An Analysis of Urban Heritage Conservation Approaches in Bordeaux (France), Edinburgh (UK), and Florence (Italy)

Francesca Giliberto and Federica Appendino

Managing Change in Historic Urban Environments: A Landscape Approach

Managing historic urban environments is one of the biggest challenges in heritage conservation as they constitute critical sites where forces of change and continuity collide (Pendlebury and Strange, 2011; Dormaels, 2012; Gambino, 2013). This complex management is amplified by increasing pressures—rapid urbanisation, commercial and infrastructure development, climate change, socio-functional changes, mass tourism, among others—which may have irreversible impacts on long-term urban heritage conservation (Civilise, 2012; Bandarin and Van Oers, 2015; Leifeste and Stiefel, 2018). In this context, existing conservation tools have often proved to be inadequate or insufficient in handling urban change all over the world (Bandarin and Van Oers, 2012, 2015; Labadi and Logan, 2016; López Sánchez, Tejedor Cabrera, and Del Pulgar, 2020).

In particular, there is still a gap between theoretical approaches that recognise continuous change as an intrinsic characteristic of historic urban environments which are recognized as living systems (Duché, 2010; Jokilehto, 2010; Gabrielli, 2011; Gambino, 2013), and current practice, unable to fully operationalize this flexible conservation approach on the ground through adequate measures for managing change (Van Oers, 2009). In fact, the conventional approach to urban conservation interprets heritage as static and fixed over time, promoting a general attitude of "prevention of change" or "intolerance to change" (Veldpaus and Pereira Roders, 2014). This is reflected in urban heritage conservation processes that generally attempt to maintain the historical integrity and authenticity of the urban fabric, without recognising the urban dynamics of change; neglecting the preservation of its intangible aspects and causing urban fragmentation and deterioration of urban values and meanings (Zancheti and Loretto, 2015). Furthermore, urban heritage conservation practices tend to be implemented in isolation from broader development issues and more interdisciplinary and integrated approaches are envisaged by several

DOI: 10.4324/9781003195238-19

authors (Teutonico and Matero, 2003; Bandarin and Van Oers, 2015; Labadi, 2018).

Since the beginning of the 21st century several international organisations have addressed these issues by providing an overall framework for a renewed approach to sustainable urban management able to overcome the persisting dichotomy between heritage conservation and (sustainable) development (Council of Europe, 2000; ICOMOS, 2011; UNESCO, 2015; United Nations, 2015; Labadi et al., 2021). In particular, the *Recommendation on the Historic Urban Landscape (HUL)* adopted by UNESCO in 2011—also known as the *HUL Recommendation*—promotes a paradigmatic shift in urban conservation by applying a landscape approach to the implementation of a comprehensive and integrated urban heritage management framework for the entire city and its surrounding landscape, considered as a whole (Ginzarly et al. 2019). Applying the "cultural landscape" concept into the urban sphere (Taylor, 2016), the *HUL Recommendation* provides the basis for a more holistic and participatory approach to the identification and assessment of urban heritage tangible and intangible attributes. The concept of historic urban landscape is not new as it is deeply rooted in European theories of urban conservation (Veldpaus, Pereira Roders, and Colenbrander, 2013; Martini, 2013; Greco, 2016). Nevertheless, the UNESCO definition of the "historic urban landscape" is characterised by a growing complexity in the processes of understanding, preserving, and managing heritage, giving greater relevance to its wider urban and geographical context, to intangible dimensions of heritage, and to the dynamic components of historic urban environments.

Therefore, the HUL definition expands the concept of urban heritage, moving from single objects and historic areas to include the multi-layered characteristics of the entire historic urban landscape, linking the urban and man-made environment with its natural setting. Recognising the need to carefully consider social, cultural, environmental, and economic processes in the conservation of urban attributes and values, the *HUL Recommendation* encourages a more integrated, long-term, flexible, open-ended, and people-driven approach (Bandarin and Van Oers, 2015). In this way, urban heritage conservation can be envisaged as the "management of change" (Araoz, 2013), paving the way for the implementation of adaptable approaches to urban conservation, and considering urban environments as living spaces for sustainable communities (Martini, 2013). In practice, the *HUL Recommendation* suggests the implementation of localised tools—including civic engagement tools, knowledge and planning tools, regulatory systems, and financial tools—to be developed through participatory processes involving private and public actors at different scales (local, national, regional, international). However, the recommendation is not intended to substitute existing doctrines or conservation strategies and, wherever possible, it encourages the integration between policies, tools, and practices that already exist, or the development of innovative tools.

Recent research and practical case studies have shed light on how the HUL approach has been implemented in a variety of contexts at a global scale (Fayad et al., 2016; Pereira Roders and Bandarin, 2019). However, comparative studies are required to understand how similar approaches work in different countries and how it is possible to integrate the HUL approach into existing and consolidated systems, as well as to identify good practices and current challenges (Ripp and Rodwell, 2016; Giliberto, 2018; Rey-Pérez and Pereira Roders, 2020). This chapter addresses the following research questions: how do existing urban conservation approaches cope with change in different European historic urban landscapes? And to what extent do they take into consideration the guidance of the *HUL Recommendation*? This chapter discusses the findings of a qualitative analysis of existing urban conservation policies, legislation, and tools operating on the three World Heritage (WH) cities of Bordeaux (France), Florence (Italy), and Edinburgh (United Kingdom). Moreover, it highlights good practices and critical challenges in supporting current urban conservation systems to better handle contemporary challenges.

Analysing Different Urban Conservation Approaches: Materials and Methods

Starting from the definitions and principles of the *HUL Recommendation*, this chapter presents the results of a qualitative analysis of urban conservation approaches implemented in three medium-size European cities: Bordeaux (France), Florence (Italy), and Edinburgh (UK). These case studies were selected because they are characterised by an outstanding urban and architectural heritage—with a large portion of their urban heritage inscribed in the WH List (Figure 19.1.).

These living historic cities have in place consolidated and multi-layered regulatory frameworks and tools for urban heritage conservation. Moreover, they belong to three countries that have strongly contributed to the definition of the HUL approach through the ideas and experiences of some of the most important theorists and practitioners in the field of urban heritage conservation (Bandarin and Van Oers, 2012; Veldpaus, Pereira Roders, and Colenbrander, 2013). However, they share common challenges for urban heritage preservation and management, such as over-tourism, climate change, gentrification processes, and the provision of new buildings and infrastructures in historic environments (Figure 19.2.). Moreover, the participation of the three cities in the European project "Atlas World Heritage",[1] which aims to develop integrated and participatory strategies for the sustainability of urban WH sites (De Luca et al., 2020), raises questions about the relevance of existing urban conservation systems facing contemporary challenges.

Our analysis focuses on planning tools and regulatory systems for urban conservation and management in force in each case study. These documents, presented in Table 19.1., were examined through a desk-analysis supported by the use of an analytical framework to facilitate the comparison of the results in terms of: urban heritage definition and interpretation; protection perimeters and heritage regulations; orientations and prescriptive measures for managing change; integration with other policies, plans, and tools. These findings were

Figure 19.1. The three historic urban landscapes of Florence (top), Edinburgh (centre), and Bordeaux (bottom)

also complemented by interviews carried out with relevant stakeholders. A critical discussion of the key insights emerged from this investigation is provided in the section below which combines them into three major issues correlated with the *HUL Recommendation*: recognising urban heritage as historic urban landscape; urban heritage conservation as management of change; and integration of urban conservation tools, policies, and sectors.

Figure 19.2. Contemporary challenges in historic urban environments: mass tourism in
piazza della Signoria, Florence, Italy (top); new St James Quarter and 'W
Edinburgh' hotel seen from Calton Hill, Edinburgh, UK (centre); and new
tramline in the historic centre of Bordeaux, France (bottom)

Implementing the HUL Approach: Good Practices and Current Challenges

Recognising Urban Heritage as Historic Urban Landscape

The urban heritage of Florence, Edinburgh, and Bordeaux constitutes a complex historic urban landscape. It does not include only the cities' WH

Table 19.1. Essential information about the case studies and related urban conservation and management policies, legislation, and tools

	Bordeaux (Aquitaine, France)	Edinburgh (Scotland, UK)	Florence (Tuscany, Italy)
Name of the WH property	Bordeaux, Port of the Moon	Old and New Towns of Edinburgh	Historic Centre of Florence
Year of inscription in the WHL	2007	1995	1982
Brief description (source: WHL)	The Port of the Moon, port city of Bordeaux in southwest France, is inscribed as an inhabited historic city, an outstanding urban and architectural ensemble, created in the age of the Enlightenment, whose values continued up to the first half of the 20th century .... Its urban form represents the success of philosophers who wanted to make towns into melting pots of humanism, universality and culture.	Edinburgh has been the Scottish capital since the 15th century. It has two distinct areas: the Old Town, dominated by a medieval fortress; and the neoclassical New Town, whose development from the 18th century onwards had a far-reaching influence on European urban planning. The harmonious juxtaposition of these two contrasting historic areas, each with many important buildings, is what gives the city its unique character.	Built on the site of an Etruscan settlement, Florence, the symbol of the Renaissance, rose to economic and cultural pre-eminence under the Medici in the 15th and 16th centuries. Its 600 years of extraordinary artistic activity can be seen above all in the 13th-century cathedral (Santa Maria del Fiore), the Church of Santa Croce, the Uffizi and the Pitti Palace, the work of great masters such as Giotto, Brunelleschi, Botticelli and Michelangelo.
Resident population	239,157	482,005	382,533
Protected urban heritage attributes	• WH Core Zone (1,731 ha) • WH Buffer Zone (11,480 ha) • Safeguarded Sector • Area of Architectural and Landscape Enhancement (AVAP) • Historic Monuments • Ville de Pierre (PLU) • Historic Monuments' Environs	• WH Core Zone (444 ha) • Scheduled Monuments • Listed Buildings • Conservation Areas • Gardens and Designed Landscapes	• WH Core Zone (505 ha) • WH Buffer Zone (10,480 ha) • Listed Architectural Heritage • Landscape and Archaeological Areas

	Bordeaux (Aquitaine, France)	Edinburgh (Scotland, UK)	Florence (Tuscany, Italy)
National legislation for heritage protection	• *Code du Patrimoine*, 2020 • *Code de l'Urbanisme*, 2020 • *Law for Historic Monuments*, 1913 • *Law for the Protection of Natural Monuments and Sites*, 1930 • *Law for Historic Monuments' Environs*, 1943 • *Law Malraux*, 1962 • *Law for Creativity Freedom, Architecture, and Heritage (CAP Law)*, 2016	• *The Ancient Monuments and Archaeological Areas Act*, 1979 • *The Planning (Listed Buildings and Conservation Areas) (Scotland) Act*, 1997 • *The Town and Country Planning (Scotland) Act*, 1997	• *Cultural and Landscape Heritage's Code*, 2004 • *Law n°77, Special Measures for the Protection and the Fruition of Italian WH Cultural, Landscape and Natural sites*, 2006
Territorial planning tools	• Greater Bordeaux Metropolitan Area, *Territorial Cohesion Plan (SCoT)*, 2016 • Nouvelle-Aquitaine Region, *Regional Plan for Spatial Planning, Sustainable Development and Equality (SRADDET)*, 2020	• Scottish Government, *Scotland's Third National Planning Framework (NPF3)*, 2014 • Scottish Government, *Scottish Planning Policy (SPP)*, 2014	• Tuscany Region, *Regional Orientation Plan (PIT)*, 2014 • Province of Florence, *Territorial Coordination Plan (PTCP)*, 2013
Urban planning tools	• Municipality of Bordeaux, *Safeguarding and Enhancement Plan (PSMV)*, 2021 • Municipality of Bordeaux, *Local Urban Regulation Plan (PLU) Ville de Pierre*, 2016	• The City of Edinburgh Council, *Edinburgh Local Development Plan (LDP)*, 2016	• Municipality of Florence, *Structural Plan*, 2014 • Municipality of Florence, *Town Planning Regulation*, 2015

	Bordeaux (Aquitaine, France)	Edinburgh (Scotland, UK)	Florence (Tuscany, Italy)
WH Management Plan	• Municipality of Bordeaux, *WH Management Plan*, 2007	• The City of Edinburgh Council, Historic Environment Scotland and Edinburgh World Heritage, *WH Management Plan*, 2017	• Municipality of Florence (UNESCO Office), *WH Management Plan*, 2016
Other Urban Conservation Tools	• Municipality of Bordeaux, *Bordeaux [Re] centres*, 2010 • Greater Bordeaux Metropolitan Area, *Guidelines on Heritage Protection and Development*	• The City of Edinburgh Council, *Skyline Policy*, 2008 • Historic Environment Scotland, *Managing Change Guidance*, 2016 • The Edinburgh Partnership, *Locality Improvement Plan*, 2017 • The City of Edinburgh Council, *Planning Guideline on Listed Buildings and Conservation Areas*, 2019	• Municipality of Florence, *Building Regulation*, 2015 • Municipality of Florence, *Measures for the Protection and Decorum of the Cultural Heritage in the Historic Centre*, 2016

properties as described in Table 19.1. (see "Brief description"), but also their setting, their relationship with the surrounding landscape (urban and natural), their particular urban character and spatial organisation, visual and historical relationships, local social and cultural practices, economic processes, and all the other elements that define their identity.

The analysis showed how the urban conservation and management policies, regulatory frameworks, and tools operating in the case studies apply a landscape approach for heritage identification in accordance with the *HUL Recommendation*. This approach is mainly incorporated into broader territorial and regional planning tools, which provide long-term orientative management directions, moving beyond the preservation of specific historic areas to include their broader built and natural environments, as well as the tangible and intangible interrelationships with their surrounding landscapes. These directions are deemed to be practically implemented by operational and prescriptive tools in force at smaller scales, from single monuments, listed buildings, and conservation areas to larger urban zones.

However, this approach challenges the management of the historic urban landscape as a whole. In this framework, the perimeters of the WH properties and the recognition of their Outstanding Universal Value (OUV) encourage a more comprehensive approach to urban heritage, going beyond the monumental conservation of the historic centre to include a greater number of urban heritage attributes and values. This is particularly relevant for the case of Bordeaux, where the WH boundary is much wider than in the other two cases, covering almost its entire municipal territory and including more recent urban areas. Nevertheless, Ragot (2008) outlines how the OUV of the WH property marginalises the role that contemporary architecture, often neglected in UNESCO nomination dossiers, plays in the definition of urban heritage values.

In Florence, the buffer zone, adopted to provide additional protection to the WH property, comprises the entire historic urban landscape, exceeding the municipal border and including four neighbouring municipalities. The buffer zone was defined according to the principles of the *HUL Recommendation* and taking into account: the broader systems of historic centres surrounding Florence; relevant public visual axes and vistas connecting the historic centre with the surrounding hills; and different historic layers and cultural relations between the WH property and the rest of the city (Bini, Capitanio, and Francini, 2015). In the case of Edinburgh, the city adopted a different approach—not applying the buffer zone as the existing layers were considered to be adequate to protect the WH site (Giliberto, 2018). In fact, a *Skyline Policy*—used as a model for the definition of Florence's buffer zone—provides supplementary planning control for the safeguarding of key views, silhouette, and topographic features, and regulates the impact that new tall buildings could have on the WH property. However, in both cases, the attempt to apply a HUL approach is done in a very aesthetic manner, mainly considering the visual relationships between the WH property and its surrounding context as well as between relevant buildings of historic and architectural value, rather than other urban heritage elements.

Urban Heritage Conservation as Management of Change

In all case studies urban heritage is understood as a complex living and evolving entity. The investigation revealed how general dynamics of structural and socio-functional change are identified and taken into consideration in urban heritage policies and conservation tools, and different approaches are implemented to managing change. Noteworthy aspects include strategies for infrastructure development, inner city regeneration, reconnection of urban public spaces with the natural environment, and the integration of contemporary buildings in historic contexts. The documents analysed provide measures to handle change not only in relation to heritage tangible aspects, but also to intangible dynamics constituting part of local culture and identity as suggested in the *HUL Recommendation*. However—particularly in the case of Florence and Edinburgh—this approach gives a larger consideration to material aspects of conservation and heritage physical structures rather than to more intangible elements that convey cultural significance.

Different degrees of protection and conservation exist for diverse elements of the three historic urban landscapes: limits of acceptable change vary from a very limited possibility of transformation for listed buildings, conservation, and landscape areas to a careful management of change for distinctive zones characterised by similar heritage features. However, this approach contributes to the urban heritage protection as separated elements—often as special districts—from the rest of the city. As a consequence, the major problems of uncontrolled development commonly occur outside the protection boundaries, particularly in their adjacent districts which are not often sufficiently regulated. The case of Bordeaux illustrates how the definition of protective boundaries—that is the safeguarded sector, the most prescriptive tool in place—provides different safeguarding measures and responsible actors for the urban heritage depending on its location. This process may lead to a conservation paradox as it is applied also when the urban heritage presents very similar characteristics within and outside the preservation perimeter (Appendino, 2017a).

Another limitation was found in the case of Florence, which reflects a very conventional and conservative approach to urban conservation. In fact, priority is given to the preservation of the structural integrity of the urban heritage and to its aesthetic and historic values rather than to its socio-functional integrity and ecological values. This overly prescriptive and normative approach limits the possibilities for new developments, and causes damage in terms of the design quality of new contemporary projects. On the other hand, the more flexible approach encouraged in Edinburgh presents some limits too. Surprisingly, the historic centre is one of the areas where the highest degree of change is admitted to maintain the city's appeal and living standards, being the most vulnerable zone in relation to new development pressures, like for example "W Edinburgh"—a new luxury hotel in St James Quarter located in the WH core zone (see Figure 19.2.). This approach favours economic development and job creation, but seriously threatens the safeguarding of the urban heritage over time.

A more balanced approach between protection and development is implemented in Bordeaux. Similarly to Florence, the very high level of heritage protection makes the intervention of the superintendence, a peripheral body of the Ministry for Culture, necessary for most interventions (Callais, Jeanmonod, and Barlet, 2017). However, Bordeaux has always opted for a more flexible approach that can be defined as "inventive conservation" (Donadieu, 1995). In a battle against the risk of museification, Bordeaux's conservation policies aim to ensure the continuity of a living city and its capacity to develop and evolve over time even in the most protected sectors of the city. It is possible to appreciate this approach in the UNESCO nomination dossier for the WH site (Duchene, 2008), which is keen on balancing heritage protection and contemporary architectural design, and in the latest large-scale projects realised in the city. This is particularly evident if we consider for example "*[Re]centres*", an urban regeneration programme for the sustainable rehabilitation of the entire historic urban area in response to local residents' new requirements and needs (Appendino, 2017b); the implementation of the tramway in the historic centre; and the reconfiguration of the Garonne river's banks. In addition, the *PSMV* was recently revised to incorporate sustainability's targets defined in the *PLU* and contemporary lifestyle requirements, that is, environmental protection, economic development, attractiveness, green mobility, social equity, and buildings' energetic retrofit. In this way, the extremely conservative approach that applies to the safeguarded sector is shifting towards a more flexible attitude reconciling urban preservation with quantified targets for meeting the above-mentioned requirements.

Integration of Urban Conservation Tools, Policies, and Sectors

A lot of complexity is involved in the urban conservation and management of these three historic urban landscapes, which is reflected in the number of overlapping policies, protection perimeters, and tools that are designated to meet this scope at different scales. This is particularly relevant for the case of Florence and Bordeaux, whose documents provide very detailed information about urban heritage attributes and values recognised at different levels, as well as transformation dynamics and critical factors affecting or potentially affecting the urban heritage. The result is a superimposition of perimeters, plans, and tools, each one providing specific directions and prescriptive measures to be implemented by different responsible institutions, actors, and departments. This approach over-complicates the understanding of the historic urban landscape and may lead to confusion and contradictions in urban heritage conservation (Appendino, 2017a; Giliberto, 2018). On the other hand, Edinburgh's urban management policies provide very concise information for the identification of territorial and urban elements, and more straightforward measures for implementation, simplifying their understanding. However, they poorly inform local managers, developers, architects, and designers about the city's heritage significance, and contemporary dynamics, which may result in inadequate urban and development planning processes compromising the long-term heritage safeguarding.

Furthermore, even if forms of collaboration between different urban stakeholders are increasing in all cases, there is still a need to move beyond each disciplinary boundary for sustainably preserving, managing, guiding transformations of, and enhancing these complex urban environments as suggested by the *HUL Recommendation*. Moreover, our findings reveal that local communities are not always (or meaningfully) involved in the definition of urban heritage attributes and values to be safeguarded over time—a process which remains driven by "experts" and institutional officers. In this context, the WH properties, buffer zones, and their related management plans play a unique role. In fact, the WH perimeters overlap with other safeguarding boundaries and urban areas, adding another layer of protection that needs to be ensured through the involvement of different actors, and with the integration of diverse urban management tools. The WH management plans appear to be the most colla-borative and cross-sectoral tools for coordinating heritage-related projects and actions as they constitute a shared and interdisciplinary field for urban heritage decision-making processes. A positive example is shown by the case of Edin-burgh, where the WH management plan was complemented by a *Locality Improvement Plan* sharing common aspirations for managing the complex range of issues facing the city centre, including the WH site. However, despite these promising aspects, the management plans are not prescriptive plans and are consequently poorly taken into account by more operational tools (Lo Piccolo, Leone, and Pizzuto, 2012). An attempt for greater integration is provided by the case of Bordeaux, where the *Cap Law* establishes that the WH perimeter and related management plan must be integrated into urban planning and conservation tools in the next few years to ensure the overall consistency of urban heritage protection and enhancement measures.

Conclusion

Since the adoption of the *HUL Recommendation* in 2011, national and local governments are called on to adapt, disseminate, and facilitate its implementa-tion in their territorial jurisdictions, as well as to monitor its impact on the conservation and management of historic urban environments. This chapter highlighted how the three case studies have incorporated some of the principles expressed in the *HUL Recommendation*. Nevertheless, our analysis showed how this is not always a comprehensive and straightforward process, and more inte-grated, people-driven, and value-based approaches are yet to be developed and implemented. The fragmentation and overlapping of various tools and policies over-complicates the understanding of the historic urban landscape—which should be considered as a whole and not divided into distinctive components—as well as the development of concrete actions that need to be undertaken for its sustainable safeguarding and management over time. This is particularly evident when considering the limits of existing strategies for managing change presented in this chapter. Overcoming these criticisms requires a shift toward a greater balance and flexibility able to meet both heritage conservation and transformations requirements, and a more consistent definition of limits for acceptable change.

Finally, a multidisciplinary and cross-sectoral approach is today more timely than ever to handle the development challenges that these cities are currently facing, the recovery from the COVID-19 pandemic, and the countdown to achieve the Sustainable Development Goals set by the United Nations by 2030. Bordeaux, Florence, and Edinburgh are currently tackling some common chal-lenges related to the need for a greater socio-economic balance and accessibility of services and infrastructures between historic centres and more peripheral urban areas, more efficient tourism management strategies, and more inclusive and coordinated systems for urban management governance (Consorcio de la Ciudad de Santiago de Compostela, 2018). As part of the ATLAS project, they are expected—together with Porto and Santiago de Compostela—to ensure sustainable models for urban heritage management and monitoring by the end of 2021. This chapter showed how the HUL approach applied in these three cities can be improved through the creation and efficient implementation of more comprehensive, integrated, and participatory plans for managing change in the historic urban landscape, able to bridge different disciplines and sectors (e.g., heritage conservation and climate action, energy efficiency, social inclusion or inequalities reduction), and to drive the overall urban management toward the same direction.

Note

1 More information about the project is available at www.atlaswh.eu/

References

Appendino, F. (2017a). *Sfide e Opportunità per la Tutela del Patrimonio Urbano nel XXI secolo: Città Storica e Sostenibilità. Dall'Esperienza Francese al Caso di Parigi.* Turin-Paris: Polytechnic Institute of Turin and Paris-Sorbonne University. PhD dissertation.

Appendino, F. (2017b). Balancing Heritage Conservation and Sustainable Development – The Case of Bordeaux. *IOP Conference Series: Materials Science and Engineering*, 245(6).

Araoz, G. (2013). Conservation Philosophy and its Development: Changing Understandings of Authenticity and Significance. *Heritage and Society*, 6(2): 144–154.

Bandarin, F. and Van Oers, R. (2012). *The Historic Urban Landscape: Managing Heritage in an Urban Century.* Oxford: John Wiley and Sons.

Bandarin, F. and Van Oers, R. (eds.) (2015). *Reconnecting the City: The Historic Urban Landscape Approach and the Future of Urban Heritage.* Oxford: Wiley-Blackwell.

Bini, M., Capitanio, C., and Francini, C. (2015). *Buffer Zone: The Safeguarding Area for the Historic Centre of Florence*, UNESCO Site. Florence: University of Florence.

Callais, C., Jeanmonod, T., and Barlet, A. (eds). (2017). *Bordeaux, la Fabrique du Patrimoine. Paysages d'une Cité Historique Vivante.* Bordeaux: Editions ensapBx.

Civilise, A. M. (2012). Patrimoine et Développement Durable: un Atout?. In Collectif Confluences (ed.) *Patrimoine et Développement Durable*, Bordeaux: Editions confluences.

Consorcio de la Ciudad de Santiago de Compostela. (2018). *Diagnosis Study of Urban WH sites in the AA.* ATLAS-WH Consortium.

Council of Europe. (2000). *European Landscape Convention.*

De Luca, G., Shirvani Dastgerdi, A., Francini, C., and Liberatore, G. (2020). Sustainable Cultural Heritage Planning and Management of Overtourism in Art Cities: Lessons from Atlas World Heritage. *Sustainability*, 12(9).

Donadieu, P. (1995). Pour une Conservation Inventive des Paysages. In A. Roger (ed.) *La Théorie du paysage en France, 1974–1994*, Seyssel: Champ Vallon.

Dormaels, M. (2012). Repenser les Villes Patrimoniales: Les "Paysages Urbains Historiques". *Téoros*, 31(2): 110–113.

Duché, D. (2010). De l'objet mobilier à la gestion des paysages urbains historiques - Les pratiques françaises, *Managing Historic Cities*, World Heritage Papers, 27.

Duchene, M. (2008). L'enjeu urbain de l'Unesco pour Bordeaux. In J. Boisseau (ed.) *Bordeaux-UNESCO: Les enjeux du patrimoine mondial de l'humanité*, Talence: Editions Bastingage.

Fayad, S., Reeves, K., Zhou, J., Verdini, G., Jiaotong, X., Rogers, A., Juma, M., Re, A., and Veldpaus, L. (2016). *The HUL Guidebook. Managing Heritage in Dynamic and Constantly Changing Urban Environments.* Shanghai: WHITRAP.

Gabrielli, B. (2011). 50 anni ANCSA: le idee di ieri, le responsabilità di oggi. In F. Toppetti (ed.) *Paesaggi e Città Storica. Teorie e politiche del progetto,* Firenze: Alinea.

Gambino, R. (2013). Historic Urban Landscape: dai Centri Storici al Territorio Contemporaneo. In Comune di Alberobello, Istituto Superiore Sistemi Territoriali per l'Innovazione (SITI), and Comune di Matera (eds.) *Historic Urban Landscape: dalla Raccomandazione Unesco all'Ambito Applicativo.* Alberobello: Tipografia A.G.A.

Giliberto, F. (2018). *Linking Theory with Practice: Assessing the Integration of a 21st Century Approach to Urban Heritage Conservation, Management and Development in the World Heritage Cities of Florence and Edinburgh.* Turin-Canterbury: Polytechnic Institute of Turin and University of Kent. PhD dissertation.

Greco, E. (2016). Preserving and Promoting the Urban Landscape. The French and Italian Debates of the Post-World War II Decades. *plaNext,* 2, Retrieved from: http://journals.aesop-planning.eu/volume-2/article-12/.

Ginzarly, M., Houbartb, C., and Teller, J. (2019). The Historic Urban Landscape Approach to Urban Management: A Systematic Review. *International Journal of Heritage Studies,* 25(10): 99–1019.

ICOMOS (2011). *The Valletta Principles for the Safeguarding and Management of Historic Cities, Towns and Urban Areas.* Paris: ICOMOS.

Jokilehto, J. (2010). Notes on the Definition and Safeguarding of HUL. *City and Time,* 4(3).

Labadi, S. (2018). Historical, Theoretical and International Considerations on Culture, Heritage and (Sustainable) Development. In P. Larsen and W. Logan (eds). *World Heritage and Sustainable Development,* London: Routledge.

Labadi, S., Giliberto, F., Rosetti, I., Shetabi, L., and Yildirim, E. (2021). *Heritage and the Sustainable Development Goals: Policy Guidance for Heritage and Development Actors.* Paris: ICOMOS.

Labadi, S. and Logan, W. (eds.) (2016). *Urban Heritage, Development, and Sustainability.* Abingdon: Routledge.

Leifeste, A. and Stiefel, B. L. (2018). *Sustainable Heritage. Merging Environmental Conservation and Historic Preservation.* Abingdon: Routledge.

Lo Piccolo, F., Leone, D., and Pizzuto, P. (2012). The (Controversial) Role of the UNESCO WH List Management Plans in Promoting Sustainable Tourism Development. *Journal of Policy Research in Tourism, Leisure and Events,* 4(3): 249–276.

López, S., Tejedor Cabrera, A., Del Pulgar, M. L. G. (2020). Guidelines from the Heritage Field for the Integration of Landscape and Heritage Planning: A systematic Literature Review. *Landscape and Urban Planning,* 204, article 103931.

Martini, V. (2013). *The Conservation of Historic Urban Landscapes: An Approach.* Slovenia: University of Nova Gorica. PhD dissertation.

Pendlebury, J. and Strange, I. (2011). Centenary Paper: Urban Conservation and the Shaping of the English city. *Town Planning Review,* 82(4): 361–392.

Pereira Roders, A. and Bandarin, F. (eds.) (2019). *Reshaping Urban Conservation. The Historic Urban Landscape Approach in Action.* Singapore: Springer.

Ragot, G. (2008). Bordeaux port de la lune. Une occasion manquée pour le patrimoine et la création contemporaine. In J. Boisseau (ed.) *Bordeaux-UNESCO: Les enjeux du patrimoine mondial de l'humanité,* Talence: Editions Bastingage.

Rey-Pérez, J. and Pereira Roders, A. (2020). Historic Urban Landscape: A Systematic Review, Eight Years after the Adoption of the HUL Approach. *Journal of Cultural Heritage Management and Sustainable Development*, 10(3): 233–258.

Ripp, M. and Rodwell, D. (2016). The Governance of Urban Heritage. *The Historic Environment: Policy and Practice*, 7(1): 81–108.

Taylor, K. (2016). The Historic Urban Landscape Paradigm and Cities as Cultural Landscapes. Challenging Orthodoxy in Urban Conservation, *Landscape Research*, 41(4): 471–480.

Teutonico, J. M. and Matero, F. (eds.) (2003). *Managing Change: Sustainable Approaches to the Conservation of the Built Environment*. Los Angeles: The Getty Conservation Institute.

UNESCO. (2015). *Policy Document for the Integration of a Sustainable Development Perspective into the Processes of the WH Convention*. Paris: UNESCO.

UNESCO. (2011). *Recommendation on the Historic Urban Landscape*. Paris: UNESCO.

United Nations. (2015). *Transforming Our World: The 2030 Agenda for Sustainable Development*. New York: United Nations.

Van Oers, R. (2009). Gestion des villes historiques et conservation des paysages urbains historiques. In *"Paysages urbains historiques: Une nouvelle recommandation de l'UNESCO à l'appui de la Convention du patrimoine mondial" Synthèse des journées techniques*. Bordeaux.

Veldpaus, L., Pereira Roders, A., and Colenbrander, B. J. F. (2013). Urban Heritage: Putting the Past into the Future. *The Historic Environment*, 4(1): 3–18.

Veldpaus, L. and Pereira Roders, A. (2014). Learning from a Legacy: Venice to Valletta. *Change Over Time*, 4(2): 244–263.

Zancheti, S. M. and Loretto, R. P. (2015). Dynamic Integrity: A Concept to Historic Urban Landscape. *Journal of Cultural Heritage Management and Sustainable Development*, 5(1): 82–94.

20 What cultural landscape for Bamiyan (Afghanistan)?

Observations on the UNESCO site protection practices

Mirella Loda

Premise

The case of Bamiyan (Afghanistan) – included in the World List of Heritage in Danger in 2003 owing to its exceptional "Cultural Landscape and Archaeological Remains" – offers an interesting example to think about the UNESCO approach to protecting the cultural landscape as well as the problems accompanying the practices to put this into effect. Furthermore, it offers cues for reflection on the entanglement between landscape protection and regional planning.

In the following pages we briefly go through the main stages through which UNESCO has focused its attention on the topic of the landscape and thereafter the action put together by UNESCO in this field in Bamiyan; we then proceed by illustrating how the topic of protecting the cultural landscape has been included in the extension of the new Bamiyan Strategic Master Plan and conclude by underlining the need for concepts and operations to pass from sectoral outlooks to integrated heritage management perspectives.

The approach of UNESCO to the topic of landscape is outlined in three fundamental documents: *Recommendation Concerning the Safeguarding of the Beauty and Character of Landscapes and Sites* from 1962; *Convention Concerning the Protection of the World Cultural and Natural Heritage* from 1972, the document founding the World Heritage Convention and relative list; and the *Budapest Declaration* from 2002, to which all the subsequent operational guidelines make reference. None of the three texts defines the concept of landscape in itself, or includes any trace of the long scientific (in particular geographical) debate on its nature which has pitted culturalist and substantialist visions against each other. Instead, they make – even if implicitly – reference to the idea of landscape developed by the French Regional Geography at the beginning of the 20th Century, spread in the US by Carl Sauer, and that set down in everyday language as an equivalent of beautiful scenery. This idea proved to be very useful for describing forms and organization of the territory as shaped by the traditional agricultural (European) civilization. However, it is ineffective as analytical and, most important, as operational tool to set out landscape protective plans.

In the *Recommendation*, the term landscape never appears alone but always in association with the word "site". Hence the effect of the conceptual device "landscape and site" is to place the specific object of interest (the site) in a fundamentally

DOI: 10.4324/9781003195238-20

aesthetic. At the same time the interchangeable use of the terms "site" and "land-scape" projects onto the latter the idea of a physical entity, to be delimitated and preserved with the same principles applied to the preservation (or museumization) of a site. Article 1 of the 1972 Convention identifies cultural heritage as "groups of separate or connected buildings which, *because of* their architecture, their homo-geneity or *their place in the landscape*, are of outstanding universal value from the point of view of history, art or science" (my italics). Again, the landscape, is understood reductively as a portion of physical, a (harmonious) context that sub-stantiates the exceptional value of a particular heritage.

The "cultural landscape" concept appears for the first time in the 1992 version of the "Operational Guidelines for the Implementation of the World Heritage Convention", that is, 20 years after the Convention itself,[1] to then be reused in all the following updates. The concept takes up the idea of a whole, a single context, which already belongs to the concept of landscape, while strengthening the sense of continuity with a historical-cultural construct and a universe substantially inside traditional farming societies. Last, the *Budapest Declaration* (2002) also proposes a similar formulation, hinging around an almost interchangeable use of the terms site and landscape, but where the second term more explicitly assumes the sense – very close to the meaning assigned to it in French regional geography – of the visual projection of a particular cultural context: "We care for these sites from the dee-pest forests to the highest mountains, from ancient villages to magnificent build-ings, so that the diverse landscapes and cultures of the world be forever protected".

The short quotations transcribed here document how the establishment and then the management of the World Heritage landscape took its cue from the fundamentally visual sense that the term landscape had for the French Regional Geography and from the aesthetic meaning it assumes in everyday language.[2] As such, the WHL has been able to absorb all the different meanings and evocative power of the term landscape, to go beyond an idea of heritage as a collection of single events/assets and read their value in contextual terms. At the same time, it has inevitably paid for the elusive nature of this conception of landscape which makes its translation in operational terms – that is, its identification, delimitation, protection, and management – extremely complex and fragile.[3]

The criticalities resulting from the adoption of quite lax basic definitions in UNESCO practices relating to landscape heritage have, moreover, been accentuated by the need to satisfy the criteria of authenticity and integrity[4] which have been a condition for nomination to the list since the *Budapest Declaration*. What is more, it has augmented the already tough task of identify-ing shared and so-to-speak transcultural criteria to distinguish between the categories of cultural and natural landscape.[5]

Among these issues, subject to broad debate at international level, I would like to recall the following problems owing to the significance they assume in the case of Bamiyan (Afghanistan) presented in this article:

1   The difficulties connected with identifying the constitutive elements of a cultural landscape and defining its boundaries;

2   The competition between subjects/territories prompted by processes for inclusion on the World Heritage List;

3   The unstable balance between protection of the landscape and transformation of the territory.

The observations that I will make in the following pages are the result of the experience gained as part of a cooperation project – funded by the Italian Agency for Development Cooperation (AICS) and implemented by LaGeS, the University of Florence Laboratory of Social Geography. The project – whose aim was to make a Strategic Master Plan (SMP) for the valley of Bamiyan – started in February 2017 and ended in September 2018.[6]

What cultural landscape for Bamiyan?

Bamiyan is a city of 50,000 inhabitants located 2,500 metres above sea level in a mountainous area of central Afghanistan (Hazarajat). The town became sadly famous in March 2001 when the Taliban government decreed the destruction of two giant (38 and 57 metres) statues of Buddha dating from the sixth and seventh centuries. The two statues, sculpted into the rock on the northern border of the Bamiyan valley, were the westernmost testimonies of Buddhist culture (Figure 20.1.).

Immediately after the Taliban defeat, the Bamiyan valley was placed on the World Heritage List (2003) – owing to its exceptional "Cultural Landscape and Archaeological Remains" – as the reasons for its inclusion read. Bamiyan was nevertheless put in the "in danger" category due to the risks connected to the general conditions of insecurity and structural instability of the archaeological remains and Buddha niches.

From that moment on, the Bamiyan valley became the focus of a vast system of operations to protect the cultural heritage, with the engagement of numerous donor countries, in particular Japan, Korea, Italy, France, and Germany, under the umbrella of UNESCO, to protect the archaeological remains. Among other things, this allowed the niches that had hosted the Buddhas to be made safe and the partial recovery of the wall paintings.[7]

These favourable conditions, together with the population's great expectations of an improvement in their economic and housing conditions, sparked a positive dynamism in the region, but inevitably exercised growing pressure on resources and generated potential conflicts as to their use.

In terms of the UNESCO goals, there is no doubt that these various dynamics made the landscape a particularly sensitive point. But despite its explicit mention in the title of the application document, the attention and protection actions following Bamiyan's inclusion on the list in actual fact concentrated exclusively on the archaeological remains, which were rapidly marked off along with the protection areas. The protection of the cultural landscape, on the other hand, found itself relegated to an afterthought.

Between 2005 and 2007, the University of Aachen, supported by UNESCO, set up a survey of the territorial resources which, as well as adding to the census of archaeological heritage, enabled the recognition of important elements of the landscape and offered a very detailed description of the geographical and physical features of the territory, the settlement and architectural structures, water resources, and water regulation systems.

Nevertheless, the resulting Cultural Master Plan (CMP) – beyond the ambitious title – was more a stocktake of landscape elements[8] than a structured reconstruction and identification of invariants to use as the grounds for the rules for transforming the landscape framework, in other words, as a real planning tool. The upshot was that it had no influence in terms of standards to protect and enhance the cultural landscape (ACDC, 2013).

In line with this approach, UNESCO's most recent intervention in Bamiyan with AICS funding, is to be centred around creating an archaeological park in the valley bottom, immediately at the base of the rocky wall with the niches which used to host the Buddhas.

In sum, we can conclude that 18 years after Bamiyan's inclusion in the heritage of humanity list, the action by UNESCO has without doubt been effective in protecting and promoting the archaeological heritage. On the landscape level, however, there has been a lack of clear planning directions.

One of the main causes of this situation is the abovementioned difficulty to put into operational terms a concept that is extremely complex, intrinsically holistic, and that, last, has an aesthetic basis, such as that of cultural landscape adopted by UNESCO. Indeed, it is no coincidence that the areas of archaeological interest and the relative protection areas are clearly marked off, while no UNESCO property for the cultural landscape has yet been defined.

First of all, the elements identified by the CMP as making up the local cultural landscape are distributed in a vast area of around 32 km^2, equivalent to the whole valley area. Hence, it could be quite problematic to identify the whole of this area as UNESCO property but at the same time it cannot be reduced to a portion of it, except by way of totally arbitrary and questionable operations of landscape analysis. The topic is highly sensitive owing to the consequences that its delimitation would have on the scenarios of future development of the areas falling either inside or outside the property perimeter.[9]

Furthermore, and above all, placing the stress on the preservation of single components/elements of the landscape risks losing sight of the fact that protection can only begin by being considered the outcome of processes. In the case of Bamiyan, these processes consist basically in farming activities.

In this connection, Gambi's concept of structural landscape, which probably constituted a crucial point of geographical reflection on the matter (Gambi, 1966), can be taken as a theoretical standpoint for the formulation of planning tools whose goal is to protect and enhance the cultural landscape.

Separating the concept of landscape from the topographical and visual dimension typical of the neo-positivist substantialist approach, and at the same time from the aesthetic value that it holds in everyday language, Gambi frames the notion of landscape as the visible outcome of underlying structures that govern the transformation of the territory. Hence, the attention and potential protection should concentrate on these structures rather than on the visible outcome (the landscape).[10]

Moreover Gambi's vision – albeit within a historical-materialist approach – tied the notion of landscape to that of transformation. Hence, he anticipated the recent reflections on the landscape as a "becoming" cultural concept, in a perennial state of deconstruction and reconstruction (Kelly and Norman, 2007), which is crucial for the policies aimed at managing and protecting cultural landscape.

In the case of Bamiyan, this means reflecting on the farming practices that have forged the rural landscape in the valley bottom, whose practicability and profitability are essential to ensure that the plots of land, buildings, cleaning of the channels, and, in short, the care of the land, are not abandoned. However, we must not overlook the problems connected to the dynamicity of the farming landscape. Bamiyan's rural landscape has undergone profound transformations during recent history: until the 1970s, the typical crop was wheat,[11] while at present the totally dominant crop is the potato. This change to a typical "cash crop" resulted from the progressive integration of Bamiyan agriculture into the national and international markets, recently facilitated by the improvement of the road infrastructure and the connections with Kabul and Herat. The shift from extensive wheat to potato cultivation, which demands much more water, had a decisive impact in broadening the irrigation system that shapes the current rural landscape. Finally, the trees that today make such a rich contribution to the valley landscape are also a recent acquisition, as shown by comparing the present appearance with earlier images.[12]

In this context, it appears objectively complex (and perhaps questionable) to select a specific rural landscape as Bamiyan's legitimate cultural landscape. In the same way, it becomes tricky to define it – as the so-called Cultural Masterplan tried to do – through a stocktake of single elements (objects) to protect. Nevertheless, there is no question that, along with limitation of the urbanization processes, the landscape values in the valley bottom require urgent protection. Indeed, it has been greatly affected by the transformative pressure of recent years, with the rapid expansion of the bazaar and the consequent demand for parking places, also for the trucks transporting potatoes.

The search for a balanced position between the conceptual and operational difficulties posed by the definition and protection of the cultural landscape on one hand, and the consideration of the landscape-making role of the farmers on the other, was the inspiration for the guidelines contained in the new SMP, in force since the end of 2018 (LaGeS, 2018).

At the other extreme to Gambi's line of reflection (or more in general to the "cognitively perfect landscape"),[13] the aesthetic dimension inherent in the concept can be reclaimed as part of a new culturalist approach which reads the landscape as a stratification of meanings, a system of signs and a narrative text with aesthetic value (Duncan and Duncan, 1988; Socco, 1998). In this perspective, it becomes central to understand how semiosis structures the perceptive information we receive from the external space as it translates it into landscape, that is, something to which we give a meaning and aesthetic value. So, semiosis – namely, the act of signification with which we associate "meanings" with "significant" portions of perceptive information using a "code"– is situated at the centre of attention for the management, planning (and protection) of the landscape.

This approach to interpreting and protecting the landscape is extremely interesting because of the link with the community's own identity recognition processes. Nevertheless, it is very difficult to put into practice,[14] as shown by the difficulties to use its principles even in a moment when the application of the European Landscape Convention (Council of Europe, 2000) was pushing towards the exploration of subjective landscapes (Vecchio, 2011). Still, it outlines a path to follow in the future, especially in a case such as that of Bamiyan, where the object of protection is a "cultural landscape" which first of all needs to be identified and understood from the perspective of the local collectivity.

The adjective "cultural" further denotes the already dense concept of landscape as the complex outcome of intricate processes of territorialization and implicitly recalls a specific socio-cultural-territorial matrix. The concept's use in the ambit of World Heritage protection should therefore not be separated from reflection on how the Western global perspective transmitted by international bodies (Smith, 2006) interfaces with the local culture, visions and systems of values that are quite distant and different from it, or from careful consideration as to which local collective identity-building strategy it goes to support.

In this connection, the results of some preliminary studies carried out in preparation for the SMP are cause for concern – and deserve suitable investigation. These results shed light on the lack of correspondence between the two perspectives – international and local – and the relative marginality of the UNESCO sites on the map of favourite (therefore symbolically more significant) places for the local population.[15]

Alternative landscapes?

Ever since its inclusion in the list, the action to protect the cultural landscape in Bamiyan has therefore worked in a somewhat negative direction, in that on the basis of the CMP the UNESCO representatives have opposed locally promoted initiatives or development plans with potentially problematic impacts on the heritage.

An example of this action is the pressure exercised on the local authorities, with the threat to cancel Bamiyan from the WHL in order to prevent the outward or upward expansion of the farms in the valley bottom, which is restricted by the Afghan law of 2004 on the protection of the cultural heritage (Law on the Protection of Archaeological and Cultural Properties). The UNESCO interventions here have without doubt reinforced the effectiveness of the restrictions imposed by that law to a much greater degree than in the rest of the country, but at the cost of a great increase in conflict not only between insiders and outsiders, but also differences in opinions among the various components of the local collectivity.

The CMP – also thanks to the tenacity of the authors and UNESCO staff in illustrating its usefulness – set the standard for the protection of the yet-to-be-clearly-defined "cultural landscape", in contrast to the proliferation of built-up areas in the most precious and sensitive parts of the valley. Nevertheless, the political feasibility of the restrictive action did not lie in widespread sensitivity towards protecting the heritage – although this was certainly strengthened among the local community by UNESCO's efforts. At its basis, instead, was the expectation of tourism development fuelled by the valley's inclusion in the World Heritage List, and the great promise of avant-garde urban transformation reserved primarily for those operating in the local sectors of trade, craft, and services.

For other sectors of the population the restrictions issued by the CMP were instead an obstacle to their economic activities and efforts to improve their living conditions. This was especially the case of families of farmers living on the valley floor, close to the UNESCO sites and the protected areas, who were prohibited from increasing the height or volume of their homes.

This contrast brings us to reflect on the difficulties deriving from the different positions on the topic of protecting the heritage, which in Bamiyan are also charged with particular tension owing to the interference of ethnic factors. Hence, the cultural landscape debate inevitably becomes a political confrontation. The situation here is that the Hazara population, whose economic base lies in the trade and craft of the "new bazaar", is in favour of protective action, while the families belonging to the Tajik group, whose economic base is agriculture in the most sensitive landscape areas of the valley, are strongly against it.

The potential conflict between the two groups is further exacerbated by the Tajik population's fear of so-called ethnic substitution, stemming from the recent drastic drop in their demographic weight.[16]

The intricate relationship between a readiness to protect the landscape, ethnic belonging, and economic base nevertheless only became evident by crossing over the data collected in the direct surveys carried out during the project. The surveys in question were a comprehensive investigation of the characteristics of the activities and operators present in the bazaar,[17] showing the overwhelming presence of Hazara shops and workers, and the mapping of the agricultural lots in the buffer zones with the name and ethnic group of the owners,[18] indicating that the vast majority of the plots belong to Tajik families.

Last, documentation of the facts and not just the ideology at the basis of a great part of the resistance to protecting the landscape enabled reflection on the dangerous side effects of an excessively abstract and restrictive protection policy. Similarly emblematic of UNESCO's difficulties in working to protect the cultural landscape was the position assumed with regard to the projects to build a bypass crossing the valley for the heavy through traffic on the east-west route linking Kabul with Herat via Chest-e Sharif. The harsh criticism levelled by

UNESCO against the plans initially proposed by the Ministry of Public Works in Kabul had the merit of highlighting the dramatic consequences that they would have had on the protection of the cultural heritage owing to the closeness to the site protection zones, in particular Gholghola and the farming area in the Kakrak valley, which are an integral part of the "cultural landscape". Nevertheless, the criticism was not accompanied by acknowledgement of the effective necessity to improve the routes for vehicles to cross the valley, thereby denying the population's legitimate aspirations for modernization and a generally more efficient urban system.

Landscape directions in the new Strategic Master Plan

Concerning the three issues in the UNESCO landscape heritage practices quoted at the beginning of this article – namely, 1. solving the problems posed by an imprecise definition and outlining of the cultural landscape of Bamiyan, 2. mitigating conflicts among different social groups and 3. reconciling the landscape heritage protection goals posed by its place on the WHL with the local population's legitimate claims for modernization – the new SMP has turned to solutions founded on the basic principles of protecting the territory and town planning regulations.

With no explicit definition or delimitation of the cultural landscape to protect, the SMP goes on to identify the *cultural landscape* with the *rural landscape* of the valley floor,[19] which hence becomes a sort of buffer zone extended around the sites of archaeological interest, but obviously managed with town planning-type tools.[20]

The first objective of the plan therefore consists of safeguarding the farming vocation of the flat land on the valley floor. To this end, the whole valley bottom has been included in the "planning district"[21] no. 1 (Figure 20.1.), for which the plan prescribes particularly strict and restrictive regulations. In district 1, the plan does not allow for the settlement of inhabitants (and therefore dwellings) in addition to those already existing.[22] Moreover, the plan does not permit the existing buildings to be raised, hence protecting the views over the sites of archaeological interest. At the same time, by enabling the existing farms to expand/consolidate their agricultural outbuildings, the SMP nevertheless aims to safeguard the feasibility of the farms themselves and avoid their abandonment, thereby ensuring the continuation of the practices to take care of the territory.

The farming vocation of the valley bottom and the rural landscape are also defended through the solution identified to resolve the delicate question of vehicles crossing through the valley, around which a highly tense public discourse has grown up between those wanting to protect the landscape and those urging modernization. The bypass project proposed by the Ministry in 2013 had quite rightly aroused strong opposition from UNESCO because – by cutting across the valley floor – it would have swallowed up a lot of farming land and rapidly and intensely urbanized the portion of the valley to the east of the

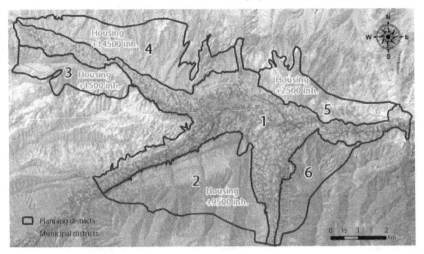

Figure 20.1. Planning districts
Source: LaGeS (2018)

site of Gholghola. Nevertheless, the opposition to the project quashed the local authorities' efforts to guarantee a more efficient crossing of the valley for vehicles in transit on the east-west route joining, respectively, Bamiyan to Kabul to the east and Herat (via Chest-e Sharif) to the west. Improving the road system would have been to the advantage of the through traffic, which at present flows at the foot of the UNESCO property that contains the Buddha niches, as well as vehicles transporting the potato crops outside the region and finally the host of business activities linked to Bamiyan's central importance as a city. The relevance of the farming base for the local economy has indeed not prevented a general urban turn in the population's lifestyles or the spread of a growing demand for more modern infrastructures and services. This is also due to the typically urban central functions that the city provides for a vast area of central Afghanistan, the Hazarajat, as well as, on a more cultural level, the ongoing interaction with international staff working on the archaeological sites and development cooperation projects in the area.[23]

The SMP deals with the matter by drawing up a variant of the ministerial bypass project which frees up the eastern part of the valley of Kakrak by taking the road along the sides of the rocky mountains until it joins the road for Kabul further east (Loda and Tartaglia, 2020) (Figure 20.2.).

The strategy adopted by the SMP to protect the rural landscape of the valley hence does not intervene on the question of which structural invariants of the cultural landscape to protect in relation to the WHL nomination. Nor, prior to that, does it touch on which collective memory the heritage process helps to build.[24] These aspects should instead be central in the Management Plan, the document that all World Heritage sites are requested to provide and that is

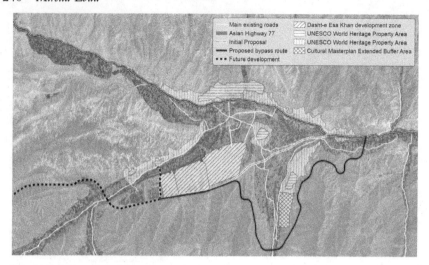

Figure 20.2. Proposed bypass route
Source: Loda and Tartaglia (2020)

going to be set out for Bamiyan, hopefully with the intensive involvement of the local population.

In this connection – and owing to the obstacles that have arisen, thus far impeding the actions to protect the cultural landscape in the WHL perspective – I believe we should ask ourselves whether we should reconsider the goal of protecting the cultural landscape within a more openly integrated approach. It could be similar to the Globally Important Agricultural Heritage Systems (GIAHS) view developed in 2002 by the Food and Agriculture Organization (FAO) which interprets the topics of landscape protection and rural development at the same time (Koohafkan and De La Cruz, 2011).

The focus on protection could thus shift from landscape with "Outstanding Universal Value" towards the farming system that that landscape has produced. In addition, greater and more direct attention could be paid to the production needs that are responsible for and guarantee the (re)generation of the landscape and its necessary transformation.

By dampening the contrast between calls for protection and transformation and at the same time reducing the ever-present risks of museumization of the heritage, this perspective could provide more suitable and effective tools to operate in the context of a "living" or "continuing landscape" such as that of Bamiyan.

However, the events that took place in Afghanistan in the month of August 2021 have profoundly altered the geo-political and economic picture surrounding the protection action. Hence, at the time of writing, there is no certainty as to if and how the protection of the Bamiyan cultural landscape will be undertaken in the new context.

Notes

1 Interesting reflections on the historical background of the meeting of the World Heritage Committee which took place at La Petite Pierre (France) in 1992 are found in Brown (2018).

2 On this topic, see the interesting research from the 1970s in which Gerhard Hardt demonstrated how the modern concept of "landscape" corresponds to the idea of "beautiful scenery" (Hardt, 1970). In effect, the abstract idea of landscape is associated with concepts such as "harmony", "totality", "context", and "synthesis". Hence, it defines a semantic field that corresponds to an abstract ideal of beauty applied to the landscape, originating in the context of bourgeois cultural tradition.

3 According to Peter Fowler (2003, p. 42), despite having the requirements, many sites do not request registration on the cultural landscape list owing to the definition and management difficulties that this would imply. The same reflection was made by Fowler in his contribution to the UNESCO conference on cultural landscape held in Ferrara in 2002.

4 On the elusivity of the concept of integrity and the problems connected to its evaluation, especially in rural settings, see Gullino and Larcher (2013).

5 As shown by the recent appearance of hybrid concepts such as "naturecultures". See ICOMOS (2017).

6 The SMP was presented to the High Council for Urban Development on 27 June 2018, signed by president Ashraf Ghani and officially adopted on 10 November of the same year.

7 For a detailed reconstruction of the UNESCO interventions to protect the Bamiyan heritage, see ICOMOS (2009), ICOMOS (2016) and LaGeS (2018), ch. II.4.I and Masanori (2020).

8 Criticism of the "stocktake" approach to landscape values seeped into the town planning debate. In the last years of the twentieth century, this resulted in defining "structural invariants" as the baseline for outlining the landscape transformation rules. For a critical reflection on the concept of structural invariant and the difficulties accompanying its practical implementation in the Italian context, see Maggio (2014).

9 Puleo (2013) very effectively illustrates the mechanism in connection with the case of the Valtellina (Italy).

10 Gambi's reflection is part of the debate on landscape (at that time more historiographical than geographical) that developed in "continental" Europe in the 1960s.

11 While on one hand UNESCO appreciates the "continuing landscapes", "closely associated with traditional ways of life" (Roessler and Lin, 2018, p. 4), particularly if connected to the permanence of traditional crops, the transformative dynamics of farming practices pose very great challenges to application of the integrity principle (Gullino and Larcher, 2013).

12 For example, see the photo taken in November 1885 by the Afghan Boundary Commission, reproduced by LaGeS (2018) in Fig. II.3.3 on p. 14, which depicts a much less intensively farmed valley. The change in this condition is confirmed at least since the first decades of the last century, as results from numerous photos taken in the 1930s by DAFA (Délégation Archéologique Française en Afghanistan).

13 This effective expression was proposed by Socco (1998) to designate the scientific approach to studying the landscape.

14 The recent evolution of these reflections has progressively shifted some branches of landscape studies from the reference to actual places towards more subjective categories of interpretation such as the affective quality of the memory: this evolution will probably further complicate the use of this approach to the operational management of cultural landscapes.

15 The figure was found in a survey on a random sample of 2,048 inhabitants, carried out in preparation for the SMP (LaGeS, 2018).
16 For further information, see Loda and Tartaglia (2020).
17 Carried out in the period of March and April 2018.
18 Carried out in spring 2017.
19 Jansen and Toubekis also agree on this option – albeit at a late stage and curiously without ever quoting the SMP: "The title of the World Heritage nomination 'Cultural Landscape and Archaeological Remains of the Bamiyan Valley' can be misleading, since the cultural landscape under the protection of the Convention is covering only a small fraction of the total cultural landscape" (2020, p. 82).
20 Furthermore, this choice complies with the UNESCO praxis according to the interpretation provided by Peter Fowler: "'Cultural landscape' is used in practice by the Committee to mean 'rural landscape'" (Fowler, 2003, p. 27).
21 The SMP divides the municipality of Bamiyan into six "planning districts", each of which is designated an acceptable number of additional inhabitants, infrastructure, and town planning regulations.
22 The SMP aims to limit the demographic. expansion and consequent housing demand in the valley to around half of the increased forecast up to 2037, while directing the remaining part towards the new city of Pasnaw, located on the strategic road that will connect Bamiyan with Shaidan and Shebartu (the site allocated for the new airport) (LaGeS, 2018). The demographic increase to be hosted in the valley is directed towards planning districts 2, 3, 4, and 5.
23 Therefore, the strict opposition between rural and urban followed by Jansen and Toubekis (2020, p. 86) and above all the nostalgic and impracticable hypothesis of freezing the valley in an improbable rural state seem sterile.
24 On the relationship between landscape and heritage, please see the interesting text by Harvey and Wilkinson (2019).

References

ACDC, Aachen Center for Documentation and Conservation (2013). *Cultural Masterplan Bamiyan, Campaigns 2003–2007* (omnibus volume). Aachen: Aachen University.

Brown, S. (2018). World Heritage and Cultural Landscape. *Heritage and Society*, 11: 19–43.

Duncan, J. and Duncan, N. (1988). (Re)Reading the Landscape. *Environment and Planning D: Society and Space*, 6: 117–126.

Fowler, P. (2003). *World Heritage Cultural Landscapes 1992–2002*. Paris: UNESCO.

Gambi, L. (1966). *Critica ai concetti geografici di paesaggio umano*. Faenza: Fratelli Lega.

Gullino, P. and Larcher, F. (2013). Integrity in UNESCO World Heritage Sites. A Comparative Study for Rural Landscapes. *Journal of Cultural Heritage*, 14: 389–395.

Hardt, G. (1970). *Die 'Landschaft' der Sprache und die 'Landschaft' der Geographen. Semantische und Forschungslogische Studien*. Bonn: Dümmler Verlag.

Harvey, D. and Wilkinson, J. (2019). Landscape and Heritage. In P. Howard, I. Thomson, E. Waterton, and M. Atha (eds.), *The Routledge Companion to Landscape Studies*. Abingdon: Routledge, pp. 176–191.

ICOMOS (2009). *The Giant Buddhas of Bamiyan. Safeguarding the Remains*. Berlin: Hendrik Bäßler.

ICOMOS (2016). *The Giant Buddhas of Bamiyan II. Safeguarding the Remains 2010–2015*. Berlin: Hendrik Bäßler.

ICOMOS (2017). *Learnings and Commitments from the Culture Nature Journey*, Delhi: 19th General Assembly.

Jansen, M. and Toubekis, G. (2020). The Cultural Master Plan of Bamiyan: The Sustainability Dilemma of Protection and Progress. In M. Nagaoka (ed.), *The Future of the Bamiyan Buddha Statues: Heritage Reconstruction in Theory and Practice*. Cham: Springer, pp. 71–98.

Kelly, K. G. and Norman, N. (2007). Historical Archaeologies of Landscape in Atlantic Africa. In D. *Hicks, L. McAtackney*, and G. *Fairlough* (eds.), *Envisioning Landscape: Situations and Standpoints in Archeology and Heritage*. Walnut Creek: Left Coast Press, pp. 172–193.

Koohafkan, P. and De La Cruz, M. J. (2011). Conservation and Adaptive Management of Globally Important Agricultural Heritage Systems (GIAHS). *Journal of Resources and Ecology*, 2(1): 22–28.

LaGeS-Laboratorio di Geografia Sociale (2018). *Bamiyan's Strategic Master Plan*. Firenze: Polistampa.

Loda, M. and Tartaglia, M. (2020). Developing the Bamiyan Master Plan between Cooperation and olitics. *Rivista geografica Italiana*, 127(2): 29–50.

Maggio, M. (2014). *Invarianti strutturali nel governo del territorio*. Firenze: Firenze University Press.

Masanori, N. (ed.) (2020). *The Future of the Bamiyan Buddha Statues. Heritage Reconstruction in Theory and Practice*. Cham: Springer.

Puleo, J. T. (2013). Parasitizing Landscape for UNESCO World Heritage. *Geoforum*, 45: 337–345.

Roessler, M. and Lin, R. (2018). Cultural Landscape in World Heritage Conservation and Cultural Landscape Conservation in Asia. *Built Heritage* 3: 3–26.

Smith, L. (2006). *Uses of Heritage*. Abingdon: Routledge.

Socco, C. (1998). *Il paesaggio imperfetto. Uno sguardo semiotico sul punto di vista estetico*. Torino: Tirrenia Stampatori.

UNESCO (1962). *Recommendation Concerning the Safeguarding of the Beauty and Character of Landscapes and Sites*.

UNESCO (1972). *Convention Concerning the Protection of the World Cultural and Natural Heritage*.

UNESCO (2002). World Heritage Committee, Twenty-sixth session, *The Budapest Declaration on World Heritage*.

UNESCO (2002). *Cultural Landscapes, Challenges of Conservation*, Ferrara, Italy, Paris: UNESCO.

UNESCO (2019). *Operational Guidelines for the Implementation of the World Heritage Convention*, World Heritage Center, WHC.19/01 10 July 2019.

Vecchio, B. (2011). Convenzione Europea del Paesaggio e progettazione paesaggistica. Alcuni problemi aperti. In G. Tesio and G. Pennaroli (eds.), *Lo sguardo offeso. Il paesaggio in Italia. Storia geografia arte letteratura*. Atti del Convegno internazionale di studi, Vercelli-Demonte-Montà, 24–27 settembre 2008, Torino: Centro Studi Piemontesi, pp. 305–325.

21 The "obsolete structures" in the outstanding landscape of the UNESCO Dolomites World Heritage Site

Values, disvalues, and management practices

Viviana Ferrario and Benedetta Castiglioni

Introduction

Since 2009 the Dolomites (Italian Eastern Alps) have been included in the UNESCO World Heritage List as a natural site according to criteria VIII, relating to geological processes and the consequent physical forms significant for Earth's history, and VII, relating to natural beauty (UNESCO, 2005). In 2011 an expert from the International Union for Conservation of Nature (IUCN) – UNESCO's advisory body responsible for examining the applications and periodic checks for the natural properties of the World Heritage List – drew up an evaluation report. It addresses some specific requirements for maintaining landscape integrity to the Fondazione Dolomiti UNESCO, the institution in charge of managing the World Heritage Site (WHS). One of them was implementing "actions to remove obsolete infrastructure and equipment" (Worboys, 2011).

Between 2013 and 2018 the Fondazione Dolomiti UNESCO involved the Universities of Udine, Padua, and Iuav of Venice in various research activities on the subject of "obsolete structures" (which, for brevity, we will call "str.obs", based on the Italian *strutture obsolete*) for the purpose of cataloguing them in view of their removal. This chapter discusses some questions that arose alongside this research in which the authors were involved.[1]

The removal of str.obs is not a new concept for the Alps; in the early 2000s the NGO Mountains Wilderness had already launched a campaign for the removal of "installations obsolètes" in order to obtain a "requalification paysagère" in some protected areas of the French Alps (Mountain Wilderness, 2002).[2] Originally a voluntary activity, this operation was soon institutionalized in protected areas' plans and in local authorities' action plans in different parts of the Alps, drawing the attention of scholars. According to French geographer Laslaz (2013), the removal of str.obs is mostly a device for accentuating, by reaction, the value of the context. Laslaz subjects the operation to a close criticism summarized in three main points: the removal does not "save" nature but conforms it to certain aesthetic norms and certain ideological expectations which express an idealized, elitist, and urban conception of the Alps; removal

DOI: 10.4324/9781003195238-21

selectively denies the right to memory ("dénégation patrimoniale") and particularly affects some products of modernity; and, presented as an exemplary action often carried out with heavy vehicles, removal is an operation of power through which the volunteers and institutions involved build their own rights over the "cleaned-up" areas.

While we largely agree with Laslaz's arguments, some issues need to be further investigated. The exceptional nature of the UNESCO Dolomites site and the relevance of the players involved in the strategy of removing str.obs in this area allow us to focus on two fundamental questions: starting from a reflection on the concept of obsolescence, on what other bases can the strategy of removal be questioned? Can a greater awareness about obsolescence and removal lead to improved management of natural heritage?

The issues at stake

The topic of str.obs and their removal calls into question the debate on some more general issues. A first theme concerns considering nature as heritage: from a general point of view, it is in fact a question of culture, linked to social, anthropological and ethical arguments. Often in an unconscious way, this implies a dichotomy between humans and nature as separate domains that leads to considering the human presence as always being a threat to nature (Olwig and Lowenthal, 2006; Papayannis and Howard, 2007). In the debate on environmental aesthetics, the role of aesthetic judgment – typically of cultural derivation – in formulating nature-conservation policies has been emphasized (Brady and Prior, 2020): UNESCO's recognition of the Dolomites as a "natural" heritage for their aesthetic value (according to criterion VII) and the resulting need to protect aesthetic integrity – even before natural integrity – therefore appears to contain a strong cultural connotation.

A second reflection concerns the concept of obsolescence: in the debate on material culture, the concept refers to common objects considered no longer useful because, for example, they are out of fashion. This is expected when the cultural context leads to paying increasing attention to the new and forgetting everything old and useless, even if those things persist. However, obsolescence is considered a field of possibilities in which creative practices can give new life to what is no longer needed, thanks to the loss of its original function (Tischleder and Wassermann, 2015). A partially similar approach can be found in the architectural field (Abramson, 2016).

The debate on obsolescence is therefore linked to reflections on our relationship with the past, and particularly with the concept of aging. The attitude is ambivalent, since in some cases we wish to forget, hide, remove, and replace those parts of the past that we consider outdated (therefore considering them obsolete); in other cases, we consider the past important for its intrinsic value, within a process of heritagization (Lowenthal, 2015).

Due to this link between obsolescence and heritagization, the case of the str.obs in the natural landscape of the UNESCO Dolomites can also be analysed through the debate on cultural heritage. The Authorized Heritage Discourse (Smith, 2006) selects from the past the material and immaterial elements that should be considered as heritage. In so doing, it denies the same possibility of becoming heritage to other elements: this happens to the str.obs too, as Laslaz had already noted. On the one hand, what is considered "traditional" becomes heritage – given a difficult univocal definition of "traditional" (Stenseke, 2016), often referring to a generic "simpler, happier time" (Cameron, 2010: 211). On the other hand, the objects produced by modernity – perceived as problematic – are instead more easily "erased in favour of a nostalgic reference to a lost past" (Tilley, 2006). Only in some cases, such as industrial heritage valued for tourism purposes, what is functionally obsolete can acquire heritage dignity (Somoza-Medina and Monteserín-Abella, 2021). More often, what bears the signs of neglect and abandonment is difficult to recognize and accept as heritage (Garcia-Esparza, 2018). Both obsolescence and heritage reflect the material dimension of landscape change and the immaterial processes through which value or disvalue is attributed to the landscape; these processes themselves continuously change (Herring, 2019) and depend on the diversity of points of view (Swensen et al., 2013).

The gaze on the Dolomites landscape is strongly influenced by the history of their discovery by European travellers: since the 18th century, "the process through which such a scenery becomes a heritage landscape relates to a strategy to shield an orthodox way of seeing, treasured by temporary sojourners, from the potential harm provoked by permanent dwellers" (Bainbridge, 2018: 259). Both the very designation of this "heritage landscape" as a UNESCO WHS and the "set of conditional norms for the appreciation of a landscape, and a set of behavioural protocols for its conservation, management, and sustainability would depend on this 'privileged act of looking'" (ibid.). In this framework, the str.obs appear as inappropriate for the "picturesque" and the "sublime" landscape of the Dolomites.

The removal of the str.obs can therefore be considered a practice of landscape restoration and reinstatement of lost naturalness, a debated issue: "Rewilding as activist practice attempts to erase human history and involvement with the land and flora and fauna, yet nature and culture cannot be easily separated into distinct units" (Jorgensen, 2015: 487).

The "obsolete structures" in the UNESCO Dolomites

In setting up the work of cataloguing the str.obs, the research group considered it useful to classify them into systems according to the different activities from which the structures themselves originate: agro-pastoral, forestry, tourism, border/military, mining/industrial, energy and communication (Table 21.1.).

The research was based on cartographic analysis, field surveys, collecting signalization by public and private bodies, NGOs and web sources (web communities, newspapers, blogs). It made it possible to identify and map about 200 str.obs within the core area of the UNESCO site, in the buffer area or in close

Table 21.1. Str.obs Systems

System	Structure
agro-pastoral	Alpine hut, cattle byre, barn, fountain, drinking trough, watering hole, shelter, storage, irrigation canal, terrace, fence, etc.
forestry	Sawmill, telpherage, forest service road, penstock, etc.
tourism	Alpine lodge, hotel, restaurant, café, path, hiking sign, advertising board, ski area, ski jump trampoline, ski lift, snow cannon, via ferrata, rock piton, steel rope, steel step, picnic area, road, parking, etc.
border/military	Boundary stone, trench warfare, military fort, barrack, military road, fortified line, military base, bunker, tunnel, etc.
mining/industrial	Mine, quarry, mill, furnace, industrial plant, shed, etc.
energy and communication	Hydropower station, reservoir, penstock, dam, intake, pylon, cable, antenna, repeater, roadman's house, rockfall barrier, avalanche protection, garage, warehouse, weir, etc.

proximity: remains of old power lines, stretches of abandoned roads, ruined bridges, neglected quarries, abandoned military structures, plants of abandoned ski lifts, and a rather large series of other disused artefacts linked to the tourism or infrastructural sectors. This list does not include the numerous str.obs already affected by some heritagization processes (WWI military and agro-pastoral artefacts) because the UNESCO Dolomites Foundation had promptly and explicitly asked to prioritize the str.obs systems considered "critical" for the landscape – infrastructural, mining/industrial and tourist systems – from which a more probable disturbance is expected: the structures built after 1950. This moment actually corresponds in the common sense to a sort of temporal watershed between the "traditional" cultural landscape and the "modern" anthropic transformations that create negative impacts and "disturbances". These are certainly reasonable criteria in view of removing disturbances, as recommended by IUCN: most of the str.obs identified during the research are small, abandoned, temporary objects (for example, disused construction site shacks), very visible and easily accessible. Their removal is certainly the most desirable solution. However, in more complex cases removal can be questioned. In the followings, we present some examples of str.obs identified in the research, even in the light of what happened in the last few years, that allow us to critically discuss the strategy of removal.

Abandoned hotel in Passo Rolle (TN). This is a mountain pass hotel dating back to the early 20th century that was enlarged and heavily transformed before being left in disuse. The structure was decrepit at the time of the research. Opinions online have a strong negative connotation and identify the hotel as a significant component of the degradation of the pass itself. Patrimonio del Trentino S.p.A (the company that manages the properties of the Autonomous

Province of Trento, owner of the land of Passo Rolle) had acquired the hotel "abandoned, dilapidated and a real problem for the safety of citizens to demolish it ...." The abatement remedies a state of degradation that is unacceptable for an area of this environmental quality".[3] The hotel was demolished at the end of 2017. The press reported unanimous satisfaction, underlining that demolishing the "decrepit wreck that had marred the place for years" has been "a benefit for everyone".[4] The media framed it as the beginning of a new life and a sign of the willingness to revive Passo Rolle for tourism.

Ruins of the Pineland tourist complex, Forni di Sopra (UD). These are the remains of an unfinished building designed in the early 1960s by the Italian architect Marcello D'Olivo; it "was supposed to be a tourist residence hotel commissioned by a London company in 1964, which was abruptly interrupted due to the bankruptcy of the company".[5] Only the reinforced concrete skeleton of the complex's most imposing structure (an arched building about 100 metres long) remains. The unfinished work was then abandoned, and it is now almost completely hidden by vegetation, despite being close to a main road. The structure, which the NGO Mountain Wilderness in 2011 included in a report about obsolete structures in Friuli, is not a common str.obs, but an "artistic" ruin, one of the few examples of Marcello D'Olivo's organic architecture in Italy, thus valuable for the history of architecture.

Plinths of old chair lifts and ski lifts on the Marmolada Mountain (TN). From the very beginning of tourism development in the Marmolada area, several ski lifts have been built, demolished, and re-built to reach the glacier, which today is in rapid retreat due to global warming. Some of the lift foundations (concrete pillars) remain, such as those distributed along a straight line that, from the Fedaia Pass (2,057 m asl), reaches an altitude of 2,650 m near the Pian dei Fiacconi refuge. Some are more disturbing due to their size and the presence of exposed iron, pipes, and concrete retaining walls; others have a lower visual impact, as they blend in with the surrounding rock; and some of them have found a new use as hiking trail markers. In the same area (outside but very close to the WHS perimeter) there is a project to replace the lift disused in 2019 with a new bigger cable car. During 2020, the local environmentalist associations asked that any new ski lifts were authorized after a complete dismantling of the remaining disused lifts. On this occasion, 4,500 signatures were collected to ask that "the useless and disfiguring memory of the ancient structures be erased" on the Marmolada; the public administration listened to this petition.

The roadman's houses. During the research, some str.obs belonging to serial systems were also highlighted, such as the roadman's houses once occupied by the families of the workers in charge of maintaining the state roads and their equipment. The roadman's houses have not been used for some time due to the cessation of their original function and are often in a poor state of conservation. Although these are objects dating back prior to 1950, they have been included in our survey due to their significant dimensions, position close to the core area, great visibility and – a crucial topic that we will return to later – full

Figure 21.1. Str.obs in the Dolomites. One of the plinths remaining from old chair lifts
on the Marmolada slopes
Source: Photo by Chiara Quaglia, 2016

Figure 21.2. Str.obs in the Dolomites. One of the plinths remaining from old chair lifts
on the Marmolada slopes, now reused as trail sign
Source: Photo by Chiara Quaglia, 2016

potential for new uses. During the research, eight houses were mapped, some
of which were reduced almost to ruins.

Alongside these examples, we also report the interesting case of *the plinths of the
ski lift in Danta di Cadore (BL)*, slightly outside the WHS. From 2008–2009, the
concrete plinths of the old ski lift's pylons were removed as part of a Life project[6]
with the purpose of environmental restoration and tourist enhancement (adding

signs, equipped paths, etc.). The project documents are very explicit: "These are obviously artefacts that are not suited to the natural and landscape characteristics of the place and which can negatively affect the overall image of the site"; "The impact is exclusively of landscape type, but significant because the peat bog, beyond the ecological and naturalistic peculiarities of wetlands, is located in an area of high aesthetic value ... and with appreciable wilderness characteristics"; "Even the interventions with a prevalent aesthetic-landscape orientation, such as the elimination of cementitious artefacts, are part of the philosophy of offering a fruition that contributes to recovering the sense of naturalness, of coexistence with the nature that surrounds us to avoid new violence". However, the unique disvalue attributed in official documents is questioned on a blog of cable car enthusiasts,[7] where a user explicitly expresses regret for the removal of the plinths, the last trace of a plant whose story he is trying to reconstruct.

Removing obsolete structures: a critical discussion

These examples suggest that the very concept of obsolescence, and therefore the definition of str.obs, deserves further study. According to MW (2002) the str.obs are abandoned objects built with "exogenous" materials and which "disfigure" the mountain landscape. Laslaz (2013) questions the uncertainty of these criteria, coming to the conclusion that the definition of str.obs does not precede but follows the choice of removal. Basically, a str.obs would be an "abandoned artifact, identified and inventoried, for which a dismantling operation is envisaged by associations, organizations or public bodies, upon agreement with the owners" (ibid.: 355). As Laslaz notes, removal expresses the aspirations of those who support it: an aesthetic preference; a lesson in respect for nature; the reparation of damage; a reminder of the responsibility of decision makers and owners; a self-legitimation for the promoters of removal (ibid.). It emerges from the Dolomites case that the return to the "natural" state would also be a deterrent for subsequent anthropogenic interventions, which is more difficult to accept in an "intact" place than in a man-made place. In short, it is an attempt at *damnatio memoriae*.

Certainly, the removal, as in the case of the hotel in Passo Rolle, can have a cathartic effect and bear a palingenetic action, which allows restarting with a new project. However, localized str.obs removal becomes problematic if uncritically applied as a generalized strategy for managing the UNESCO WHS. Examining the 2011 mission report, the IUCN experts' approach emerges between the lines: human activities represent a form of exploitation and a disturbance to conserving the outstanding beauty of the core area of the Dolomites' natural heritage, which ideally should remain intact. Thus, protecting the WHS must translate into visible and measurable actions to be credible. The ultimate aim – as absurd as it may sound – would be to eliminate all human activities, cancel the disturbance or stop exploitation. In the Dolomites, however, there are plenty of signs of human activities especially connected to tourism, even at high altitudes. It would not be politically credible to pretend to eliminate them unless we deeply question the current development model. Therefore, the strategy focuses on the str.obs, a small subset of signs that correspond to activities that are no longer ongoing. Removing the str.obs is politically acceptable because it only asks to remove "dust", to throw away things that (at least apparently) are no longer needed. As it is unviable to eliminate the active functions, it is proposed to remove the signs of inactive functions represented by the str.obs. Yet, this reveals a trap: the visual impact of the disused ski lift plinths on the Marmolada, for example – however much disturbance it may cause – disappears in the presence of the long ski slope that significantly marks the landscape and whose existence no one even dreams of questioning.

A critical reading of the requests and proposals put forward by the actors involved allows us to identify some preconceived positions that can lead to

Table 21.2. Some preconceived positions and their related narratives inherent in the strategy of removing str.obs, and the resulting paradoxes

Preconceived positions	Related narratives	Resulting paradoxes
1. Eco-aesthetics	Integrity is nature without humans; human activity is interpreted as exploitation. Removing the str.obs is an "eco-aesthetic" cleaning (narrative of renaturalization).	To justify removing the str.obs, which are considered to disturb the *natural* heritage, *cultural* arguments are used (explicitly mentioning, for example, aesthetic or visual integrity).
2. Ethical compensation	Removing the str.obs means not only cleaning the Dolomites, but also compensating them for the damage suffered before. Removal is a kind of ethical compensation (Laslaz, 2013) (narrative of restitution).	The symbolic value of removal may exceed its concrete effect. By also bearing the costs of removal, the local community actually risks "paying" twice.
3. Un-do	Removal seems to have a sort of "magic power" to go back in time, returning to a state of "uncontaminated" nature in the Dolomites (narrative of restoration).	Removal may be irrational if its impact is greater than the benefit. Removal may be economically wasteful when the outdated structure is potentially reusable.
4. One perception	It is assumed that everyone shares the same negative perception of the str.obs (narrative of disvalue).	Some people may perceive removal as loss. There is a conflict in the attribution of value between experts/populations, insiders/outsiders and interest groups.
5. No heritage	Str.obs are painted as "ugly" and "dirty": as such, they lose the right to become heritage (Laslaz, 2013), or the right to curated decay (DeSilvey, 2017) (narrative of degradation).	Contemporary artefacts are denied any possible heritage value. The process of heritagization of the context prevents any form of heritagization of the object.

paradoxical situations. We have summarized them in Table. 21.2. with the intentionally provocative purpose of building greater awareness of the relationship between attributions of value (and disvalue) and consequent actions, also with a view to better and more consistent management of the WHS. These preconceived positions, which we have named *eco-aesthetics, ethical compensation, un-do, one perception,* and *no heritage,* are supported by certain specific narratives (renaturalization, restitution, restoration, disvalue, and degradation) and justify a priori removing the str.obs without a real convenience assessment or considering any alternative attributions of value.

Concluding remarks

The processes of attribution of value/disvalue that drive the protection policies and the management of landscape change are particularly interesting in the case of UNESCO sites, where the concept of "outstanding universal value" faces the practices and processes of use/disuse. In the Dolomites WHS this issue is amplified by the contrast between the exceptional natural elements and the signs of human activity, mostly interpreted as detractors. Among these detractors, the str.obs represent a set that is both obvious and problematic, as shown by the research experience described above, which questions the institutionalized strategy of their removal.

In many cases removing the str.obs is a desirable solution; it can have a cathartic value in the framework of the consumer society, represent an exemplary reminder of the responsibility of those who built them in the past (according to the "polluter pays" principle), and produce a deterrent effect with respect to future intervention projects. A greater awareness of the processes of attribution of value and disvalue, however, can help to avoid falling into the paradoxes discussed above and encourage evaluating the effective convenience (including the environmental one) of removal, even with respect to a possible "curated decay" (DeSilvey, 2017) and avoiding the trap of an Authorized *Anti*-heritage Discourse.

The removal, in turn, can involve some risks: the loss of information, energy and work potentially incorporated in the str.obs; costs disproportionate to the value of the result; the risk of distracting attention from the much more significant impacts caused by functioning structures (sometimes close to the str.obs) that it would not be politically admissible to request removing; and finally, the risk of losing opportunities for reuse or recycling that could emerge in the future.

Explaining preconceived positions makes it possible to consider the str.obs' presence not only as a factor of degradation, but as an opportunity in protected areas and UNESCO sites, inviting a more coherent and effective strategic approach to managing exceptional landscapes. Given the plurality of functions/dysfunctions and values/disvalues that can be associated with the str.obs, reflecting on the destiny of the single structure and the definition of the actions to be taken represents a valid opportunity for citizens to participate in constructing a shared project for the Dolomites area.

The research group insisted on the opportunity given by an investigation based not on the choice of a priori removal, instead suggesting to enlarge the observation field to all those abandoned or underused artefacts whose recovery could represent an opportunity for managing the UNESCO Dolomites site. A recent sign in this direction is encouraging: in 2020 a roadman's house in Cortina d'Ampezzo found a new function as an information centre for the Fondazione Dolomiti UNESCO, and is also in view of the Winter Olympics to be held in the area in 2026.

A critical reflection on the str.obs should finally be an occasion for forward-looking considerations on anthropic activity in sensitive areas that include the consequences that global warming could entail, even in a short time, for certain types of uses and infrastructures. In particular, the infrastructures for winter sports that are being built lately in the Dolomites as a function of global sporting events could be destined to rapidly transform into str.obs due to the rapid climatic changes of the context in which they are inserted.

Acknowledgements

The authors thank the Fondazione Dolomiti UNESCO and the Province of Pordenone that financed the research that identified and mapped the str.obs in the WHS and have always been open to debate. They also thank Chiara Quaglia, who contributed in str.obs' identification and mapping and gave an important contribution in the general discussion.

Notes

1 This chapter results from the common work of the authors. Viviana Ferrario wrote section 1 and 4, Benedetta Castiglioni wrote section 2 and they wrote sections 3 and 5 together.
2 The Mountain Wilderness "Obsolete Facilities" campaign won the UIAA Mountain Protection Award in 2016 and continues to this day: www.theuiaa.org/uiaa/mounta in-wilderness-marks-two-decades-of-removing-obsolete-facilities-from-mountain-areas/ (Retrieved on 14 November 2020).
3 *Il Trentino. Quotidiano online della Provincia Autonoma di Trento*, Press office, press release 31992017, November 28: www.ufficiostampa.provincia.tn.it/Comunicati/Pa sso-Rolle-consegnati-i-lavori-per-la-demolizione-dell-albergo (Retrieved on 15 November 2020).
4 www.ladige.it/territori/valsugana-primiero/2017/12/19/addio-allecomostro-che-deturpava-passo-rolle (Retrieved on 15 November 2020).
5 *Il Piccolo*, 16 December 2015: https://ricerca.gelocal.it/ilpiccolo/archivio/ilpiccolo/ 2015/12/16/nazionale-riscopriamo-l-incompleta-pineland-dell-architetto-d-olivo-39. html (Retrieved on 30 April 2021).
6 2006–2007 LIFE project "Danta2004" (Life04 NAT/IT/000177) – Technical report. The project website (http://torbieredanta.info) has been discontinued, but quoted documents can be downloaded at the Internet Archive (https://a rchive.org).
7 www.funiforum.org/funiforum/node/3623 (Retrieved on 5 October 2021).

References

Abramson, D. M. (2016). *Obsolescence: An Architectural History*. Chicago: University of Chicago Press.

Bainbridge, W. (2018). Mountains Run Mad: Picturesque Signatures in the Dolomites. In C. Kakalis and E. Goetsch (eds.), *Mountains, Mobilities and Movement*. London: Palgrave Macmillan, pp. 255–283.

Brady, E. and Prior, J. (2020). Environmental Aesthetics: A Synthetic Review. *People and Nature*, 2: 254–266.

Cameron, C. (2010). The Unnatural History of Heritage: What's the Future for the Past? *Journal of Heritage Tourism*, 5(3): 203–218.

DeSilvey, C. (2017). *Curated Decay: Heritage beyond Saving*. Minneapolis: University of Minnesota Press.

Garcia-Esparza, J.A. (2018). Are World Heritage Concepts of Integrity and Authenticity Lacking in Dynamism? A Critical Approach to Mediterranean Autoptic Landscapes, *Landscape Research*, 43(6): 817–830.

Herring, P. (2018). Valuing the Whole Historic Landscape. In P. Howard, I. Thompson, E. Waterton, and M. Atha (eds.), *The Routledge Companion to Landscape Studies*, Abingdon: Routledge, pp. 192–207.

Jorgensen, D. (2015). Rethinking Rewilding. *Geoforum*, 65: 482–488.

Laslaz, L. (2013). Renaturaliser sans patrimonialiser. Bannir les "installations obsolètes" et les points noirs paysagers dans les espaces naturels protégés alpins. *L'Espace géographique*, 42(4): 354–369.

Lowenthal, D. (2015). *The Past Is a Foreign Country – Revisited*. Cambridge: Cambridge University Press.

Mountain Wilderness (2002). En finir avec les installations obsolètes ... Analyse de la situation dans les espaces protégés des montagnes françaises et propositions d'actions pour une requalification paysagère. Retrieved from: www.mountainwilderness.fr/IMG/pdf/guide_installations_obsoletes.pdf.

Olwig, K. and Lowenthal, D. (eds.) (2006). *The Nature of Cultural Heritage, and the Culture of Natural Heritage*. Abingdon: Routledge.

Papayannis, T. and Howard, P. (2007). Editorial: Nature as Heritage. *International Journal of Heritage Studies*, 13: 298–307.

Smith, L. (2006). *Uses of Heritage*. Abingdon: Routledge.

Somoza-Medina, X. and Monteserín-Abella, O. (2021). The Sustainability of Industrial Heritage Tourism Far from the Axes of Economic Development in Europe: Two Case Studies. *Sustainability*, 13: 1077.

Stenseke, M. (2016). Integrated Landscape Management and the Complicating Issue of Temporality. *Landscape Research*, 41(2): 199–211.

Swensen, G., Jerpåsen, J. B., Sæter, O., and Sundli Tveit, M. (2013). Capturing the Intangible and Tangible Aspects of Heritage: Personal versus Official Perspectives in Cultural Heritage Management, *Landscape Research*, 38(2): 203–221.

Tilley, C. (2006). Introduction: Identity, Place, Landscape and Heritage, *Journal of Material Culture*, 11(1–2): 7–32.

Tischleder, B. and Wasserman, S. (eds.) (2015). *Cultures of Obsolescence. History, Materiality, and the Digital Age*. New York: Palgrave-Macmillan.

UNESCO (2005). Operational Guidelines for the Implementation of the World Heritage Convention.

Worboys, G. (2011). *Mission Report*. Reactive monitoring mission The Dolomites (Italy) 2–8 October 2011. UNESCO – IUCN.

22 A heritagescape in the Appalachians

When a tornado came to Kinzua

Katherine Burlingame and Philip Burlingame

Introduction

Deep in the mountains near the remote Allegheny National Forest of Penn-sylvania in the United States lay the twisted ruins of the Kinzua Bridge. Built in 1882 from wrought iron and later rebuilt using steel, the railroad viaduct was the highest and longest in America (and the world's highest) at the time, earning it the temporary title of the "Eighth Wonder of the World." For nearly 70 years, the bridge provided an important transportation link between the coal, oil, and timber resources of Pennsylvania to the Great Lakes ship-ping lanes. Though the bridge fell out of use in the late 1950s and faced the scrap heap, its enduring historical value led to the opening of the Kinzua Bridge State Park to promote tourism and highlight the region's history and exceptional natural landscapes. In 2002, with growing concerns over the condition of the bridge, the state initiated a $12 million restoration project. However, tragedy struck in 2003 when a rare tornado tore across the valley and toppled 11 of the bridge's 20 towers. With renewed national attention and a rise in visitors who were eager to see the mangled remains in the valley below, the state opted to build an overlook known as the "Sky Walk" on the remaining towers rather than either demolishing or fully reconstructing the bridge. With a visitor center added later, it was estimated that the park would bring in roughly $11.5 million in new tourism revenue for the region (PA DCNR, 2011).

While there was much debate and discussion leading up to the landscape's transformation, the transformation itself and how the park is experienced today have remained largely unexamined. Therefore, set within a wider discussion of the development of heritagescapes, the Kinzua Bridge State Park provides a unique example of a landscape transformed by industrial, recreational, and heritage use values over time. In this chapter, we investigate the political, eco-nomic, and sociocultural factors that led to the heritagization of the landscape, and we explore the disparities between local and state perspectives and valua-tions. Given that heritagescapes are intrinsically linked with nature, we also show how natural disasters and climate change can play a significant role in the heritage-making process.

DOI: 10.4324/9781003195238-22

Defining heritagescapes

While a vast and diverse range of literature explores ruins through, for example, discussions of power (DeSilvey and Edensor, 2012), performativity (Lorimer and Murray, 2015), and memory (Olsen and Pétursdóttir, 2016), we shift our focus to the heritagescape encompassing the ruin and the heritage-making processes that emerge when bringing new life to a ruinous landscape.

Noting that every heritage site carries unique qualities connected with broader heritage-making practices, Mary-Catherine Garden developed the heritagescape concept and method to challenge the tendency of imposing a "veneer of sameness" (Garden, 2004, p. 199) on similar heritage sites. Positioning heritage sites as individually dynamic, experiential landscapes, Garden attempts to bridge the divide between research focusing on the visitor experience and research exploring the materiality of a site, particularly arguing for a more critical approach to the role of the landscape in the heritage-making process (Garden, 2004, 2006).

Yet, landscape is a fickle term (Cosgrove, 2006), and scholars have long debated its wide range of meanings and the complexity of its intertwined layers of material, symbolic, and affective dimensions that are constantly reproduced and renegotiated over time (Burlingame, 2020). As the meaning of heritage and the experience of the landscape are also shaped by these forces of change, heritagescapes must be understood as occupying the contested space between progress and preservation. They are therefore always produced landscapes, which can involve "the destruction of real places, real communities, [and] real landscapes" (Mitchell, 2008, p. 42).

A heritagescape assessment model

In order to analyse the different layers and decision-making processes of heritagescapes and their production, we use Garden's heritagescape concept while also employing Katherine Burlingame's Triangle of Landscape Engagement (or TRIOLE model) (2020). In response to the lack of interdisciplinary approaches combining landscape geography, heritage research and practice, and tourism studies (Burlingame, 2022; Carman and Sørensen, 2009), the TRIOLE model builds on previous models of landscape assessment (Bender, 1998; Garden, 2004; Granö, 1997; Ryan, 2012), weaving together the empirical with the conceptual through three methodological perspectives: Locale, Story, and Presence. Locale focuses on the tangible, material landscape, Story takes a more critical look at the history of the landscape and how it is communicated, and Presence explores the lived experience of being in the landscape including the emotional and affective qualities that are not easily accessed through traditional tourism encounters. As Garden's heritagescape methodology neglects a more critical analysis of the landscape itself beyond its material and aesthetic qualities, the TRIOLE model allows for a more nuanced investigation into the contested nature of the production, experience, and transformation of heritagescapes over time.

Transformation of the Kinzua heritagescape

The Kinzua Bridge State Park is the result of decades of decision-making torn between the enduring historical significance and cultural value for local communities and the gradual decline in the park's use value due to the increasingly dilapidated bridge. In a strange twist of fate, while restoration was finally under way, the damage from the 2003 tornado led to an entirely different heritagescape developed around the ruins of the bridge. Following the TRIOLE model, we first explore the physical landscape (Locale) followed by the history of the landscape and its development over time (Story). Outside of these more formal decision-making processes, we also investigate local residents' perceptions on how the park has changed, how it is experienced today, and if and how local communities have been involved in the planning and development process (Presence). In particular, we seek to understand the potential conflicts or positive outcomes that can emerge during the heritagization process of a landscape with deeply rooted local significance. Because the Kinzua heritagescape emerged from a natural disaster, we also present it as a unique example of adaptive re-use for landscapes threatened by climate change.

Locale: the Appalachian landscape

The land in what is now McKean County in Pennsylvania was first occupied by itinerant hunting and fishing camps of indigenous Native Americans, most recently the Seneca people. Characterized by a relatively high-elevation plateau rising to over 2,200 foot (671 metres) above sea level, the topography of the landscape includes deep valleys eroded by abundant streams and rivers (Pennsylvania Natural Heritage Program, 2008). The winter season is relatively harsh for Pennsylvania with bitter cold temperatures and annual snowfalls averaging 84 inches (2 m) (NOAA, n.d.), which is perhaps why no permanent Native American settlements have been identified there. Historically, the Seneca people spearfished along the Allegheny River and its tributary streams; they called the region Tgëdzó:a', or Kinzua, meaning "fish speared there" (Chafe, n. d., p. 92). The first Europeans were drawn to the region after treaties between the federal government and the Iroquois Confederacy were established in the 1790s, which permitted large tracts of land in northwestern Pennsylvania to be purchased from the government and sold in smaller parcels. Farming, timber harvesting, and the trapping and hunting of fur-bearing wildlife were the most important economic activities until the next century, when industries developed around sawmills, gristmills, glass production, tanning chemical manufacturing, and oil/natural gas extraction and refining (Leeson, 1890).

Story: the Kinzua Bridge

In 1882, Civil War hero General Thomas Kane, then president of the New York, Lake Erie and Western Railroad and Coal Company, aimed to create a more efficient rail line in western Pennsylvania to transport coal to the Great Lakes and beyond by bridging the deep Kinzua Gorge – cut by the Kinzua Creek, a small tributary of the Allegheny River. Anticipating an engineering challenge, the railway company employed civil engineer Octave Chanute (whose glider research would later inspire the Wright brothers) and Adolphus Bonzano to design the wrought iron bridge (Allegheny National Forest Visitors Bureau, 2013).

The bridge's sandstone foundation piers were excavated on-site, and the iron bridge sections were transported by rail from a prefabrication foundry in Phoenixville, Pennsylvania. The bridge was an ambitious engineering feat using the "Phoenix Column" to prevent vibration and buckling under the weight of the steam-powered freight trains. A construction crew of 125 workers, most of whom were underpaid immigrants, assembled the structure in just 94 days at a cost of $237,000 ("The Kinzua Viaduct," 1882, p. 765).

At 301 ft (92 m) high and 2,052 ft (625 m) long, the bridge was then the highest and longest railway viaduct in America (and briefly the world's highest). With a rise in curious visitors, excursion trains began to run across the length of the bridge (Devlin, 2004). By the turn of the century, freight train load weights had increased dramatically, and in 1901, the wrought iron bridge structure was replaced with steel girders. The original wrought iron metal casing and anchor bolts embedded in the sandstone supports were not replaced, which would later prove to be a fatal error (Leech, 2005). Again, workers were overworked and underpaid, and the reconstruction was completed in just four months.

For 60 more years, the bridge fulfilled Kane's dream to quickly transport coal, oil, and timber resources to the Great Lakes shipping lanes connecting to the Atlantic Ocean and the American Midwest. In 1959, the aging steel structure was deemed unsafe to handle increasingly heavy freight trains. It was closed to all rail traffic and purchased by a scrap dealer who initially planned to tear it down. However, recognizing the bridge's historical value, the dealer convinced Pennsylvania's Department of Conservation and Natural Resources (PA DCNR) to buy the structure in 1963. In an effort to bring tourism back to the region, the PA DCNR opened the Kinzua Bridge State Park in 1970. In 1977, the bridge was listed on the National Register of Historic Places and, in 1982, on the National Register of Historic Civil Engineering Landmarks.

In 1987, the Knox and Kane Railroad revived the passenger rail service powered by a steam locomotive, transporting some 20,000 passengers over the bridge annually (PA DCNR, 2021). Within two decades, the park attracted more than 160,000 visitors each year (PA DCNR, 2011). The bridge once again became a centerpiece of tourism and continued to be recognized as a significant landmark woven into the fabric of the region's identity.

The tornado

In the summer of 2002, bridge inspectors found structural deficiencies caused by rusting metal in the century-old bridge girders. An engineering firm was

hired to make necessary repairs, and the restoration was planned to be docu-
mented in the short film Tracks Across the Sky (Devlin, 2004). Work and
filming were well under way when tragedy struck on 21 July 2003. Weather
radar showed a strong storm system moving in from the west, and at 3:20 pm,
a category F1 tornado hit the bridge with 90 mph (145 kph) winds (Markowski, 2003; NOAA, 2003). The corroded 1882 anchor bolts had broken
away from the force of the wind, and in less than a minute, 11 of the bridge's
20 towers lay mangled on the valley floor. Steel train rails on both sides of the
remaining sections were left torn apart and bent downward to the "yawning
chasm below" (Devlin, 2004).

Almost immediately, work began to determine the precise cause of the collapse and to secure the safety of the curious public who came to visit the
destroyed structure. The documentary film team returned the day after the
tornado to document the damage. Executive Producer Linda Devlin from the
Allegheny National Forest Visitors Bureau noted, "Our documentary went
from Disney to a 'disaster' film in which Mother Nature changed history"
(personal correspondence, 7 May 2021). In the film, Devlin states her disbelief
that "a structure that had ... withstood time and numerous catastrophes, at the
point of being saved, could fall," and that they were so close "to saving it for
the next generation" (2004). The damaged bridge's notoriety also increased
significantly when it was featured in the History Channel documentary film
Life After People, which explored what would happen if humans suddenly disappeared from Earth (de Vries, 2008). After 200 years without people, the film
shows an "era of collapses," using the Kinzua Bridge as an example of an
unmaintained man-made structure that fell victim to the forces of nature.

The Kinzua Bridge State Park Sky Walk and Visitor Center

Due to the safety concerns of increased visitor numbers and the fact that pieces
of the ruined bridge were being illegally picked away as souvenirs, state,
county, and local officials began to focus on the future of the venerable bridge
and state park (Thomas, 2003). In February 2009, an extensive management
plan drafted with public involvement proposed numerous potential redevelop-
ments of the region, predominantly centred around the Kinzua Bridge State
Park (McKean County Planning Commission, 2009). A further community
effort was launched to encourage the state government to completely rebuild
the bridge; however, this was quickly rejected due to high estimated costs and
an unwillingness to rebuild a rail structure to the historic standards of 1900-era
engineering technology. After several years of discussion, at a cost of $4.3 mil-
lion, the PA DCNR decided to build a viewing platform with a glass-floor 624
feet (190 m) out onto the longest remaining terminus of the bridge and 225
feet (69 m) above the valley below. In September 2011, the new Sky Walk
opened for visitors (PA DCNR, 2011) with the remaining ruins left on the
valley floor (Figure 22.1.).

Figure 22.1. Ruins of the Kinzua Viaduct
Source: Photo by Katherine Burlingame

Plans for further development involved additional hiking trails and a visitor centre to be built on newly-cleared woodland overlooking the bridge. In September 2016, costing $8.9 million, the visitor centre opened to tell the story of the landscape's "history, construction, and destruction" (PA DCNR, 2011, 2014, 2016; see also Allegheny National Forest Visitors Bureau, 2017). The entrance to the visitor centre is framed by sections of the bridge's original, fallen steel girders, and the building includes a tourist information desk, classroom space, park administrative offices, public restrooms, and two large exhibits with a Victorian design to reflect the era when the bridge was first built. Interactive elements engage visitors with the bridge's history and the flora and fauna found in the park. The visitor centre is frequently supported by the Kinzua Bridge Foundation, created in 1993 "to increase awareness of, and visitation to, the State Park" (Kinzua Bridge Foundation, 2011). In 2019, during the last full year prior to the COVID-19 pandemic, more than 262,000 visitors toured the Sky Walk and Visitor Center, an astounding 100,000 more than before the bridge was damaged (Allegheny National Forest Visitors Bureau, email correspondence, 12 May 2021).

Presence: understanding local perspectives

In order to collect a more nuanced view of local perceptions and experiences in the landscape over time, an online survey was distributed across five Facebook groups for local communities. Respondents were asked to verify their current or previous residency in McKean County and to attest that they had visited the park both before the bridge was damaged and after the construction of the Sky Walk and Visitor Center. The survey consisted of two open-ended questions asking for a memorable experience in the park before the tornado and their reactions upon hearing the bridge was damaged. There were nine questions asking the respondents to react to different statements about the current park using a Likert scale, and two multiple choice questions asked about their thoughts on the reconstruction of the bridge and if they were involved in any discussions (informally or formally) about what to do with the park after the bridge was damaged. The survey ended with a space for additional comments.

In total, there were 229 valid responses from the survey that unveil a complex history of how local communities have experienced the heritagization and transformation of the landscape. Amplifying even a small sample of local voices reveals how the lived experience of a landscape is shaped and renegotiated by locals shifting heritage valuations and landscape encounters over time. We therefore frame our analysis around two main themes: the emotional and affective qualities of heritagescapes and local pride and stewardship.

Emotional and affective qualities of heritagescapes

The reflections of past experiences in the landscape reveal deeply embedded memories with both material and intangible dimensions. In particular, respondents indicated a strong sense of belonging and identity within the landscape, recalling a wide range of stories visiting the park before the bridge was damaged including walking across the bridge and then hiking back on the trail underneath, seeing or riding a train across the bridge, spending time with family and friends, participating in different recreational activities, and enjoying the park as a secluded place with beautiful scenery. As one noted, "We would sit on the bridge swinging our feet off of the bridge and sing songs, have long talks, throw stones off the bridge." The connection with childhood memories was a significant source of nostalgia once the bridge was damaged, with some worried that their own children or future generations "will never truly see it for what it was" and that their experiences will only be kept alive through storytelling if the bridge is never reconstructed.

The destruction of the bridge was therefore met with a very visceral feeling of loss where some described it as an "end of an era" or as if they had lost a part of themselves, a home, a friend, or a loved one. It was difficult for many respondents to accept the abrupt change in such a familiar place, and many continue to miss the "old days when it was quiet and peaceful" when one "could pitch a tent and be there for days without seeing anyone. ... Just us, the wildlife and the beauty of nature." A select few respondents were very vocal about their dissatisfaction of the transformation of the landscape arguing that it has become too busy and more for tourism purposes than for "local enjoyment." While one noted they are "glad the visitor center encourages tourism to support the local economy," they nevertheless "miss the days of peaceful solitude [they] used to find [there]." Another respondent was cautious in accepting any further changes to the landscape, arguing that "progress is not always good" and they "hope it doesn't become too commercialized and lose what we always loved so much about the area." Quoting Joni Mitchell, they argued that through the redevelopment of the park, "they paved paradise and put up a parking lot." The vast majority of respondents, however, expressed positive remarks about the transformation of the park.

Local pride and stewardship

Before the construction of the Sky Walk and Visitor Center, many respondents noted that they were worried about the loss of an important historical landmark and they had supported reconstructing the bridge to its original structure. However, only 20 per cent indicated that they had formally expressed their opinions about reconstruction plans for the park by signing a petition, attending a public meeting, or contacting a government leader. Once the Sky Walk and Visitor Center were constructed, while still recognizing the tragedy of losing the bridge, most respondents appreciated the new developments, with many arguing that the park, and particularly the experience of going to the bridge, are even better than before.

Given that the bridge and surrounding natural landscape have long been a source of pride for the local area, respondents also reflected that they are happy that the new developments attract a wider range of visitors. Several commented that the park has become more welcoming, educational, and accessible, and that building the Visitor Center and Sky Walk brought visitors back to the area to enjoy both the history and scenic qualities of the park. Citing the work of the PA DCNR, one respondent noted they have "done a wonderful job tastefully developing and promoting this park" and that "anything that brings tourism and showcases this beautiful area is of great benefit." One respondent also specifically noted that they were "saddened" by locals who verbalize their resentment regarding traffic, visitors, sharing space and this remarkable treasure. While some respondents still hold on to the hope of reconstructing the bridge, there is a general understanding that the landscape has irrevocably changed, and reconstructing the bridge no longer makes sense given the cost as well as the different building materials that would be used that would distance it from its original unique architectural value. While holding onto nostalgia for what has been lost, a majority of respondents indicated that they are actively invested in the heritage-making process by recognizing the value of the park in attracting visitors to the area, and they themselves continue to return to the park to create new experiences. As one respondent noted, they "will always have past memories and look forward to more."

The local communities' continued attachment and sense of stewardship for the park were also illuminated through the efforts of our research project. As news of our research spread around the remote mountain communities of McKean County, we were approached with several offers to help, including sending pictures and suggesting potential people to contact who have been involved in different capacities in the park's development over time. Our research also made the front page in the local newspaper (Wankel, 2021). Though the destruction of the bridge left an indelible mark on the region, the landscape is perpetually embedded with profound value and meaning, and the memory of the bridge is fervently kept alive by the people who grew up climbing over its rusted rails and decaying planks high above the valley floor.

Future heritagescapes and climate change

While we have shown that change is inevitable in heritagescapes both through tangible and intangible valuations, unexpected changes, particularly from an unpredictable climate, will increasingly create challenges of how to balance enduring layers of meaning with the limits and costs of adaptive re-use. Though one option for the Kinzua heritagescape would have been to tear down the bridge and allow the natural landscape to rewild itself just as was suggested in the 1960s, as one respondent argued: "They created something wonderful from a devastating act of nature." In considering different pathways forward, the construction of the Sky Walk and Visitor Center proved a successful reinvention with over 100,000 more annual visitors than before the tornado. The Kinzua Bridge State Park therefore provides a unique example of embracing loss and finding an adaptive solution bridging progress and preservation.

Climate change research increasingly emphasizes strategies focused on adaptation as it is not possible to stop the changes that many landscapes will inevitably face. In line with the argument that transformation occurs "through embracing changes as positive and necessary" (Harvey and Perry, 2015, p. 10), the evolution of the Kinzua heritagescape shows the value in letting go of what has been lost and finding innovation and reinvention through a tragic event. As Moscardo (1996) suggests, focusing on creative adaptation, effective interpretation, and offering a variety of experiences and different possibilities of interaction within the landscape resulted in a better distribution and representation of visitors while encouraging more sustainable behaviors and attracting prolonged support from the public and other stakeholders.

Though some argue that we should sometimes simply accept "oblivion" and that "permanence is not a viable and necessary feature of valued heritage" (Harvey and Perry, 2015, p. 11; see also Morris, 2014), creative adaptations can also be viewed as an acceptance and recognition of the natural processes of time while still acknowledging the affective and emotional dimensions embedded in heritagescapes. While many communities have failed to "acknowledge the possibility inherent in the transformation from one phase of existence to another" (Morris, 2014, p. 211), we position the Kinzua Bridge State Park as a successful example of creative reinvention and transformation.

The de/regeneration of heritagescapes

Harvey and Perry argue that "heritage is haunted by a sense of uncertainty" (2015, p. 11, original emphasis), and recognizing its transient nature makes it easier to accept change and allow heritagescapes to evolve over time. This (re) production, or de/regeneration, of heritagescapes is a testament to the constantly renegotiated values and layers of meaning embedded in places of heritage, and the Kinzua Bridge State Park exemplifies a heritagescape that has never been stagnant and never will be. Guided by the TRIOLE model, we investigated the different phases of the heritagescape, revealing a complex, non-linear process influenced by local, state, and national valuations. The bridge faced the scrap heap numerous times, with suggestions that there was more value (both economically and logistically) in simply returning the landscape to its natural state. Yet, the emotional and affective value of the place always prevailed. Exploring the lived experience in the landscape over time uncovered the local communities' enduring attachments of emotion, nostalgia, sense of pride, and stewardship in keeping the history alive. This attests to the resilience of local communities to evolve with, and adapt to, the changing landscape even when the heritagization of the landscape is a highly contested process.

While a tornado in Kinzua was an unforeseen natural disaster, it resulted in the unique creation of a heritagescape that shows the possibilities of creative reinvention in a rapidly changing and unpredictable climate to bring new life into threatened landscapes. In his book In Ruins, Christopher Woodward argues, "When we contemplate ruins, we contemplate our own future" (2002, p. 2), and the twisted ruins of the Kinzua Bridge entrenched within the landscape have provided the foundations of a new heritagescape that will continue to change.

References

Allegheny National Forest Visitors Bureau. (2013). Walk the Tracks Across the Sky. Retrieved from: https://visitanf.com/wp-content/pdf/ANFVB-Kinzua-Sky-Walk-Brochure.pdf.

Allegheny National Forest Visitors Bureau. (2017). Allegheny National Forest Travel Guide and Map. Retrieved from: http://visitanf.com/wp-content/pdf/ANFVB-VG-2017.pdf.

Bender, B. (1998). *Stonehenge: Making Space*. Oxford: Berg.

Burlingame, K. (2020). *Dead Landscapes – And How to Make Them Live* [Doctoral dissertation, Lund University]. Lund University Research Portal. Retrieved from: https://portal.research.lu.se/portal/en/publications/dead-landscapes–and-how-to-make-them-live(7470a71d-d10b-4163-b75b-84111066273d).html

Burlingame, K. (2022). Presence in Affective Heritagescapes: Connecting Theory to Practice. *Tourism Geographies*, 24(2–3): 263–283.

Carman, J. and Sørensen, M. L. S. (2009). Heritage Studies: An Outline. In M. L. S. Sørensen, and J. Carman (eds.), *Heritage Studies: Methods and Approaches*. Abingdon: Routledge, pp. 11–29.

Chafe, W. (n.d). English–Seneca Dictionary. Seneca Language Department. Retrieved from: https://senecalanguage.com/wp-content/uploads/2014/04/SENECA-DICTIONARY-FINAL.pdf.

Cosgrove, D. (2006). Modernity, Community and the landscape Idea. *Journal of Material Culture*, 11(1–2): 49–66.

DeSilvey, C. and Edensor, T. (2012). Reckoning with Ruins. *Progress in Human Geography*, 37(4): 465–485.

Devlin, L. (Executive Producer). (2004). *Tracks Across the Sky* [Film; Video]. Allegheny National Forest Vacation Bureau and Penn State Public Broadcasting. YouTube. www.youtube.com/watch?v=qinUza6H61I.

de Vries, D. (Director) (2008, January 21). *Life After People* [Film]. History Channel.

Garden, M.-C. E. (2004). *The Heritagescape: Exploring the Phenomenon of the Heritage Site* [Doctoral dissertation, University of Cambridge]. Apollo: University of Cambridge Repository. www.repository.cam.ac.uk/handle/1810/244822.

Garden, M.-C. E. (2006). The Heritagescape: Looking at Landscapes of the Past. *International Journal of Heritage Studies*, 12(5): 394–411.

Granö, J. G. (1997). *Pure Geography*. Edited by O. Granö and A. Paasi. Translated by M. Hicks. Baltimore: Johns Hopkins University Press.

Harvey, D. C. and Perry, J. (2015). Heritage and Climate Change: The Future Is Not the Past. In D. C. Harvey and J. Perry (eds.), *The Future of Heritage as Climates Change: Loss, Adaptation and Creativity*. Abingdon: Routledge, pp. 3–21.

Kinzua Bridge Foundation. (2011). Kinzua Bridge Foundation History. www.kinzua bridgefoundation.com/history.html.

Leech, T. (2005). The Collapse of the Kinzua Viaduct: A Combination of Design Oversight and Material Fatigue Left a Century-old Railroad Bridge Vulnerable to an F-1 Tornado. *American Scientist*, 93(4): 348–353.

Leeson, M. A. (1890). *History of the counties of McKean, Elk, Cameron and Potter, Pennsylvania*. Armstrong County: J. H. Beers and Company.

Lorimer, H. and Murray, S. (2015). The Ruin in Question. *Performance Research*, 20(3): 58–66.

Markowski, P. (2003). Meteorological Aspects of the 21 July 2003 Kinzua Viaduct Storm. Pennsylvania State University, Department of Meteorology. Retrieved from https://web.archive.org/web/20120922031605/http://www.dcnr.state.pa.us/info/kinzuabridgereport/app/appb.pdf.

McKean County Planning Commission. (2009). Kinzua Bridge Byway Corridor Management Plan. Retrieved from www.dot.state.pa.us/public/Bureaus/Cpdm/Byways/KinzuaBridgeBywayCMP_final.pdf.

Mitchell, D. (2008). New Axioms for Reading the Landscape: Paying Attention to Political Economy and Social Justice. In J. L. Wescoat, Jr. and D. M. Johnston (eds.), *Political Economies of Landscape Change: Places of Integrative Power*. Cham: Springer, pp. 29–50.

Morris, B. (2014). In Defence of Oblivion: The Case of Dunwich, Suffolk. *International Journal of Heritage Studies*, 20(2): 196–216.

Moscardo, G. (1996). Mindful Visitors: Heritage and Tourism. *Annals of Tourism Research*, 23(2): 376–397.

NOAA. (n.d.). Records. State Climate Extremes Committee (SCEC). Retrieved from: www.ncdc.noaa.gov/extremes/scec/records/pa.

NOAA. (2003, July 21). Event Record Details. NOAA Satellite and Information Systems. Retrieved from: http://www4.ncdc.noaa.gov/cgi-win/wwcgi.dll?wwevent~ShowEvent~513297.

Olsen, B. and Pétursdóttir, þ. (2016). Unruly Heritage: Tracing Legacies in the Anthropocene. *Arkæologisk Forum* (35): 38–45.

Pennsylvania Department of Conservation and Natural Resources (PA DCNR). (2011, September 28). Visitors Invited to Walk Out and Observe Valley Below on Restored Portion of Viaduct at Kinzua Bridge State Park in McKean County. *Resource*

Newsletter. Retrieved from: www.apps.dcnr.state.pa.us/news/resource/res2011/11-0928-kinzuabridgesp.aspx.

Pennsylvania Department of Conservation and Natural Resources (PA DCNR). (2014, August 4). DCNR Announces Contract for Kinzua Bridge State Park Office/Visitor Center. *Resource Newsletter.* Retrieved from: www.apps.dcnr.state.pa.us/news/resource/res2014/14-0806-kinzuabridgesp.aspx.

Pennsylvania Department of Conservation and Natural Resources (PA DCNR). (2016, August 17). DCNR, partners to hold dedication for Kinzua Bridge State Park Visitors Center and park office on Sept. 15. *Resource Newsletter.* Retrieved from: www.apps.dcnr.state.pa.us/news/resource/res2016/16-0817-kinzuabridgesp.aspx.

Pennsylvania Department of Conservation and Natural Resources (PA DCNR). (2021). History of Kinzua Bridge State Park. Retrieved from: www.dcnr.pa.gov/StateParks/FindAPark/KinzuaBridgeStatePark/Pages/History.aspx.

Pennsylvania Natural Heritage Program. (2008, February). McKean County Natural Heritage Inventory. Retrieved from: www.naturalheritage.state.pa.us/CNAI_PDFs/McKean%20County%20NHI%202008%20WEB.pdf.

Ryan, A. (2012). *Where Land Meets Sea: Coastal Explorations of Landscape, Representation and Spatial Experience.* Abingdon: Routledge.

The Kinzua Viaduct. (1882, December 15). *Railroad Gazette.* Retrieved from: https://babel.hathitrust.org/cgi/pt?id=mdp.39015013053650andview=1upandseq=839andq1=237,000.

Thomas, L. (2003, July 27). Officials Are Warning People to Stay Away from the Damaged Kinzua Viaduct. *Pittsburgh Post-Gazette.* Retrieved from: www.post-gazette.com/localnews/20030727kinzuareg4p4.asp.

Wankel, J. (2021, April 30). Area Natives Researching for Book, Create Survey for Local Input. *The Bradford Era.* Retrieved from: www.bradfordera.com/news/academics-researching-for-book-that-will-include-kinzua-bridge/article_ba008052-ce4b-5c81-b3cd-df4023f24ec5.html.

Woodward, C. (2002). *In Ruins.* New York: Vintage.

23 Heritagization between nature and culture

Managing the Sečovlje salt pans in Slovenia

Primož Pipan and Maja Topole

Introduction

Heritage is a concept that is adaptable to current flows, building on the past but shaping itself in the present, and being selectively used for contemporary purposes (Nic Craith 2012: 11). Heritage has always been with us and has always been produced by people according to their contemporary concerns and experiences (Harvey 2001). Heritage is subjective and filtered with reference to the present, whenever that "present" actually is (Harvey 2001).

The landscape is a place where natural and cultural heritage meet. In order to protect important cultural landscapes, the European Landscape Convention was introduced in Europe. According to the Danish geographer Kenneth Olwig, landscape means not only a piece of land (region, territory), but also the community (population) associated with the region and its collective traditions and customs. Customs related to the ownership and land use play a key role in the landscape. Spek, Brinkkemper, and Speleers (2006) argue that the rise in educational attainment has led to a growing interest in the "story of the landscape". Previously uninteresting landscapes have been transformed into living heritage. Landscape management should therefore integrate nature conservation and heritage management and engage the public in a collaborative way. This is especially true for areas where a "new nature" is being introduced, a nature that cannot exist without human management.

There is often a gap between the heritagization of (new) nature and culture in the same landscape. We will show this with a case study of the Sečovlje salt pans in Slovenia. We studied the Sečovlje salt pans through literature, films, videos, volunteer work, participant observation, and extensive visits. One of the reasons for the gap between the heritagization of (new) nature and culture goes back to the professional and official designation resulting from the legislation. In Slovenia, the 1999 Nature Conservation Act divides large-scale protected areas into "national, regional or landscape parks". The Slovenian term for English "landscape park" is "krajinski park". It comes from the word "(po) krajina" in Slovene (Landschaft in German and landscape in English). The Institute of the Republic of Slovenia for Nature Conservation also uses the term "nature parks" for large-scale protected areas. We believe that this English

DOI: 10.4324/9781003195238-23

translation for the term "landscape park" is not appropriate. Instead we use the term "Designated Landscape Area" for a protected area where the result of a high degree of human impact interferes with nature.

Today, two most important actors in heritagization of Sečovlje salt pans are:

1   *Krajinski park Sečoveljske soline* (the Sečovlje Salt Pans Designated Landscape Area – SSPDLA). Its main goal is to protect nature and culture. Its concessionaire for the period 2001–2021 is the salt production company *Soline, pridelava soli, d.o.o.* (from now on: Soline d.o.o.), an economic entity, owned by the Slovenian national telecommunications company *Telekom Slovenije.*
2   *Muzej solinarstva* (the Museum of Salt-making) – a part of the *Pomorski muzej "Sergej Mašera" Piran* ("Sergej Mašera" Maritime Museum Piran).

This chapter studies heritagization of the landscape of the Sečovlje salt pans. It focuses on the inadequate management of the landscape as heritage, particularly the lack of coordination between different actors and managers – (new) nature and culture. We want to encourage the integration of nature and culture in order to preserve the heritage from further decay.

Outline of the saltworks in the Sečovlje salt pans

The Sečovlje salt pans are located on the Istrian peninsula in the northeast of the Adriatic Sea. With an area of 593 hectares, they are the largest salt pans on the eastern Adriatic coast. The written sources date back to the 13th century (Pahor and Poberaj 1963). In the past they belonged to and were managed by the town of Piran. During the Venetian Republic, the Piran salt pans produced as much as a third of the sea salt on the eastern Adriatic coast (Savnik 1951; Savnik 1965; Bonin 2016). One of the most important technological milestones of the Piran salt workers is 1377, when they took over the production of *petola* from Dalmatian salt workers from the island of Pag. This biosediment at the bottom of crystallization basins prevents sea mud from coming into contact with salt crystals.

The work in the salt pans was seasonal: in winter the levees were rebuilt and the canals cleaned, and in summer salt was harvested. Every April, on the day of St. George, the patron saint of Piran, the salt workers moved with their families to the south-eastern coast of the Piran Bay to the salt-pan houses 10 km away. Seasonal migration involved over 400 families (3,800–4,200 people). Until the beginning of the 20th century, one family was responsible for obtaining salt in an individual salt field, the basic production unit. The stone masonry salt-pan houses, located in the middle of salt pans, on the embankments along the navigable canals, are today mostly in ruins. The Drnica river (*Canal Grande*) divides the salt pans into Lera and the Fontanigge area. In 1912 the medieval way of extraction of salt in Lera was abandoned. The Austro-Hungary began to reorganize the salt pans into a single large salt-pan (Muzej Solinarstva 1992). The modernization of the work process was completed under Italian government in the mid-1920s. It introduced a typical industrial division of tasks between specialized professions (watermen, carpenters, salt harvesters), and replaced wind pumps with diesel and later electric ones. The constant presence of salt workers was no longer necessary, but daily manual salt harvesting was still mandatory. After World War II, nearly 200 sea salt pans on the northern shores of the Mediterranean were closed, as they could not compete with the salt pans from the African shores. There, in the drier climate, salt was harvested only once a season, mechanically. In the Fontanigge area, the medieval structure of the salt pans with salt-pan houses and the way of working were preserved for 55 years

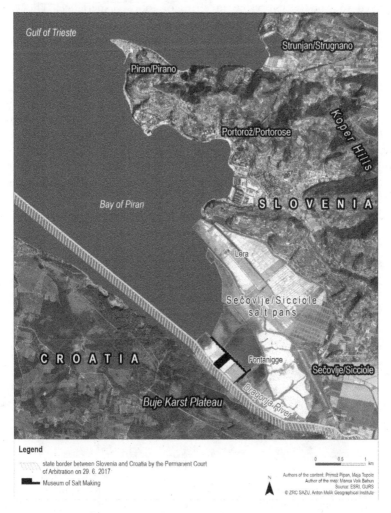

Figure 23.1. Part of the Istrian peninsula with the Bay of Piran and the Sečovlje salt pans

longer: the production was stopped in 1967. When the medieval salt production technology in Fontanigge finally collapsed, the path to its heritagization was open.

Heritagization of salt pans

The Museum of Salt-making – heritagization of medieval salt-making

The idea of the Museum of Salt-making was designed by the "Sergej Mašera" Maritime Museum Piran in connection with the local tourist economy immediately after the salt pans were abandoned in the 1960s. The area was thus expected to gain greater value in terms of tourist experience. The "Sergej Mašera" Maritime Museum Piran and the Intermunicipal Institute for the Protection of Natural and Cultural Heritage Piran in 1985 determined its location in the Fontanigge area of the Sečovlje salt pans.

In 1990, the Municipality of Piran established the SSPDLA and set protection regimes and development guidelines. On these foundations, the Museum of Salt-making also came to life in 1991 (Muzej Solinarstva 1992). Together with the Designated Landscape Area it was granted state protection status in 2001. The open-air museum in the Fontanigge area still displays the medieval way of extracting salt and boasts the only functioning traditional wooden wind-powered brine pump on the entire Adriatic coast.

The heritagization of medieval salt-making also took place through voluntary work. Summer international work camps were held at the Museum of Salt-making in the period 1999–2014. Maintenance work was carried out and

Figure 23.2. Sečovlje salt pans from the southeast. In front, Dragonja River and Fontanigge area with renovated salt-pan houses at the Museum of Salt-making
along the Giassi Canal. Followed by the ruins along the Curto Canal, the
Lera area and the Koper hills
Source: Photo by Maja Topole, 2019

dozens of newspaper, radio, and television articles were published in local, national, and international media. The participants filmed material for the documentary "Zgodba o soli" in 2004 and the English version "The Story About Salt" in 2006. In 2007, the film was published as a didactic tool for teachers. Besides the volunteers, there were also students of ethnology on study practice and researchers evaluating the sustainability of the salt production method (Laganis and Debeljak 2006).

The Museum of Salt-making received the Europa Nostra Medal in the category of Cultural Landscapes for the year 2003 "for the exemplary and sensitive revitalization of the cultural landscape, including the restitution of facilities for traditional salt production technology, architectural restoration, and educational activities, all in close harmony with the natural environment". This was the first time that any institution from Slovenia received the European Union Prize for Cultural Heritage/the Europa Nostra Award.

Heritagization by art, the tourist industry and other related stories

The salt pans landscape is often used in screenplays or as a set of various films: for example the 1957 Italian drama by František Čáp "La ragazza della salina" (*Sand, Love and Salt*); two Croatian documentaries by Krsto Škanata "Bjele žetve" (*White Harvests*) and "Morska Solana" (*Sea Saltworks*), respectively in 1958 and 1959; the fourth of five episodes of the Slovenian teen film based on Astrid Lindgren's book by Staš Potočnik, *Erazem in potepuh* (*Rasmus and the Vagabond*), in 1971; the cult Slovenian teen film by Tugo Štiglic *Poletje v školjki* (*A Summer in a Sea Shell*), in 1985, and many other videos and commercials.

In 1999, Telekom Slovenije took over the concession for the extraction of salt in the Lera area from the food company Droga Portorož, established the Soline d.o.o. and designed the brand *Piranske soline*. In 2001, it also acquired the concession for the management of the SSPDLA for 20 years. Today, the traditional Piran salt and salt flower for gourmets, a wide variety of salt-based cosmetics, and salt-related souvenirs are high-quality items that are known all over the world. Piran salt was registered in the European Union with a protected designation of origin in 2014. In 2015, the traditional sea salt production was granted the status of intangible cultural heritage in the Slovenian National Register.

One of the ways of heritagization of the Sečovlje salt pans is also the use of salt mud for the treatment of skin diseases. Thalassotherapy is a centuries-old method that was introduced here by the Benedictines from the monastery of St. Onofrio from Krog above Sečovlje (1432–1957). Today, their tradition is continued by the *Lepa Vida* Thalasso Spa, managed by the Soline d.o.o. Thalassotherapy is also offered by many hotels in Portorož and Piran. Spa activities based on salt mud and brine are the foundations of the tourist development of the Municipality of Piran. In 2019, only the Slovenian capital city of Ljubljana surpassed it in the number of overnight stays.

Portorož Airport in Sečovlje is also taking part in the competition for salt pans landscape. Its beginnings are connected with the Cosulich family and date back to 1921, when tourist panoramic flights by seaplanes were introduced in Portorož. In 1922, the private airline SISA – Societa Italiana Servizi Aerei in Trieste was founded. In 1962, the first airport runway was built in Sečovlje, in 1980 it gained international status and has constantly been modernized and expanded at the expense of the salt pans.

Interested parties who want to take advantage of the proximity of the salt pans landscape are still multiplying. In relation to adventure tourism linked to this landscape, the planned resort next to the salt pans, on the site of the abandoned Sečovlje black coal mine (it operated in the period 1935–1973), and the planned Sečovlje golf course will probably develop. Today, the story about salt-making is included wherever possible in the touristy neighbourhood. It is presented through selected art photographs, reproductions of old photographs and statues, and especially illustratively during the Salt-Making Festival, organized by the Municipality of Piran and various co-organizers since 2003.

New nature – heritagization of nature and biodiversity

In recent decades, the importance of salt pans has constantly been changing. The economic function of the salt pans prevailed for centuries. Soon after the cessation of salt production and maintenance of the levees in Fontanigge, the nature conservation function gained in importance and the heritagization of nature and biodiversity took place. The area began to take on the appearance of a wetland again. Over a period of a few decades, habitats such as the sea swamp, the salt marsh, the salt grass, the tidal flat and the reed bed gradually formed. As many as 45 plant species have settled in them, included also in the Slovenian red list, in addition to 291 bird species, more than 80 of which nest here either permanently or occasionally.

The Sečovlje salt pans are the largest Slovenian coastal wetland and its most important ornitho-faunal locality. In 1993, the saltworks in Fontanigge were the first in Slovenia to be included in the List of Ramsar wetlands. Upon Slovenia's accession to the European Union in 2004, the Sečovlje salt pans and their surroundings became part of the Natura 2000 protected area. The Habitats Directive from 1992 protects 366.22 hectares, while the Birds Directive from 2009 protects 891.94 hectares. The areas partially overlap.

In two decades, the SSPDLA with the help of European Union funds has arranged numerous routes for visitors, bird observatories and information boards. Its headquarters with a visitor centre is in Lera.

Fontanigge – discord in the management of medieval saltworks heritage

The decay of the heritage of the medieval saltworks in Fontanigge is happening due to the lack of coordination between the different managers and the lack of maintenance. An important current solution would be to maintain the embankments, thus preventing the museum's salt field from flooding due to meteor or seawater intrusion. The floods threaten the foundations of the restored museum salt-pan houses, and even more the other unmaintained ruins.

The map of the Sečovlje salt pans from the middle of the 19th century shows 493 salt-pan houses, while there are only 118 in the map from 1984. In 2019, the Fontanigge area offered a view of 70 former salt-pan houses predominantly in ruins.

The Museum of Salt-making does not have the appropriate status or conditions for sufficient maintenance of salt-pan embankments. It no longer produces salt because it does not have a permit. The state concession for the extraction of sea salt is operated by the Soline d.o.o. Both museum salt fields came under its administration and care. The entrance fee to the Designated Landscape Area now includes entry to the museum. Thus, the Museum of Salt-making can no longer charge the entrance fee, issue tickets, or keep statistics on the number of visitors. This is the reason for the drastic drop in the number of visitors to the Museum of Salt-making. In 2005, there were 25,000, so it financially covered its own activities. Today, the museum can be accessed on foot, by bicycle, or by electric train with zero carbon emissions and no noise that would disturb the birds. But in 2019, it only had about 3,000 visitors. The saltworks open-air museum thus no longer has any real function. Only four renovated salt-pan houses remain under its administration.

Heritagization of nature and heritagization of culture in coexistence, separately or one against another

Landscape is a multi-layered phenomenon, integrating past and present functions, ideologies, and physical contexts (Urbanc et al. 2004). Landscape has an important influence in shaping people's minds, ideas, emotions, and identities. It can be viewed as "a palimpsest, a document that has been written on and erased over and over again" Crawford (1953 p. 51). "Some landscape elements have remained the same through all the changing socio-economic formations. Some others have been forgotten or destroyed by the emerging formations. Some have been replaced by other objects. Yet others have retained their physical structure but the meanings have changed. Landscape is thus the collection of inscriptions by all formations, where one can still recognize the signs of different time periods (Urbanc et al. 2004)".

Harvey and Waterton (2015) distinguish between a natural landscape, which is "protected" as a heritage by the interests of colonists or later settlers; in contrast, there is an "indigenous landscape" associated with "indigenous knowledge". The first emphasizes the tangible and the visual which is characteristic of Eurocentric understandings, the second emphasizes the intangible, the experimental, and the emotional (Harvey 2015). We suggest that the 700-year practice of medieval salt-making at Fontanigge, following the example of Clarke and Waterton (2015), be understood in terms of indigenous knowledge systems. Thus the Museum of Salt-making plays the role of indigenous landscape, and nature protection plays the role of natural heritage. The museum has successfully carried out the heritagization of medieval salt-making in the past. In 1990, the Intermunicipal Institute for the Protection of Natural and Cultural Heritage Piran designed the museum in the spirit of "collaborative conversation", as Harvey and Waterton (2015) term the coexistence of natural and cultural heritage. It was set in the abandoned Fontanigge – the marginal area where it would not interfere with the tourist development of the most tourist-developed municipality in Slovenia. Eventually, the area without modern infrastructure became a hot spot in terms of biodiversity and natural heritage.

The story of this landscape consists of collaborative stories of natural and cultural heritage. In the case of the Fontanigge area in the Sečovlje salt pans, the cultural heritage is subordinated to the "new nature". Unlike in the Netherlands, where the new nature has been systematically introduced since 1990, the new nature in Fontaniggie has emerged spontaneously and naturally. According to Kenneth Olwig, the practice of medieval salt-making at Fontanigge could be classified as "customary law" – common law; while nature conservation would fit into the category of Roman law – imposed on the region and the population by a higher external power (nation, ruler) (Spek, Brinkkemper, and Speleers 2006).

In Slovenia at the time of Yugoslavia, a single organization was in charge of the protection of nature and culture. After the independence of Slovenia in 1991, the two areas began to diverge. Nature conservation got separated from the once unified organization. The Nature Conservation Act 1999 established the Institute of the Republic of Slovenia for Nature Conservation. It changed diction; the former "natural heritage" was renamed to "natural value". Decrees and regulation on the establishment of individual designated landscape areas do not contain official translations into English. Instead of translating them into "designated landscape areas", they are most often translated into "landscape parks". This is practiced also by professionals in the field of environmental protection in Slovenia. "Landscape parks are the most common type of large protected areas (IUCN category V) in Slovenia. There are 44 of them altogether, covering 5.7% of Slovenian territory. They are the result of a long-lasting interconnection between man and nature, and are comprised of areas with great ecological, biotic, or landscape value. Landscape parks permit the highest degree of human impact, which together with the natural environment ultimately helps create diversity" (Smrekar, Polajnar Horvat and Ribeiro 2020: 318). Even the same authors alternate between the two in different cases: "landscape park" (Smrekar et al. 2016b) and "designated protected landscape area" (Smrekar et al. 2016a).

The official Slovenian term for the Designated Landscape Area – krajinski park – is not problematic, as primarily the point at issue is not strict protection of nature but the intertwining of human activity and nature in cultural landscapes. The challenge for the discourse on the relationship between nature and culture is obviously the English translation of the Slovenian term for landscape (*krajinski*) in the official names of individual designated landscape areas in Slovenia. Sometimes it is translated as "landscape park", and in other cases into "nature park", with no official recommendations about the translation. Does the choice about how to translate *krajinski* implicitly suggest the priority of its protection regime: landscape or nature? What is in the foreground – nature or culture? It is interesting that the professional organization that unites Slovenian designated landscape areas is called "*Skupnost naravnih parkov Slovenije*"; the English translation is unambiguous here – "The Community of Nature Parks of Slovenia".

This inconsistency is clearly seen in the example of the English translation of the neighbouring Strunjan Designated Landscape Area (*Krajinski park Strunjan*) – the Strunjan salt pans are part of the Piran salt pans. On its official website in English, it is called "Nature Park Strunjan", however, as part of "The Community of Nature Parks of Slovenia", it is called "Strunjan Landscape Park".

Would the process of heritagization of the Sečovlje salt pans be different if the official English name of the SSPDLA was "landscape park" instead of "nature park"? Is the perception of natural heritage, on the one hand, and of cultural heritage, on the other, crucial for the relationship between the two – for the dominance of one over the other or for a balanced treatment of both?

The question arises as to whether the English *nature* park and the *landscape* park are only labels for the marketing of (tourist) products, which depend on the target group of a designated landscape area. But this is already a step into the field of territorial branding or place branding.

In the absence of a coexistence between nature and culture, the museum became a hidden narrative of the heritagization of the Sečovlje salt pans. In the middle of Europe, there is a discourse on the lack of space for the "non-elite and indigenous voice" (Harvey and Waterton 2015) presented by the Museum of Salt-making – revealing a conflict of interest between different users of this landscape. The two predominant narratives in the heritagization of the SSPDLA are the "*Piranska sol*" brand and natural heritage. The latter generate a popular romantic imagination of the ruins of salt-pan houses. These, of course, are not frozen in time, shrinking every year due to decay. The ruins of the salt-pan houses in Fontanigge have become an object of aesthetic valuation of landscape forms, despite their current disappearance. This is confirmed by the findings of Urbanc et al. (2004) and Pipan and Kokalj (2017) – preserved visible landscape elements in new circumstances can acquire new meaning for future generations.

In the period 1967–1991, Fontanigge became what Mares, Rasin, and Pipan (2013) call an "abandoned landscape". Due to the growing importance of nature conservation or the protection of biodiversity, and blaming the legislation in this area, it is impossible to protect the small part of the former "factory" of sea salt Fontanigge. Within this area, the museum salt fields are, according to today's Slovenian protection classification, a unit of cultural heritage, and its wider surroundings are protected as a natural heritage.

The existing contradictions between the interests of nature conservation and cultural conservation are only apparent. The dilemma of the discourse between cultural and natural heritage is nicely addressed by Harrison (2015). He claims that the critique of the separation of natural and cultural heritage is well established – many acknowledge this as an artificial separation. He illustrates this point with a statement by Phil Sullivan, a Ngiyampaa man and Aboriginal Sites Officer in National Parks and Wildlife Service in New South Wales, Australia: "The 'natural' and 'cultural' heritage of National Parks is not separate. This is an artificial white-fella [western culture] separation. They are still boxing the whole into sections, we need to integrate management into a holistic view of the landscape" (Harrison and Rose, 2010, cited in Harrison 2015: 30).

We suggest that landscape should be looked at more broadly in Europe as well, similarly to what Harrison (2015: 30) suggests for Australia, where "within an indigenous ontology in which 'culture' is everywhere, not only is there no boundary between nature and culture, there is no mind-matter binary. This contrasts with a modern Cartesian dualism that sees the mind and body as separate, and the mind itself as non-physical." Land management bureaucracies go about managing and protecting endangered plant and animal species. We should consider as many components of the landscape as possible. In the discourse between nature and culture in Fontanigge, the domain of nature and biodiversity conservation prevailed over the domain of cultural heritage of the salt pans and the domain of built heritage conservation – the ruins of salt-pan houses. The landscape is a complex intertwining of nature and society, which also stands out in the case of the Sečovlje salt pans. The natural heritage of Fontanigge is a result of the Anthropocene epoch. Centuries-old salt canals and basins of varying depths today allow different species of birds to live. As Harrison (2015) points out, heritage-making is about preserving values and objects in the future. Different heritage domains are engaged in the work of assembling and caring for the future. The future will show what layers, composing the palimpsest that Anthropocene writes into the landscape of the Sečovlje salt pans, will be preserved.

Acknowledgements

We thank Flavio Bonin from the "Sergej Mašera" Maritime Museum Piran, who made it possible for Service Civil International to conduct international volunteer work camps in the Museum of Salt Making in Sečovlje, and for a detailed insight into the history and operation of the museum. We acknowledge financial support from the Slovenian Research Agency research core funding Heritage on the Margins: New Perspectives on Heritage and Identity within and beyond the National (P5-0408).

References

Bonin, F. (2016). *Belo zlato krilatega leva: razvoj severnojadranskih solin v obdobju Beneške republike*. Piran: Pomorski muzej "Sergej Mašera".

Clarke, A. and Waterton, E. (2015). A Journey to the Heart: Affecting Engagement at Uluru-Kata Tjuta National Park. *Landscape Research*, 40(8): 971–992.

Crawford, O. G. S. (1953). *Archaeology in the Field*. London: Dent and Sons.

Harrison, R. (2015). Beyond "Natural" and "Cultural" Heritage: Toward an Ontological Politics of Heritage in the Age of Anthropocene. *Heritage and Society*, 8(1): 24–42.

Harrison, R. and Rose, D. (2010). Intangible Heritage. In T. Benton (ed.) *Understanding Heritage and Memory*. Manchester: Manchester University Press, pp. 238–276.

Harvey, D. C. (2001). Heritage Pasts and Heritage Presents: Temporality, Meaning and the Scope of Heritage Studies. *International Journal of Heritage Studies*, 7(4): 319–338.

Harvey, D. (2015). Landscape and Heritage: Trajectories and Consequences. *Landscape Research*, 40(8): 911–924.

Harvey, D. C. and Waterton, E. (2015). Editorial: Landscapes of Heritage and Heritage Landscapes. *Landscape Research*, 40(8): 905–910.

Laganis, J. and Debeljak, M. (2006). Sensitivity Analysis of the Energy Flow at the Solar Salt Production Process in Slovenia. *Ecological Modeling* 194: 287–295.

Mares, P., Rasin, R., and Pipan, P. (2013). Abandoned Landscapes of Former German Settlement in the Czech Republic and in Slovenia. In I. Rotherham (ed.) *Cultural Severance and the Environment*. Dordrecht: Springer, pp. 289–309.

Muzej solinarstva (1992). *Katalog št. 7*. Piran: Pomorski muzej "Sergej Mašera".

Nic Craith, M. (2012). Europe's (Un)Common Heritage(s). *Traditiones* 41(2): 11–28.

Pahor, M. and Poberaj, T. (1963). *Stare Piranske soline*. Ljubljana: Mladinska Knjiga.

Pipan, P. and Kokalj, Z. (2017). Transformation of the Jeruzalem Hills Cultural Landscape with Modern Vineyard Terraces. *Acta Geographica Slovenica*, 57(2): 149–162.

Savnik, R. (1951). Solarstvo Šavrinskega primorja. *Geographical Bulletin*, 23: 137–156.

Savnik, R. (1965). Problemi Piranskih solin. *Acta geographica Slovenica*, 9: 59–82.

Smrekar, A., Šmid Hribar, M., and Erhartič, B. (2016a). Stakeholder Conflicts in the Tivoli, Rožnik Hill, and Šiška Hill Protected Landscape Area. *Acta geographica Slovenica*, 56(2): 305–319.

Smrekar, A., Šmid Hribar, M., Tiran, J., and Erhartič, B. (2016b). A Methodological Basis for Landscape Interpretation: The Case of the Ljubljana Marsh. *Acta geographica Slovenica*, 56(2): 279–290.

Smrekar, A., Polajnar Horvat, K., and Ribeiro, D. (2020). Slovenia's Protected Areas. In D. Perko, R. Ciglič, and M. Zorn (eds.) *The Geography of Slovenia: Small But Diverse*. Cham: Springer, pp. 313–320.

Spek, T., Brinkkemper, O., and Speleers, B. P. (2006). Archaeological Heritage Management and Nature Conservation: Recent Developments and Future Prospects, Illustrated by Three Dutch Case Studies. *Berichten van de Rijksdienst voor het Oudheidkundig Bodemonderzoek*, 46: 331–354.

Urbanc, M., Printsmann, A., Palang, H., Skowronek, E., Woloszyn, W., and Konkoly Gyuró, É. (2004). Comprehension of Rapidly Transforming Landscapes of Central and Eastern Europe in the 20th Century. *Acta geographica Slovenica*, 44(2): 101–131.

24 The UNESCO evolving and living heritage of the Nord-Pas de Calais Mining Basin

Post-industrial landscape heritagization as a territorial healing process

Lucas Monsaingeon

Introduction

The Nord-Pas de Calais Mining Basin in the North of France is 100 km long and 18 km wide, populated by more than 1 million inhabitants around major cities including Valenciennes, Douai, Lens, Béthune, and Bruay-La-Buissière. To the North and South, it is bordered by Lille, the biggest city in the area, and by the historic city of Arras. The coal seam of the basin extends and grows in Belgium and Germany while in the West it disappears, to appear again much farther on the other side of the Channel in England.

The Mining Basin area is characterized by a landscape shaped by the mining industry, which extracted more than 2.4 billion tons of coal from the ground in nearly two centuries of activities. This includes large-scale "neo-natural" sites such as *terrils* (slag heaps, artificial mountains of mining residues) some of which are more than 100 m high, making them major landmarks in the flat plains of Northern France. There are also subsidence ponds, canals, and railroad tracks, as well as a major heritage of buildings, comprising technical buildings related to mining, community facilities (churches, schools, town halls, swimming pools, hospitals, etc.) and over 20,000 workers' housing units (Figure 24.1.). When the mines were shut down between 1970 and 1990, it was a hard-hitting economic, social, and cultural trauma for the area, leaving behind it a post-industrial landscape in decline and a state of change, whose conservation raised many questions (Kourchid and Melin 2002).

In 2012, two decades after the closure of the last mine, this mining area became a World Heritage Site. Listed by the United Nations Educational, Scientific, and Cultural Organization (UNESCO) as an "organically evolved and continuing (living) cultural landscape",[1] it is an area of 3,943 hectares, 89 municipalities and 100,000 inhabitants closely interweaving industrial and rural worlds, now recognized and protected, as well as the buffer zone which covers 18,804 hectares and 124 towns with 720,000 inhabitants.[2] The French Nord-Pas de Calais Mining Basin is the only mining site to have been designated as a World Heritage Site on this scale, putting it in an important position in the geography of post-mining sites all over the world (Fiori, Mariolle, and Poli 2020).

DOI: 10.4324/9781003195238-24

Figure 24.1. Aerial view of pit n° 6 at Bruay-La-Buissière in 1989, when the mines closed
Source: © Altimage Philippe Frutier

Ten years after the UNESCO nomination, this chapter aims to take a critical look at this case study in order to analyse: (1) the specificities and the stakes of the heritagization of this post-industrial landscape, and (2) the issues and the stakes of management and preservation that this raises today for the stakeholders and professionals of the conservative sector.[3]

The Mining Basin included in the World Heritage List as a living landscape: peculiarity of this post-industrial landscape

An anti-picturesque landscape: a countertrend process of heritagization

The first specificity of the Mining Basin post-industrial landscape, which is obvious when compared to other protected cultural landscapes, is its anti-picturesque nature. Today, most of the cultural landscapes recognized and protected in France and in the world remain associated with a romantic and aesthetic tradition of the landscape, where a certain vision of nature, wild or carefully cultivated, predominates. However, the heritage recognition of the Mining Basin concerns an industrial cultural landscape that is far removed from the usual canons of beauty and from the very definition of landscape (Figure 24.1.): repetitive alignments of brick workers' dwellings, slag heaps of black shale devoid of any vegetation, industrial wastelands, and so on.

In France, the progressive protection of landscapes during the 19th and 20th centuries is closely linked to the mobilization of artists in order to safeguard landscapes of artistic, legendary, or picturesque value. This landscape heritagization process is historically connected with its scarcity and disappearance (Tricaud 2010), dating back to the first Industrial Revolution which erased entire sections of the pre-industrial rural and agricultural landscape. Ironically, through the inscription of the cultural landscape of the Mining Basin of Nord-Pas de Calais, it is precisely a landscape characteristic of this Industrial Revolution which has been recognized as heritage, a landscape which was largely built on the erasure of pre-existing rural structures.[4]

In the context of this peculiar industrial landscape, and while the recognition of industrial heritage is still recent, it is easy to understand the difference in perception and attractiveness of a site like the Mining Basin for the general public, compared for example to the French wine landscapes of the Loire Valley or the Italian Cinque Terre, and this despite some important assets such as the establishment of a branch of the Louvre Museum in Lens in 2012. This lack of attractiveness, despite a progressive change in perception, can also be seen in some ways as an asset for the territory, leading to a focus on local development through its own resources. While international research increasingly points out the complexity of the relationships between World Heritage Sites and their consequent tourism share with local communities (Bourdeau, Gravari-Barbas, and Robinson et al. 2017), the Mining Basin used its designation as a local and political design tool for its community, rather than a marketing tool for touristic attraction. By setting up a needed transversal governance, by betting on the feeling of pride and belonging that this world-wide recognition would arouse in its inhabitants, its aim was to "redevelop emotional ties with the mining heritage and strengthen their sense of belonging to the territory" (Mortelette 2019) rather than dwelling on the economic spinoffs of the tourism industry. Perhaps one day tourists will come from all over the world to visit the industrial remains of the Mining Basin, as in the example of the buses disgorging tourists at the foot of a slag heap in Luc Moullet's ironic short film from 1991, *La cabale des oursins.*[5] But for the time being, gentrification and tourist pressure are far from being a threat to the territory. Jean-Francois Caron, mayor of Loos-en-Gohelle and initiator of the nomination process, clearly stated that tourism was not their objective, as he said in a conference: "Of course UNESCO brings back tourists, but that's not why we did it. For us, it is a therapy".[6]

An ever-living landscape: heritagization as a territorial healing process

After the trauma of the shutdown of the mines, the UNESCO nomination was conceived from the beginning as a force of resilience for the territory to move forward, rather than as a museum-like constraint with a historical-tourist vocation in mind (Monsaingeon and Prost 2020). It was therefore supported by the stakeholders of the territory as a way of reconciling the two "contradictory temptations" at work (Fontaine 2016), between the erasure and the over-valuation of mining remains: a possible reconciliation made possible through the concept of an evolving and living landscape.

During the nomination process, the question of mining heritage, and therefore of post-industrial heritage, encompassed the notion of landscape. The mining post-industrial landscape has thus become increasingly important, until it became the central issue of the nomination (Alessandri 2018). The Mining Basin is protected today as a *cultural landscape*, a "combined work of nature and of man" illustrating "the evolution of human society and settlement over time, under the influence of the physical constraints and/or opportunities presented by their natural environment and of successive social, economic and cultural forces, both external and internal" (World Heritage Committee 2021). Within this category, the Mining Basin was listed as *an organically evolved landscape*, being a palimpsest territory that has never stopped in its transformation, starting with the upheavals that the mines wrought on the rural landscape in which they were inserted, and as *a continuing (or living) landscape*, as opposed to being categorized as *relict (or fossil) landscape*, like in the case of the Blaenavon industrial mining site in Wales.

In fact, not only do the industrial landscape and architecture of the Nord-Pas de Calais Mining Basin bear witness to a bygone activity but they are also the living support of an energy and a territorial transition at work. Unlike other French cultural landscapes, mainly winegrowing and still active, such as the Loire Valley, the Saint-Emilion jurisdiction, the Champagne hillsides or the Burgundy *climats*, the final cessation of any mining extraction since 1990 leads us to read the notion of living our heritage differently: no longer as a framing tool to perpetuate a historical structural activity, but as a resilience force and a support for inventing a new activity and a new way of life. The point here is to meet the challenge of the Third Industrial Revolution, to move from extractive economy to heritage ecology (Debary 2002), from predatory urbanism and management of mining resources, to the sustainable development of the territory making way for inhabitants and natural elements (Chautard and Zuindeau 2001). Recycling the remains of the mining heritage can help to repair the territorial legacy of centuries of intensive industrial exploitation (Monsaingeon and Prost 2020).

From theory to action: issues and lessons from post-industrial landscape heritagization

The heritagization process of the Mining Basin landscape has made it possible to raise and overcome a certain number of cultural and economic territorial issues in order to accompany the societal transition at work: to initiate a change in the way we look at these spaces and landscapes, which are considered as "ugly" and uninteresting, and to make this heritage a resource and a lever for local development. But this also raises many issues of concrete implementation in the daily management of this property, which are still valid ten years after its nomination on the World Heritage List. How to involve the inhabitants who live in this territory, and avoid that this label is perceived as an additional constraint? How to overcome territorial fragmentation through the landscape approach? How to concretely translate the preservation of a living landscape into a project that respects the outstanding universal value?

Fragmented territories and stakeholder interplays: landscape as a negotiation process

One of the major interests and challenges of the nomination was, and still is, to set up a transversal governance that did not previously exist. Split between two departments, four inter-municipal authorities and several hundred municipalities, the mining area has always suffered from its fragmentation. In 1946, the dozens of mining concessions, as many numbers of partitioned private mining companies, were grouped together and nationalized within a new structure, which disappeared in 1993 just after the end of mining, leaving behind a scattered heritage of hundreds of pits and tens of thousands of miners' dwellings. As far back as in 1996, the Nord-Pas de Calais Region,[7] aware of the need for territorial management, convened in the *Conférence Permanente du Bassin Minier* more than a thousand people to consult the inhabitants and actors of the territory, leading to a White Paper for "a shared territorial ambition for the post-coal era" in 1998. In the process, the association known as *Mission Bassin Minier Nord-Pas de Calais* was created in 2000 to support the implementation of an overall program of urban, social, economic, and ecological restructuring, while at the same time, the *Bassin Minier Uni* association was created in 2002 to set up the World Heritage candidacy to be completed 10 years later. The two associations merged in 2013 and are the designated manager of the inscription of the Mining Basin on the World Heritage List, in close collaboration with the French State services. This association integrates representatives of the various public structures (State, regions, departments, inter-municipal structures) and associated members (including the Caisse des Dépôts and regional natural parks) in a partnership structure which was sorely lacking in the fragmented territory of the Mining Basin.

In addition to monitoring the management plan submitted in the course of the application, approved and regularly appraised by UNESCO experts, the *Mission Bassin Minier* association is responsible for setting up a monitoring, support, and awareness policy, and plays a central role as coordinating actors, the need for which is still prevalent ten years after registration. It participates in the collective search for "balances between preservation and revitalization of heritage and territory", where "heritage retains its identity and integrity but also finds an active role" (Alessandri 2018). It has conducted several studies on the mining landscape[8] and supports local authorities in defining their "Landscape

Quality Objectives", to orient their development around the preservation, development, management, and enhancement of their landscapes.

The place of the associative world, the local actors, and communities appears central in the management of the heritage of the Mining Basin, whereas the French State traditionally closely monitors the national heritage through the Ministries of Culture and Environment, in a top-bottom approach. The specificities of a very large-scale fragmented heritage such as the Mining Basin, of which only a small part is really protected as national historical and natural landmarks, and the approach specific to the landscape, understood as a negotiation process (Donadieu 1994), raises the question of heritage conservation in a different way. By placing the inhabitants and local actors at the center of the process, this challenges the authorized official discourse of heritage, in line with current critical heritage studies.

Landscape, urbanism, architecture, and preservation: a collaborative conversation

The heritagization of cultural landscapes has led to a disciplinary rapprochement between the fields of landscape and heritage studies, opening a new space for "collaborative conversation" (Harvey and Waterton 2015). The critical approach induced by the notion of a living cultural landscape, whose definition is still recent, and the paradox between a conservative and evolving approach that it highlights are also inducing managers and preservation professionals to reconsider their tools and actions, beyond these disciplines.

For the preservationists, architects and urban planners working on this territory, the approach of an evolving and living cultural landscape questions what could or should be an evolving and living built heritage that it often embodies. Can the built heritage be approached as a living organism? What specific actions of maintenance, repair, and restoration does this imply? How can we conserve the 27,000 miners' dwellings listed by UNESCO, most of which are social housing and still inhabited? Can the demolition of an existing building to make room for a new construction be seen as an act of preservation in some way?

In the specific context of the preservation of a landscape or a heritage garden, the fact that the plants grow back every spring is not perceived as a loss of authenticity, but rather as a necessary and welcome cyclical renewal operation. For several decades, the reflection on the conservation and restoration of historic gardens has thus raised many questions in France and internationally in the field of professional practice as well as in that of research, confronting the theory and practice of critically restoring architectural heritage to historic gardens. Pierre-Marie Tricaud's PhD thesis, "Essay on a theory of dynamic preservation of heritage", defended in 2010, is a significant example: this landscape-architect and agronomist investigates the concept of heritage from his reflections on the landscape. Indeed, as he reminds us, "the notion of living heritage is in itself an oxymoron" (Tricaud 2010), because the living is perishable and mortal, whereas the conservation of heritage implies being able to make the historical substance endure and survive for future generations, beyond time. Landscape-architects have therefore already gone beyond the simplistic opposition between conservation and transmission, by integrating the operations of transformation that this implies: pruning, soil amendment, irrigation, reseeding, and so on.

Looking at the question of the preservation of the living, it is interesting to compare the Venice Charter (International Charter for the Conservation and Restoration of Monuments and Sites, 1964), which constitutes the basis of the doctrine of intervention on the built heritage for ICOMOS (International Council on Monuments and Sites) and is focused "on the respect of the ancient substance",[9] with the more recent Florence Charter (International Charter for the Conservation and Restoration of Historic Gardens, 1981), its counterpart for historic gardens, which deals with the plant heritage:

> The historic garden is an architectural composition whose constituents are primarily vegetal and therefore living, which means that they are perishable and renewable. Thus, its appearance reflects the perpetual balance between the cycle of the seasons, the growth and decay of nature and the desire of the artist and craftsman to keep it permanently unchanged.[10]

The Florence Charter (1982) also encourages punctual replacements and cyclical renewal of plants, that is, scheduled felling and replacement of trees (ICOMOS, 1982, article 11, Maintenance and Conservation).

From an architect's point of view, the heritage approach is often centered on the primacy of conservation, the authenticity of the material, and the integrity of a hypothetical original state. But this approach therefore comes up against the specificities of the heritage of the Mining Basin. This chapter hypothesizes that, in some respects, the Florence Charter would be better suited to the specificities of the Mining Basin, including its built heritage. The approach to these buildings, and in particular to the many miner's dwellings, raises very concrete questions of bringing this housing up to current standards of thermal renovation, of habitability and of management of external spaces. In this context, does changing an exterior window or building a new extension still constitute an attack on the authenticity and integrity of the heritage property? All these issues lead to an overall shift in the prevailing paradigm, from the presupposition of building conservation to focus on the global quality and cohesion of the urban landscape (Monsaingeon and Prost 2020). This implies moving from a linear and fixed conception of time to a dynamic and cyclical approach, capable of integrating the notions of repetition, reproduction, change and evolution: the cycle of the four seasons, that of the generations, and the inhabitants, that of the small and big rehabilitation works which follow one another and overlap. These reflections remain theoretical at this stage, their application to concrete preservation cases must be analysed on a case-by-case basis, as is always the case in the field of heritage.

Moreover, the scalar opening offered by the heritagization of this post-industrial landscape calls for a holistic approach to industrial heritage, in all the complexity of a spatial system, reaching out beyond the only outstanding buildings and equipment. Indeed, one does not approach a castle or an isolated and unique industrial building, however large it may be, in the same way as one would the typological multiplication of workers' dwellings reproduced in thousands of copies. The late invention of industrial heritage has long been a transposition of a Western conception of the monument, inherited from the nineteenth century (from the castles of royalty to the castles of industry). Thus, the question of the inclusive scale of the cultural landscape hybridizing nature, industry, infrastructure, and housing allows us now to broaden the field of industrial heritage and go beyond the single productivist framework of the workplace to address the impact of industry on social and family organization, services, leisure and transportation. Like the American company towns, "the territorial, economic and social extension that they introduce into industrial heritage, and therefore into heritage in general, certainly seems to be promising" (Morisset 2018) and leads to a revaluation of the notion of use and re-appropriation by the community, making heritage a dynamic and iterative process.

Conclusion

The case study of the post-industrial landscape of the Mining Basin of the Nord-Pas de Calais is a representative example of a scalar and typological turn in the heritagization process. If the preservation of landscapes on a very large-scale participates in a global form of "heritage inflation" (Heinich 2009) in France and internationally, the extension to the domains of industrial remains and the associated "commonplace" habitat implies a renewal of views and heritage values. The living dimension of this cultural landscape heritage, which is still inhabited and in full mutation, is hardly compatible with a conservative Western approach to restoration, with a need for innovation "in managing the complex interaction between people and nature which is considered to be of outstanding universal value, but also in maintaining the integrity of these places in a world of global socio-economic change and climate change" (Mitchell, Rössler and Tricaud 2009). The critical approach to heritage through the concept of cultural landscape as heritage, and particularly of living and evolving landscape, opens up the way to new reflections for the professional conservation sector, allowing the opening up of a whole area of reflection for architects, preservationists, and beyond that, for the inhabitants, users, and stakeholders of the territory on the question: what makes heritage?

This case study highlights and identifies several lessons taken from heritagization. On the one hand, we have the appearance of the notion of living heritage, linked in particular to the vegetation embodied in the landscape, leading to a reconsideration of the current conservation paradigm in order to re-question – but not to abandon – the notions of integrity and authenticity, in favour of the quest for a perpetual balance between the cyclical movement of occupations, development, and decay of the architectural elements that compose it. And on the other hand, we have the change of scale induced by the landscape calling for a renewed attention to the context, to the territory and to the social and human dimension of the living and inhabited heritage, by passing from an analytical approach to a systemic one, necessarily multi-disciplinary. In this way, it makes it possible to overcome the territorial fragmentation, to be more in touch with the communities concerned, in reversal of (or rather as a complement to) the vertical approach of the experts.

If the conservation of an evolving and living heritage might first appear as an impossible paradox for preservationists, architects, and urban planners, it leads in fact to shifting the gaze, to be inspired by the work of landscape-architects to put back the maintenance and the value of use in the center of the concerns, and to demonstrate that a dynamic approach of the heritage can participate to the repair of the living.

Acknowledgements

This work was supported by the Paris Seine Graduate School Humanities, Creation, Heritage, Investissement d'Avenir ANR-17-EURE-0021

Notes

1   The category of "cultural landscapes" was adopted by the World Heritage Committee in 1992. The official name of the subcategory is in English "continuing landscape", but I find more suitable in this case the French translation of *paysage vivant* since this landscape is still inhabited, without continuing the industrial mining activity; I will rather use the expression "living landscape" in this chapter.

2   For more information on the specifics of the nomination, and a more detailed description of the territory, its history, and its heritage, one can refer directly to the specific literature (Fagnoni 2014; Alessandri 2018; Fontaine 2018; Monsaingeon and Prost 2020; Céleste 2020; Tost et al. 2021 etc.), as well as the complete UNESCO application file or to the many resources kept by the Mission Bassin Minier online.

3   The author is a PhD candidate and an architect who, for the last ten years, has been working on design, rehabilitation, restoration, and extension projects as well as prospective urban and heritage studies in the Mining Basin, at the Philippe Prost architecture workshop (AAPP), based in Paris.

4   Although the UNESCO nomination file insisted on the richness of the evolving cultural landscape of the Mining Basin, where the industrial and the rural are closely interwoven, the strict delimitation of the property has sought to exclude any trace of the rural to preserve only the traces of the mining industrial past.

5   In this short film, filmmaker Luc Moullet imagined that perhaps one day tourists will come to visit the slag heaps. Twenty years before the UNESCO nomination, this film was an ironic criticism of the abandonment and disregard of the slag heaps at the time.

6   Jean-François Caron, TedX, 2015, *Changer de regard pour se redonner un futur | TEDxVaugirardRoad*, 2015, www.youtube.com/watch?v=uZFNNN7i734.

7   Since the 2016 reform, this region has merged with Picardy and is now called *Hauts-de-France*.

8   See in particular the study "Les paysages du Bassin minier Nord-Pas de Calais, Dynamiques d'évolution et enjeux de protection d'un paysage culturel évolutif

vivant inscrit au Patrimoine mondial de l'Unesco" by Mission Bassin Minier and Urbicand, *Cahiers techniques de la MBM*, 2016 [online, January 2022] www.bassinm inier-patrimoinemondial.org/wp-content/uploads/2016/12/cahier_technique-paysa ge-internet.pdf.

9 Petzet and ICOMOS 2004.
10 Petzet and ICOMOS 2004.

References

Alessandri, R. (2018). *Le Bassin minier du Nord et du Pas-de-Calais: une stratégie d'aménagement et de développement fondée sur la protection et la valorisation d'un paysage industriel inscrit sur la Liste du patrimoine de l'UNESCO.* In F. Hachez-Leroy (ed.) *Le patrimoine industriel au XXIe siècle, nouveaux défis. Actes du congès TICCIH Lille Région 2015*, Paris: CILAC.

Baudelle, G. (1994). *Le système spatial de la mine: l'exemple du bassin houiller du Nord-Pas-de-Calais.* PhD Thesis, Université Paris 1.

Donadieu, P. (1994). Pour une conservation inventive des paysages. In A. Berque (ed.) *Cinq propositions pour une théorie du paysage.* Seyssel: Champ Vallon.

Bourdeau, L., Gravari-Barbas, M., and Robinson, M. (eds.) (2017). *World Heritage Sites and Tourism: Global and Local Relations.* Abingdon: Routledge.

Céleste, P. (2020). Le bassin minier du Nord-Pas-De-Calais pris dans les rets de l'aménagisme généralisé. *Cahiers de la recherche architecturale, urbaine et paysagère*, 7, online. Retrieved from: https://journals.openedition.org/craup/3912.

Chautard, G. and Zuindeau, B. (2001). L'enjeu d'une reconversion durable des territoires de tradition industrielle: l'exemple du bassin minier du Nord - Pas-de-Calais. *Espace Populations Sociétés* 19(3): 325-339.

Debary, O. (2002). *La fin du Creusot, ou, L'art d'accommoder les restes.* Paris: Ed. C.T.H.S.

Fagnoni, E. (2014). Faire patrimoine, et, faire territoire. L'exemple du Bassin minier uni / UNESCO. In M. Gravari-Barbas and S. Jacquot (eds.) *Patrimoine mondial et développement: au défi du tourisme durable.* Québec: Presse de l'Université du Quebéc, 87–114.

Fiori, S., Mariolle, B., and Poli, D. (2020). Repairing post-mining territories through territorial, landscape, architectural and artistic approaches. *Cahiers de la recherche architecturale, urbaine et paysagère*, 7, online. Retrieved from: https://journals.openedition. org/craup/4261.

Fontaine, M. (2016). Visible/invisible: Ce qui reste des mines. *Techniques and Culture*, 65–66: 74-91.

Fontaine, M. (2018). Regional identity and industrial heritage in the mining area of Nord-Pas-de-Calais. In C. Wicke, S. Berger and J. Golombek (eds.) *Industrial Heritage and Regional Identities.* Abingdon: Routledge.

Harvey, D. and Waterton, E. (2015). Landscapes of heritage and heritage landscapes. *Landscape Research*, 40(8): 905–910.

Heinich, N. (2009). *La fabrique du patrimoine: de la cathédrale à la petite cuillère.* Paris: Maison des sciences de l'homme.

Houbart, C. (2014). Deconsecrating a Doctrinal Monument: Raymond M. Lemaire (1921–1997) and the Revisions of the Venice Charter. *Change Over Time*, 4(2): 218–243.

ICOMOS (1964). *International Charter for the Conservation and Restoration of Monuments and Sites – Venice Charter.* Paris: ICOMOS.

ICOMOS (1982). *The Florence Charter*. Paris: ICOMOS.

Kourchid, O. and Melin H. (2002). Mobilisations et mémoire du travail dans une grande egion: le Nord-Pas-de-Calais et son patrimoine industriel. *Le Mouvement Social*, 199(2): 37–59.

Melin, H. (2002). *La construction d'un patrimoine industriel dans le Nord-Pas-de-Calais: du travail de mémoire au développement local*. PhD Thesis, Université de Lille I. Retrieved from: www.theses.fr/2002LIL12007.

Mitchell, N. J., Rössler, M., and Tricaud, P. (2009). *World Heritage Cultural Landscapes: A Handbook for Conservation and Management*. World Heritage Papers 26. Paris: UNESCO World Heritage Centre.

Monsaingeon, L. and Prost, P. (2020). Le bassin minier du Nord-Pas-de-Calais, un patrimoine évolutif et vivant: Entre conservation et évolution, enjeux et nouveau paradigme pour les projets d'architecture. *Cahiers de la recherche architecturale, urbaine et paysagère*, 7, online. Retrieved from: https://journals.openedition.org/craup/3786.

Morisset, L. K. (2018). *Le territoire par-delà les monuments: les leçons patrimoniales de l'obsolescence industrielle*. In F. Hachez-Leroy (ed.) *Le patrimoine industriel au XXIe siècle, nouveaux défis, CILAC hors-série*, 1: 16-27.

Mortelette, C. (2019). *Culture-led conversion of former mining sites: Territorial issues and appropriation in the Nord-Pas-de-Calais mining basin*. Theses, Université d'Artois. Retrieved from https://hal.archives-ouvertes.fr/tel-02478106.

Petzet, M. and ICOMOS (eds.). (2004). *International Charters for Conservation and Restoration: Chartes Internationales Sur La Conservation et La Restauration*. München: Lipp.

Tost, M., Ammerer, G., Kot-Niewiadomska, A., and Gugerell, K. (2021). Mining and Europe's World Heritage Cultural Landscapes. *Resources*, 10(2): 18.

Tricaud, P. (2010). *Conservation et transformation du patrimoine vivant*. PhD Thesis, Université de Paris-Est. Retrieved from: www.projetsdepaysage.fr/images/documents/tricaud_these.pdf.

25 Landscape as heritage in museums

A critical appraisal of past and present experiences

Maria Luisa Sturani

Introduction

During the closing decades of the twentieth century, landscape received full recognition in international heritage policies. The well-known cornerstones of this process have been the introduction of "cultural landscape" as a new category by UNESCO's World Heritage guidelines in 1992, and the adoption of the European Landscape Convention by the Council of Europe in 2000, the two official statements that thereafter have to varying degrees guided most heritage and landscape policies. This "heritagization" of landscape is one expression of the ongoing transformation and widening of the idea of heritage (Graham, Ashworth, and Tunbridge, 2000: 1; Harvey, 2001), although the move from general statements of principle to their application raises many questions.

Those questions arise, first, from the complex and ambiguous nature of the concept of landscape in itself, which has been abundantly discussed within the tradition of geography (Wylie, 2007) and is expressed by the opposition between the tangible nature of landscape, when considered as the material result of interacting natural forces and human labour, and its intangible dimension as a pictorial image and a form of representation. Problems also arise from the intrinsically dynamic nature of landscape, both as the product of past and continuing ecological and social processes and as a perceived and lived-in territory, with the diverse and changing values attributed to it by people. An additional source of problems derives from the difficulty – at an operational rather than theoretical level – of applying to the management of the landscape the methodologies and tools that have been developed for other kinds of heritage acknowledged earlier, which – unlike landscape – are confined to single objects, monuments or sites.

In this chapter, the manifold challenges posed by the "heritagization" of landscape will be explored, focusing on the specific issues raised by its inclusion in the sphere of the activity of museums, at the intersection between the perspectives of geography and museology. The first part retraces the steps through which – both in the geographical tradition and in museum studies – a rapprochement between museums and the issue of landscape has emerged in over

DOI: 10.4324/9781003195238-25

a century. The following part offers a critical review of different museum experiences: they are generalised into different models and their respective potential in dealing with landscape is critically discussed. In conclusion, the crucial role recently played by landscape in museum theory and practice is acknowledged as a result of these experiences and tradition.

Museology, geography and landscape

Although the reference to the official definition of a museum contained in the Statutes of the International Council of Museums (ICOM) compresses the variety and dynamism of real museum experiences into a standardised formula, it is nonetheless an inevitable starting point for exploring the relationship between museums and landscape. Through its subsequent reformulations, the definition has in fact established the canon on which the regulatory frameworks and museum policies of many countries have been modelled since the Second World War (Brulon Soares, 2020). Until the 1970s this definition emphasised the constitutive link between a museum and a collection of objects, the ownership of which was acquired by the institution in order to gather them together inside its walls, extracting and separating them from their original context. This emphasis on "musealia" or collections of museum objects (Van Mensch, 1990) has been diluted since 1974 into a more general reference to the "material evidence of man and his environment" (Brulon Soares, 2020: 18). Finally, in the 2007 revision even intangible heritage enters the domain in which the various functions of museums are performed:

> A museum is a non-profit, permanent institution in the service of society and its development, open to the public, which acquires, conserves, researches, communicates and exhibits the tangible and intangible heritage of humanity and its environment for purposes of education, study and enjoyment.
>
> (ICOM, 2007: Article 3, Section 1)

Even with the progressive expansion of the definition of a museum, the persistent foundational centrality played by collections is clear, and the connected practices of de-contextualisation remain implicit in the transformation of things into "musealised" or "heritage objects", even in the case of immovable or intangible assets (Jallà, 2017: 10). This concept of a museum has therefore long been an obstacle to the inclusion of landscapes – one of the dimensions of the context itself – among the objects of museum activities. Indeed, the very idea of "musealising" the landscape has often been used in a negative sense in the discourse of heritage planning, to emphasise the impossibility of freezing its change through the application of preservation policies to extensive areas.[1] Nonetheless, the very evolution of the official definition of a museum and the heated debate regarding its revision[2] express a growing openness on the part of museums to context: a trend that has gradually also come to involve the landscape and has ultimately resulted in the explicit assumption of the relationship between *Museums and Cultural Landscapes* as the central theme of the 24th ICOM General Conference, held in Milan in 2016.

Signs of interest in the landscape were evident in museological debate and in the initiatives of various museums well before that date. However, such opportunities for contact did not arise from consolidated relationships between museums and academic disciplines that include the landscape within their objects of study, such as geography. In fact, since the nineteenth century, other disciplines close to it, like the natural sciences, anthropology and archaeology, have established stable relationships with certain types of museums – natural history museums, ethnographic museums and museums of antiquity – enriching their collections through their own fieldwork and offering them sources of inspiration for the arrangement and display of objects, in addition to supplying curators and external consultants. In the case of geography, on the other hand, attempts to establish specialised museums in which the landscape could have its own space have been few and far between, and short-lived.

The earliest and best-known experiment of this kind was begun in 1892 by Patrick Geddes in the Outlook Tower in Edinburgh, on the basis of which a plan for a larger Geographic Institute and Museum was formulated, albeit never realised (Geddes, 1902; Withers, 2001: 225–232). A few other experiments were subsequently launched, making reference to this precedent, which did not survive the death of its originator. In 1919 the Central Geographical Museum opened in Leningrad on the initiative of the geographer Veniamin Petrovič Semenov-Tian-Šanskij. This was initially conceived as a reconstruction of environments inspired by Scandinavian open-air museums, and then reorganised into a more traditional indoor structure, before being closed in 1937 (Semenov-Tian-Šanskij, 1929). The *Museum für Länderkunde* was instead active in Leipzig between 1929 and 1945, in an indoor form and under the direction of the geographer Rudolf Reinhard (1934). These three enterprises, despite having their own special features, had in common the fact that they were not so much based on displays of collections of objects as on the extensive use of a variety of visual media employed to illustrate the regional diversity of the Earth: a terrace roof with a view of the surrounding landscape and a *camera obscura* in the Outlook Tower, along with maps, models, globes, panoramas, paintings, photos and, in the case of Leipzig, even films. There emerged a plan for a new type of museum that was very innovative for the time, being capable of condensing and making available to the public, within a limited space, the representation of the entire world ordered according to the schemes of contemporary geography: a discipline for which the observation and classification of landforms constituted a fundamental aim of research. And a discipline for which the use of visual means of communication was a powerful tool for popular education. However, the rapid decline of these experiences and their largely shared removal from both geographical disciplinary memory[3] and from museological studies testify to the failure of the attempt to create an institutionalised relationship between geography and museums.

After the failure of geographic museums, human and historical geographers engaged in research on European landscapes continued to collaborate on projects promoted by well-established indoor and open-air ethnographic museums, especially in the field of the cataloguing and the protection of the settlement components of the landscape.[4] However, since the 1980s, the dematerialisation of the landscape as an object of geographical research, a product of the affirmation of the New Cultural Geography (Cosgrove and Daniels, 1988), has reduced opportunities for operational collaboration between academic geography and museums, which in that period were still oriented solely towards the care of material assets. If anything, museums are now attracting the interest of geographers as new objects of study due to the role they play in the processes of building national identities or in tourism development, with the inclusion of the discipline in the field of heritage studies (Hertzog, 2004; Geoghegan, 2010).

At the same time, and relatively independently of developments in geographical research, in the second half of the twentieth century the theoretical reflection of museology was instead marked by a tendency to extend the functions and responsibilities of museums beyond the walls that enclose them, which ultimately ended up involving the landscape. The process – the stages of which can be easily be reconstructed through official ICOM documentation (Jallà, 2015) – began in the 1950s and 1960s, when the urgency attached to the environmental question in public opinion drove museums of natural history and, to a lesser extent, museums of science and technology to go beyond the traditional tasks of caring for their own collections in order to make a broader educational commitment to safeguarding the natural environment (Davallon, Grandmont and Schiele, 1992). In the following decade, in the political climate that opened in May 1968 and with the disruptive entry of issues of decolonisation and development into the museological debate, sensitivity towards environmental problems combined with a more marked openness towards society and the traditional concept of the museum itself was radically questioned by the development of New Museology.[5] The result was a drive towards the democratisation of museums, which finds expression in the idea of the *museo integral* that emerged from the Round Table in Santiago de Chile in 1972, in the experience of the Anacostia Community Museum in Washington DC, and in the development of ecomuseums, all conceived as participatory initiatives in the service of local communities (De Varine, 2000 and 2017: 15–35). Museums thus came to accept a growing commitment to society and the issues of its future development, rather than limiting themselves to the conservation of the material heritage inherited from the past, and they now operate through innovative methods based on protection in situ, outdoors, and extended over the territory.

It is precisely on these foundations that since the 1990s the landscape – the visible sedimentation of history and culture in a given territory and an element of identity rootedness for the population that inhabits it – has also become part of the theoretical reflections of museology. However, this recognises the difficulties posed by the treatment of an object that is scarcely compatible with its traditional canons:

> If museums have seldom been engrossed with matters of landscape, maybe it is because it is necessary changeable, difficult to grasp, to identify, and impossible to divide into classified elements … it is in fact a complex system of mobile connections, baffling any arranging attempt, and percei- vable through countless ways.
>
> (Bellaigue, 1990: 26)

As a result, the awareness of the complexity of the concept of landscape is also gaining ground among museologists, with reference to its dynamism and the tension between the material dimension and the perceptive and symbolic one, on the basis of the reflections already matured by geography (Delarge and Hilaire, 1996; Gestin, 1996). After the start of the reflection on how to inte- grate this complexity in a new "landscape museum" (Bellaigue, 1990: 27), in the following phase museology's interest in the landscape has been consolidated under pressure from two factors: it has been fuelled by the centrality that the landscape has assumed in heritage policies and, at the same time, it has been encouraged by the quashing of the approach that had hitherto confined the activities of museums to movable objects only, leaving the conservation of the cultural built heritage to other institutions.[6] Landscape thus joins with full rights the other objects which museums attend to on the basis of the consonance between the guidelines of international policies, which emphasise the role of perceptions and the involvement of the population in the definition and man- agement of the landscape itself (Rössler, 2006; Jones, 2007; Olwig, 2007), and the concept of a participatory museum open to the needs of society, that was affirmed in the latter part of the twentieth century. On this basis, ICOM has finally come to acknowledge the safeguarding of cultural landscapes as a new "general priority" for contemporary society, for which reason museums must mobilise accordingly (Jallà, 2017: 8).

Landscape in museums/museums for landscape

The transition from the idea of museum/collection to that of museum/context expressed by the museological debate is reflected in the many museum experiences which, more or less explicitly, have placed the landscape at the centre of their activities. These can be connected to a number of models of which will be provided a critical review with regard to the solutions they offer to the problems posed by the museums' action on the landscape.

The oldest of these models is that of the open-air museum, which derives from the prototype of Skansen, Stockholm, which was established in 1891 by Artur Hazelius, and which then became widespread in central-northern and eastern Europe and in non-European countries (Rentzhog, 2007). In its origi- nal form this type of museum appears as an outdoor collection of original buildings (mostly rural, but also urban and industrial) that have been dismantled, transported and reassembled on the site of the museum. These are sometimes accompanied – or completely substituted when documenting more remote historical periods – by replicas constructed on the basis of historical and archaeological studies. Visits to these buildings, complete with their furnishings and equipment and sometimes brought to life by the reproduction of former daily activities by costumed figures, offer the public an immersive experience of past lifestyles, combining education and entertainment in a highly successful formula. These museums have often been criticised for tending to convey static and holistic representations of the past, from which all references to change and social conflict have been expunged, as well as for being infused with feelings of anti-modernist nostalgia and conservative romanticism (Bennett, 1988; Crang, 1999; Overdick, 1999: 18). Nevertheless, they suffer from more acute limitations relative to the re-enactment of landscapes: in the examples closer to the original model the landscape experienced by visitors on the museum site is, unlike the buildings and objects, neither authentic nor conceived as a faithful replica of a specific historical landscape. Arranging buildings between greenery or along a road creates a generic rural or urban setting specially designed to make the "time machine" effect of the visit more evocative and to act as a backdrop for the staging of the past (Conan, 2002; Young, 2006). The artificiality of the open-air-museum landscape is also accentuated by the space-time implosion effect caused by concentrating many buildings from areas and periods remote from each other within a few hectares of land, all extracted from their respective real contexts and presented as regional types (Cuisenier, 1984: 134–135; Young, 2006: 329).

In response to these criticisms, however, in the second half of the twentieth century various open-air museums ventured into larger re-enactments of the original landscapes within which the buildings on display were located, starting with the vegetable plots and gardens that surrounded them, up to extensive attempts to reconstruct entire swathes of landscapes representative of specific regions and periods.[7] In this way an attempt is made to attenuate the de-contextualisation effect underlying the logic of collection, which in this type of museum is applied to buildings rather than objects, and which is incompatible with the conservation of landscapes as manifestations of systems of integrated and dynamic relations.

The interest in re-enactment for educational purposes and for the protection of past landscapes rather than individual buildings is given its most advanced expression in the evolution of German open-air museums. Since the 1970s the traditional *Freilandmuseum* – an exhibition of a collection of vernacular buildings in a park – has in fact been the subject of profound critical rethinking, resulting in the development of the new model of the *Landschaftsmuseum*, which was applied in the following two decades to various newly founded open-air museums thanks to close collaboration with the discipline of historical geography (Overdick, 1999: 19; Denecke, 1999 and 2009). The *Landschaftsmuseum* is based on the reconstruction of a realistic model of settlement (by relocating original buildings or preserving them in situ) and of landscapes connected to an agrarian system of the past reproduced in its fundamental material features (in addition to buildings and gardens, fields, woodland and pasture areas, rural roads, canals, fences, etc.) and kept active through the application of land uses and historical agricultural techniques. This artificially reconstructed "museum landscape" is offered to visitors as a small-scale model through which to envisage the functioning and shaping of the landscapes in the museum's area of reference. The museum acts both as an interpretation centre for regional contemporary landscapes, through the promotion of thematic itineraries, on-site conservation and dissemination activities in the surrounding area. The aim is thus to train visitors to recognise evidence of historical change in contemporary landscapes: a visit to the museum is not conceived as an immersion in the "good old days" of a past that is concluded and always equal to itself, but rather as a stimulus for a dynamic interpretation of landscape change (Denecke, 2009).

A different model is that of the ecomuseum, which was invented in France by G.H. Rivière and H. De Varine at the end of the 1960s and spread widely afterwards, with different generations and adaptations both in France (Hubert, 1985) and now on a global scale (Davis, 2011; De Varine, 2017). As a theoretical model, the ecomuseum, while drawing inspiration from the tradition of open-air museums, quickly detaches itself from it, abandoning practices of dismantling and transferring buildings in favour of protecting in situ movable and immovable tangible assets and the intangible heritage that characterise a territory. The territory, in its relationships with the community that has moulded it over time, now becomes the whole and integrated focus of the museum's activity, which is no longer centred on individual and isolated elements. The ecomuseum looks at the territory with a retrospective eye aimed at protecting memory and historical heritage, but at the same time it also serves as a place in which to reflect on the problems of the present and formulate future development strategies for the local community. These objectives, expressed in the well-known "evolutionary definition" of the ecomuseum (Rivière, 1985), are reflected in new organisational solutions. The museum is no longer enclosed in the limited dimensions of a building or park, but its "collection" is ideally spread within the entire territory of the community it seeks to serve (De Varine, 2017: 190), from urban districts to extremely large areas within which museum activities are carried out through decentralised structures (*antennes*). Furthermore, the ecomuseum, embodying the participatory principles of New Museology, is based on the systematic involvement of the local population in all museum activities at all levels – management, research and cataloguing, education and exhibiting – with minimal support from professional staff and external consultants and, especially in the most recent examples, is intended to be a bottom-up initiative and a tool for local development (De Varine, 2017: 215–217).

It is difficult to fit all the changing manifestations of the ecomuseum movement into a single model, and several studies (Hubert, 1985; Desvallées, 2000;

Howard, 2002; Chaumier, 2003) have discussed its numerous weak points and possible deviations: from the difficulty of maintaining high levels of participation in the local population over time, to the frequent outbreaks of conflict on the interpretation of heritage and its management between different groups of local actors and between them and professional curators, to the interpretation of community and tradition in terms of local insularity and a misleading reconstruction of the past, to the retreat towards institutionalised, traditional museum models or towards mere economic-tourist enhancement initiatives. Yet despite these points of criticism, the ecomuseum model has significant potential for the treatment of landscape. The definitive defeat of the rationale of collecting that is the principal characteristic of the ecomuseum lays the foundations for an interpretation of the landscape as an integrated system, rather than a set of individual components (buildings) or isolated fragments (reconstructed historical landscapes). Moreover, the adoption of a diachronic perspective in the interpretation of relationships between communities and their territories can support interpretive strategies aimed at revealing the processes underlying the landscape rather than using it as a static setting. Finally, the ecomuseum movement's determined insistence on participation and community constitutes the prerequisite for the protection of the landscape, which can only be achieved through an active and conscious management of its changes by a population that is its custodian. However, even initiatives specifically dedicated to the landscape by ecomuseums starting from the 1980s and 1990s – there have been numerous in Italy in particular (Pressenda and Sturani, 2007; De Varine, 2017: 129–131) – are often blighted by a significant gap between theoretical potential and practical achievements.

While it is not possible to draw together hitherto sporadic experiences into a further generalised model, there are also a number of museum initiatives dedicated to the intangible dimension of the landscape to be considered. These have arisen in Italy, which since the early twentieth century has witnessed the growth of a movement for the protection of "natural beauty" and the prevalence of an aesthetic conception of the landscape. A guiding step was made in that direction by the *Museo del paesaggio* (Museum of Landscape), created in Verbania in 1914 and still operating as a museum exhibiting collections of paintings and sculptures. The museum was born – in the intentions of its founder Antonio Massara, a teacher and enthusiast of local culture and history – not so much to protect material objects as to safeguard the "soul of the landscape of Verbania"[8] and the traditional aesthetic values of the Lake Maggiore landscape, which was coming under threat by the incipient development of industry and tourism and which the museum celebrated through the exhibition of a collection of paintings and iconographies.

Almost a century later, another venture with the same name was launched in 1999 in Castelnuovo Berardenga (Siena), based on a project drawn up by the geographer Bruno Vecchio (2009). This second landscape museum is contained within a small indoor space and does not exhibit collections, but uses panels and audio-visual methods to transmit its discourse on the landscape in two different ways. On the one hand, it aspires to be an interpretation centre that guides the public towards the surrounding material landscape (i.e. the "beautiful Tuscan landscape"), providing explanations on its ecological foundations and the historical-social processes that have shaped it over the centuries. On the other, the museum aims to stimulate its visitors' reflection on the landscape as a "way of seeing", outlining the idea of landscape in the arts and sciences and infusing the perspective of New Cultural Geography into a new type of museum, based on the exhibition of ideas rather than objects.

Conclusion

The approach to landscape by museums has been long hindered by the constitutive link between the latter and the collection, deeply rooted in the European tradition, that tended to enucleate, extract and separate the objects of museum's concern from their original contexts, isolating them from the living cultural landscape. The first steps to overcome the divide between museums and landscape can be traced back to the end of the nineteenth and the beginning of the twentieth century – with the ephemeral attempts to build geographical museums or the more successful foundation of open-air museums – and continue during the last century with the development of different types of museums acting as centres and tools for the interpretation of material or symbolic landscapes: the *Landschaftsmuseum*, the ecomuseum, the museum of landscape as an idea.

Simultaneously, from the second half of the last century the emergence of an interest towards landscape can be detected also in the theoretical debate of museology, with the challenging of the traditional idea of museum/collection and the increasing openness to the context, with the attention for environmental, social and development issues. From the 1990s this opening expressly refers to the landscape as a new museum object. The turning point of this debate is represented by the New Museology, with the claim for the democratisation of museums through the involvement of people and grass-roots participation, that resonate with the guiding principles of recent policies that, like the European Landscape Convention (2000) and the Faro Convention (2005),[9] stress the participation of people for the effective safeguarding of landscape and heritage.

In light of these developments, the most recent museological debate seem to go beyond the search for the best formula of landscape museum, tending towards a wider engagement of museums with the landscape. Alongside the experiences reviewed in the second part of this chapter – which express a variety of efforts to capture and consider some of the multiple dimensions of the landscape within specific museum types – the declaration on *The Responsibility of Museums Towards Landscape*, which concluded the 24th ICOM General Conference,[10] opens in fact innovative possibilities of interaction between museums and landscape. Indeed, it commits all museums, not just the specialised ones we have described, to the safeguarding of cultural landscapes, stimulating the search for new forms of organisation and action. These have been identified through the challenging idea of the "heritage responsibility centre", an institution that combines the functions of the museum with those of the archive and the library and collects, develops and communicates knowledge about the landscape in its entirety, in order to "preserve the promiscuity value of the heritage, the vital coexistence between heritage and landscape, including its dissonances and contradictions" (Jallà, 2017: 15).

Notes

1 The distinction between preservation (intended as the protection of isolated objects, monuments and sites from change and damage through care and restoration) and conservation (aimed at maintaining a useful continuity through the maintenance of the links between form and function, that is applicable to large areas) has long been affirmed by heritage planning (Ashworth, 2011).

2 A new official definition of a museum to update the one issued in 2007 was supposed to be approved during the 25th ICOM General Conference (Kyoto, 2019), following preparatory work lasting two years. However, lack of agreement has delayed its elaboration with further consultations, to be concluded before the next General Conference in August 2022 (Brulon Sares, 2020: 22–24 and https://icom.museum/en/resources/standards-guidelines/museum-definition/).

3 The total absence of references to such museums appears significant in the two reports dedicated to the theme of the relationship between geography and museums in the French (Hertzog, 2004) and British (Geoghegan, 2010) contexts.

4 As in the case of H. Deffontaines and A. Demangeon's involvement in the activities dedicated to the rural house by the *Musée d'Ethnographie* and then of the *Musée des Arts et Traditions populaires* in Paris (Trochet, 1995), and in that of the collaboration of M.R.G. Conzen with the Beamish open-air museum, or in that of the German historical geography with the *Freilandmuseum*, which will be discussed later.

5 Movement advocating a strong social engagement of museums, emerging in the museological debate during the 1970s and finding a formal recognition with the establishment of MINOM/Mouvement International pour la Nouvelle Muséologie in 1985 (Brulon Soares, 2015 and www.minom-icom.net/).

6 This is a fracture sanctioned at the institutional and operational level by the division of competences between ICOM and ICOMOS/International Council on Monuments and Sites (Jallà, 2015: 12–13).

7 Interesting projects to reconstruct gardens and portions of rural landscapes have been carried out by the *Frilandsmuseet* in Lingby, Denmark and by the Beamish open-air museum, United Kingdom.

8 Brief mentions on the Verbania Landscape Museum and its founder are provided by www.museodelpaesaggio.it/en/our-history/.

9 Convention on the Value of Cultural Heritage for Society (2005): www.coe.int/en/web/culture-and-heritage/faro-convention.

10 https://icom.museum/wp-content/uploads/2018/07/ICOMs-Resolutions_2016_Eng.pdf.

References

Ashworth, G.J. (2011). Preservation, Conservation and Heritage: Approaches to the Past in the Present through the Built Environment. *Asian Anthropology*, 10(1): 1–18.

Bellaigue, M. (1990). Museum and Protection of the Landscape. *ICOFOM Study Series – Museology and the Environment*, 17: 25–27.

Bennett, T. (1988). Museums and 'the People'. In R. Lumley (ed.), *The Museum Time Machine: Putting Cultures on Display*. Abingdon: Routledge, pp. 63–85.

Brulon Soares, B. (2015). L'invention et la réinvention de la Nouvelle Muséologie. *ICOFOM Study Series, 43* a: 57–72.

Brulon Soares, B. (2020). Defining the Museum: Challenges and Compromises of the 21th century. *ICOFOM Study Series*, 48: 2.

Chaumier, S. (2003). *Des musées en quête d'identité: écomusée versus technomusée*. Paris: L'Harmattan.

Conan, M. (2002). The Fiddler's Indecorous Nostalgia. In T. Young and R. Riley (eds.), *Theme Park Landscapes: Antecedents and Variations*. Washington, DC: Dumbarton Oaks Research Library and Collection, pp. 91–117.

Cosgrove, D., and Daniels, S. (eds.) (1988). *The Iconography of Landscape: Essays on the Symbolic Representation, Design and Use of Past Environments*. Cambridge: Cambridge University Press.

Crang, M. (1999). Nation, Region and Homeland: History and Tradition in Dalarna, Sweden. *Ecumene* 6(4): 447–470.

Cuisenier, J. (1984). Exhiber et signifier. Sémantique de l'exposition dans les musées d'agriculture. *Museum*, 36: 130–137.

Davallon, J., Grandmont, G., and Schiele, B. (1992). *L'environnement entre au musée*, Lyon: Presses Universitaires de Lyon.

Davis, P. (2011). *Ecomuseums. A Sense of Place*. London: Leicester University Press.

Delarge, A. and Hilaire, P. (1996). Musées et paysages: une introduction. *Publics & Musées*, 10: 31–32.

Denecke, D. (1999). Kulturlandschaftgenese in Freiland- und Landschaftsmuseen: Konzeptionen der Dokumentation und Vermittlung. In R. Aurig (ed.), *Kulturlandschaft, Museen, Identität. Protokollband zur Tagung "Aufgaben und Möglichkeiten der musealen Präsentation von Kulturlandschaftsrelikten"Angewandte Historische Geographie vom 7.- 9.3.1996 in Plauen/Vgtl*. Beucha: Sax-Verlag, pp. 37–57.

Denecke, D. (2009). Open-air and Landscape Museums: Interpreting Histories of the Agricultural Landscape. *Rivista Geografica Italiana*, 116(4): 403–418.

Desvallées, A. (ed.) (2000) Special issue: L'écomusée: rêve ou réalité. *Publics & Musées*, 17–18.

De Varine, H. (2000). Autour de la table ronde de Santiago. *Publics & Musées*, 17–18:180–183.

De Varine, H. (2017). *L'écomusée singulier et pluriel. Un témoignage sur cinquante ans de muséologie communautaire dans le monde*. Paris: L'Harmattan.

Geddes, P. (1902). Note on Draft Plan for Institute of Geography. *The Scottish Geographical Magazine*, 18: 142–144.

Geoghegan, H. (2010). Museum Geography: Exploring Museums, Collections and Museum Practice in the UK. *Geography Compass*, 10(4): 1462–1476.

Gestin, J.-P. (1996) Un objet du musée: le paysage. Le paysage un concept ambigu. *Publics & Musées*, 10: 43–50.

Graham, B., Ashworth, G.J., and Tunbridge, J.E. (2000). *A Geography of Heritage: Power, Culture and Economy*. London: Arnold.

Harvey, D.C. (2001) Heritage Pasts and Heritage Presents: Temporality, Meaning and the Scope of Heritage Studies. *International Journal of Heritage Studies*, 7(4): 319–338.

Hertzog, A. (2004). Quand les géographes visitent les musées, ils y voient des objets … de recherche. *L'espace gèographique*, 33(4): 363–368.

Howard, P. (2002). The Eco-museum: Innovation That Risks the Future. *International Journal of Heritage Studies*, 8(1): 63–72.

Hubert, F. (1985). Les écomusées en France: contradictions et déviations. *Museum*, 37: 186–190.

ICOM (2007). *Statutes*, art. 3, section 1, 2007 (Retrieved from: https://icom.museum/wp-content/uploads/2018/07/2017_ICOM_Statutes_EN.pdf).

Jallà, D. (2015). *Musei e "contesto" nella storia dell'ICOM (1946–2014): una prospettiva di analisi in preparazione della 24a Conferenza generale del 2016.* unpublished document. (Retrieved from: www.academia.edu/16082823/Musei_e_contesto_nella_storia_dell_ICOM_1946_2014_una_prospettiva_di_analisi_in_preparazione_della_24a_Conferenza_generale_del_2016_2016_).

Jallà, D. (2017). Cultural Landscapes and Museums. *Museum International*, 69(1–2): 8–17.

Jones, M. (2007). The European Landscape Convention and the Question of Public Participation. *Landscape Research*, 32(5): 613–633.

Olwig, K.R. (2007). The Practice of Landscape "Conventions" and the Just Landscape: The Case of the European Landscape Convention. *Landscape Research*, 32(5): 579–594.

Overdick, T. (1999). Landschaft und Museum. Theoretische Überlegungen zur Musealisierung von landschaft. *Museologie Online*, 1: 1–40.

Pressenda, P. and Sturani, M.L. (2007). Landscape and Museums: Some Critical Reflections on Initial Developments in Italy. *Die Erde*, 138: 47–69.

Reinhard, R. (1934). The Museum of Regional Geography in Leipzig. *Geographical Review*. 24(2): 219–231.

Rentzhog, S. (2007). *Open-air Museums: The History and Future of a Visionary Idea*. Stockholm: Carlsson.

Rivière, G.H. (1985). Définition évolutive de l'écomusée. *Museum*, 37(4): 182–183.

Rössler, M. (2006). World Heritage Cultural Landscapes: A UNESCO Flagship Programme 1992–2006. *Landscape Research*, 31(4): 333–353.

Semenov-Tian-Šanskij, V.P. (1929). The Geographical Museum. *Geographical Review*, 19(4): 642–648.

Trochet, J.R. (1995). Sciences humaines et musées: du Musée d'ethnographie du Trocadero au Musée national des arts et traditions populaires. *Géographie et Cultures*, 16: 3–30.

Van Mensch, P. (1990). *Annual Conference 1990: Museology and the Environment*. ICOFOM Study Series - Museology and the Environment, 17: 13–24.

Vecchio, B. (2009). Comunicare un'idea. Riflessioni a margine del Museo senese del Paesaggio. *Rivista Geografica Italiana*, 116(4): 463–482.

Withers, C.W.J. (2001). *Geography, Science and National Identity: Scotland since 1520*. Cambridge: Cambridge University Press.

Wylie, J. (2007). *Landscape*. Abingdon: Routledge.

Young, L. (2006). Villages that Never Were: The Museum Village as Heritage Genre. *International Journal of Heritage Studies*, 12(4): 321–338.

26 British and European Meanings of Landscape as Heritage, and the Nationalistic Elephant in the Landscape

Opening New Paths to Landscape Heritage Research

Kenneth R. Olwig

This is an important book because it assembles an insightful international collection of studies of the under-researched relationship between landscape and heritage. It is also significant because the authors largely have an international, multi-disciplinary, cosmopolitan educational background, and collaborate with others with similar backgrounds, perhaps due partially to the European Union. Though the empirical examples are from many parts of the world, most of the authors are of Continental European background, or have European connections. The chapters are thus written largely by authors from non-anglophone countries, but they have been published in English by a major international publisher. English is the contemporary international scholarly lingua franca, comparable to Latin in the Renaissance and Enlightenment, and this means that the book can reach not just a world readership, but also native English readers who have been spared having to read "foreign" languages because theirs *is* the lingua franca.

There is, however, a catch to the use of English as a lingua franca because national languages are not a neutral media, they frame and shape discourse. As Pierre Bourdieu puts it (1991: 48):

> Thus, only when the making of the "nation" … creates new usages and functions, does it become indispensable to … undertake the work of normalizing the products of the linguistic habitus. The dictionary is the exemplary result of this labour of codification and normalization.

An imperial national language is a dialect with an army and navy. The British Empire had a powerful navy, and this is why so many speak English.

A number of the book's authors write of the difficulty in pinning down the meaning of landscape. This can be clarified by arguing that landscape has a double meaning, as Marjeta Pisk and Špela Ledinek Lozej do in Chapter 12: "Cross-border landscape as heritage? Insights from Slovenian borderlands." Here, mobilizing Yi-Fu Tuan's neologism of the "diaphoric," they write:

DOI: 10.4324/9781003195238-26

The landscape – in its synthesised diaphoric meaning, as domain or land inhabited, and as a scenery perceived (Tuan 1978; Olwig 2006) – is hence at the same time the backdrop for human and non-human agencies and an active foreground in borderlands' agencies and institutional development.

Tuan amplified this argument writing (Tuan 1978: 366):

> Domain belongs to the vocabulary of political and economic discourse. A domain or an estate can be surveyed and mapped; it can be viewed objectively from a theoretical point high above. Scenery, on the other hand, is an aesthetic term. It is an individual and personal perspective from a position on the ground.

Taking a philological approach,[1] combining language, literature, and geographical history, I will argue that this dual character derives from the differences between the historically prior pan-European meaning of landscape as material domain, that is the subject of political and economic discourse, and the British definition of landscape as spatial scenery, which originated around 1600, and which subsequently spread to much of the world, including "Europe" (British English excludes Britain from Europe (O.D.E. 2017)). This distinction, in turn, provides a useful way to comprehend the fertile panoply of differing, yet potentially complementary, approaches to the relation between landscape and heritage found in this book.

The definition of landscape in the Oxford English Dictionary (O.E.D), the standard British dictionary, states: "The word was introduced as a technical term of painters ...." The historically and etymologically first meaning listed is: "A picture representing natural inland scenery, as distinguished from a sea picture, a portrait, etc." The earliest example given is from a 1603 reference to "The cunning Painter. Limning [illuminating] a Land-scape, various, rich, and rare." The second example does not refer to painting but is taken from a 1605 theater piece called *Masque of Blackness* which reads "First for the Scene, was drawn a *Landschap*, consisting of small woods." The word scene derives from the theater via the Italian *scenario*, referring to the stage background for a performance, and it is thus from the theater that the word scenery comes. The second meaning is: "A view or prospect of natural inland scenery, such as can be taken in at a glance from one point of view: a piece of country scenery." These first two meanings define landscape as modes of representation. With the third definition, however, the meaning of landscape shifts from a mode of representation to the object represented: "In generalized sense (from 1 and 2): Inland natural scenery, or its representation in painting" (O.E.D. 1971: landscape). Compare this definition to the one found in the Council of Europe's "European Landscape Convention" (ELC), here quoted from Chapter 14: "Damming the past: interplay between landscape heritage and water management," by Mesut Dinler and Özgün Özçakır:

According to the Council of Europe, the term "landscape" "means an area, as perceived by people, whose character is the result of the actions and interaction of natural and/or human factors" (CoE, 2000). ... this document locates the role of people, citizens and communities at the core of landscape.

The English definition clearly belongs within the realm of the scenic and aesthetics, whereas the ELC definition belongs to the "substantive"[2] material realm termed "domain" by Tuan. The ELC definition also includes the material interaction between people and nature, and hence between the human and non-human agents that transform the landscape, making nature not simply an object of the aesthetic gaze.

I will look first at examples of chapters that use a largely British landscape definition, in harmony with the largely British literature on "critical heritage." Then I will examine examples of chapters that understand landscape in a more classically European way. This leads to consideration of the value of crossing the border between the two definitions. Finally, there will be a concluding hunt for the nationalist "elephant" in the landscape, which today marauds the world's material and linguistic borderlands.

"British" Modes of Landscape Heritage

The New Zealand-based landscape architects, Shannon Davis and Jacky Bowring, in "Heritage landscapes and cues to care: exploring the concepts of guardianship and care within a forgotten rural New Zealand cemetery" (Chapter 15), couple "critical heritage" theory to landscape in a discussion of the way "in which heritage is perceived and framed in design terms." Their approach underlines the ties to the British aesthetic definition of landscape as a form of spatial scenery. Words like "performance" signal a connection between the scenic meaning of landscape and theater, where actors perform the script, as when the authors write: "Critical Heritage Studies suggest that 'the discourses that frame our understanding of heritage are a performance in which the meaning of the past is continuously negotiated in the context of the needs of the present' (Gentry and Smith, 2019, p. 1149)." Since the Renaissance, stage scenery spatially framed and marked the stages in the plot recounted in the text of the play's script. This connection between theater landscape and text is brought out when the authors write, citing, among others, Steven Daniels and Denis Cosgrove (who conceptualized landscape in visual scenic terms): "Landscapes can be seen as kinds of texts, symbolic arrays that are intentionally or unwittingly broadcasting values and meaning to observers." It is thus natural to approach landscape as scenery from the humanistic perspective of art, literary and cultural criticism (e.g. Raymond Williams), and to analyze the way landscape heritage can be interpreted in terms of the politics of identity. For the authors landscape heritage can, as argued in critical heritage studies, "stabilise or destabilise issues of identity, memory and sense of place."

A good example of the scenic conception of landscape is Chapter 6, "Storytelling and online media as narrative practices for engaging with the Historic Urban Landscapes (HUL). The case study of Porto, Portugal," by Ana Rita Albuquerque, Maria Leonor Botelho and Dominique Crozat. Here the authors "analyze the performative process behind these online narratives as part of a multivocal approach to the Historic Urban Landscapes' representation and preservation." This approach is perfectly suited to Porto because the city itself, with its imposing facades, reflects a time when theater design was an important influence on urban architectural design, and wandering historic Porto is like wandering a theater stage. This is reflected in the online interviews they made:

> For me, the most representative place of Porto is the viewpoint of Fontainhas. When I was young, I used to come here to visit my grandmother. She told me stories about this place. We used to walk around and visit the abandoned chapel and the vegetable gardens in the middle of the ruins.
>
> (Interview, 2020)

When I wandered the streets of Porto in 2014 the city's crumbling facades were a visceral danger. Now, however, gentrification and tourism are leading to both a heritagization and much needed restoration of the city's scenic landscape that is threatening the identity, memory and sense of place of its ordinary citizens. The authors state that "Heritage 'from below' (HFB) is often simply addressed as a counter-narrative of what constitutes one's heritage." Moreover, such "counter-narratives are particularly useful in revealing the partiality and selectivity of official versions of the past or in representing counter-sites that the 'authorised heritage discourses' (AHD) (Smith, 2006) have excluded or forgotten (Robertson, 2016)." Nevertheless, they argue, there is reason to believe that "HFB and AHD should not necessarily be seen as antithetical but possibly [as] complementary to one another." A theater piece can be directed to multiple audiences and be open to multiple interpretations, allowing for multiple truths. This is also true of the scenic landscape of Porto.

Just as the heritage of the scenic landscape of Porto, the original Portuguese capital that gave its name to the nation, is vital to Porto's and Portugal's identity, the perceived heritage linked to landscape is vital also to the identity of Britain, and was built into the British conceptualization of landscape as scenery from the very start. The 1605 theater piece, *The Masque of Blackness*, quoted from above by the O.E.D., was performed (somewhat delayed due to a pandemic) to celebrate the English coronation of King James I, who already was king of Scotland. Its text was by Ben Jonson, and the stage scenery and costumes were by the pioneer designer, architect and urban planner, Inigo Jones, who introduced the British Palladian style of architecture to what was to become widely known as "Britain" (in part due his efforts). The masque was performed as part of a campaign to (successfully) re-introduce the Roman name Britain, and with it the imperial heritage of Roman Britain, and to foster the absorption of Scotland into a "British" national body, unified by the body of the island as represented by maps and its organic landscape scenery with its rivers perceived then as comparable to blood veins. The masque's zany plot, concocted under the direction of James' very blond and pale skinned Danish Queen Anne, concerned the efforts of a bevy of black African princesses (performed in blackface by the queen and members of her court) to become white, and thereby "faire" and beautiful, by sailing to the island of Britain. Here the island's mild sun, a reflection of its sun-king (James), would turn their skins white. This may have been the first linking of the landscape's soil and climate to a nation's racial blood. (*On The Masque of Blackness and Landscape*, see Olwig 2002).

This original twinning of landscape and national/imperial heritage makes clear how important it is for critical heritage studies to parse the differing ways, positive and negative, that scenic landscape and heritage define each other (Mitchell 1994; Bluwstein 2021). It also suggests the need to examine the historically primary European understanding of landscape, which sees it more as a human domain than a natural scene.

European Modes of Landscape Heritage

In Chapter 14, the authors cite not only the definition of landscape in the ELC, as quoted above, but also a 1998 article by Eugenio Turri entitled "Il paesaggio come teatro. Dal territorio vissuto al territorio rappresentato" (The landscape as a theatre: From the lived territory to the represented territory). Turri describes the landscape as "the reflection of our actions, the measure of our living and working in the territory." The chapter itself is concerned with the way, using a Turkish example, "Dam projects have, historically, played an immense role in completely transforming (terminating, in most cases) the relationship between communities and their environment." In this way they have become "deheritagised" (and "damned"!). The chapter discusses how Turkish modernists uprooted communities and destroyed the cultural landscape of a Turkish area, inspired by the U.S. Tennessee Valley Authority's (TVA) 1930s damming projects.

In a similar vein to the Turkish case, Cecilia Paradiso in Chapter 5, "A vineyard landscape, a UNESCO inscription and a National Park. A historical-anthropological analysis of heritagization and tourism development in the Cinque Terre (Italy)," is concerned with landscape understood as an area as perceived by people in which the interaction between nature and society plays a significant role. Here, it is the survival of a functioning terraced cultural landscape and its populace that is seen to be threatened by heritagization in all its forms. Paradiso makes a similar argument as David Lowenthal, a founder of heritage studies (see: 1996), in arguing that it is heritage's muddying of history that is a problem.

These chapters arguably fall within the historically European understanding of landscape discussed above. Tuan has also "diaphorically" counterpoised the scenic, theatrical landscape to that of the lived territory (Tuan 1974: 133):

Scenery and landscape are now nearly synonymous [in English]. The slight differences in meaning they retain reflect their dissimilar origin. Scenery has traditionally been associated with the world of illusion which is the theater. The expression "behind the scenes" reveals the unreality of scenes. We are not bidden to look "behind the landscape," although a landscaped garden can be as contrived as a stage scene, and as little enmeshed with the life of the owner as the stage paraphernalia with the life of the actor. The difference is that landscape, in its original sense, referred to the real world, not to the world of art and make-believe. In its native Dutch, "landschap" designated such commonplaces as "a collection of farms or fenced fields, sometimes a small domain or administrative unit." Only when it was transplanted to England toward the end of the sixteenth century did the word shed its earthbound roots and acquire the precious meaning of art.

In Chapter 11, "Remains of privileged spaces: moral landscapes in Delfland, the Netherlands," Maurits W. Ertsen refers to "Delfland, one of the oldest water managing agencies (water boards) in the Netherlands." The name of these boards in Dutch is "*watershap*," and the "administrative unit" referred to above by Tuan is called a *landschap*. In Dutch the term landscape does not mean scenery, but first a region and what it looks like in a certain region and second a painting of it. In the Netherlands, where much of the country is near or below sea-level, the collective management of water and land was of critical importance to the survival of the community, and this is why there was a moral imperative for all to manage both the water and the land. In the Turkish case, also about water, "'landscape's preservation' is similarly described as 'a civic duty since its degradation is interlinked with social degradation'."

The meaning of the Dutch word *landschap*, which is similar to cognate words found throughout Northern Europe and parallel words in the Romance languages, thus approaches the ELC's definition of landscape. Ertsen refers to the power of the nobility in regulating the *watershap*, but the *landschap* communities, linked by waterborne mobility, were known, particularly in Friesland to the north, for their rule by representative bodies of the people. The Danish topographer Jens Peter Trap thus writes in 1864 of the Frisian *landschap* of *Eiderstedt* that "no other district in the duchy of Schleswig is equipped with a district constitution which expresses such a high degree of freedom and independence." "It has gradually, developed into its present state," he continues, "and it rests just as much upon rules which have developed through autonomy and custom as through law and privilege" (quoted in Olwig 2002: 12). The word moral derives from the Latin *moralis*, meaning custom, so Ertsen is right in linking morality to *landscape* in its historically original sense. The link of custom to a morally bound community, furthermore, is suggested by the fact that Ferdinand Tönnies, whose work was foundational to the sociological study of community, was himself from *Eiderstedt*.

The Nationalist Elephant in the Landscape

In Chapter 20, "What cultural landscape for Bamiyan (Afghanistan)? Observations on the UNESCO site protection practices," Mirella Loda is concerned to show the difficulties of harmonizing the UNESCO approach to landscape as heritage with local agricultural practices. Bamiyan is the location of the valley where the Taliban gained notoriety for destroying ancient Buddhist statues, and the UNESCO goal was to help ameliorate this world heritage loss. The author concludes the chapter with the unhappy comment:

> However the events that took place in Afghanistan in the month of August 2021 have profoundly altered the geo-political and economic picture surrounding the protection action. Hence, at the time of writing, there is no certainty as to if and how the protection of the Bamiyan cultural landscape will be undertaken in the new context.

The Taliban's iconoclastic destruction of the ancient statues might well be seen by the Taliban as justifiable as "heritage from below," following more recent occupations by the British and the Soviets, with the statues symbolizing both ancient and modern invaders. The authorized Western heritagization of the statues' landscape by an international body, can thus be perceived to threaten the "truths" of Afghani HFB, much as the destruction of the statues of slave owners and traders can be perceived as an expression of solidarity with African-American resistance to a repressive HFA and AHD. The violent, despotic acts of the Taliban regime are nevertheless difficult to relativize in terms of alternative heritage truths.

The Brexiters cannot be fairly compared to the Taliban, but the populistic Brexit movement exhibits a similar polarizing, sometimes violent and racist tendency, in which Brexit was perceived to be a justified response to an alien European threat to native British heritage. And Brexit is just one example. On U.S. southern border, and along the fault lines between Eastern and Western Europe, and between Europe and the Middle East, the polarized ideas of blood and soil national heritage that split the world apart notably with WWII are resurfacing. The result is that hopeful projects to heal the wounds along Europe's internal borders from earlier wars risk being made as redundant as the Afghanistan example.

Conclusion: What are the lessons to be learned for future research?

One avenue for future research might be for research in landscape heritage to consider the literature on landscape, law and justice that has been inspired, in part, by the ELC. The Council of Europe was created in the wake of WWII as a means of upholding human rights, democracy and the rule of law in Europe and countering the blood and soil nationalism that broke Europe apart. The

ELC, fostered by the Council, has helped to stimulate a movement for landscape rights and democracy which is highly relevant to critical landscape heritage (Jones and Peil 2005, Mitchell and Olwig 2009, Egoz and Jalla Makhzoumi 2011, Jones and Stenseke 2011, Waterman, Wall and Wolff 2021).

Another avenue for future research might be to explore, and break down, the borders between the British and European concepts of landscape. Yi-Fu Tuan is an example of a scholar who has done work in both areas. Tuan wrote his dissertation in geomorphology at the University of California, Berkeley's geography department. The historical geographer Carl Sauer founded the department beginning with a state-of-the-art survey of European geography in which landscape was a key concept. His approach to landscape and geography was inspired by American Cultural Anthropology as pioneered by the secular Jewish-German anthropologist Franz Boas, who had fled German nationalism and anti-Semitism for the U.S. He began as a geographer, but since European geography and anthropology largely grew out of anthropogeography, it was natural to shift to anthropology, while maintaining common ground with geography. Boas incorporated anthropology, history, ethnology and archaeology, along with language (philology) as a non-racial, cultural expression of people's interaction with their environment. Sauer, following Boas, used the concept of culture to replace the concepts of race and evolutionary environmental determinism – approaches that then dominated geography and anthropology. Berkeley's geography, following Sauer, was particularly focused on the landscapes and heritage of the indigenous populations of Central and South America as being worthy of equal interest to that of their imperial conquerors. Tuan studied southwestern U.S. desert landscapes and was struck by the ways in which differing visual and material perceptions of the desert landscape resulted in disparate heritages, and behavior, on the part of the indigenous population, the Spanish and the American Yankee settlers. Thus was born his contribution to the founding of the study of landscape perception and humanistic geography.

Another key scholar whose approach might help guide landscape heritage researchers in navigating between the British and the European approach to heritage, whilst avoiding nationalism, is David Lowenthal. Luca Muscarà has described Lowenthal's approach to landscape and heritage as "transatlantic" owing to the role of his early contact with the French geographer Jean Gottmann. Lowenthal first met Gottman in the United States through Lowenthal's jurist father (see Olwig 2020), and then in Europe during WWII. Lowenthal experienced the war as a soldier doing, in part, a photographic study of Europe's landscapes (Muscarà 2022). Lowenthal, like Gottmann, was of secular Jewish background and the war experience made him critically aware of the potential dangers of heritage more generally. He went on to study geography at Berkeley, and he, along with other Berkeley associates, such as Tuan and J.B. Jackson, became founders of the study of landscape perception (1961), which was concerned with both scenic and substantive domain approaches to landscape. He also wrote and published a dissertation, at Sauer's behest, on the life of the 19th-century American geographer and philologist George Perkins Marsh. Marsh's command of many European languages made possible his studies of the perception of nature/society relations as manifested in landscape and helped him, thereby, lay the foundations for the conservation movement and the later idea of the anthropocene. As a founder of the Smithsonian Institution, and then through his experience of Italian heritage in Torino (as the first and longest serving United States minister (ambassador) to Italy), Marsh developed ideas on heritage that influenced Lowenthal's pioneering development of heritage studies.

In some ways the British and European approaches to landscape mix like oil and water, the one focusing on spatial scenery and the other on substantive places, their material environment and their interconnections through movement. On the other hand, as seen in the Dutch example, landscape could be both a region or place, and a depiction of how it looks. Conceptualized diaphorically, or perhaps dialectically, the two approaches, counterpoised to each other, could provide a fruitful future common ground in critical landscape heritage studies that also hunts the marauding elephant in the landscape of blood and soil nationalism. The cosmopolitanism that made possible the variety and depth of this book is, in the end, threatened by the barriers erected by the chauvinism and xenophobia of the new nationalism.

Notes

1 On the philological approach to landscape see: (Ingold, 2021: 207–210; Olwig, 2019: 1–17).
2 "Substantive" means "real rather than apparent," "belonging to the substance of a thing." It is also used in the legal sense of "creating and defining rights and duties. A substantive concept of landscape is more concerned with the economic, the political, law and justice than with natural law or aesthetics (see Olwig, 2019: chpt. 1, pp. 18–49).

References

Bluwstein, J. (2021). Colonizing landscapes/landscaping colonies: from a global history of landscapism to the contemporary landscape approach in nature. *Journal of Political Ecology* 28(1).

Bourdieu, P. (1991). *Language and Symbolic Power*. Cambridge: Polity Press.

Egoz, S. and G. P. Jalla Makhzoum (eds.) (2011). *The Right to Landscape: Contesting Landscape and Human Rights*. Aldershot: Ashgate.

Gargano, P. and F. Veldman (2013). *Prisma handwoordenboek Nederlands-Engels*. Houten-Antwerpen: Spectrum.

Ingold, T. (2021). *Correspondences*. Cambridge: Polity Press.

Jones, M. and T. Peil (eds.) (2005). *Landscape, Law and Justice*. Oslo: Institute for Comparative Research in Human Culture and Novus Forlag.

Jones, M. and M. Stenseke, (eds.) (2011). *The European Landscape Convention: Challenges of Participation*. Dordrecht: Springer.

Lowenthal, D. (1961). Geography, Experience and Imagination: Towards a Geographical Epistemology. *Annals, Association of American Geographers* 51(3): 241–260.

Lowenthal, D. (1996). *Possessed by the Past: The Heritage Crusade and the Spoils of History.* New York: The Free Press.

Mitchell, D. and K. R. Olwig (eds.) (2009). *Justice, Power and the Political Landscape.* New York: Routledge.

Mitchell, W. J. T. (1994). *Imperial Landscape: Landscape and Power.* Chicago: University of Chicago Press.

Muscarà, L. (2022). Transatlantic Landscapes: Gottmann and the Roots of Lowenthal's Intellectual Heritage. *Landscape Research.* doi:10.1080/01426397.2021.2021162.

O.D.E. (2017). *Oxford Dictionary of English.* Oxford: Oxford University Press.

O.E.D. (1971). *Oxford English Dictionary.* Oxford: Oxford University Press.

Olwig, K. R. (2002). *Landscape, Nature and the Body Politic: From Britain's Renaissance to America's New World.* Madison: University of Wisconsin Press.

Olwig, K. R. (2019). *The Meanings of Landscape: Essays on Place, Space, Nature and Justice.* New York: Routledge.

Olwig, K. R. (2020). David and Max Lowenthal – and Marsh: Public Intellectuals and Advocates in the Political Landscape. A Personal View. *Landscape Research.* doi:10.1080/01426397.2020.1791811.

Tuan, Y.-F. (1974). *Topophilia: A Study of Environmental Perception, Attitudes, and Values.* Englewood Cliffs: Prentice-Hall.

Waterman, T. and E. Wall and J. Wolff (eds.) (2021). *Landscape Citizenships.* New York: Routledge.

Index

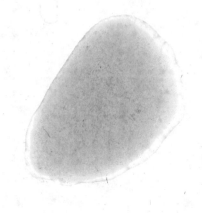